W9-CYT-900

GUNNY

Memoirs of Mobile's South Side

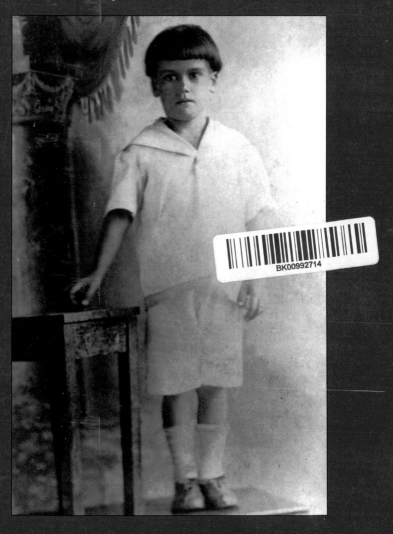

Riding Alabama's Tide of White Supremacy

JAMES JOULLIAN GONZALES

GUNNY

Memoirs of Mobile's South Side
Riding Alabama's Tide of White Supremacy

JAMES JOULLIAN GONZALES

ACADEMY BOOKS 📖
Colorado

GUNNY
Memoirs of Mobile's South Side:
Riding Alabama's Tide of White Supremacy

Published in Centennial, Colorado by
ACADEMY BOOKS, LLC
P. O. Box 3801
Greenwood Village, Colorado 80155

Library of Congress Control Number: 2007902299

Gonzales, James Joullian, 1947-

GUNNY: Memoirs of Mobile's South Side: Riding Alabama's Tide of White Supremacy

Includes bibliography and index.

ISBN-13: 978-0-9794714-1-4
ISBN-10: 0-9794714-1-9

Front cover design by James Joullian Gonzales. Photograph of Emanuel Joseph (Gunny) Gonzales, Jr., Mobile, 1919 (Brown's Studio).

Back cover design by James Joullian Gonzales. Photograph of Emanuel Joseph (Gunny) Gonzales, Jr., January 27, 1981 (Courtesy, *Mobile Register*, photographer Roy McAuley, January 28, 1981).

Cover and layout graphics by Rebecca Finkel, F + P Graphic Design, Inc., Colorado.

In Memory of

GUNNY and ANNE

About the Author

A native of Mobile Alabama, James Joullian Gonzales graduated from McGill Institute High School, class of 1965. He received his Bachelor of Science degree and Second Lieutenant Commission from the U.S. Air Force Academy, Juris Doctor from Vanderbilt University Law School, Master of Laws from George Washington University Law School, and M.A. Theology from St. Thomas Seminary. Colonel Gonzales served as a Judge Advocate in the active and reserve U.S. Air Force, retiring in 1999 with decorations including the Legion of Merit, Meritorious Service Medal, Air Force Commendation Medal, and Vietnam Service Medal. He resides in Colorado and practices law in the Rocky Mountain region.

CONTENTS

PREFACE

Charles Joullian sank his weary 73 year-old bones into a cushioned rattan chair, savoring what would be our last visit in this life. Despite Mobile's hostile July sun, Charles had lingered in his garden at 24 Westwood, posing with two of Gunny's grandchildren Kimberly, very much a Gonzales, and Brian, a striking blue-eyed Joullian. Family tradition dictated presenting offspring to Uncle Charlie and Aunt Myrtle.

As children, we paid our respects each Christmas, nibbling on Aunt Myrtle's spicy cheese crackers and patiently awaiting a modest present. Charles and Myrtle, blessed with no children of their own, displayed abiding patience with nieces and nephews. Not one to squander good money on mere fancies, Uncle Charlie rewarded those who came by to greet him and Myrtle over the holidays with a crisp new dollar bill. No visit, no dollar. We heard from good authority that Charlie Joullian still had the first nickel he ever earned, and pinched every dime after that. It was common knowledge he housed in the shed out back a new Plymouth that he seldom and Myrtle never drove. His frugal ways, honed from living hand-to-mouth, became legendary among his nieces and nephews. That Charlie Joullian would share his cache of new dollar bills with us, one at a time, added mystique to his eccentricities. As we aged, Christmas rituals also came to include sipping a jigger of Charlie's favorite store-bought whiskey, which he ceremoniously measured. He joked that the cork was off should anyone care for another shot, but we never dared ask for a second round.

Relaxing alone in the Florida room that summer of 1979, I noticed how Uncle Charlie had aged but kept his wit intact, those crystal blue eyes sparkling with humor and mischief. We reminisced in a drowsy sort of way, turning leaves on the family tree like bees combing azaleas. He seemed uneasy to hear that I would be writing about his nephew and the family. That seed had been planted earlier in 1976 when Emanuel Joseph "Gunny" Gonzales, Jr. spoke with me over a bowl of black *roux* gumbo about penning his memoirs. Gunny had been quite a political figure. Anyone from Mobile to Montgomery who could read knew of him. His name became a household word, often laden with conflicting sentiments. Thousands heard about what he did, but very few really understood why.

Probing into the distant past, I rummaged through Uncle Charlie's mental attic until stumbling over a trunk he would not open. Our eyes locked for a spell. Then he leaned forward, putting aside the sweet iced tea. He murmured in a raspy hush, a condition since birth, to leave both the living and the dead undisturbed. Something in Charles Joullian's emotional baggage had shifted, uncomfortably opening a mental scar. I had no clue what memories he guarded, but Uncle Charlie clearly planned on taking them to his grave. That July afternoon with Charles Joullian fundamentally affected the course of this story.

What began as a narrow tale of post-war political intrigue deep within the Heart of Dixie evolved into a journey about survival, challenge, and courage spanning most of a century. Until I wrote *GUNNY*, I did not fully understand my father or those who crossed his path. Over the years, chapters emerged, slowly crawling off the drafting table until the day finally arrived to assemble a working manuscript. Though he closely followed newspapers, pasting articles into scrapbooks, Gunny Gonzales was not known to read a book from cover to cover. I doubted he would sit still long enough. But for three days and nights he nursed each page, lips moving silently over the words, one by one. When asked his thoughts, Gunny simply said what he read was true. He seemed subdued by it all, relieved that this story, warts and all, would see the light of day once his long journey ended.

Gunny and other have-nots from Mobile's hand-to-mouth world carried their share of life's baggage. Galvez Park, rising from history's ashes in 1921, symbolized the spirit of their passage through Mobile's south side. This hallowed plot became a touchstone of character, setting apart those whose mettle survived the crucibles of want and despair. Nothing more aptly explains Gunny Gonzales than that he thrived on the hard knocks of Galvez Park.

GUNNY traces the life and times of a baseball champion, walk-on football star, savvy political ward heeler, thorny Democratic Party firebrand, daring state registrar, voting rights populist, and Mobile's most controversial figure. When asked what moment he cherished most, Gunny happily recalled his championship baseball season with the 1930 Whippets. Yet history records a more stunning and profound moment 18 years later in Judge John McDuffie's United States District Court where Gunny confronted Alabama's high tide of white supremacy.

Some years ago I interviewed Gunny on a wharf overlooking Mobile Bay's western shore as he cleaned mullet for a family reunion. Seagulls squawked above, eyeing raw fish carcasses about to be trashed overboard. Against the background of lapping waves under the wharf, Gunny scaled fish after fish, a grating sound much like a rough dry shave. I paused after hours of questions and abruptly changed direction, asking how his tombstone should read. The fish-scaling stopped. Gunny stared thoughtfully at the shore, hoisted a beer, and grinned: "Tell it like it is." For good or ill, that is what he did best.

These memoirs of Mobile's south side tell it like it was. Along the way, some surprising fragments of history fell into place, solving riddles that nearly went to the grave unanswered. Charles Joullian did right by the family. I suspect Uncle Charlie will tell me someday whether I have done as well.

James Joullian Gonzales
January 2007

PART ONE

There are

only two families

in the world,

the Haves and the

Have-nots.

—Miguel Cervantes

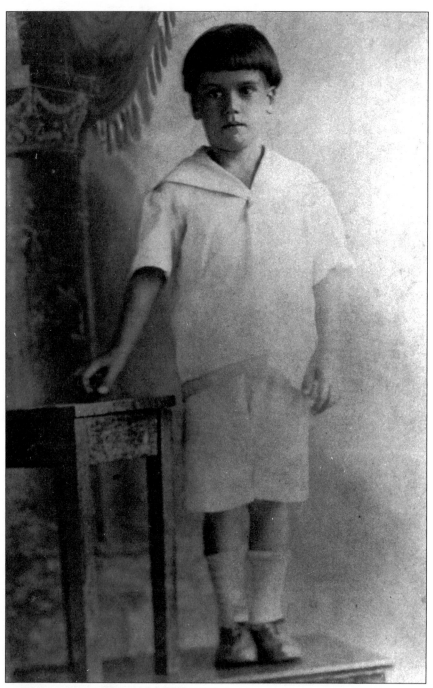

1. *Emanuel Joseph (Gunny) Gonzales, Mobile, 1919 (Brown's Studio).*

CHAPTER 1

Sunset on the Have-nots

Generations of Mobile's rugged south side and many a stray pig followed their common instincts to Horace Cunningham's door. Long a neighborhood crossroad on the northeast corner of Hamilton and Madison, Cunningham's grocery tended the daily needs of familiar faces and ran tabs for Have-nots surviving on credit. Horace's family kept house above the fray of open vegetable bins, canned shelf stock, curios, chickens, and whatnot. Just beyond the grasp of small hands that might lack a coin, a wooden counter displayed jars of hard candy. Youngsters freely wandered about downstairs, their calloused feet shuffling slowly along cool planks worn smooth by the constant ebb and flow. Under the grocery's floorboards, a patient band of rats awaited nightfall to forage undisturbed.

Between the store and north fence, weathered chicken coops slumped next to broken barrels and crates. The chickens were gone and their empty cages soon would follow. Rodents would surely overrun the place and pester adjoining neighbors if the yard were not purged ever so often. A store hand piled some debris near the fence. The sun-bleached wood burst into flame, fanned by warm northwesterly gusts. In minutes the fire began to spread. Nettie Sullivan resided on Hamilton just over the north fence from Cunningham's grocery. Her azalea beds stretched east and west along the fence, their gentle fragrance diluting the pungent odor of seasoned chicken coops. Flames from Cunningham's fire quickly raced the length of the fence, crawled through Nettie Sullivan's azalea bushes, and found her coal bin.

South of Madison past the Charleston Street trolley, clapboard houses armored with hurricane shutters huddled closely, showing little to nothing of a front yard. Long shallow ditches waited to catch the runoff of occasional spring showers, though the unusually dry wind dispelled any notion of rain. Some school boys had gathered to romp around the horse trough pump where Claiborne, Conception and Canal streets meet. The broiling afternoon sun did not much bother them. Several blocks east of Conception an afternoon paddle wheeler nudged away from its dock into the river channel for a routine bay crossing. A slower pace had settled over Mobile's south side since Europe's killing fields fell silent on November 11, 1918. The collapse of German, Russian, and Ottoman empires commanded scant attention among those eking out a living in a port once ruled by France, Great Britain, and Spain. Simpler concerns about next month's rent, White Sox pennant hopes, and Ku Klux Klan marches in Oakdale occupied their thoughts.

Mobilians pledged their allegiance at one time or another to European kingdoms, the United States of America, the 1861 Republic of Alabama, and the Confederate States of America. Those Have-nots who survived the War Between the States and endured the blight of Reconstruction entered the new century alongside empty-handed immigrants south of Church Street. Whatever their story or fate, though, none trifled with the memory of Mobile's ancestors who braved the War. Confederate Rest still kept vigil on Mobile's southern flank. Cradled in the bosom of Magnolia Cemetery, Alabama's fallen heroes bore witness to a wound not yet healed. Foot soldiers who mastered no one mingled amid the ranks of hallowed stone epitaphs with those who once mastered many. Undisturbed since the dusk of Reconstruction, they patiently faced east awaiting the scriptural Second Coming. On the horizon beyond Oakleigh Plantation, Confederate Rest watched a telltale plume slowly rising much as a ghost leaving its grave.

Joseph Gonzalez knew little of gray soldiers who battled under the Confederacy's Stars and Bars. He stepped off a boat onto Mobile's waterfront at age 36 in 1887, expecting never again to see his *papa* Carlos, *mama* Louisa, the Balearic Islands, or the rivers of Galicia. Joseph did not acquire a drawling Alabama dialect. Mobile's premier oyster monger trafficked in Spanish, the mother tongue his old mule understood well enough to make deliveries. Joseph's prosperous trade began each morning shucking oysters with hired Coloreds under a simple backyard shed and finished the day from the bed of a worn dray cart. Despite his 68 years, Grandpa Joe still made the daily delivery of fresh shucked oysters to Mobile's finer hotels and taverns.

At the turn of the century, Joseph moved into an impressive three story property at 407 south St. Emanuel between Canal and Charleston overlooking St. Vincent Church to the west. Though Joseph fared better than some, Sebastian's side of the Gonzalez family fared better than most. Joseph's older brother Manuel Gonzalez had arrived in Alabama at the end of Republican Reconstruction in 1874 with five year-old twins Sebastian and Louisa. Señor Manuel plied the coastal seafood trade and by 1885 he and son Sebastian operated *Manuel Gonzalez & Son* out of a Southern Market stall and the Church Street fish house between Commerce and Water. Joseph initially lived with his brother Manuel at 156 South Royal, clerking with nephew Sebastian across the street at the Southern Market fish stall. But bachelor Joseph soon caught the eye of Lucinda, one of the Point Clear Varedo girls from Mobile Bay's eastern shore. Seventeen year-old Lucinda consented to marry prosperous 40 year-old Joseph in 1891, giving birth on June 6, 1892 to Manuel Joseph. Once a name found favor in the family, its use became tribal despite inevitable confusion. That same year Papa Joseph opened his own Southern Market oyster shop and moved down the street to 205 South Royal. When Lucinda christened Manuel Joseph in May 1895, nephew Sebastian stood godfather. Sebastian's wife Leopoldina Perez de Gonzalez, a Campeche Mexico beauty, became *la madrina* and *tia Leo* to Lucinda's firstborn. By 1900 Sebastian and Aunt Leo's brother Charlie E. Perez, Jr. were operating *Gonzales Fish and Oyster Company*, the largest shipper of fish in the Gulf states, out of their Southern Market stall. Joseph and Sebastian Gonzalez found Mobile uncommonly hospitable.

Fire Company No. 3 took Horace Cunningham's call just after 3:30 p.m. Centrally located on Franklin Street between Church and Monroe, Company No. 3 enjoyed the distinctive honor of being Mobile's only motorized firefighting unit. It stood ready to support slower horsedrawn companies should a serious emergency arise west of town past Michigan Avenue. A trash fire posed no particular challenge for this Company's seasoned fighters, but allowed them to race about town with sirens wailing. Fire Engine No. 3 stirred a great commotion southbound on Franklin. The five year-old grandson of Joseph Gonzalez sat at play amid the street's clay ruts. Gunny, as he came to be known, faced the trolley rails with his back to the sun and gusting wind. His eyes rose to the noisy excitement of an amazing machine wildly rushing at him. Too fascinated to move, the boy simply watched in awe. Fire Engine No. 3 suddenly made a sharp right turn heading west on Madison, the grocery now but a block away. As the mighty fire engine raced out of sight, Gunny looked over his shoulder to find the front porch empty. His mother, Ursulene Joullian Gonzales, did not step outside to see what all the fuss was about.

Company No. 3 arrived within several minutes of Horace Cunningham's call. Nettie Sullivan and her neighbors followed the smell, smoke, and noise to the middle of Hamilton in time to watch the roof of Cunningham's store surrender to a flapping sheet of flame. Horsedrawn Company No. 6 arrived later amid much less fanfare. Despite the effort of Mobile's finest, Madison street started to fill with men, women, children, and animals. The Pickett's and Vaughan's emptied their homes as flames engulfed nearby Parker's Pressing Club. Clouds of smoke rolled east down Canal Street past Franklin all the way to Conception. An appetizing whiff spewed from Campbell's Oyster Shop when several bushels of unshucked oysters collectively belched their salty juices into the steaming heat. Beds, chiffarobes, barefoot children, and old women on cots watched from the street as a roaring inferno stalked them. On Canal, the Miller's and Wilson's stripped rooms of furniture before their roofs crackled and popped. Figures slipped through walls of smoke like visitors from the nether world. Freed from their bondage, flames leapt from house to house, block to block, between Madison and Canal on an easterly course toward the L&N Railroad shops.

Further up Canal the Ott's and Bradley's stood in the street praying the path of the fire would change. But the wind steadily fanned white cinders eastward onto the roofs of their homes. Resigned to disaster, folks from Hamilton to St. Emanuel began to pile their few keepsakes in the street, in vain. Persistent tongues from hell lashed past weary firemen, scorched the newly homeless, and set upon all that lay heaped outdoors. In a strange chorus, beds, dressers, and other earthly baggage collectively hissed in the streets before exploding into flames and scattering bewildered refugees in all directions. In but a couple of hours tragedy became monotonous and the bizarre commonplace. Only happenstance distinguished the favored from the condemned. With hasty intimacy, anxious victims opened their homes to unfamiliar faces that appeared on doorsteps to offer help. Soiled helping hands heaved onto crowded streets what moments earlier had been untouchable family treasures. Some of those hands also helped themselves. Looters and refugees alike, weaving under the burden of stuffed sheets, fled slowly to distant safety.

Homeless crowds gathered midstreet in disbelief. Their lashes and eyebrows crumbled in the painful heat. When explosions hurled burning debris into clogged streets, faces turned with renewed alarm as shrieking children jumped from flaming furniture. There was no safe path for their bare feet to tread. A few lucky soles sloshed about in the horse trough on Claiborne at Canal. Most of the horses were gone, having smartly fled in terror. A few lay still in the street, mortally lashed by electrical wires dangling from burning street poles. Red Foster balanced on one of his short ten year-old legs as two skinny men wobbled nearby under the weight of a huge piano. Amid the excitement, Red had planted a not so calloused bare foot on a white cinder, quickly raising ugly blisters and sending the youngster into the water trough.

Flames crept up Canal toward Franklin. Gunny now stood mute next to the trolley rails in the middle of the street. No taller than a fireplug, he stared curiously over the rooftop into a darkening sky. Gunny squinted as the family's monthly rental house at 308 Franklin wheezed and coughed. His mother crouched nearby clutching her two year-old daughter Luthia. The little girl only answered to "Dit", though, as her given name wore thin very quickly. Amid stacks of scorched furniture along Franklin, Ursulene's first born son disappeared into thick clouds of choking smoke. His stubby bowed legs arched out of the ash that mostly covered both feet. With one arm warding off the searing heat, Gunny watched a charred skeletal foundation slowly emerge from where he had lived only moments earlier. The wall of fire then crawled past Franklin to Claiborne, consuming Gunny's nearby birthplace at 205 Madison. From Claiborne the blaze torched creosote blocks that paved Conception Street, igniting hot oils under the bare feet of wild-eyed children. As the fire crept further east, a thousand railroad and dock workers met the blaze at Canal and Royal, stopping its advance. Within only a few hours, Cunningham's fire covered more distance than Gunny Gonzales had traveled in all his five years.

Through an open parlor window at 407 south St. Emanuel, Grandpa Joe stared in amazement as the street filled with women, children, animals, and furnishings. Just one block west, Conception Street already appeared overcome with refugees. Joseph Gonzalez looked about the parlor, wondering what to do. This past Sunday he and Sebastian had gathered in the parlor after Holy Mass to drink sherry and play poker with Antonio Caminas, Señor Gabriel, and Señor Castro, *el Cubano*. Lucinda outdid herself when Grandpa Joe's friends came to play cards. Tortilla balls of stuffed mashed potato fried on one side of the stove while oysters stewed among onions in a clear milk broth on the other side. Within the parlor, kerosene lamps at high wick revealed layers of yellow and green cigar smoke near the ceiling. Grandpa Joe leaned back in a wicker chair, absently brushing ashes off his smoking jacket, as Señor Gabriel's muscular hands shuffled the deck. They spoke in lyrical Spanish of Havana, Andalusia, Galicia, and

Menorca. Ever so often Sebastian left Mobile for Menorca. He returned with a handful of young Spaniards to work a year for Sebastian's Star Fish & Oyster Company. Señors Castro and Caminas managed a ceramic tile plant west of Duvall Street across the railroad tracks in Oakdale, where they practiced Andalusian tile crafts amid great vats of clays, colors, and glazes. The Spaniards' weekly rite of cigars, poker, and sherry would resume next Sunday after Mass, God willing. Grandpa Joe watched the approaching inferno. It seemed that God might not be willing.

From the bow of the ferry in the bay, Mobile appeared to reel under a warlike siege. Angry flames soiled the sky with smoke, turning the afternoon sun into an apocalyptic dusk. Gusting winds tossed the remains of Franklin and Madison streets into the Mobile River and spread an eerie dark canopy over the bay. Mesmerized by the orange and black sunset that covered the city, the paddle wheeler treaded water, unsure of its destination.

North of Dauphin Street, a hospital orderly removed Arthur Gonzales' lunch tray, leaving the 6 year-old alone until his mother Leopoldina visited later. Leopoldina and Sebastian made their home with Nelo, Marietta, Emilie, Victor, Arthur Sebastian, and Margarita amid a compound of houses near the foot of Eslava, just off the Mobile River. Sebastian had christened Leopoldina's firstborn son Manuel Joseph to honor Sebastian's father Manuel and uncle Joseph. The constant confusion of multiple identities proved too much for the third Manuel Joseph, though, and resulted in changing his name to Nelo. Arthur Sebastian at least got a name of his own.

Young Arthur whiled away the afternoon daydreaming through his open hospital room window, watching oaks sway in the gusty wind. Across town he saw a black plume arching over the river. Below his window, horse drawn wagons and people afoot hurried to the south part of town. Everyone except Arthur seemed headed to the rising cloud of smoke. As the horizon darkened, Arthur marveled at brightly glowing trees. Pockets of light flashed on and off, silently, like midsummer heat lightning. Arthur stayed at the window until more than 36 blocks lay in rubble, but could not see whether fate steered the fire south of Eslava, sparing his home.

A portrait of Grandpa Joe, Lucinda, and their family stood proudly on a sideboard in the parlor. Lucinda bore another 7 children between 1892 and 1914 after the birth of her son Manuel Joseph. Lucinda's second son came amidst much fanfare the Thanksgiving of 1902. Only two years later on Christmas Eve, though, son Joseph Gonzalez, Jr. died at home in Grandpa Joe's lap and lay in wake in the parlor Christmas morning. Twelve years and five daughters later, baby Alphonse arrived under the shadow of World War I on November 21, 1914. Older sisters Pauline, Amelia, Juanita, Frances, and Josie seemed like aunts to Alphonse. Baby Al was even younger than his nephew Gunny.

The images of Lucinda's offspring bore meaning much deeper than a two dimensional photograph. They each dressed to the nines for baby Al's christening on January 3, 1915. Cradled in Lucinda's arms and dressed in a long white christening gown, Al calmly watched the camera flash. Josie at Mama's right and pretty Pauline to the left proudly boasted white winged bows above their thick dark hair. With her left hand claiming Mama's shoulder and right hand pressing Juanita's lap, Josie nestled just below Frances near Al, a position of honor. Beyond Josie and Mama, flourishing long cascades of brown hair to the waist of her velvet dress, teenage Juanita showed poise and elegance.

However beguiling, Lucinda's attractive girls could not upstage their older brother. Darkly handsome in 1915 at 23, Manuel Joseph subtly dominated the family portrait. Blushes of light across his proud brow and piercing eyes betrayed darker emotions within. Garnished with formal finery, the family heir's moody presence commanded deference. Standing patiently at his side, sister Amelia abides the moment, denying the photographer a glimpse of her thoughts. Tucked behind her pleasant smile were still fresh images of a private ceremony two years ago when Amelia, William Blalack, and Father Daniel Brady stood in St. Vincent's rectory one Saturday evening to witness her brother Manuel Joseph exchange simple marriage vows with Ursulene Joullian. Ursulene's 7 year-old brother Charles Joullian and sister Clarice Joullian, the twins, stood near Ursulene, quietly absorbing the affair. Clarice thought Ursulene pretty and liked the large bow tying off her sister's dress in the back. Ursulene's mother, though, wore a look of mixed feelings. Lucinda and Lena, as Leona Joullian preferred to be called, spoke on the back porch some weeks before the wedding. The two mothers paid little heed to Clarice, who hung on every word. Neither Lucinda nor Lena favored the marriage, though for reasons 7 year-old Clarice found complicated. Miss Nettie Pocase, a thin spinster by appearance, hovered near Charles and Clarice during the ceremony without offering a hint of emotion. Ursulene's father, about whom no one spoke, did not attend his daughter's wedding. Grandpa Joe also was notably absent. Afterwards, Amelia walked with the small wedding party north on Franklin to Lena Joullian's house on Madison to drain a couple of beer kegs donated by Lucinda. The newlyweds did not honeymoon.

Neither Ursulene nor Grandpa Joe's grandson Gunny appeared in Lucinda's 1915 family portrait. Four years later, little had changed. No picture of Ursulene and her son, no photograph of Lucinda's first grandchild, graced the sideboard in the front parlor on May 21, 1919. Lucinda's family portrait revealed much by what it left out.

At four years old, Al Gonzales understood the notion of hell. Father Brady often spoke from St. Vincent's pulpit about hell. Al now beheld the jaws of hell. From his front porch at 407 south St. Emanuel, Al watched flames and smoke belching east across Conception at him. Al looked to the peak of the roof where his aging father was hoisting another water bucket up the ladder. But water could not quench the fires of hell. What little water made it to the shingles turned to vapor shortly before the shingles turned to fire. Al had never before seen Papa Joe's face despair, hapless against a dark power that casually reduces a man's place in life to naught. The old Spaniard cursed as he flung the wet bucket against hissing clapboard walls. Lucinda gripped Al by the wrist. His feet moved along St. Emanuel in one direction as he watched Papa splash the burning roof in the opposite direction. Joseph Gonzalez's house seemed eager to join its neighbors and fly away. Stumbling backwards and sideways, Al crept through the darkness to Aunt Mary Soutullo's place, escaping the fiery plague that had come for them all. Al wondered if he would ever see home or Papa again.

On the morning of May 21, 1919 Grandpa Joe had much to show for his 32 years in the new world. Come sundown he had little. Years of carting muddy oysters from the river docks, day-in day-out shucking by hired Coloreds under the shed out back, and gallon upon gallon delivered all about town disappeared in one afternoon. The old Spaniard watched his three story castle crumble to its foundation, sickened by the sight yet unable to look away. In the few moments before flames devoured all his life's baggage, Grandpa Joe rescued his family portrait from the sideboard. With stuffed knapsack weighing heavily against his bony shoulder, an aged Joseph Gonzalez struggled through Mobile's littered streets, an immigrant again.

From St. Vincent Church to the L&N Railroad shops off Royal Street, blackened chimneys hovered like tombstones over the scorched remains of Mobile's south side. Coloreds from Our Alley commingled with Whites in silent grief, stirring ashes for memories that suddenly perished the afternoon of May 21, 1919. Southern brethren extended condolences to Mobile's sudden homeless, opening doors to strangers, preparing meals, and offering donations. For its part, though, the fire department felt obliged to blame low water pressure in reply to criticism about the caliber of its response. Speculation abounded how a simple trash fire could wreak such havoc, even with the help of steady warm winds. Attention focused on how Cunningham let the fire spread out of control, wondering if kerosene carelessly fueled its progress. Understandably, Horace Cunningham denied knowing how the fire started. He suggested an unknown person must have dropped a cigarette into some trash. Horace claimed that his "attention was first attracted to the fire by a negro man calling me that my back yard was on fire." To those rummaging amid their ruins, talk of blame, excuses, and denials did not much matter.

The chore of surviving overcame the shame of taking handouts. Mobile had two families, the Haves and the Have-nots. Cunningham's chicken coops added a lot more Have-nots, who were now common as gully dirt on the south side. Losing everything meant losing the little that once tempered their poverty. Before May 21 it was no disgrace to be poor. Folks latched screen doors to keep dogs and babies from wandering off and pigs from wandering in. There was little worth stealing below Madison Street. No one latched doors to keep thieves out. After May 21, there were no doors to latch.

Within the week, hundreds of two-room tents from Camp Shelby Mississippi sprouted like saplings from Charleston south to Savannah Street and Royal west to St. Emanuel. Until their new house rose from the ashes, Lucinda, Papa Joe and Al gathered each night in one of the Army tents near Charleston and St. Emanuel. Home became wherever Al put his head when darkness fell. In time, Al came to know the trolley that wormed its way down Royal and turned west onto Charleston near Ben Cody's restaurant. In daylight, the trolley reminded Al of the Spanish tile factory where carts on narrow-gauge rails ran through the production areas, offering Al a solitary ride on Mobile's smallest railroad. The trolley's routine measured the passing days. In the darkness west of the L&N Railroad yards, Al would lie on a tent cot, sensing the rumble of trolley wheels. Somewhere in the shadows the clatter changed cadence. The trolley hesitated. Al's eyes bolted open in the dark Army tent. A bright light stared at him through the canvas wall as the trolley charged. He trembled with fear, certain the train would leave its tracks and come for him. Al pulled the blanket around his neck, praying for the rumble to go away. Each night the demon trolley spared Al, wandering off through the crop of tents where Gunny and the rest of Mobile's Have-nots awaited sunrise.

2. Joseph Gonzalez family: (1st, l-r) Juanita, Josie, Alphonse, Lucinda Varedo Gonzalez, Pauline, Joseph Gonzalez (Gunny's grandfather); (2nd, l-r) Frances, Emanuel Joseph (Gunny's father), Amelia, January 3, 1915 (photographer unknown).

3. Sebastian Gonzalez family: (1st, l-r) Manuel Joseph (Nelo), Arthur Sebastian, Leopoldina Perez (Mama Grande & Tia Leo), Marguerita (Peggy), Sebastian Gonzalez; (2nd, l-r) Victor A., Marietta (Cushie), Emilie (Mil), c. 1921 (photographer unknown).

4. Great Fire, Mobile's south side, May 22, 1919 (Courtesy, Erik Overbey Collection, University of South Alabama Archives).

5. *Great Fire, Mobile's south side, May 22, 1919 (Courtesy, Erik Overbey Collection, University of South Alabama Archives).*

6. *Great Fire, Mobile's south side, May 22, 1919 (Courtesy, Erik Overbey Collection, University of South Alabama Archives).*

7. *Great Fire, Mobile's south side, May 22, 1919 (Courtesy, Erik Overbey Collection, University of South Alabama Archives).*

8. Mobile's south side in 1891 from Charleston north to Eslava and from Cedar east to St. Emanuel, showing St. Vincent Church and school, Cunningham's grocery at Madison and Hamilton, Gunny's birthplace on Madison east of the Franklin street trolley, and Grandpa Joe's house on the east side of St. Emanuel south of Canal, but omitting Our Alley and Colored dwellings from Palmetto south to Texas between Conception and Franklin (Courtesy, C. J. Pauli, University of South Alabama Archives).

9. *Mobile's town center in 1891 showing (l-r) the Cathedral (6), Bienville Square, and Battle House Hotel (48) (Courtesy C. J. Pauli, University of South Alabama Archives).*

10. GONZALES FAMILY 1924

CARLOS GONZALEZ (Galicia, Spain)
——*married* Louisa Fernandez (Spain)
|
> Manuel Gonzalez [b. 1838 (Galicia, Spain); d.7-21-1907 (Mobile)]
> ——*married* Maria Moll de Gonzalez [b. 1836 (Menorca, Spain);
> d. 11-5-1897 (Mobile)]
> |
> > Johanna Gonzalez [b. 3-10-1873 (Spain)]
> > Louisa Gonzalez [b. 12-1-1869 (Spain)]
> > Sebastian Gonzalez (Uncle Sebastian) [b. 12-1-1869 (Spain)]
> > ——*married* Leopoldina Perez (Mama Grande, Tia Leo)
> > [b. 10-24-1870 (Campeche, Mexico)]
> > |
> > > Manuel Joseph (Nelo) Gonzales
> > > Marietta (Cushie) Gonzales
> > > Emilie (Mil) Gonzales
> > > Victor Armand Gonzales
> > > Arthur Sebastian Gonzales
> > > Margarita (Peggy) Gonzales

|
JOSEPH GONZALEZ (Gunny's grandfather) [b. 5-25-1851 (Galicia, Spain)]
——*married* Lucinda Varedo [b. 9-16-1869 (Point Clear)]
|
> Joseph Gonzales, Jr.
> Juanita Gonzales
> Frances Gonzales
> Josie Gonzales
> Pauline Gonzales
> Amelia Gonzales
> Alphonse C. Gonzales
> Emanuel Joseph Gonzales (Gunny's father)
> ——married Ursulene Pond Joullian
> |
> > **EMANUEL JOSEPH (GUNNY) GONZALES, JR.**
> > Luthia (Dit) Gonzales
> > Joseph V. Gonzales
> > Leona Gertrude (Nonie) Gonzales

CHAPTER 2

Ursulene Joullian

Nine months of pregnancy and four children left Ursulene Joullian Gonzales every bit as tired as she looked. Carrying a fourth baby while keeping up with Gunny, Dit and Joseph wore her wit thin. Ursulene's 26 year-old grin and robust laugh faded with the years. Sitting at the kitchen table in the small frame rental at 218 South Cedar, the young mother pondered what to do. For the past four years, Ursulene and her kids moved from house to house, sometimes just a step ahead of the landlord. It was a familiar story, with the monthly $10 rent due faster than money coming in to pay it. Of course, half the neighborhood shared the same boat. Sitting on the porch step at dusk, Ursulene and Gunny often watched neighbors pack households onto street carts around the end of the month. Gunny did not have to ask why folks came and went like the tide. This was the nature of things on the south side.

The morning sun crested above shiny tin roofs, casting a shaft of light onto Ursulene's kitchen floor. Eight month-old Nonie, namesake of her Irish Ma, Leona Gertrude Joullian, consumed what freedom and youth Ursulene still had. Three year-old Joseph and 6 year-old sister Dit would be up soon, wanting to eat. They also were likely to ask when Manuel would be coming home from Irish Ma's house, unaware that Ursulene gave away their older brother last night. After supper with Leona, brother Charles, and Miss Nettie, Ursulene walked Joseph,

Dit, and Nonie home and tucked them in bed. Gunny did not walk home with them. Ursulene's 11 year-old stayed the night with Irish Ma, Uncle Charlie, and Aunt Nettie. Gunny would not be coming home again. Ursulene gave up her firstborn. No one talked of adoption. That did not seem fit. The family would take care of its own. This was something long in the making, something that finally had to give.

Four children left Ursulene with options somewhere between bad and worse. Feeding the children's mouths no longer seemed to be a blessing of motherhood. Ursulene fooled herself into thinking she and husband Manuel Joseph could smooth over their ups and downs. They married each other twice. As a tugboat engineer, Manuel Joseph proved smart and skillful hauling trees and cargo downriver. As a businessman, he ran oyster shops and clerked for Grandpa Joe. He even worked a spell at the fire house. When work cycles played out, though, he drank. When words were exchanged, he drank. Booze seemed to make bad times tolerable, until the next day. Layoffs came and went. The only steady jobs in the south part of town ran with locomotives at the GM&N shops near Royal and Charleston.

Ursulene's mother had heard most of this before, as had Charles Joullian. Ursulene's younger brother was not yet 18, but his word in Lena Joullian's house carried weight. Ever so often Ursulene did not make the rent and had to move. Young Gunny could not help but overhear Ursulene and Manuel Joseph arguing about this, that, and the other. Sometimes Manuel Joseph stayed over at his mother's house. Lucinda Gonzalez knew her grandchildren often did without, but seldom spoke to Ursulene and never paid a visit. Gunny and Dit took to calling grandmother Lucinda Grandma Sin. Gunny and Dit played with Al Gonzales over at Lucinda's house, but come suppertime Grandma Sin did not offer Ursulene's kids a bite to eat. Lucinda called Al in for supper, leaving Gunny and Dit waiting on the steps outside until Al returned to play.

Whether Ursulene divorced, separated, or accepted her fate would make little difference paying rent at the end of the month. Ursulene had made her bed and now had to lie in it. The scandal and expense of divorce served no practical purpose. Even if it did, Church law did not recognize civil divorce except as a prelude to annulment. Civil remarriage without negotiating the theological hurdles of a canonical annulment would draw an automatic excommunication. That was more than Ursulene could handle at the moment. She figured that Gunny could live with his Irish Ma and Aunt Nettie, run errands, and help out around the house. Both Lena and Miss Nettie already were in their 50's. Ursulene figured that Gunny could mostly take care of himself, though keeping up a household of three adults already proved tough enough without an 11 year-old under the roof. There would be no one to watch over Gunny when school let out. Miss Nettie, Lena, and Charles worked most of the day just to make ends meet. Lena was long past raising kids, though Miss Nettie lent a hand rearing Charles and Clarice. Charles did not know the first thing about looking after children, especially one who already had a mind of his own. If Gunny stayed with Irish Ma, he had to toe the line with Uncle Charlie.

For the last two years, Miss Nettie and the Joullian's shared the west side of a double tenement at 408 Charleston. Henry Bresewitz's family lived on the east side of the common wall at 406 Charleston. The Waldstrom's house, at the northeast corner of Hamilton and Charleston, flanked the Joullian's to the west. The double tenement was a step down from where the Joullian's had lived at 210 Charleston east of Franklin. With Charles' twin sister Clarice married off, the luxury of some elbow room momentarily made the tenement somewhat more habitable. On February 26, 1923, the day before she turned 17, Clarice Joullian and her boyfriend Ernest James went off to Pascagoula with Lena's reluctant blessing to get married. Lena's baby girl was not of age under Alabama law, but met what few standards existed in Mississippi. Clarice made it clear to everyone that she did not have to get married. Her sweetheart wanted to take a hard-to-come-by federal job upstate in Tuscaloosa, and could not bear the thought of leaving Clarice in Mobile. Next morning, Clarice celebrated her birthday and left home, promising Lena that she would visit every month. Clarice kept her word, at least until Ernest James, Jr.'s birth on May 1, 1924, a month after Ursulene delivered Nonie.

With Clarice in Tuscaloosa, Ursulene figured the time was right for Gunny to move in with his Irish Ma. Lena, Ursulene and the twins had made do in even closer quarters years ago in a two room rental back of the Pocase Grocery on Elmira at Lawrence, and later when Ursulene gave birth to Gunny under Lena's roof at 205 Madison. The Joullian's temporarily left the south side in 1916 for a modest place at 55 Springhill Avenue near the farmers' market, only to move back to 210 Charleston before the Great Fire of 1919. But for the grace of God, the Joullian's would have lost what little they had. Still, they stayed only a step ahead of the poorhouse. As an apprentice in the composing room at the *Mobile Register*, Charles sometimes earned $9 a week if he had work. Lena Joullian worked for one of Mobile's leading hotels, the St. Andrew, right next to the Battle House. At $5 a week, she kept up guest rooms. The work never got easier, the pay never got better, and she never got younger. Miss Nettie had been with Hammel Drygoods Company on south Royal Street for some time, also taking home $5 per week. Together, they might see $11 to $19 in a good week. Each dime mattered for all of them to make do.

No one needed to ask young Gunny's thoughts about leaving home. He preferred being over at Irish Ma's house. But taking in Gunny might not make life easier for anyone, and Gunny probably would never return home. Lena needed a no-nonsense surrogate father, not just Miss Nettie, to help raise a boy. Without Charles' say so Lena could not take on the responsibility for Gunny that Ursulene wanted to surrender. No Joullian had ever given away a child, even to relatives, and there would be no turning back.

11. Ursulene, Clarice and Charles H. Joullian, 300 Elmira, Mobile, 1909 (photographer unknown).

12. *Clarice and Charles H. Joullian, 300 Elmira, Mobile, 1910 (photographer unknown).*

13. Emanuel Joseph (Gunny) Gonzales, Jr., 210 Charleston, Mobile, 1917 (photographer unknown).

*14. Gunny Gonzales, First Communion, Mobile, May 7, 1922
(photographer unknown).*

15. *St. Vincent Church, Lawrence Street, Mobile, 1994 (Copyright © 2007 James J. Gonzales).*

*16. Leona Pond and Charles H. Joullian, 210 Charleston, Mobile, c. 1919
(photographer unknown).*

17. JOULLIAN FAMILY—1924

JACQUES (JACOB) JOULIN [b. 1768 (France); d. 11-26-1844 (Mobile)]
|
Francis Charles Joullian [b. 1800 (France); d. 1837 (Macon, Georgia)]
——*married* Sophia Beulah (Beulat)
[b. 5-1-1801 (Berne, Switz.); d. 1-7-1891 (Mobile)]
|
Charles Alexander Joullian [b. 1823 (N. Y.); d. 1895]
——*married* Mary J. Pierce Jordan [b. 1833 (Ireland)]
|
CHARLES EDWARD JOULLIAN [(b. 1867]
——*married* LEONA GERTRUDE POND (Irish Ma)
[b. 7-15-1870]*
|
Clarice Joullian [b. 2-27-1906]
——*married* Ernest James

Charles Henry Joullian (Uncle Charlie) [b. 2-27-1906]

URSULENE POND JOULLIAN (Nannie)
[b. 12-11-1898]
——*married* Emanuel Joseph Gonzales
|
EMANUEL JOSEPH (GUNNY) GONZALES
Luthia (Dit) Gonzales
Joseph V. Gonzales
Leona Gertrude (Nonie) Gonzales

*Nettie G. Pocase (Aunt Nettie) [b. 4-12-1870]

CHAPTER 3

Oysters a la Cart

Old Mule lived at 355 south St. Emanuel in a small shed behind the house Grandpa Joe rebuilt after the Great Fire. The animal stood nearly a hand taller than its master, and each moved with the deliberate pace of increasing age. Some twenty years earlier, Grandpa Joe and his mule began their now familiar routine. At daybreak, the two trotted up St. Emanuel to Eslava and then down to the river to meet incoming boats. Old Mule picked its pace and turned corners without a touch of rein. It knew where Grandpa Joe bought oysters and where he sold them. The mule's ritual never changed.

"Vamos, Manuelito!" The old Spaniard shouted, slapping the empty bench seat at his side. Gunny walked from Irish Ma's place on Charleston to ride with Grandpa Joe. His short, stubby legs took their time covering four blocks. Grandpa Joe was already on board, on time, when Gunny appeared in the shell driveway. The youngster scampered onto the dray next to the old Spaniard. Grandpa Joe twisted his full moustache and nodded *andale*. Old Mule shook its bonnet and the two-wheel dray cart rolled slowly onto St. Emanuel. Grandpa Joe glanced sideways at his dark grinning grandson and mumbled something in Spanish. The Spaniard addressed his grandson as Manuel, and only in the mother tongue. Gunny understood. For the most part, though, neither had much to say. Being together said plenty. Clopping mule hooves and creaking wooden wheels spoke for both of them. Riding high with Grandpa Joe down the streets of Mobile was enough. The noise of words would only break the spell. They rode in earnest silence.

The old Spaniard handed soft, worn reins to Gunny. It mattered little whether anyone held the reins, for the aging mule knew its own mind. But Gunny brimmed with excitement. The cart bounced over the same ruts and through the same mud holes the veteran mule had stepped over yesterday. The little oyster drover gasped with each bump and splash. His grandfather barely noticed the ride. The Spaniard eyed his family namesake, his first grandson. Lucinda harbored no ill feelings against Gunny. She simply harbored no feelings at all. Whatever the distance between Lucinda Varedo and Ursulene Joullian, their common issue now rode down St. Emanuel on a dray cart with his grandfather.

Old Mule turned right at Eslava. A few blocks remained to the foot of the street and the river's edge. In the distance, mast riggings wobbled near the wharf. Several fishing and flat-bottom oyster boats huddled close to creosote pilings. Mounds of oysters waited on the bows, the oyster shells still bearing wet blue-gray mud from the reefs off Bon Secour and Pascagoula. The cart hesitated as it neared the wharf. Grandpa Joe jiggled the left rein against the mule's ear. Old Mule moseyed off to the right and came to rest on a comfortable sandy spot atop smooth pebbles.

The Spaniard stepped off the cart and ambled over to the oyster barges for closer study. Gunny kept his bare feet in the cart, gripping the reins and watching Grandpa Joe. A lifetime of marketing oysters made this a routine matter for the old man. The boy stared curiously as his grandfather sniffed the catch, then shucked a sample at random. A knife flashed quickly and tossed the hapless oyster into the old man's mouth. He chewed thoughtfully, glancing up as seagulls swooped low over the wharf. Grandpa Joe did not spit out the oyster. That was a good sign. Queasy stomachs fared poorly when the old Spaniard sampled a stale catch. It could get ugly.

From the cart, Gunny inhaled the briny seaweed aroma cast off by oysters on board and fish under ice. As Grandpa Joe stepped from barge to barge, lapping waves cast a rhythmic spell over the boy and the mule. Even the ritual haggle down to 35 cents a bushel did not disturb the morning's peaceful mood. It merely added ceremony to the spectacle. Old Mule dozed in place until four heavy baskets of oysters, still weeping with water and mud, crashed loudly aboard the cart. Grandpa Joe regained his seat on the cart and talked Old Mule back to life. An even slower and more deliberate pace over bumpy clay streets led back to the shed behind Joseph Gonzalez's new house. The ride ended too soon for Gunny. As the cart creaked into place under the shed's awning, Colored shuckers removed the heavy live cargo. Each shucker pulled up to a bushel astride a stubby slanted bench that seemed ever ready to collapse on its shorter legs.

The Spaniard and his grandson watched double-edged shucking knives slip expertly into rock-like shell. As mother of pearl flashed open, the knife rolled under the fat gray oyster and severed its chewy muscle from the eye of the shell. With a flick of the shucker's wrist, the homeless oyster fell into a gleaming pail. Hands and shucking knives repeated this cycle again and again, creating a cadence all by themselves. Shucking done, the Spaniard and his grandson went about delivering the oysters. The dray cart followed Old Mule over wooden paving blocks up Royal Street across Government. Grandpa Joe stopped at the Royal St. Cafe between Conti and Dauphin, leaving Gunny holding the reins. Next on his rounds were the St. Andrew Hotel and Battle House oyster bars, where gentlemen who could afford to pay more for the best did. By noon, day was done. Tomorrow and after tomorrow, Grandpa Joe would retrace these steps as he had for years. He and his mule were older and his cart slower. But grandson Gunny did not notice such small matters. Riding next to the old Spaniard on a dray cart down the middle of Royal Street, pulling right up to the fanciest hotels in Mobile, etched memories for many a morrow. Grandpa Joe filled the gap in Grandma Sin's family portrait.

CHAPTER 4

Aunt Nettie

Including thick eyeglasses and high-top laced shoes, Nettie G. Pocase weighed all of 94 pounds. A hard sneeze could throw Miss Nettie off balance, but no one pushed her around. Though a spinster of no particular kin to the Joullian's, Nettie was family. She and Leona had known the other since the administration of Ulysses S. Grant, Nettie dating from April 12, 1870 and Leona three months later.

Leona, Ursulene and the twins lived with the Pocase's on Elmira, renting out two rooms of the corner grocery run by Nettie's mother, Mariah. Not long after Mariah passed away from consumption, Miss Nettie lost both home and store for non-payment of a small amount of taxes that infinitely exceeded her means. Leona made room for her spinster companion in the rowdy world of Leona's pubescent Ursulene and precocious 5 year-old twins. In 1912 the Joullian's and Miss Nettie moved from Elmira eight blocks north between Claiborne and Franklin, settling down at 205 Madison. Miss Nettie stepped through the looking glass into the shoes of *Aunt* Nettie. A year later, in the dusk of a Saturday evening, the spinster found herself standing uncomfortably in the rectory of St. Vincent Church, watching Ursulene exchange vows with the darkly handsome Manuel Joseph Gonzales. Wrapped in white with a broad sash tied off boldly in the back, Ursulene's well-developed young figure looked deceptively older and mature.

Ursulene delivered her firstborn in Irish Ma's bed. No matter how often the Joullian's moved about after that, Gunny found himself at home with his Irish Ma and Aunt Nettie. However deep the tricycle ruts Gunny carved into the Joullian's porch on Charleston before the Great Fire, Aunt Nettie abided him patiently. After Ursulene gave Gunny to his grandmother in 1924, Aunt Nettie staked her territory. White haired, wizened, and thin as worn socks, Nettie cast a protective eye on her surrogate nephew and a jaundiced one on those around him. The passage of time had not yet dimmed her wit or vigilance.

"Manuel, what all did you learn in school today?" Nettie mumbled as she sometimes did while starting supper. Like the old Spaniard, Nettie called the boy Manuel, never Gunny.

"Nothin'." Manuel stared at the back of her tightly wound hair bun, wondering what she might be getting at. He had long since learned not to underestimate Aunt Nettie's never-you-mind questions that came out of nowhere. He also had learned the hard way to tell Aunt Nettie the truth, though only as little as possible. Unlike Irish Ma, Aunt Nettie could be hell on wheels when she caught someone in the cross-hairs. Trifling with Irish Ma was one thing, for Lena Joullian idolized her grandson, but messing around with Nettie Pocase proved mostly stupid. Aunt Nettie said nothing when Irish Ma wanted Manuel to explain all the E's on his report card. Grandson convinced grandmother that E meant excellent. Irish Ma swallowed that worm, hook, line, and sinker. But Nettie's eyes narrowed at Manuel over the bridge of her large glasses, as they did before she swatted a fly. She didn't buy any part of that smooth talk. Gunny knew he had a way to go to outsmart Aunt Nettie.

Nettie stirred the dinner pot and then stepped over to the icebox, a large knife in hand. Without a word she trimmed what little meat still clung to an aging ham bone, and muttered about the ice block being nearly gone. Every day or so Manuel pulled his wagon over to People's Ice House to collect ice scraps for the icebox. Whenever he could rub 35 cents together, Manuel also hauled home a bucket of oysters and shucked them for his Uncle Charlie. Charles never seemed to get the knack of shucking, but had no trouble slurping the critters off the half shell. Aunt Nettie preferred to starve instead. She would have nothing to do with a raw oyster. Nettie faced the stove, dropping a slice of fatty pork and a pinch of sugar into the pot of steaming collards. "Did school let out late today?"

Gunny looked for a way out of this. He knew what she was getting at, but pretended otherwise. A telltale stomach growl broke the silence. Nettie leaned on one leg and scanned the kitchen ceiling for his answer. She squinted hard. Gunny could see it coming. He managed a half-truth: "Well, Sister Helena got mad at me about somethin' and kept me after school."

"I reckoned you might say that," Nettie put another quarter into the gas meter to feed the stove. "What would Sister Helena want with you? Doesn't she see you enough already?"

"I dunno. I guess she was mad at me before I even got to school this mornin'. My name's still on the chalkboard for not payin' tuition. She talked about me right there in front of all the kids. I told her I already told you and Irish Ma about tuition, and as soon as y'all can afford to make me lunch, y'all can afford to pay tuition. I told her that's what y'all said. She didn't like that none at all. Said I was smartin' off again. She whacked me good and told me to stay after school." Manuel figured he had said the wrong thing to Sister Helena, and probably too much to Aunt Nettie.

Nettie set the lid on the pot and turned off the burner. She stared absently at Gunny for the longest time, plumbing for the truth. He braced for the worst. The old woman walked over and leaned into his face, close up.

"Where did Sister Helena whack you?" She measured the words slowly.

Gunny held out his left hand. Bright red lines scored an open palm.

"You didn't get into any fights, did you Manuel?" Nettie wanted to be sure what happened.

"No ma'am. Not today. I swear." Manuel usually owned up to fighting, that being a fairly respectable sport and survival skill on the south side.

"Manuel, I've told you before not to swear. You can't afford to get on the Lord's bad side. Get on your shoes. You're coming with me."

Nettie tossed off her apron and marched through the screen door with Manuel in tow.

"Where're we goin', Aunt Nettie?" Manuel feared getting Nettie riled, and by the look on her face he had reason to worry. The old spinster marched down the middle of Charleston, stepping over deep runoff ruts. Faster than a *Hail Mary*, she swept through St. Vincent school's south door and found Sister Helena in the courtyard. Miss Nettie was not one to mince words, especially with nuns and clerics. She harbored a bitter suspicion that a priest long ago had beguiled her parents out of their humble savings for a donation to the church.

"Sister Helena, Manuel here tells me he stayed after school today and got spanked in class for smartin' off to you."

The nun gave the boy a solemn look and pitied his misfortune. "Yes, I reminded Manuel of his place and manners. Boys his age must be corrected, don't you think?" The nun turned on a hapless Manuel, smiling condemnation all over him. He tried to catch Aunt Nettie's eye, but she paid him no mind. The skinny spinster carefully studied the nun through mental cross-hairs. Manuel breathed rapidly, dreading the what-for that awaited him at home. Nettie came by her reputation honestly.

One old maid puckered her lips at the other old maid, as though testing a poorly seasoned stew. "Sister Helena, if Manuel needs a good whackin', let me know. You rest assured, I'll give it to him myself. And if I can't, his grandmother will. As long as he's under our roof, he'll toe the line. But we don't plan to take the boy down a notch for not paying what we don't have and he don't owe. When we see fit to send Manuel to school with lunch, you can start looking for tuition money. But if you lay another hand on this boy, I'll be back over here to knock that hat right off your head. We understand each other?" Nettie spoke her piece and turned to go. Sister Helena had nothing to say that Nettie cared to hear, so the meeting ended. Manuel kept his bulging eyes on Sister Helena, who looked especially pale beneath her starched veil. He had never seen Aunt Nettie punch a grownup, much less a Sister. But Aunt Nettie did not make idle threats. Gunny admired that.

From the look on Sister's face, Nettie's promise sounded convincing. Gunny tried to imagine Aunt Nettie hurling the nun's habit across the courtyard, with Sister Helena still attached. Of course, Nettie would surely go straight to hell if she hit Sister Helena. Gunny had no doubts about that. But Aunt Nettie did not seem to fret about the Devil. She would cross that bridge when the time came. For the moment, Nettie Pocase seemed fit to deal with hell itself. Manuel resolved never to cross the old spinster on this Earth.

Nettie grabbed a stunned Manuel by the arm and marched out the south door into the dusty street. "Them collards oughta be done," she muttered. "Your Uncle Charlie and grandmother will be home for supper any time now. Get a move on. I've got to get the cornbread in." Gunny stumbled, looking over his shoulder to see if Sister Helena might be coming after them. All he saw were two sets of footprints down the middle of Charleston. Sister Helena never whacked Manuel again. None of the sisters did. They took Nettie Pocase at her word.

Even so, *Manuel Gonzales* stayed on the chalkboards for the rest of the year. The $1.50 monthly tuition the Joullian's owed but could not pay kept adding up. "Tuition'll get paid when we've got the money, Manuel," Irish Ma said time after time. "Putting food on the table and shoes on your feet comes first."

"But I'm still up there on the blackboard and Sister makes everybody stop and see who's paid and who ain't," her grandson explained.

Irish Ma could think of nothing more to say. There was hardly enough money left over to feed the lot of them each night. Aunt Nettie paused in the rocker. "Manuel, you know I walk all over town to save a penny or two on something for dinner. And unless it's too cold out there in the shed, I fire up that little charcoal furnace and iron clothes so we don't have to spend on electricity. It ain't amountin' to much yet, but it'll go for your schoolin'." Nettie liked to get out and walk all over town. Gunny traipsed around with Nettie from the Southern Market to Stokes Grocery at the corner of Charleston and Franklin looking for cheap soup bones. What few pennies Nettie pocketed at a butcher's block barely took care of Gunny's hunger from all that extra walking.

"Course, we might just get lucky come Mardi Gras and win the $100 costume prize," she fancied. Each Fat Tuesday, Nettie and Gunny packed a lunch, got all gussied up, and went over to Bienville Square to watch floats and enter the costume contest. They never won.

"Can I take something for lunch at school?" Manuel changed the subject. "Al and them bring a lunch and eat at recess. I don't have anything to eat."

"Manuel, there just ain't anything to fix for lunch. We're expectin' your mama, Joseph, Dit, and baby Nonie to be comin' over again for supper tomorrow. Your brother and sisters don't eat much of anything twice a day. It's about all we can do just to make ends meet for us and them too. But I'll fix something special this weekend, like bread pudding with lemon sauce. How'd you like that?" Irish Ma's gray eyebrows arched into question marks. It amazed Gunny how Irish Ma could turn stale bread nose ends into pudding. "See if Alphonse Gonzales or one of your cousins'll share something with you." Gunny did not like to mooch lunch at school. His buddies did not bring much to eat, and he usually ended up with whatever nobody wanted.

"It's late now, off to bed with you." Irish Ma patted Gunny on the back and waited until he left the room. As little as Manuel had to eat for lunch, others had it worse. There was no secret about Gunny's father eating and staying at Lucinda Gonzalez's house. Ursulene often had no milk in the icebox for baby Nonie. Dit and Joseph lived mostly on beans and rice. Leona recalled having words with Lucinda Gonzalez about the wisdom of the marriage, but eventually resigned herself to the inevitable. Of course, Leona could not foresee that Lucinda would hold onto her oldest son, mothering him while his own kids did without. They were Lucinda's grandchildren, but they were Ursulene's brood first. Ursulene would have to tend them. The Spanish matriarch, the young Irish child bearer, and Gunny shared a common son, husband, and father, but not a common family.

Thoughts of Ursulene mingled with memories of Leona's own youth, marrying Charles Edward Joullian so many years ago, bearing Ursulene in 1898 and then Charles and Clarice on February 27, 1906.

Of them all, only Charles still lived at home. He was her bonus baby, an unanticipated Mardi Gras favor. After delivering Clarice at 3 in the afternoon, Leona lay exhausted in her bed feeling the pain of continuous contractions. She mumbled to her Colored midwife that something inside was not right, something was still moving. Doctor Parish, who left just after delivering Clarice, already had rejoined the mystic revelry in the streets downtown but rushed back to Leona's bedside. As the semiconscious mother and midwife carried on about the pain inside, the surprised doctor noticed Charles' bluish crown emerging. Neither doctor nor mother anticipated twins. Charles nearly got lost amid all the fuss of Fat Tuesday. Doctor Parish plucked Charles' motionless blue body from his mother, quickly pinching an eerie membrane that smothered his face. The fetal veil dissolved into a spate of coughs and wails, changing Charles to a ruddy shade of pink.

Charles' spoken word still carried that telltale catch, a breathless rush, an urgency forever reminding Leona of Charles' gasping birth. She treasured the sound of his voice in the heavy silence of her husband's long absence. Charles Edward Joullian, a plumber by trade but gambler by choice, once proudly plied his craft in the bowels of Mobile's City Hall before honing skills more suitable at gaming tables. The Joullian family fortune ebbed for the worse when Charles Edward failed to return to Mobile from one of his frequent sojourns in the Crescent City. Leona lost her husband to the lures of the New Orleans gambling joint he ran on a narrow rue in the *Vieux Carré* known as Our Alley. She could have packed up the kids and followed him, but her roots lay deep within Mobile's south side. Leona never saw Charles Edward again. To make ends meet, she took up pressing clothes at White Swan laundry until the St. Andrews Hotel offered work cleaning guest rooms. Leona felt the toll of the years, yet found comfort in her son and best friend. She treasured the sparkle in Charles' crystal blue eyes and the honesty of Nettie Pocase.

Nettie figured that Manuel would have to make do. She did not intend to fret about the monthly $1.50 tuition they did not have. If need be, she would have another word with Sister Helena. There was nothing else to do. Nothing changed the next morning. Nettie did not prepare a lunch for Gunny. Within an hour of noon, the squirming in class signaled that lunch was not far off. Sister Alphonse could almost tell time by the restlessness. Gunny's belly growled to everyone's amusement. The hungrier he got, the louder he talked, and the more his stomach growled. Sister Alphonse did not like the boys talking in class. It was a malady, for which Sister Alphonse had a cure. Quinine awaited those who talked in class. Only medicinal, undiluted quinine was good enough for these boys. She gave them a choice of sticking out a tongue for a good dose or staying after school. After two years in her class, the boys were mostly immune to malaria. Despite the odds, Sister would teach the neighborhood riffraff to behave. Compared to Sister Alphonse, Sister Helena was a gentle soul. Sister Helena even let crazy Sherwood Harrison roll up his pants and dance on top of his desk in religion class. For that, Sister Alphonse would have force-fed Sherwood a bottle of quinine.

Sister Alphonse apparently got word about Miss Nettie Pocase from Sister Helena. Sister Alphonse thought better of dosing Manuel with quinine. Instead, she banished him from class. "Manuel Gonzales, you are disturbing everyone. Go to the cloakroom and think about working quietly." A pause interrupted the squirming and whispering. The boys expected Gunny to get quinined. Everybody got quinined. Gunny was getting special treatment. They had reason to be disappointed. Gunny walked to the rear of the class and disappeared around the bookcase into the cloakroom. On the shelf above the coat hooks, amid sacks and boxes, he smelled peanut butter, jelly, scrambled egg, and fried chicken. He peeked into one sack, then another. By the time class recessed for lunch, Gunny had finished his. He was ready to go out and play. Sister Alphonse noticed the positive effect exile had on the boy. This would not be his last trip to the cloakroom.

18. *Gunny Gonzales, Ernest James, Jr., & Mrs. Waldstrom's calf,*
408 Charleston, Mobile, 1925 (photographer unknown).

19. St. Vincent School, Charleston Street, Mobile, 1994 (Copyright © 2007 James J. Gonzales).

20.Ursulene Joullian Gonzales, 1928 (photographer unknown).

CHAPTER 5

Pigeons
& Pouldoux

Ancient live oaks shaded Government Street all the way past Michigan Avenue to the Gulf Mobile & Northern Railroad line at the western end of town. Sprouting from massive gray arms, a web of thinner branches mingled midway in a green arch over the street. Through long shadows and splashes of sunlight, horses, carts, and motorcars moved about below. Civic elders had not yet seen fit to pave many downtown streets, and even then seemed partial to creosote blocks. Except for dust, ruts, and mud holes, most folks could not come up with good reason to pour money into concrete streets. After all, trolleys ran just fine on gravel beds, and the thought of horses relieving themselves on concrete put the whole silly matter to rest.

A one-way trolley ride out to Michigan Avenue cost only eight cents, but the boys seldom had a nickel between them. Gunny and Pat Healey usually took the trolley at night when fares were more affordable. Crouching low and holding tight to the outside running bar, the boys hitched rides without the conductor being any the wiser. As it turned out, the smoothest pavement in town stretched west down Government to Michigan Avenue. With a touch of luck, the boys could skate the twenty blocks from Franklin to Michigan Avenue, capture some pigeons, and be home by supper. Or, they could wind up in the Catholic Boys Home out on Old Shell Road. Gaining admission to the Boys Home did not require being a delinquent, though that helped. Being poor was enough.

"Pat, there ain't enough shoe left to keep my skate from slippin'. I can't tighten it no more. It's gonna come off for sure, probably right in the middle of Broad Street." Gunny sat on Pat's front porch on Canal Street fitting his skates. "Last time I scraped my knee up somethin' awful, and Irish Ma wasn't none too happy about the holes in them stockings. She don't want me messin' up my shoes and knee socks again. Says she can't spare for any new ones." Gunny fully expected a trip to the shed out back of Irish Ma's house for coming home again with torn up clothes.

"Manuel, what in tarnation happened to you? You look like somethin' the cat drug in!" Pat mimicked Aunt Nettie.

"Don't call me Manuel. I hear that enough at home." On the street, Manuel was known only as Gunny. Gunny would heel when Aunt Nettie hissed his christened name, but he would not abide being teased by others. He wore his nickname well, and few outside St. Vincent's even knew a Manuel Gonzales. He was just Gunny. "How many of them pigeons are there?"

Pat had seen pigeon lofts in the backyard of the house on Michigan. "About eight or so. And they've got funny little hairs stickin' straight up on top their heads, kinda looks like a fan."

Gunny tugged hard on his left shoe to be sure it was snug. "I bet they're king pigeons or something like that. They'd probably find their way back home if we let 'em go. I hear armies used pigeons in the war to fly messages over trenches during battle. King pigeons are probably a lick smarter than regular homing birds, don't you think?"

"Guess so. Don't really know how they find their way back home, though. Can't figure why they'd want to anyway. Should go live in Bienville Square like other pigeons. Maybe they like livin' in cages. Sure don't sound so smart to me." Gunny and Pat started walking up Conception Street to Government with skates dangling over their shoulders. They skated past the whitewashed facade of antebellum Barton Academy, but paid no mind to Alabama's oldest public school. Neither planned ever setting foot inside the front door anyway.

In the distance just beyond Washington Avenue, a rambling brick wall guarded tenants of the Church Street cemetery. By choice, the boys stayed clear of the cemetery. Over a hundred years of death, mystery, and yellow fever kept most heathens, chicken thieves, and pigeon poachers at a distance. Gunny and Pat heeded omens from the afterlife. They heard of the executed Charles Boyington and the prophetic oak that sprang from Boyington's grave as proof of his professed innocence. The boys would not trifle with restless spirits, whose favor in the hereafter the boys might need. Their skates hurried past the Scott Street gate in the cemetery's north wall. Once on the other side of Bayou Street, they paused in front of Admiral Raphael Semmes' home. Even fifty years after his death, the Confederate States blockade runner's exploits aboard *CSS Alabama* sustained his memory. Pat and Gunny were mindful not to disturb Mobile's legendary hero, though he was no longer at home.

Beyond the trolley tracks at Broad, old mansions stood proudly amid great lawns of mossy oaks. People of means lived west of Broad. They could afford to keep pigeons just for fun, even though Bienville Square already had more pigeons than anyone could shake a stick at. The boys had tried stalking pigeons in the Square, but those were wily birds. As soon as Pat and Gunny took aim with sling shots, the purple-heads in the Square fled in all directions. Some folks downtown would gladly cane young hooligans for trying to harm Bienville Square's wild birds. A safer hunting ground for the boys lay under the eaves of the school just south of the Church Street cemetery between Washington and Bayou Streets, where thousands of pigeons roosted at dusk. When startled, the great flock filled the sky and presented a mass target for slingshots. With luck, a couple of meals fell to earth. Today's prey should be easier.

Michigan Avenue joined Government just west of Ann Street and ran south a couple of miles down to the GM&N tracks. After twenty long blocks, Pat and Gunny turned south onto Michigan, skated across Selma and Elmira and stopped at Texas. Only their grinding steel wheels disturbed the afternoon quiet. For a long while, they rested in the ruts of a driveway that ran the length of a deep clapboard two-story house. A high wooden fence and gate enclosed the back yard and obscured any view of the pigeon lofts. The boys scanned porches down both sides of the street.

"Front porches are all empty. Maybe it's dinner time around here. I don't see anybody. Kinda early for dinner, don't you think?" Gunny strained to catch sounds of dishes or radios. A slight breeze rustled nearby live oaks, masking over any life noises from behind the wood fence. "What if somebody's home?"

"We came all this way to get king pigeons, Gunny. I ain't goin' home without 'em. Come on." Pat held his breath and tiptoed toward the gate on the skates' front wheels. Shells crunched sharply under each step and betrayed their presence. Pounding heartbeats and cracking shells drowned out any pigeon coos and people noise. Pat trusted his luck. Pushing through the tall gate, the boys found their quarry. Two stacks of cages rested on the back porch just twenty feet away.

Unlike chickens, the pigeons sounded no alarm. Huddled in their nests, they eyed two strangers tiptoeing on skates to the porch's edge. Suddenly, doors flew open and thin brown arms raided the cages, snatching the birds and tucking the feathered bundles into the warm darkness between bare skin and T-shirts. With four pigeons each stuffed under their shirts, Gunny and Pat stalked like cranes along the drive, out the gate and into the street. Bowing low to keep balance, they gained speed and headed north. Neither returned the trolley conductor's wave as their wheels rounded the corner east on Government toward Broad. Clutching themselves about the waist, both skaters wrestled feathered spirits as they passed Bayou Street and the cemetery. Except for the trolley crossing at Broad, the return trip went about as well as could be expected. Catching a wheel in the groove of the track bed, Pat lost his balance. Though avoiding a spill on the rails, his sudden change of motion so alarmed the birds that they tried to fly. Gunny watched Pat making a spectacle of himself through the intersection. Inside Pat's shirt, though, the picture turned nasty. The boys were not quite sure how thirty-two claws, eight wings, and four beaks should feel against bare skin. Now they had a better understanding of that and the unexpectedly runny sensation of warm pigeon waste.

Once safely inside the shed behind Pat's house on Canal, the pigeons fluttered from sticky T-shirts into a cage. The boys took stock of the damage. It was not pretty. The pigeons fared much better than did their handlers. Gunny would not begrudge a bath tonight. Pat wiped his belly, but managed only to smear the green-gray deposits. Pat smelled positively ripe.

"What are you gonna say if your folks find out about them?" Gunny nodded at the birds.

"Nothin. They never bother with stuff out here anyway. If they find out where we got 'em though, I wouldn't be able to walk much less skate again. They'd probably hand me over to Officer Dumas or the Boys Home."

"Just don't say anything around Aunt Nettie." Gunny measured his risks. "She don't mind my bringing home pigeons I shoot at the school. She won't clean 'em and won't eat 'em though. Chicken's okay, but not pigeons. Aunt Nettie would just as soon walk all over hell's half acre to find a ten cent soup bone than eat a pigeon. And she wouldn't cotton to my eating somebody else's pigeons. If she gets wind that we got house pigeons here, there'll be hell to pay. And after she gets finished with my behind she'll come looking for yours." Pat had heard of Miss Nettie's visit with Sister Helena. He got the picture. Pat decided it safer to roost the pigeons behind Charlie O'Boyle's house.

Gunny left for home with skates and shoes dangling over his shoulders. Near the corner of Franklin and Canal, he caught sight of a muddied heavy-set figure pushing a wheelbarrow down the middle of Canal. It was old man Kramer. Gunny could tell by the duck-like waddle. As the gap between the boy and the man closed, Gunny noticed a shotgun barrel pointing out the front of the bouncing wheelbarrow. It must not be loaded, Gunny figured, or it would have gone off by now.

In the bed of the barrow, under the shotgun, thirty or so birds sprawled in a blood-speckled heap. Gunny had never been this close to so many killed game. More than once he had seen old man Kramer pushing an empty wheelbarrow alone in the early morning hours down Canal to the river near Star Fish & Oyster. But that was not much more than just a minor curiosity in the south part of town. Gunny had frequently heard Lala Kramer, the youngest of old man Kramer's boys, talk about cleaning birds for dinner. Lala sometimes had a funny smell about him, but then most of the boys smelled funny at one time or another.

As the bow-legged man neared, Gunny stopped and waited.

"Hi, Mr. Kramer," Gunny began, "sure got a big pile of birds there. Those quail or somethin'?"

"Well son, these here birds are pouldoux," the old man paused to rest and humor the boy.

"Pouldoux, huh?" The unusual sound of *pole-doo* intrigued Gunny. "Don't remember ever seeing pouldoux before."

"You won't find pouldoux in a store window, son. Most folks don't like the taste. It's kind of bitter. If you don't cook 'em right, they taste like they smell." Gunny shifted between the old man and the birds. The same smell came from both directions. Old man Kramer had not said pea-turkey to any other living soul since rising at dawn to go hunting. He sized up the scrappy barefoot kid, and noticed the uneasy look he and his birds were getting. There was a long night of cleaning yet to be done. Three dozen birds had to be scalded, plucked and dressed before supper, after which old man Kramer intended to soak himself.

"Where do you go huntin' pouldoux?" The boy wondered.

"Well, I got my places, but once I tell you, then they won't be my places anymore, will they now?" Old man Kramer grinned and posed a riddle. "Let's just say I go sit on an island and them birds come to me."

Word of the Kramer clan's taste for pouldoux held wide currency south of Eslava Street. What the Kramer's did not eat, they sold off the front porch. Given a choice between something and nothing, folks would try pouldoux at least once. The wild bird is to chicken what collard is to lettuce. Some things are worth eating only for the sake of proving how good other things taste. Pouldoux met that test, but the Kramer's did not complain. Old man Kramer never thought twice about packing the barrow, loading the shotgun and filling the coffee bottle for the island. He kept a flat-bottomed boat tied up at the foot of Canal near Uncle Sebastian's wharf. In the early morning hours before boat traffic churned up the river, Kramer paddled across to Blakely Island. From the western bank of the river the old man and his small boat seemed to disappear mid-channel, slipping south into the narrow that separates the northwestern spit of Pinto Island from the eastern edge of Blakely Island. Once out of view, Kramer paddled another half mile southeast until the narrow opened into a large shallow surrounded by marsh rushes. At high tide, Kramer beached on the eastern side of Pinto Island and stalked pouldoux. At low tide, he would round Pinto Island and land at Little Sand Island. He did not ask for two-legged company and rarely found any. Old man Kramer went into the marsh of Mobile Bay to be alone, and to come home with dinner.

"How do you fix 'em?" Gunny asked.

"Well, you just drop 'em in hot water and pluck. No need to worry about it jumping out of the pot like a chicken. You come over sometime and try one, you hear? Bet you'll want seconds." Old man Kramer winked, lifted the barrow, and waddled off. It was nearly sunset and close to supper. Between the pigeons and pouldoux, Gunny had lost most of his appetite.

Halfway through the week Pat took one of the pigeons out of hiding. He held it gently, stroking the folded wings and bobbing neck. He walked the pigeon around the yard and sat with it on the front porch a long while just talking. Then he stood, raised his arms, and let the bird go.

Come Friday, Gunny found Pat in the pigeon shed. "There're only seven pigeons here. What happened to the other one?"

"I wanted to see if they might be homers. I fed them real good all week long. I took one out and showed it around the shed, the house, the whole damn yard. I talked to a stupid pigeon nearly an hour so it knew my voice and where I lived. I let it go. It ain't a homin' pigeon. It didn't come back. It's just a funny lookin bird with a comb in its hair."

"So what're we gonna do with 'em?" Gunny asked.

"They ain't gonna get any fatter than they are right now. We can't fly 'em, and we can't just put 'em back on the porch where we got 'em. We're gonna eat 'em." Pat salivated as he talked. "You know how to clean pigeons, don't you?"

"Yep. Just wring their necks, dip 'em, pluck 'em and fry 'em. Not much to it really, except I've never cooked one before. Aunt Nettie always does that. She'd get to wondering if we just walked in with seven pigeons for her to cook. She won't believe I'm that good a shot with my sling. And they don't look a thing like purple-heads." Gunny narrowed the options down to one. "Let's eat at your house." Pat and Gunny stared at seven king pigeons. Their pecking order on the food chain had been decided. Birds of fancy became birds of prey. Pat and Gunny ate what they killed, fancy or otherwise. Any pigeon in Mobile, king or purple-head, remained fair game as long as Irish Ma served soup bones for dinner.

CHAPTER 6

A Nickel's Worth

Early thunderstorms had all but wrung themselves out into a soft drizzle as St. Vincent's steeple summoned the faithful. Under umbrellas and scarves, a handful of early risers made their way along the stone steps up to the church's main door. Mass would begin in minutes. Though Church law decreed that Catholics attend Sunday Mass, few hurried to be early. They were content to be on time or, if late, at least not draw attention when the door hinge creaked open. Nettie and Gunny slipped through the main door, crossed themselves with holy water, and knelt in an empty pew off to the right of the offertory box.

Pockets of cool air beneath the high vaulted ceiling had not yet warmed under the sun's hot glare. By noon any breathable air in the church would weigh heavily with charcoal fumes, incense, sweat, and the sour breath of fasting sinners. Father Brady scheduled the more ceremonial high Mass for his late-rising faithful. Elaborate liturgy played better to a full house.

Aunt Nettie's prayers before Mass lasted only as long as her bony knees could endure the hard plank kneeler. She leaned back on the bench seat and handed Gunny an Indian head buffalo nickel for the polished oak offering box in the center aisle. That Nettie spared even a nickel was no small matter given her disposition about church donations. Except for occasionally taking Manuel to Mass, the spinster rarely set foot in church anymore, though she found no particular fault with Father Brady. Gunny stepped up to the box, midway between pulpit and exit, and slipped the nickel through the worn slot. News of Nettie's modest donation ricocheted wildly off the plastered ceiling and stained-glass windows. Father Brady's offertory box promptly reported every coin deposit. Nickels and dollar pieces triggered similar sonic shocks to the untrained ear. Father Brady meditated briefly in the sacristy before each Mass. His ear expertly assayed each metal offering. Listening to whispering penitents over the years through the confessional curtain had sharpened his hearing.

In the background Father Brady detected the shuffling step and heavy breathing of his most notable parishioner. Jim Martin carried a lot of weight on Mobile's south side. Successful business dealings allowed him to be gracious and charitable with less fortunate neighbors. Martin paused for air near the last two rows. These were reserved for Creoles who lived across from St. Vincent on Lawrence street. Even at this hour, though, both pews were occupied. To some white folks' way of thinking, those were the best seats in the house, far from the pulpit and close to the exit, though no one dared say such things aloud. This was, after all, the House of the Lord. Every Sunday and holyday, God's white faithful competed for premium seating in the rear of the church near the Creoles. Father Brady long ago abandoned hope of his flock huddling near the pulpit. Latecomers could always find good seating up front.

The Sisters took their place near the altar rail, surrounded by empty rows of endowed family pews. An engraved name at the end of a pew reserved seating for the donor family, which meant that uninvited occupants sat at their own risk. At high Mass, ushers were known to ask embarrassed penitents to surrender a family pew to its rightful donor. Many years had passed since an usher at low Mass had the gumption to bounce anyone from a family pew, except for Jim Martin's.

Gunny watched Mr. Martin pause at the offertory box and fumble around in the deep pockets of his huge trousers. His donation sank quietly with the distinctive crackle of paper money. Though deep in meditation, Father Brady instinctively took note. Jim Martin then found his family pew and sort of sat. The carved hardwood seat groaned when Jim Martin lowered all 350 pounds. Father Brady detected the unmistakable signal that his largest donor had settled in. Jim Martin bypassed the custom of praying on bent knee. Once down, he did not easily arise and even when sitting Jim Martin appeared to be kneeling. Mass began when the first of two altar boys reached up and rang the small bell on the sanctuary wall. Father Brady and his acolytes faced the altar and began their traditional but foreign dialogue: "*Introibo ad altare Dei.*" Behind them, the scattered audience fell to its collective knee. At first blush, the ancient Tridentine Latin Mass might leave the impression of an opera in progress. Mass could be transacted only in the arcane language of Constantine. Some of the faithful silently continued their rosary in English to the Blessed Virgin Mary. While the Lord seemed to prefer a tongue not native to Alabama, conventional wisdom regarded prayer in any language acceptable to Mary. The small congregation listened to Father Brady chant Latin in a somewhat pleasant drawl, but most followed along with a written translation in alternating shades of red and black print. Red indicated important prayers reserved to the priest, black the prayers expected of the faithful. The humble flock quietly accepted their lot in the supernatural order of things. Their hope lay in reaching God's ear through the mystical message that filled His sanctuary.

Mass reflected a carefully scripted ritual rooted in ancient scripture, faith and tradition. Though Father Brady's sermon varied from Sunday to Sunday, any connection between his message and that of the Gospel seemed coincidental. Today proved no exception. After briefly paraphrasing scripture readings, Father Brady focused on a matter of immediate pastoral concern:

> Our government is in a sorry mess. We try to elect sensible men to bring order and meaning to these difficult times. We pray that our leaders and politicians wisely exercise the power of office. We believe that the Lord hears our prayers and knows our needs. He does not abandon us, even though our own kind sometimes do. His ways challenge our weak faith. We must turn to Holy Mother Church and each other in these trying times.
>
> It is our misfortune that our government hounds us for money we don't have. Even I am told to pay more than there is in the till. I am supposed to rob Peter to pay Paul. You, my dear brothers and sisters, know this cannot be done.

> If the truth be known, those buffalo nickels are doing me in. Someone must hear all the noise in that offertory box and think it's real money. I don't want any more buffaloes. Keep them. They just get me in trouble. The good Lord knows the difference between buffalo nickels and silver dollars. You and I know the difference. But our government can't seem to figure it out. No wonder we're in such a mess. Put some real money in that box before they take me away.
>
> *In nomine Patris, et Filii, et Spiritus Sancti. Amen.*

Father Brady was preaching to the choir. Any real money this flock ever saw went to making ends meet. Father Brady might have more luck squeezing blood from a turnip. The image of poor Father Brady being hounded about taxes hit close to home, but with no effect. Only a miracle or Jim Martin could help Father Brady.

Through the rest of their Mass, Father Brady and his altar boys spoke no English. They prayed to the Lord and each other in Latin with their backs to the kneeling flock. The faithful took their cue from ringing bells and body language. As long as the script never changed, they comfortably followed along. When Mass ended, Father Brady faced his people and announced *"Ite Missa est,"* for which the people thanked God as the pastor exited right into the sacristy. When it was over, it was over. Their duty fulfilled, the faithful made for the door.

Sunlight broke through the low overcast by the time Nettie and Gunny got home. Their simple breakfast of oatmeal, toast, and the last drop of milk ended as fast as it began. Another two quarts would come in the morning if Nettie could cover the ten cents. Half the families south of Canal Street took daily milk deliveries, since few could afford an icebox, but the other half could not afford milk even at a nickel a quart. These were the poorest among the Have-nots. They did not know where the next meal might come from. Yet there were mornings when a milk bottle appeared out of nowhere on the doorstep without so much as a knock. The shame of taking handouts, even milk, passed when the mysterious donor failed to step forward.

Face to face handouts would have proved embarrassing. That also would have risked a long stay in the Boys Home. As they had done so often, Gunny, Rip Repoll, and Pat Healey arose at dawn on Saturday to follow Jackie Stokes who delivered for Stokes Grocery. Jackie picked up empties from customers' porches, topping them off from vats on the milk wagon. The boys watched from a safe distance, fully geared in their knee stockings, shoes, and skates. Holes from previous tumbles gave the stockings a seasoned feel. Only Rip did not bother to pull up his stockings or wipe his nose. He skated down-jived, not expecting to be seen by anyone important.

Once the Stokes milk wagon turned off Palmetto onto Hamilton, the boys separated and scouted porches. No two bottles would be left standing together. Swooping in slow and low, Gunny snatched an extra quart off a door step, whipped around the block, stepped quietly up to the stoop of a weathered frame house, and set the bottle down. Then he was off again. The boys left bottles on porches that could not afford delivery. If anyone saw what was going on, nothing was said about it. Not once in two years did anyone report what the boys had done. For their part, the boys did not figure on getting caught. In the whole city there were only three police scout cars, none of which was radio-dispatched. Chances were slim that a patrol car would race across town to nab these scruffy scofflaws. If Aunt Nettie ever got wind of their doings, though, no hiding place in Mobile would be safe.

After breakfast, Gunny changed into street clothes and gave his Sunday shoes to Aunt Nettie to dry. Only last week Nettie had glued new cardboard soles on the bottom of his shoes, covering holes for the next couple months or next rainfall. The soaking walk over to St. Vincent for Mass seeped through the cardboard to Gunny's stockings. So, shortly before noon, Pat Healey and Gunny shuffled into town barefoot. Walking east on Palmetto to Claiborne, the boys neared the north end of Our Alley. After the Great Fire, Coloreds had resettled into their six-block corridor sandwiched between Conception and Franklin from Palmetto south to Texas street. A high wood fence separated Coloreds from the backyards of Whites on either side. Most

Coloreds lived in the north part of town along Jefferson Davis Avenue. Those on the gritty south side lived in Our Alley, surrounded by Whites. Colored children walked from Our Alley to Marshall School at Franklin and Augusta. Gunny knew better than to go looking for trouble. There already were plenty of fights to go around on the White side of the fence. For the most part, Gunny left well enough alone and did not venture into Our Alley.

Not long after the hurricane of September 21, 1926, Irish Ma left her double tenement on Charleston and moved around the corner to 407 Franklin, which backed up to Our Alley. It was the worst storm since 1906, driven by one of the lowest barometric readings on record. Winds gusted through town, swatting down husky oaks with frightening ease, and blowing off tin roofs under which Mobile's south side huddled. Before the hurricane's eye passed over, the river flooded the streets and pried creosote wood blocks out of the road bed along Royal. The only benefit of the flood was free firewood. Creosote blocks heated homes long after the hurricane left town. Meanwhile, snakes, rats, and other critters bobbed from one yard to another. When the winds quieted and the downpour stopped, it seemed over. Bright sunshine and blue sky broke through ugly clouds to scan the initial damage. A strange calm snuffed out the normal noises of day. Mockingbirds and jays kept silent. Chickens did not cluck. Not a whisper of nature stirred, until a blast from the opposite direction turned off the sun and struck down the great oak in Irish Ma's front yard. It bowed to earth with a thunderous death-rattle. By God's will the Waldstrom's, McLeod's and Joullian's survived. But the duplex did not.

"Seems so quiet in there, don't it?" Pat looked back over his shoulder into Our Alley.

"Why shouldn't it be quiet, it's Sunday. Hell, everybody's got a right to a quiet Sunday." Gunny had never thought anything strange about Sunday afternoon in Our Alley. The Reverend M. J. Martin lived in Our Alley over the fence opposite Irish Ma's house on Franklin. "But it'll get noisy in there for church tonight." Gunny was glad Aunt Nettie took him to Mass at dawn. The best part of the day was his.

"Where're we goin'?" Pat wondered. "There's a new picture show on at the Crown, but we could try the Saenger again." The Saenger Theatre, completed in 1927, cost a dime to get in, twice the price of admission to movies at the Crown, Crescent, and Queen. Sometimes the boys collected empty shinny bottles for neighborhood bootleggers until they put ten cents together. With that dime, though, Gunny could pass through the front door, ticket in hand, and then let the rest of the boys in under the Jackson Street fire escape. Getting in without a dime took more gumption. Along the south side of the Saenger on Conti Street a separate box office sold tickets to Coloreds who entered a nearby side door and sat in the third balcony. Gunny and Pat would crawl on all fours from Jackson under the ticket window on Conti. There they waited until the side door opened between reels. In a split second they jammed the door and admitted themselves. Getting to see Al Jolson was well worth the risk of being ousted by an usher.

"Let's try the Crescent. They're showing a cowboy picture today." Gunny was partial to westerns, and getting in was half the adventure. The boys went up to Dauphin Street, and then over to Conception just shy of Bienville Square. At the eastern mouth of a narrow alley between Dauphin and St. Francis, the boys turned off Conception and walked west. From its box office on Dauphin the Crescent theater stretched north and formed part of the alley's south wall. Outdoor privies surrounded by high fencing stood outside the movie house. One roof drain pipe where the fence met the brick wall provided access from the alley to the theater.

Gunny shimmied up the pipe, getting a push from Pat who quickly followed. Leaping off the high fence near but not into the privy posed the first hurdle. Bouncing off the slanted roof onto the walk below was preferable to crashing right through the outhouse roof. Experience guided Gunny's bare feet to a solid landing near the outhouse. Pat followed closely. Except for some overfed field rats, the privy was unoccupied.

Paying patrons often tossed away ticket stubs when stepping outside to visit the outhouse. The boys tucked away a stub to flash at any suspicious usher. Gunny slipped inside the theater and found a seat. As Pat pulled the door open, a smaller boy stumbled out holding his crotch with a telltale grip. Startled at seeing Pat, and off balance from having missed the door handle, the youngster momentarily lost his grip. A grin of relief wiped the grimace off the little boy's anxious face. The show must be good, Pat figured, or else the kid would not have sat inside for so long holding himself. Pat held the door until the kid finished. That turned out to be just long enough for the smell of popcorn to flow outside and rats to race into the theatre. Pat and the rats spread out quickly once inside.

"What took you so long?" Gunny asked.

"Some little kid stood in the door and peed while a bunch of rats came in. How's the show?" Pat answered in one long breath.

"Okay. But one of them rats must be nibbling around my feet. I brushed it aside, and it just keeps coming back." Gunny peeked under his seat and kicked at a large furry shadow creeping along the sticky floor.

After the early show, Pat and Gunny boldly left through the front door on Dauphin Street. A man stood just outside the Crescent at the curb. Near his foot was a $5 bill, a hundred nickels, a lot of money. Gunny nudged Pat and nodded at the five spot.

"Hey, mister, have you got an extra penny so we can get something to eat?" Pat drew the stranger's attention while Gunny swept up the money and stuffed it in his pocket.

"Mister, you didn't lose any money around here, did you?" Gunny asked.

"No, don't think so." The man smiled and looked around for a moment. "And sorry boys, but I don't have an extra penny for you."

Pat smiled and walked off with Gunny. "What are you going to do with that five dollars?"

"I don't know. I've never had this much money before. I can't show it to Irish Ma. She'll think I stole it or something. I'll catch hell for sure. Maybe I'll get some new shoes that don't get soaking wet every time it rains. Irish Ma should be real proud of me for doing that, don't you think?" Gunny felt the small fortune burning a hole in his pocket.

CHAPTER 7

Straight Talk

Irish Ma stared long and hard at the polished leather shoes on Gunny's feet. He wiggled in her glare. "Keep still Manuel. You're gonna stand there until I hear where those really came from. And don't give me that same old song and dance again. I want the truth this time."

"But it's true. Pat and me came out of the Crescent and there it was, big as daylight, just sitting there on the ground. We asked a man if he lost any money, just in case it was his five dollar bill. He said no, and nobody else was around. It's finders, keepers." Gunny repeated his improbable story.

"Manuel, what were you and Pat Healey doing in the Crescent? Where'd y'all get money to throw away on some picture show?" Irish Ma's teeth gritted ever so lightly. Nothing added up. Nobody would just lose a whole week's salary and not be looking for it. Gunny did not answer. "I'm waitin', young man."

"Well, Pat and me walked through the door, just like everybody else. They didn't ask us for tickets, and we got to stay for a whole show." The half-truth left Irish Ma doubtful. She chose to play along.

"Okay, then, where'd the shoes come from?" She noticed the thick leather soles and marveled at the workmanship.

"Zoghby's. Cost me $4.50. I told the man my old shoes had holes and came loose when I skated. He said these could skate to Theodore and back before wearing out.

"I've got a good mind to march you back down to Mr. Zoghby and give those shoes back." Irish Ma still did not buy the story. "I won't have you thieving downtown. We don't have much, but it's come by honestly. You hear me, Manuel! You best be content with what you've got."

"Yes ma'am." Gunny shut up and stayed shut. He noticed Aunt Nettie standing in the kitchen doorway studying his shoes.

"Manuel, if your grandmother is finished with you for now, take them new shoes off and go on outside. We'll take this up at suppertime. Go on, skedaddle!" Nettie gave Gunny a reprieve until nightfall. Nettie might carry a soft spot for Gunny, but would drag him down to Zoghby's in a squall and shame him for taking something not his. She knew Pat Healey came from a nice enough family and all. His folks used to live in New Orleans, and Mr. Healey held down a good job at the air-reduction plant over on Canal. Nettie never heard about Gunny and Pat distributing radio repair business cards as though they knew something about vacuum tubes. They went out of business shortly after taking apart the first customer's radio without knowing how to reassemble the parts. Of course, Nettie did not know whether Gunny found a $5 bill, but he came straight in to show off the shoes. As Nettie figured, if Gunny had a mind to steal, he'd start with something other than new shoes. Gunny skipped down the front steps and turned toward Stokes Grocery on the northwest corner of Charleston and Franklin.

The Charleston Street trolley stopped on Conception just east of Franklin. To climb the grade to its next stop at the corner of Franklin and Charleston, the trolley had to race to gain uphill speed. For Tweet Davis, Gunny's cousin, and the rabble milling about Stokes Grocery, trolleys provided cheap entertainment. Today would differ only in degree. Before the trolley started its uphill run, Tweet and other conspirators huddled over the rails in front of the grocery. A cluster of short legs moved along the track east to west, bent backs facing the oncoming train. Dozens of slick stubby fingers massaged the full length of each rail. Sprinting west, the trolley neared Stokes. Its warning bell usually cleared children off the track, but this was goat town, the gritty south side. The little beggars ignored the speeding rail car. The conductor gripped the brake. Another warning finally got some attention. The gaggle broke up as kids backpedaled off the tracks.

In the sharp afternoon sunlight, the rails next to Stokes' grocery glowed with unusual brilliance. Two cents worth of lard, two heaping scoops of pure animal fat, lathered nearly 60 feet of track. It was an urban ambush. Behind those toothless grins and charming dimples thumped hearts of cold predators, ready to snare their first train. Amid ringing bells and waiving children, the conductor sharply yanked the trolley's hand brake. Instead of noisy shudders and lurches, the conductor felt nothing but smooth track. The Charleston Street trolley slid right through the Franklin Street stop with an ashen conductor hugging his hand brake. Its slick wheels finally ground to a stop after the neighborhood hooligans had scattered. By nightfall the Stokes Grocery trolley attack acquired legendary stature from Canal to Texas.

Amelia Gonzales Davis fretted that Gunny would influence her son Tweet for the worse. For that matter, any influence was too much for Aunt Amelia. She did her best to distance Tweet from most street delinquents. He could mix with them at Galvez Park, but nothing more. Gunny gave Sister Davis other reasons for concern. Her older brother, Manuel Joseph, weighed on the family's spirit. Gunny's father sometimes took refuge in the bottle and sympathy from Lucinda. Amelia watched her brother Manuel Joseph wither on Grandpa Joe's family tree. More than once, Amelia witnessed the old Spaniard bail her brother out of jail for bad checks and public drunkenness. After a while, Grandpa Joe shuffled out of the county jail for the last time, leaving his first born in the care of guards. Baby brother Al wrote letters asking his older brother to come home soon. As long as he was on the wagon and in confinement, Manuel Joseph usually wrote back to his kid brother. But even on the wagon, Manuel Joseph never once wrote to his own son, Gunny. None of this would have mattered much to Tweet, even had the youngster known. Gunny was a savvy five years older and much admired around Galvez. Amelia suspected that Tweet would not have a protected childhood in Gunny's company.

Tweet proudly shared with Gunny a breathless and somewhat exaggerated account of the Stokes' trolley attack. Gunny took it all in, wondering what tune Tweet would be singing once Aunt Amelia got wind of this. No matter how it all came out in the wash, a lot of the credit for turning Aunt Amelia's first-born into an urban guerrilla would probably go to Gunny. Tweet's heroic rendition, admittedly hard to top, merely whet his unquenchable story-telling appetite. No sooner finished with one tale, Tweet launched into another.

"Grandpa Joe came over the other day and took me riding on his oyster cart." Tweet never tired of Grandpa Joe stories, and it mattered little whether Gunny already had heard them. Tweet told a better story the second or third time around, anyway. "He stayed overnight, and we hitched up his old mule early the next day." Tweet lived behind Cox Drugstore at 954 Savannah, just west of Marine. "The cart barely moved no matter what Grandpa Joe said. You know how he talks to that mule all the time. I think the mule had flat feet or something. Well, when we got back home, Grandpa Joe put the dray in our yard and let the mule loose. Next morning we found Grandpa's old mule under the house, dead as a doornail. Grandpa was under the house petting it, talking to it like it was still alive. Mama wouldn't let me watch them pull it out. They were cussing up a storm under there. Don't know how that big thing got where it did. Anyway, it was stiff as a board and wouldn't budge. Had to chain it to a truck bumper and drag it out. I wanted to see, but you know how Mama is. Remember that time the guy fell out of the oak tree in the back yard? He landed right on our picket fence, and the police and everybody came over to see what happened. They said it looked like he had big arrows sticking up through his ribs. Well, Mama wouldn't let me watch that either. She locked me in the bedroom. And she worries about me being with you. I tell her we just have a good time together, but she says that's why she worries." Aunt Amelia would always worry about Tweet, especially with Gunny around.

Gunny went on his way, wandering down Conception to a large open field that stretched east to St. Emanuel. Pat Healey, Rip Repoll, and Joe O'Connor were playing cowboys, pretending the overgrown field to be a wild west prairie. Gunny squatted in the weeds next to Rip. Everybody except Gunny toted pump-action BB rifles that shot with deadly accuracy. That was the good news. Pat Healey sometimes carried his .22 rifle, but not this time. Only a short while back, Pat and Gunny were in Rip's backyard at 156 Canal, trying to get a cat out of the tree. Pat went home directly across the street at 155 Canal without saying a word, got his .22, and brought the cat down with a single shot. The boys would not let Pat play cowboys with his .22 rifle.

It was just as well that Gunny did not have his BB pistol. He had walked into a long range shoot-out, no match for a single-shot pistol. Even with their heads buried in the weeds, Gunny and Rip drew fire from Joe O'Connor's barrel. A shot caught Gunny under the eye, becoming the first and only real casualty and promptly ending the range war. Sizing up the situation, the boys grabbed their weapons and high-tailed it. Gunny held his eye tightly closed until he reached home, but it was no use. Unless he wore a mask, the ugly wound would not escape Aunt Nettie's scrutiny.

"What in tarnation's happened to you?" Aunt Nettie demanded as Gunny stepped through the door. "What have you done to your eye, Manuel? Have you been in a fight or something?"

"No ma'am. Well, yes, I guess. But I wasn't fighting. I was just playing cowboys and accidentally got shot." Gunny played this one straight.

"Got shot! What on God's green earth are you doing playing with real guns? Have you lost your mind? What riffraff did this anyway?" Aunt Nettie quickly put things in perspective.

"Well, Joe O'Connor was trying to shoot Rip, but hit me instead. He didn't mean to do it. We were just playing." Gunny could tell what he said did not make a whole lot of sense.

"Playing? You must be crazy! What if he'd hit you smack dab in the eye! I suppose you're just lucky because he's such a bad shot." Aunt Nettie reached her stride. "You wouldn't be sitting here poor-mouthing his aim if we had to put a glass eye in your empty head, now would you? Hell fire, I doubt Joe O'Connor's got the sense of a goat! That fool should be sent up-state to the reform school." Nettie cleaned and patched the dark bloody wound, muttering to herself every few seconds. She opened the screen door and held it for Gunny. "Well, don't just sit there like a bump on a log, you're coming with me, young man. It's time this Joseph O'Connor and me saw eye-to-eye. I suspect his folks'll want to know they spawned a juvenile delinquent."

Gunny trotted in the dust of Nettie's long steps. She had a single purpose in life for the moment. To his credit, Joe O'Connor knew better than to be out on the street with Nettie looking for him. Officer Charlie Dumas, the local cop on the beat, might have made a more sporting match for Aunt Nettie. But Joe cowered at home, hoping this too would pass. Nettie set the pace until she stood on the front porch of Harry O'Connor's house. She did not bother to rap politely on the screen door, but spoke right through it. Harry O'Connor answered the door.

"Mr. O'Connor, I'm Nettie Pocase. This here is Manuel. I want to see the young man who shot Manuel in the face with a BB gun." Nettie chose not to engage in small talk.

Harry O'Connor did not open the screen door, which common courtesy called for on social occasions. Mr. O'Connor correctly sensed that this was a business call. "Yes ma'am." He nodded at Nettie and summoned Joe to the door. Joe had heard everything, dreading Miss Nettie, and double-dreading his father. Joe O'Connor appeared at the screen door, stepping cautiously out on the porch. Nettie stared right through him, ignoring his father.

"You are a lucky young man, Joseph O'Connor. During the past five minutes I've talked myself out of wringing your neck like a common yard chicken. You ain't worth the effort." Nettie stepped closer to a deeply troubled Joe O'Connor, leaning down to his pallid face. "But if you ever shoot Manuel again, I'll take that BB gun of yours and whip your ass with it." Nettie's calm delivery gripped Joe with a choke hold. "You hear me, boy?" Nettie expected no response. The pale, sickly look on Joe's face was answer enough. Nettie stood tall again and looked Harry O'Connor in the eye. "Good day, Mr. O'Connor."

"Good day, Miss Pocase. Do drop by again sometime, ma'am." Harry was always the gentleman. He watched Miss Nettie until she reached the street, then turned his attention to Joe.

CHAPTER 8

Knight in White Satin

Irish Ma had not seen Manuel since morning. Gunny would have been home long ago, but he and Rip Repoll headed straight for the shipyard after school. Were it not for Bessie Rencher, they would have just skipped school altogether to get ready for tonight's big fight. Only the fear of being nabbed by Mobile's truant officer kept them in class. Somehow she seemed to find out who played hooky before the teachers knew. Repeated truancy earned a stay in the Detention Home if Officer Rencher had her say about it. Gunny so far had avoided capture. Twice this year already, Gunny leapt into ditches and hid under wooden foot bridges on Canal and Charleston. Bessie Rencher sensed when he skipped school.

Gunny had another reason to avoid getting caught. Charles Joullian brooked no embarrassment to the family. Charles gave a warning only once. He expected Gunny to stay in school and out of trouble. It would not do to get thrown in the Detention Home. Uncle Charlie might let Gunny stew there a while. Now, the Boys Home was a different story, since it did not require getting into trouble.

The old Alabama Dry Dock plate shop stood on the southeast corner of Royal and Canal, four blocks east of St. Vincent. In the rusty bowels of the aging tin barn, shipbuilders once punched rivet holes through thick steel plates, sending metallic thunder through houses across Royal. A different noise now pierced the darkness. By twilight a rowdy crowd had gathered below the rafters of the plate shop arena. Under glaring naked light bulbs that dangled from a ceiling beam, taut canvas stretched between four rigid posts. Two boxers danced off the ropes into the corners. Lean, smooth and youthful, the fighters worked themselves and their fans into a fourth round frenzy. They and other boxers from Louisiana, Mississippi, and Florida filled out this evening's card. Lead matches between newcomers paid $4, a buck a round, win, lose, or draw. In 15 minutes, contenders could earn a week's wage doing what came naturally on the street. The evening's headline bout offered a $100 prize, plus the prestige of a championship belt.

With seconds remaining in round four, *Young Joe Pagaline* in white satin trunks jabbed his way into the red trunks' corner. *Young Joe Pagaline's* bloodless face belied the fight's violence. Bruising body blows and solid jabs to the eye marked the young knight in white satin. Still, he launched a withering attack until the final bell that left both fighters clenching, exhausted but standing.

Gunny's lanky trainer cheered from the white corner. The crowd watched Brown step in the ring to wipe Gunny's sweaty face after the fighter's second impressive bout in as many outings. Though only 14, Gunny's moves and punches suggested a more seasoned boxer. The crowd applauded as the colored trainer helped Gunny through the ropes and off the stained canvas. That Brown was blacker than Gunny did not matter at ringside.

Gunny washed up and collected the $4 purse won under his boxing nom de guerre. He enjoyed the reputation of a skillful boxer. He could go toe-to-toe with anyone in his weight class, and some well beyond that over at Galvez. Boxing and street fighting provided crude but important yardsticks of respect. Gunny fought on the street because he had to. He fought in the ring because he wanted to. Between the ropes, he proved himself.

Rip had not yet entered the paying ring. Like Gunny, Rip boxed in Oakdale for sport on the vacant lot between Augusta and Savannah at Dearborne. Rip appeared on amateur boxing cards as *Dr. Pepper*. His mother never caught on to the ruse, though Mrs. Repoll suspected Gunny exerted an unhealthy influence over her boy. Gunny actually looked out for Rip, managing *Dr. Pepper's* career in the ring and standing second for any number of Rip's frequent street brawls.

Gunny hurried home, late for supper. The shiner around his eye had blossomed into a bright purple patch with a blood-shot core. Even in the dark, Gunny sensed the swelling and blurred vision. He eased quietly through the back screen door, hoping to sneak undetected into the kitchen. Aunt Nettie was waiting. She glanced up and noticed a lopsided look about Manuel's face. "Manuel, what are you doing sneaking in through that door? Get yourself over here this instant! Your grandmother has been worrying about you. Where have you been?" Aunt Nettie studied the familiar pattern of ruptured blood vessels and watched a sickly eye peek through especially fat lids. She looked in his good eye. "Lord have mercy, child, what ran into your head! Sit down before you trip over something." Nettie left the room and returned with an ice pack.

"Aunt Nettie, it's nothing to worry about. I just got hit in the face. It'll be okay by morning." Gunny mumbled under the ice pack.

"In a pig's ear, it will! Looks like you got clobbered with a horseshoe. Your Uncle Charlie's gonna be fit to be tied. You know how he feels about all the scrapping you get into." Aunt Nettie calmed down to sort things out. "What started the fight, Manuel?"

"It wasn't like that, Aunt Nettie, really. It was a guy down at the plate shop. You know, where I work out after school."

"Manuel, who hit you?" Nettie persisted.

"Robert Jackson." Gunny shrugged.

Nettie paused to connect the pieces. "You're talking about my nephew, Robert, ain't you? You and Robert were down at that arena beating each other like common street trash." Gunny nodded. "What got you two to fighting?"

"We're a pretty good match, Aunt Nettie. Robert just got in a lucky hit, that's all. We both get a dollar for each round in the ring." Gunny pulled $4 from his pocket. "See, I went four full rounds." Gunny felt proud of himself despite the black eye.

Nettie stared at the prize money. "Manuel, you listen to me. You listen real good. Right now that $4 looks like a lot of money. It takes me a long week to earn $5. But as long as there's breath in this skinny old body, you're never to set foot in a prize ring again. Tonight it's a black eye. Next time it'll be a broken nose or split lip. Letting people punch your face ugly ain't worth a dollar a round. After spending all that money, you'll just be ugly. And someday you'll wake up trying to remember my name. I won't let that happen, Manuel. You and Robert already get all the bloody noses you can handle over at that playground. Standing up for what counts might be good enough reason for fighting. But don't ever rent yourself out as a punching bag again. You're better than that." Nettie peeked under the ice pack. "And in case you ever forget, I'll come right into that boxing ring after you. Now go feed yourself something and get to bed. Just wait till your uncle sees that face."

PART TWO

I shall tell you a

great secret, my friends.

Do not wait

for the last judgment.

It takes place every day.

—Albert Camus

*21. Gunny Gonzales, Leona Pond Joullian (Irish Ma), Nettie Pocase (Aunt Nettie)
& Ernest James, Jr., 408 Charleston, Mobile, 1928 (photographer unknown).*

CHAPTER 9

Galvez Park

St. Vincent's third grade usually got fair warning of important visitors. Sister would remind her class how to behave and what to say should the pastor or the archbishop drop in to observe. To a ten year-old, that simply meant saying and stirring less than what Sister usually allowed. On an uneventful afternoon in 1923, a portly guest sporting baggy pinstripes walked unannounced into class, commanding instant attention without so much as a single word. Father Brady scurried in to settle the startled nun, his face glowing. Gunny and the class stared in disbelief at the baby-faced myth, previously unseen in the flesh, on whose name they swore with a faith larger than life.

Before Father Brady could introduce George Herman Ruth, 27 cast iron desks groaned off-balance. The boys stared open-mouth at number 3. Even the roughest hewn street urchin knew his place in the presence of the Great Bambino. They felt drawn to the grinning giant. They knew how he had been sent off as an unruly boy to the spartan halls of St. Mary's Industrial School. They felt an instant kinship. The room found its feet by the time Father Brady turned to the class. "Boys, we have a very special guest some of you might recognize." The pastor never finished.

"It's Babe Ruth!" Class spun out of control. Mister New York Yankee, baseball's hero, stood quietly next to a speechless nun enjoying the boys' unvarnished adoration. "Mister Ruth, what are you doin' here?" The class did not need Father Brady's help.

"Well fellas, I'm playing exhibition games this week. Just wanted to come by and see all of you. Hope you can make it."

"Where're you gonna be playin'?"

"Monroe Park," Babe answered, "and I want to see you there." They wanted to hear him talk and never leave. They asked about home runs, New York City, the pennant, and the Yankees. Father Brady finally broke the spell. The apparition disappeared through the door as suddenly as he had entered. What little learning Sister expected of the boys went out the door as well. Those who did not make it to Monroe Park heard how Babe Ruth came to the plate and sent the next ball sailing out of sight. Babe Ruth gave Gunny and other kids on the south side something to dream about.

From third grade on, Gunny's dreams and learning had more to do with baseball than books. He came to know another side of his father, watching older Manuel Joseph play ball at the L&N Railroad diamond on the corner of Savannah and Royal. Gunny saw little of his father, but he saw that Manuel senior played ball well, very well. And as a left-handed catcher, Gunny's father had no peers. Few players had ever seen a southpaw working behind home plate. Gunny happened to be watching the day his father became legendary in his own right. Frank Soutullo, a threatening slugger, stepped up to the plate. The right-handed batter and left-handed catcher were first cousins. Manuel Joseph checked the runner at first base taking a long lead. He smelled a steal to second. Manuel signaled for a high outside fast ball. If the runner broke, Manuel would pick him off at second. Runners who underestimated Manuel's southpaw throw never made it. The pitcher wound up and checked off first base. The ball hurtled at the inside corner of the plate, missing its intended mark. The runner sprinted for second. Frank Soutullo picked up on the steal and crowded the plate to disrupt the catcher's play to second base. Manuel's right-handed mitt snapped sharply from the shock of the ball's impact. In one fluid motion, Manuel's mask flew off and his right leg pointed to second base. Manuel's vision tunneled past Soutullo into the second baseman's waiting glove. Manuel's left hand gracefully plucked the ball from the crease of the mitt and fired a bullet. Manuel had the runner beat by two steps, but the ball traveled only two feet. Just as Soutullo collapsed face-first onto the third-base line, a crack echoed over the infield. The ball bounced oddly off the back of Frank's head and fell to the plate. Soutullo had successfully scrubbed Manuel's play at second, and any hopes of Soutullo ever getting to first. Play suspended while teammates carried Frank to the hospital. The next batter did not crowd home plate. Frank Soutullo eventually came to. Not even a point-blank bean-ball could keep Soutullo out more than a day or so.

Gunny could see himself on that diamond, squatting in red clay behind home plate like his father, playing a man's game. This was more than a sport. The diamond allowed men to measure themselves against one another, marking their worth and character with a common yard-stick that even children understood. Gunny did not want to follow in his father's footsteps or stand in his father's shadow, though. Someday, somehow he expected to do better.

Ironically, the someday and somehow in Gunny's baseball future arose out of the past. On May 31, 1921 Mobile fashioned a park out of the oddly shaped section of rubble from Franklin east to Claiborne and from Madison south to Canal. City Hall dedicated Galvez Square "to the recreation and service of the white people of Mobile" in honor of the eminent Spaniard who overcame impossible odds to free Mobile from King George III.

Some 140 years earlier, militia loyal to King George III drilled near Galvez Square on Canal and Royal, preparing for battle against American colonials. In New Orleans, captain-general Don Bernardo de Galvez, Count of Galvez, Viscount of Galveztown and Governor-General of the Louisiana Provinces, relished news that the Cabildo had formally recognized the Americans. His Catholic Majesty Carlos III declared war on England and informed General George Washington that Spain intended to seize West Florida and break England's grip on the Americans' southern flank. Galvez had been assigned the honor of seizing Mobile, Pensacola, and England's Lord Governor Peter Chester.

Don Bernardo launched his assault on Mobile from Belize through an unseasonable hurricane that scattered his fleet like flotsam. The battered remains of his exhausted armada, originally some 2000 regulars, militia, and free Negroes, straggled into Mobile Bay 11 days later, beaching near Choctaw Point. Vulnerable to attack by land and sea, his officers urged hasty retreat to Spanish New Orleans, bypassing Mobile altogether lest the British destroy what few forces remained. Don Bernardo put fate to the test and lay siege to Mobile's Fort Charlotte, raking the field of fire along Conception Street until the fort stood alone, breached and defeated amid a landscape of blackened rubble. A year later on the anniversary of capturing Mobile, Don Bernardo stood mid-deck on his defenseless brigantine *Galvezton,* rounding Santa Rosa Island into the range of Pensacola's British cannon. Fearsome Spanish warships, laden with heavily armed troops, treaded water beyond their own firing range for fear of grounding on uncharted sand bars. Galvez's daring solo attack against lethal British firepower chastened the Spanish fleet admiral to turn his flag ship into the *Galvezton's* tiny wake. Don Bernardo's brigantine passed unscathed through withering crossfire between his attacking armada and the defending fort. England yielded its Florida Territories to Galvez. For uncommon courage, Galvez won a coat of arms depicting the *Galvezton* and motto, *Yo solo,* "I alone."

Dedicating Galvez Square in 1921 reminded the south side of its nobler heritage and spirit. On April 14, 1926, the Maguire's, Greer's, Foster's, Bonham's, Busbee's, O'Connor's, Rigas's, Rooney's and other freeholders fronting Galvez Square persuaded City Hall to permit baseball, converting the peaceful square into a rowdy playground. Along Madison street the playground featured a swing set and sandbox, between which stood a water fountain on the spot where Gunny was born in 1913. Home plate rested inside the angle formed by Claiborne and Canal at the southeast corner of the park. When street urchins stepped onto Galvez, the rules of the diamond and caretaker Joe Rooney governed. But the law of the street returned after Joe Rooney left at day's end, allowing the boys to deal with their own kind in their own way.

Strays occasionally drifted into the south side at dusk to do business. A seasoned delinquent with no last name, Red often set up shop in the sandbox where he dug holes and waited. By the time park regulars gathered, Red had stuffed a rolled muggle of marijuana in each hole. Nobody asked where Red got marijuana for the muggles he rolled, figuring he trafficked with Coloreds in the north part of town. If no one seemed ready to put a quarter in his palm, Red leaned back on the concrete wall, lit up, and coached the curious to try one. After passing a muggle around, some pockets coughed up quarters. If not, Red got very weird toking up alone on all those marijuana cigarettes. That's what most of the regulars waited for. They came to see the show. One afternoon, Red struggled to his feet after smoking most of his stash and wandered off, stopping in the middle of Madison to stare at empty milk bottles on a porch across the street. Red shifted his feet and cocked his head like a pigeon to get a better look at those bottles. He strayed across the street, picked up one, studied it carefully, and hurled it through the front porch window. Then Red wandered off down Madison without uttering a word, and never returned.

By 1928, Galvez boasted a ball team with attitude. They took to the diamond to prove something to themselves and their coach, Crip Bonham. They were good, but teams from the grove north of Dauphin called them ragged-assed, and that they were. Even so, they seldom complained as long as they won. Crip knew his Galvez boys expected to win come hell or high water. None of them cared to hear that winning is not everything. Winning was the only thing. Losing was common as pig tracks in Gritney, as they called the south side.

Crip Bonham understood about winning and losing. He came by his name honestly, being crippled and all. Crip tended to call a spade a spade and got on with living, so the name stuck. The boys never thought about it much, except when some sorry no-count in the crowd snickered about the cripple. That riled them, but Crip did not flinch. He was too proud. Crip also wanted his boys to be proud, and told them so.

"Boys, our game down in Theodore is gonna be tough. They may be farmers but they ain't slouches. Don't let them hoots and hollers get you riled. You know they're gonna be raggin' on your asses from start to finish. Show 'em what you've got. Don't get angry. Get even. Whip 'em. Whip 'em good. Win or lose, keep your head. Don't give 'em reason to bad mouth you. I won't abide it." If Galvez lost, they would sort things out off the field, mostly among themselves. Despite their reputation, the boys from Galvez did not usually brawl after a game. They rarely brawled because they rarely lost, though losing disposed them to dealing with insults on the spot. That especially tended to be the case for home games at Galvez where it was best for winning visitors to leave quickly and quietly.

Most of Crip's boys had a hard row to hoe. They were crippled by what they did not have and they did not have much. But Crip saw what the boys did have. On the field they showed presence and purpose. Crip sensed their instinct, their raw talent. He also witnessed instinct gone awry. On the first away game from Galvez, half the team packed like canned sardines into Crip's old Ford. The boys lost the game and the crowd turned sour. To Crip's amazement there was no brawl. The boys did Crip proud, waiting until they got back into his car before exploding. By the time Crip limped from the field for the drive back to Galvez, the boys were waiting quietly amid the shattered glass of his windowless car. Crip went back and forth with himself about replacing the windows. He could not afford to lose another game.

Crip knew how far they had come. He no longer worried about replacing car windows. Driving down Navco Road for another away game, he sensed the boys' growing confidence. Mostly they were quiet, absently slapping a ball into a glove over and over.

"Coach?" One of the boys called out.

"Yep," Crip answered, deep in his own thoughts.

"What's that cow doing?"

Crip turned his head to see a bull charging straight at the car. He slowed but the bull kept coming. Crip hit the brakes just as the animal rammed the car broadside, lifting two wheels off the road, caving in the doors and tearing off sheet metal. The bull went in one side and the team out the other. The car would not hold both. Crip waited out the attack clutching the steering wheel. After making its point, the bull traipsed off. The boys recovered loose car parts and settled in for the rest of the ride.

22. *George Herman (Babe) Ruth, with William H. Armbrecht, Jr., John Paul Wilson, Jr., William Ross Little, Con Roberts Little, Jr., Erwin E. Little, Wilkerson V. Jones, James W. Little, and unidentified youngsters, exhibition game, Mobile (Courtesy, Erik Overbey Collection, University of South Alabama Archives), c. 1923.*

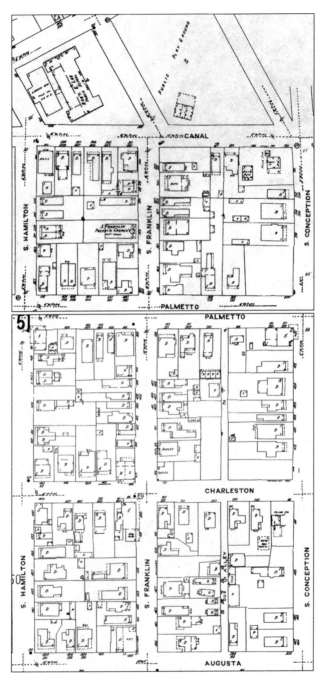

23. Mobile south side highlight showing Galvez Park and Our Alley (Sanborn Map Company 1956).

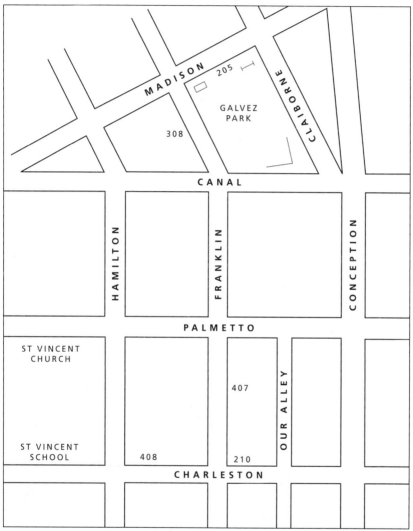

24. *Galvez Park sandbox, water fountain, swings, and ball diamond, and Gunny's addresses at 205 Madison, 308 S. Franklin, 210 Charleston, 408 Charleston and 407 S. Franklin from 1913 to 1939 (Copyright © 2007 James J. Gonzales).*

25. Galvez Park, looking southeast across baseball field toward Canal and Claiborne, Mobile, c. 1935 (photographer unknown).

26. Galvez Park, looking northeast toward John Rigas' store at Madison and Claiborne, Mobile, c. 1935 (photographer unknown).

CHAPTER 10

Whippet Athletic Club

They were a bunch of street toughs who played ball. Under a melting July sun, the south side's best baseball team sprawled out around home plate at Galvez. Practice ended early. A few balls still sat in the middle of Franklin Street. It was too hot to chase them. Leaning against the wooden backstop, a truant officer spoke firmly about each player, good and bad. For over six months he had dogged every budding athlete resting around his feet, tracking their progress and watching every move. Van Matthews knew who and what he was dealing with here. Years of herding truants gave Matthews an instinct for sizing up the likes of this group. He had their numbers. In six months Matthews had coached this Whippet Athletic Club to the doorstep of baseball fame.

Matthews studied their faces. He did not know how they would cope with the pressure of championship play tomorrow. No doubt there would be a large turnout at Lyons Park. *The Mobile Register* reported how the Whippets had surprisingly rolled over stronger opponents to earn a three-way tie for first place in the American Legion Junior League. Most teams at this level of play took years to develop. Something seemed unusual about these Whippets.

Two weeks ago the Whippets faced Little Flower in a struggle for first place. Whippet pitcher Johnnie Smith hurled an unexpected no-hitter through the sixth inning, but still trailed Little Flower 1-0. An error in the second inning set the stage for a stunning double steal and score by Little Flower from third base. Smith managed to hold the rest of the inning together. Matthews respected Little Flower's pitcher John Geary, but never figured that Geary could silence the Whippets' big guns. It looked as though Matthews' guys were choking.

In the bottom of the sixth Geary walked Rip Repoll, one of Matthews' key hitters. A walk would do though. Lamar Doyle was on deck. Only the ignorant called Doyle by his real name. There was a sissy sound to it. "Bulldog" fit Doyle much better. Bulldog was no sissy. He played infield, shortstop, and second base. He mastered double plays. With Rip on first, Bulldog was batting into a potential double play, but Bulldog knew baseball. He hit at will, lining a shot straight into right field for a single.

Gunny came to the plate with Rip at second and Bulldog pacing around first. Gunny played left field when not catching. He sported a good arm and snatched fly balls on the run. Most importantly, he did not choke. Gunny sized up the infield between second and third where Little Flower played him straight away. He swatted a single down the third base line. Only the quick arm of Little Flower's left fielder kept Rip at third base. Bulldog was causing a stir at second, even though there was no where to go. The bases were loaded. Earl Holcombe was up. At 15 and a veteran of McGill Institute and Cavalier ball teams, Earl played first base and fielded like a Southern League semi-pro, but Matthews could not rely on Earl to hit under pressure. Given his druthers, Matthews would just as soon as have Al Gonzales at the plate. Earl might choke.

Earl settled in the box and took a strike. Little Flower made hard double plays look easy. With three on base, a double play would be easy. Earl attacked the next pitch. The ball limped harmlessly right back to the pitcher. Geary cut Rip off at home for the forced out. Little Flower's catcher was no slouch. Perez pivoted and fired a bullet to first base to make the double play. Little Flower's first baseman crowded the base line. Earl made amends for his sloppy hitting. As he neared the bag, Earl heard the ball whiz past his left ear. Tucking his left shoulder in, Earl aimed at the first baseman's exposed left shoulder. The collision flushed the ball from the glove and nearly separated the shoulder from its owner. The ball went wild. The crowd went wild. Bulldog thundered over home plate from third before the ball could be recovered. Gunny had crossed second when Rip was forced out and reached third before Bulldog scored at home. Sprinting bases came easy compared to covering left field. Gunny heard the collision at first and the roar that followed. He banked off third base in full stride and sped home to put the Whippets up by one. It happened quickly. Shaken, Little Flower huddled on the mound to settle down. With Earl staggering at first base and pitcher Johnnie Smith at bat, Little Flower talked double play.

But Johnnie Smith flowed with adrenaline. He hammered the first pitch over second for an easy double, driving Earl around the bags for the score. Adding salt to the wound, Smith decided to stretch his double into a triple. The throw to third sailed high, letting Smith score the final run of the game. Matthews could sit the rest of the inning. When the side retired, Johnnie Smith returned to the mound as if nothing had happened. Johnnie pitched a no-hitter through the end of the game.

Deep down, Matthews knew that this team played beyond his coaching ability. They already had figured that out, but the rematch tomorrow against Little Flower at Lyons Park could go either way. So, Van Matthews kept on talking. It made him feel better and it did not bother the boys. They were used to it. Truant officers carried on that way.

Wednesday crept over the bay with glacial speed. Most of the team rose early enough to watch July 23, 1930 dawn. Irish Ma, Uncle Charlie, and Aunt Nettie stirred, getting ready for work. None of them would see Gunny play his championship game. Each passing hour made the boys more restless. By mid-morning, Rip, Al, Gunny, and Johnnie started milling around at Galvez. No other place felt right. Soon enough the team gathered, boasting WHIPPETS uniforms donated by McGowan & Lyons. They had a right to be proud of themselves. They were playing with the best. Time finally came to load up for Lyons Park. They rode quietly down Government to Broad and then out Springhill Avenue to the park. Coach was right. A big crowd already was there.

As Van Matthews feared, Little Flower came on strong and took an early 3 to 1 lead that held through the top of the sixth. Geary gave up very few hits. Then with two outs, the Whippets rallied to load the bases. Little Flower played in tight, ready to cover any base. Gunny stepped up to the plate for only the second time in six innings, having failed to get on base earlier. Geary looked confident.

Third baseman Douville remembered the shot Gunny nailed down the baseline in the last game. Even if he wanted to forget, Little Flower's coach brought it up for the entire infield to hear. Douville edged over a bit more than usual. There would be no repeat at his expense. Douville had time to mentally rehearse snagging a one-hopper and tagging the bag for the forced play. The crowd grew thunderous. Fans sensed this was a pivotal moment. Half the crowd wanted Geary to zip the ball past Gunny and half wanted Gunny to zip the ball past Douville. Gunny planted his McGowan & Lyons shoes in the batter's box. He panned the infield but found no gaps. He watched the first pitch miss the outside corner by a hand. Geary offered Gunny trash, but a walk equaled a run at this point. Gunny could play that game too. The next pitch was not trash. It clipped the inside corner, low and fast. Geary caught Gunny looking. Little Flower's pitcher seemed on top of the batter. The third pitch came in straight, fast and perfect. Gunny swatted at the blurry streak. He barely felt contact, but a sharp crack sliced through the air. The ball hurtled at Douville, struck the grassy apron, and bounced three feet over his outstretched glove. As Little Flower's left fielder Zieman raced to the line to corner the ball, runners scored from second and third. Earl Holcombe hustled to third from first. Gunny rounded first. Zieman fired the ball to Sweeney at second. Sweeney stared Gunny back to first base. While Sweeney held the ball, Earl took a breath and stole home, putting the Whippets up by one. Facing Gunny down at first may have cost Little Flower the game. Sheepishly, Sweeney tossed the ball to Geary.

In the bottom of the sixth, Johnnie Smith's pitching denied Little Flower any runs. Returning to bat at the top of the seventh and final inning, the Whippets could not get anything going against Geary's pitching. Trailing by two runs, Little Flower came to bat at the bottom of the seventh. Little Flower's visions of the state playoff in Talladega had about evaporated until Johnnie Smith blundered by walking Zieman. First baseman Burch, who Earl Holcombe tackled two weeks ago, then singled. Little Flower's winning run came to bat. Johnnie walked center fielder Bolling, loading the bases. Now, even a single would tie the game. A double could end the Whippets' brilliant season.

Geary the pitcher was on deck. Geary still smarted from Johnnie Smith's triple in their earlier match. Johnnie looked at his catcher, Al Gonzales, then stared at Geary. Johnnie would take it to Geary right down the middle. Johnnie shuddered when Geary slapped a solid hit over second base, driving in Zieman and Burch. Matthews had to wonder about his team choking, but Johnnie and Al seemed to handle pressure. Johnnie retired the side leaving two runners stranded on base.

Tied 5 to 5, the game went into extra innings. Johnnie Smith led off the top of the eighth with a stroll to first. Then the Whippets' artillery came to the plate. Al Gonzales hammered a single between second and third, putting runners at first and second. Earl Holcombe stepped to the plate. Earl just wanted to get the ball out of the infield. A sacrifice fly would do, but the nightmare of two weeks past returned. Earl dinked the ball again. It died in the infield. Little Flower went to first and Earl was out, though runners advanced bases.

Gunny appeared for his third and last time at bat. Geary threw trash. One mistake in the sixth inning was enough for Geary. He threw high, low, or outside. Gunny would not bite, and Geary ended up loading the bases by walking the Spaniard. As center fielder Henry Richardson came to bat, the excitement grew. Henry had been compared to Baby Doll Jacobson at the plate, but so far he was 0 for 2 at bat. Geary could not let Richardson walk in the winning run. Geary could not throw trash. Richardson did not have a good batting game, but pinch-hitting was out of the question. Matthews might have been working up a good heartburn until a solid whack hurled the ball deep into right field for a stand up double. Richardson broke the jinx, driving in Smith and Al Gonzales.

Geary had felt good about pitching to Richardson, but uncomfortable dealing with Whippets' third baseman Roy Knapp. Knapp was the fastest Whippet, usually stealing four or five bases each game. Knapp also played for the Peps when not in a Whippets uniform, and consistently hit well, already 2 for 2 at bat. That troubled Geary. Knapp liked Geary's pitching. Knapp even liked trash pitches. Knapp liked the first pitch Geary served, and reached out to greet it. The crowd unconsciously rose to follow the arc of the ball deep into center field. It should have been a home run, but there was no home run fence. Roy hustled all the way to third for a triple, bringing Gunny in for the fourth run of the inning.

Geary finally retired the Whippets, leaving Knapp on third. That was small comfort going into the bottom of the eighth trailing by four. Johnnie Smith took to the mound and threw whatever Al signaled. Johnnie retired the first two batters and then faced Adams, pinch-hitting for right fielder Blackwell. This was Little Flower's last hope. Johnnie and Al worked Adams over pitch by pitch. With a count of two strikes, Adams could anticipate low and outside on the next throw. Al dared Johnnie to split home plate. Johnnie went for the corner. Adams leaned into the pitch but held up as he watched the third strike and last out of the game sail into Al's grinning mitt. Everything beyond "steee – riiiike" died in the roar of the crowd. The umpire twisted, coiled, and jabbed his right thumb into the air, a pantomime amid pandemonium. Johnnie held the scene in his mind like the last frame of a silent feature. The spell broke when his infield converged on the mound.

Galvez had served up an unlikely plate of champions. On the front page of the Sunday *Mobile Register* Sports section, the Whippets posed for history. Poised and proud, their smooth faces masked much deeper character. Squared jaws and grinning eyes told Mobile who they were: Jack Stokes, Emanuel Gonzales, Jr., Hallet McDonough, Charles Wilcox, Al Gonzales, Lamar Doyle, Roy Knapp, John Repoll, Henry Gaines Richardson, Leo Reinhart, Earl Holcombe, William Farrar, John Smith, Anthony Perez, August Renteria, Jack Armour, and Charles Smith. They were champions. Luck had nothing to do with it. Being the best is no accident.

Whippets took being champions seriously. Folks who never before gave them the time of day now came to practices at Galvez. Neighbors looked on. Their young heroes did Galvez proud. Time finally came to head north for the Alabama State Championship series. The Whippets had traveled a bit during the regular season, but they were beside themselves about going up north to Montgomery and Talladega. A whole day in a touring car sounded just fine. A ride in any car sounded fine.

By mid-morning a commotion of cars, families, and Whippets grew on Government Street at Royal near Admiral Semmes' statue. Van Matthews counted the heads of his troops every five minutes. Al Gonzales looked up from a running board of the touring car. A stranger stood out in the middle of Government Street setting up a camera tripod. Al studied the photographer, who paid no attention to traffic. The photographer focused on a Whippet at the rear of a large black touring car. Looking over the lens box, he smiled.

"Son, how'd you like to have your picture taken?" He looked at Al.

"Me?" Al pointed to himself and looked around.

"Yeah. Aren't you the Whippets' captain?" The stranger surprised Al.

"Can I have a picture?" Al bargained.

"It's a deal," the photographer grinned. Slowly the lens framed the image of a young athlete leaning confidently against the car's trunk. In Al's eyes and toothy smile the photographer found his image of a champion. The knowing look, the foot nonchalantly braced against a shiny bumper, and the sharply shadowed face under a well-massaged baseball cap captured a universal truth. The crucible of a baseball diamond might true the mettle of a champion, but character comes from within. Fresh off the clay streets around Galvez, Al Gonzales and his team soared with character.

Most of the Whippets piled into the big black touring car captured in Al's photograph. It belonged to State Truant Officer McCauley and came equipped with an ear-shattering siren. As his land yacht approached backwoods whistle-stops along the highway, Officer McCauley triggered the siren to clear farm wagons and townsfolk off main street. Just shy of Evergreen, though, a deputy sheriff took exception to the blaring siren as Officer McCauley rumbled into town. McCauley hushed up the Whippets when the deputy approached.

"What the Sam Hill's goin' on here, mister?" The deputy studied the load of Whippets.

"Well deputy, there's no cause for concern. These here boys are from Mobile. I'm taking them all up to Talladega. They're playing for the state baseball championship this week. We've got to be up there by tonight." McCauley tried to reassure the deputy.

The deputy stared a moment. "That don't make no never mind to me. You can be taking them to see the governor for all I care. That gives you no cause to go around disturbing our peace, scarin' livestock, and drivin' through red lights. I've a good mind to put you up overnight until the justice of the peace gets back. How about you just turn around and follow me into town."

The boys never saw a truant officer get bawled out, much less arrested. McCauley's influence out in this neck of the woods was thin at best. It was time to play up to the deputy. "Deputy, I can tell you're just doing your duty. I'm just doin' mine. I'm assisting Truant Officer Matthews here to get these boys upstate before nightfall. I'm State Truant Officer McCauley." McCauley flashed his badge. "We've got a long ride ahead and sure would appreciate your helping us along. Sorry about the little ruckus we might have caused back there in town. I suspect the Governor and the Commissioner will understand. Hope you'll see fit to abide our need to hurry along, deputy." McCauley gently stroked and cautioned the deputy to let them get along.

The deputy knew he was well within his rights to haul the whole kit and caboodle back to town, but messing with truant officers and jailing a baseball team overnight could get sticky. "Mr. McCauley, you can be on your way, but I don't expect to hear that siren in town on your way back, you hear?" The deputy tipped his hat and strolled back to his patrol car. Evergreen would not see hide nor hair of them again, but McCauley was not about to silence his siren.

The Whippets made Talladega before supper time. The boys shuddered when Officer McCauley finally pulled over and stopped the car.

"Boys, we're here," Matthews announced. "Pile out and get your stuff together. This is where you'll be staying tonight."

"Coach, what is this?" Bulldog asked.

"Well, it's an asylum, an institute. This here's the institute for the deaf and dumb."

It did not matter what Matthews said at that point. Staying in an asylum clogged the Whippets' minds. An asylum and an institution sounded about the same. They were being put in an institution by two truant officers. The boys got very quiet. Matthews tried to make light of it all. "Don't worry yourselves none, nobody in there's gonna care how much racket you make. And even if they do, they can't complain about it." Matthews paused and then broke into a grin. Until then, the boys were not sure whether he was joking.

Mobile's Whippets played Birmingham the next day. Whatever the reason, the long drive, the deputy down near Evergreen, or trying to sleep in an asylum, the Whippets could not seem to find the ball. Pitching was off, hitting was off, and almost everything else seemed flat. Birmingham wasted no time running up the score. By the third inning, Birmingham led 4-0. Squatting behind home plate, Al Gonzales began to wonder if this was going to be a blowout. He dreaded the thought of going home a loser. Just into the fourth inning Al smelled rain. Within the blink of an eye, drops hit home plate and the red clay broke out in spots. Before Johnnie Smith could wind up for the next pitch, the sky opened and rained cats and dogs. It rained most of the afternoon. It rained so badly that one of the boys pulled out his harmonica and played "It Ain't Gonna Rain No More." But it did. When pools collected around home plate and first base, the umpire decided to call the game and start over the next day since the sides had not completed five innings of play.

The Whippets spent another night in the asylum, sleeping to the tune of a downpour. By rule, the game with Birmingham started over from scratch. Al was right. The game turned into a blowout. The Whippets waxed Birmingham in seven rainless innings. It was a stunning turnabout. They went on to beat Sylacauga, win the playoff, and capture the 1930 American Legion Alabama Junior Baseball Championship. The Whippets returned home as State Champions. News of their victory spread throughout Mobile. Nothing at Galvez had changed, yet everything seemed different. The Whippets had scaled the walls of the south side and returned as its heroes. They proved themselves to themselves. Old man Joe Rooney swelled with pride and disbelief. His boys were practicing now for the American Legion regional baseball championship playoffs in Palatka, Florida next week. Keeping the diamond and outfields well trimmed for his Whippets gave him purpose. This was the gritty south side, and he loved it.

The Whippets' moment in the sun faded at Palatka, down on the St. Johns River. They did not make the finals, losing to a team that spoke more Spanish than English. But the Whippets returned to Galvez no less heroes than the week before. They were recognized by judge Kennesaw Mountain Landis, the commissioner of professional baseball. They were the best ball players in the state, the most talented amateur team under seventeen Mobile ever saw. Yet within months, they were no more. Johnnie Smith, Bulldog Doyle, Roy Knapp, Jackie Stokes, Gunny Gonzales, Henry Richardson, Rip Repoll, Charlie Wilcox, William Farrar, Hallet McDonough, and Leo Reinhart turned 17 and ended their brief career as Whippets.

27. *Alabama State Champion Whippet Athletic Club: (top, l-r) manager Van Matthews, Leo Reinhart, Johnnie Geary, Earl Holcomb, unidentified, Johnnie Smith, coach Maurice Drain; (middle, l-r) Al Gonzales, Lamar Doyle, Roy Knapp, John (Rip) A. Repoll, Henry Richardson; (bottom, l-r) Jack Stokes, Gunny Gonzales, Hallett McDonough, Charlie Wilcox (Courtesy, Mobile Press Register, Sunday, July 27, 1930).*

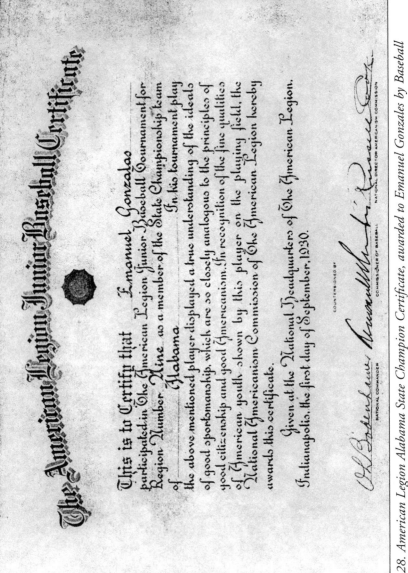

28. *American Legion Alabama State Champion Certificate, awarded to Emanuel Gonzales by Baseball Commissioner Kennesaw Mountain Landis, September 1, 1930.*

CHAPTER 11

Cowboys on Rails

Shudders rippled through the train from coal tender to caboose. On the north side of an aging westbound boxcar, four bare feet floated in the wake of the engine's smoky breath. Pat bit off one last chunk of apple and flung the core at a passing pine. He stood to watch the string of cars slow to a crawl. Gunny reached up to shut the huge sliding door. Since stealing away from the rail yard in New Orleans yesterday, Pat and Gunny kept hobos and others at a distance. Open doors attracted drifters who waited for empty cars. Sharing the boxcar meant losing it and usually everything in it. All the way from Baton Rouge to Marshall, clusters of rail people stared out from makeshift shanties when the train steamed past. Gunny remembered that look on folks amid the warm rubble of the Great Fire. The human trolls dwelling under the train's dark trestles watched Gunny's open boxcar shrink into the distance and disappear forever.

The very sound of Marshall, Texas once conjured up in Gunny's mind frontier scenes abounding with bleached steer skulls, weathered cowboys, and galloping rangers. The mystique of the old West preyed on Gunny's imagination. As the train steamed through Marshall, though, images of the rowdy West evaporated. Instead, Gunny glimpsed a dusty version of Mobile's south side, minus the shipyards. Nearly 60 years earlier, Marshall boasted being capital of war torn Missouri, the nerve-center of the Confederacy's Trans-Mississippi

Department and a crossroad of antebellum plantation life. The War Between the States snuffed out Marshall's moment of pride, leaving the town crippled until the Texas and Pacific Railroad linked it with Fort Worth. The boys kept to their boxcar until the train pulled away from the Marshall depot and headed west over the old stagecoach line buried under the tracks.

After leaving St. Vincent's in 1928, Al Gonzales and Rip Repoll went onto McGill Institute High School at Government and Joachim. Irish Ma could not cover that kind of tuition, and a high school diploma in 1929 did not make much difference anyway. Gunny hustled for a job. For the longest time he worked the Battle House Hotel, standing barefoot near the Royal Street entrance peddling newspapers. By 9:10 each night, the eastbound train from New Orleans rolled into Mobile with bales of newspapers for sale on consignment. For 15 cents, a station runner bicycled the papers to Gunny at the Battle House. A couple of hours later, Gunny had 75 cents to show for his efforts, almost a day's pay at Hammel's. He finally landed a regular job at Ibsen's seed store on Government.

Pat wondered how Gunny got off from work at Ibsen's to ride rails. "He didn't give me time off. I just decided not to go back. He's a nice old man and all, even though he's kind of funny. Comes from Norway or some place like that. Talks that Norway talk when he gets riled up. But he's been letting me open the store now for about a year or so. I stoke the fire in the morning, sweep up and move things around for some of the ladies that come in. And when I went off to play in the state championship, he never said one cross word to me. I just came back and picked up the broom right where I left it. You know, Mr. Ibsen could have hired somebody on to take my place while I was playing ball. He didn't though. Hell, I've been playing league ball while tending store." Gunny shared more with Pat about leaving Ibsen's than Irish Ma could have squeezed out in a month.

"Couple of weeks ago, Mr. Ibsen went to lunch and told me to take care of things till he got back. I did. I took care of things real good. So while he's out, a big batch of seeds comes in. I opened the boxes right up. Thought I'd get everything unpacked, you know. Well, I see all these little packets in the boxes. Never saw so many packets before. And each one of them had these highfalutin Latin words. I sure as hell couldn't make out what they said. So I opened up all them packets. Took forever, but I got it done by the time Mr. Ibsen came back. He started poking around the store like he'd lost something. Finally came up to me and wanted to know if I'd seen some seeds. Here I am standing on a floor covered with all kinds of seeds, and he's in a lather about some he can't find. Finally tells me he's been waiting for a special shipment all the way from California. The clerk down at the L&N had left Mr. Ibsen a notice the shipment came in.

"I told Ibsen those seeds came in while he was out to lunch. We went over to the bin drawer where I'd put them. He looked in the drawer and turned real pale. Started talking that Norway talk and picked up a handful of seeds. Then he looks at me like I don't have a lick of sense and says 'Manuel, where are the little packets? There should be lots of little packets!' Course, I told him not to worry because I already emptied all them packets into the drawer. Mr. Ibsen sort of choked. For the longest time he spoke at the ceiling, just like Aunt Nettie. How the hell was I supposed to know they'd put different seeds in each package? I'd mixed them all together. I didn't say a word. Just looked at Mr. Ibsen and walked out the store. Felt like a nitwit. At the end of the day Mr. Ibsen comes by the house. He talks to Irish Ma for a long time and says he wants me to come back and learn the seed business. I don't know squat about seeds. I couldn't even figure out what them packets say. There's got to be something else for me to do. That's what I told him. He looked upset but still paid me for the whole day. Irish Ma said I should let him teach me the trade, you know, because he's been so nice and all. But I just couldn't go back and sell seeds. So, here I am riding a boxcar goin' nowhere real fast." Gunny looked out the open door.

Pat still could not picture Gunny selling seeds. Pat could see him talking baseball, not petunias. "I ain't much of a judge, but I think you ought to keep playin' ball. You're already good enough to play Twilight and Central league at the same time. It won't be long before you land a spot with the Mobile Bears. Course, you're gonna go without in the meanwhile if you don't have a job." Pat had a way with the obvious.

"You're sounding like Irish Ma." Gunny shook his head. "I've been out of St. Vincent's over two years, and she still worries about me. You can guess what size a conniption fit she'd have at us bumming all over Texas and hell's half acre in a boxcar. God knows it would put her six feet under for sure. She probably figures we're in New Orleans on the St. Charles trolley right now, having an oyster loaf or something." The boys rode silently for a while.

When the train crawled into Longview, they jumped from the boxcar but did not make it into town. A fellow looking worn beyond his years, a bristle-faced man in denim coveralls, caught their attention in the rail yard. "Whereabouts you fellas from? Don't recall seeing y'all around here before."

Pat came to his wits. "We're not from around here, just visitin' for a while." His New Orleans brogue lacked Longview's twang.

One of the eyes on the whiskered face opened wide. "Now I don't suppose you fellas just come in on the freight train from Marshall, and I don't suppose you've a mind to pick up an odd job or two instead of moving on. But just in case I'm mistaken, well, you might want to know about the pea farms." Pat and Gunny grinned with curiosity. "You see, folks hereabouts got a real need for pickers this time of year, what with all them peas, beans, and corn coming in. If it weren't for the railroad, there's no telling how much crop might be lost. Ever so often, the railroad catches some of them freeloaders who don't bother to have tickets, and figures it's got some fare coming. So, the sheriff has the hobos work off their fares on the pea farms, and then work a bit longer to buy one-way tickets to Fort Worth. Usually manage to earn enough by the time all the pickin' gets done." A series of short whistles from the depot caught the boys' attention. Their train began to pull out from Longview. Pat and Gunny picked up their knapsacks, found an open boxcar door, and leapt aboard.

"Now what are we gonna do? I ain't about to go pick peas on some farm in Longview all summer. And sure as hell I don't want to keep riding boxcars to God knows where. The farther we go, the longer it'll take to get back. And Aunt Nettie will give me what for if I don't show up before long." Gunny looked into the horizon. "Let's see Amarillo and then turn around." Pat nodded and stretched out, soon falling asleep. Amarillo was a much bigger Longview in the middle of a desert. Except for the Palo Duro canyon, the boys found little of interest. Lubbock gave them even less to look at on the way back to Fort Worth. Crossing the endless prairie between Lubbock and Fort Worth made Mobile look good, real good.

CHAPTER 12

Diamonds in the Rough

Gunny and Al stopped by Elmer Guillot's house on their way to Galvez for a pickup baseball game. The Guillot's lived on the west side of St. Emanuel across the street from Al Gonzales. They were the nicest neighbors one could imagine. Elmer's house seemed like another home to the Gonzales boys until that afternoon. Al went into the back bedroom looking for Elmer's baseball glove and opened a closet door. An oddly familiar shroud caught Al's eye.

The newspaper recently carried a brief account of Klan doings south of Virginia on Washington Avenue. Only 15 blocks separated Irish Ma's front door from sheeted rabble-rousers in Oakdale. The Klan's local klavern met in the Baptist church off Garrity Street, robed up, and marched over to the park across from St. Matthew's Church for a rally. The nuns who taught school at St. Matthew's came down to Mobile from up north. No one likely mentioned anything to them about the Klan's lawn parties. The Ku Klux Klan had no problem getting a permit to march whenever it wanted. Next week the White Knights could just as soon rally at Galvez for a march over to St. Vincent's. Not even newspapers seemed beyond the Klan's influence. Some years back, a newspaper account of a daylight lynching in Monroe Louisiana reported how some local boys walked a colored fellow to the upper floor of a livery for having his way with a white girl. First the paper called it a lynching, then changed its tune claiming nobody actually pushed the Colored out the loft door. Seems he put a rope around his neck and jumped all by himself. That would make it a suicide, not a lynching, so the newspaper reasoned, printing a retraction. More recently and closer to home, Gunny witnessed a lynching on Government Street. Seems a Negro attacked a white nurse, a gal that was kin to the Mander's on Michigan Avenue. The Klan did not have a monopoly on lynching, but enjoyed a well deserved reputation that conveyed fear and intimidation. Once Hiram Evans became Imperial Wizard in 1922, the Klan began to rail even more so against Catholics. They pandered the Klan's slogan of native, white, Protestant supremacy. Oakdale's klavern rallied in front of St. Matthew's about the Church being against white people, about Spaniards and Italians trying to steal white Protestants' heritage. The message had its effect on Mobile's Catholic Spaniards.

Al Gonzales stared at the haunting image, knowing well what it meant. "Al, you coming or not?" Gunny walked into the room and peeked around the closet door. "Holy shit! He's in the Klan. Don't touch anything. Let's get the hell out of here." The ghoulish hood above the white shroud floated back into hiding. They scrambled out of the room. "You don't want old man Guillot to know we were in there. Sure as hell somebody'll show up one night and burn a cross on your lawn. Come on." Al and Gunny said nothing to Elmer about the closet. But Gunny could not leave well enough alone. He decided to embarrass the Klan through one of its own ilk.

Pickup games at Galvez lasted until dusk. When the ball could be heard before it could be seen, the game ended. No one wanted to field a line drive in the dark. Al, Elmer, and Gunny found themselves sitting on the pitcher's mound passing around a jug after the game. They had played through supper. Elmer had a taste for shinny, for which Gunny could not claim credit. Elmer could hardly get through the front door at night before Mrs. Guillot sniffed her boy for booze. Gunny knew better than Elmer to go light on corn liquor before supper. After the lips went numb, it was too late. Gunny offered Elmer first chug.

"This is good stuff, Gunny, where'd you get it?" Elmer admired Gunny's worldly connections.

"About ten of us went over the bay in a skiff to visit Willie Mastin in Fairhope. We bought about four gallons and dragged them on a line in the water behind the boat."

"What were you doin' in a skiff?" Elmer was impressed. "You can't swim a lick."

"How in the hell else am I supposed to get to Fairhope?" Gunny wondered about Elmer. "Besides, no one else in the boat could swim either."

Elmer started laughing. He tried to stop, but turned giddy instead. The shinny had captured its prey. Elmer kept nursing the jug. Numb from the neck up, Elmer stretched out, closed his eyes, and said no more.

"Look's like he's out. Elmer, you awake?" Gunny saw no response.

The headlights of a pickup truck bounced across the outfield and came to a stop next to third base. Tommy Mastin got out and walked over to the pitcher's mound. He had been delivering fish all day. After Amendment 18 imposed prohibition, peddling homebrew grew into a cottage industry that put food on many a south side table. Back porch bootlegging often made the difference between eating meat and ends not meeting. Gunny understood that a couple of Mastin's in two black Hudsons ran an enviable corn liquor business on the south side. Though nearly every block south of Madison homebrewed and bootlegged for a living, the black Hudsons provided curb service. Uncle Charlie did not mind paying the rate for premium shinny, even at $1.50 a gallon. But taking delivery at home at that price, tip included, seemed a bargain to a penny-pinching Charles Joullian. And Uncle Charlie preferred dealing with a reputable vendor. Gunny watched his normally cautious uncle stand inside the screened door and darken the porch light. In moments, a black Hudson quietly appeared and delivered fine corn liquor to one of its regular customers. Uncle Charlie closed the door, removed the jug's cap, and sniffed. Irish Ma and Nettie let Charles do the honors. Miss Nettie's restraint about oysters did not apply to shinny. Charles sipped, sloshed, and inhaled a jigger's worth, confirming the booze was okay for Irish Ma and Miss Nettie. Each weekend Charles retrieved the jug from the shed out back. His own homebrew got them through the week, but the good stuff came out each Saturday. Down the street, Ursulene stretched to make ends meet each week, dealing homebrew out of her parlor to help pay the rent. She faced plenty of competition, though. Neighbors on either side at the corner of Hamilton and Palmetto peddled homebrew off the porch, and friends across the street trafficked in shinny. The number of neighborhood vendors kept prices low and quality high. Mobile's south side was a consumer's market.

"Is that Elmer Guillot?" Tommy chuckled. "My god, he's drunk. Gunny, you know he can't hold his liquor. He'll sleep out here until morning if you don't get him home."

"Well, that's pretty much what we had in mind anyway, Tommy. Al and I found out that Elmer's dad has a hood and sheet in a closet at his house. Seems his dad rides with the Klan," Gunny explained. "We figured to play a prank on old man Guillot by getting Elmer stinking drunk and dropping him off on the front porch. That ought to give the neighbors an eyeful and keep Mr. Guillot off the streets a while. Now that you're here, how about helping Elmer stretch out in the truck on the way home?"

During the day Tommy moved seafood in the truck, which reeked of slime and fish scales. Tommy had reason to chew on Gunny's plan. Boozer Mastin would probably pin Tommy's ears back if word of this got out. No respectable seafood, homebrew or corn liquor dealer on the side south would want a burning cross in the yard. That could dry up business. But Tommy would give an eyetooth to hear Mrs. Guillot screaming at Elmer. They put Elmer in the foul truck bed. Tommy drove over to St. Emanuel and parked. Gunny and Al carried Elmer, fish scales and all, to the front porch, pounded on the door, and ran. A long silent spell broke when Mrs. Guillot finally came to the door. Tommy, Al, and Gunny heard each word nearly a block away. So did the neighbors. Only Elmer could not understand what the fuss was all about.

Come Sunday, Gunny crouched in red clay behind home plate, waiting for another fast ball. Catching for Dick Tanner's West End Barber Shop baseball team let Gunny squeeze in an extra game each week. They did not have to pay Gunny to play, though by all rights that would have been fair. The team's reward came in dark bottles after the game. If the homebrew had a ripe golden flavor, they drank it. If the beer tasted green, they still drank it. Eighteen year-old stomach walls usually recovered from green beer attacks. Ripe or not, though, the West End Barber Shop squad never said no to Dick Tanner's free homebrew.

West Enders played good but uninspired ball. Anyone who was anybody played with more than one team. Good talent could find a position in both the Twilight and Central leagues. The GM&N, L&N, and M&O railroad teams in the Twilight league played during the week, while the West Enders, the Rigas All Stars, and other Central league teams competed on Sunday. Serious semi-professionals strutted their stuff with Central and Twilight teams for a shot at one of the four teams in the premier Mobile City league. The Southern, Evangeline, Southeastern, and Cotton leagues routinely scouted City league standouts for professional careers. Dreams of getting paid to have fun during the Depression came true for some ball players.

At one time or another, Gunny caught for McGowan & Lyons, ABB's Transfer & Moving, and Rigas All Stars in the Central league. Giggy Morrison also caught for Rigas, and since Giggy was up in age at 19, Gunny played less than he liked for the All Stars. John Rigas ran a sandwich and ice cream shop on the northeast corner of Madison and Claiborne long before the Great Fire. Though Gunny liked the Greeks and eating on the house after a game, playing time came first. If he could not play, he would not stay. Gunny soon moved over to McGowan & Lyons where he flashed signals for a while to one of his favorite pitchers, Oscar Lipscomb. Though Oscar lived up north in the grove between Beauregard and Dauphin, he still threw a good ball by south side standards.

Catching for Pete Pierce was predictable. Pete won West End's pitching slot with a monotonously accurate arm. Pete could put the ball through a key hole and not touch the tumblers. Gunny just pointed the mitt and the ball found it. Catching Pete came easily. He threw one pitch, a fast ball, so signals only confused him. Pete could not throw a curve, a slider, or a knuckleball. His change-up looked more like a slower fast ball.

He did not show the change-up too much. But his fast ball burned a hole in Gunny's mitt. If the ball ever came at the batter's head, the head ducked or left the field unconscious. Pete's pitches did not break, ever.

Catching in the City league differed, and did not come so easily. It demanded that a catcher do more than just stop a fast ball. City league pitchers hurled unhittable and sometimes uncatchable balls at the target behind home plate. Only great catchers measured up to the challenge, but great catchers did not easily suffer other catchers. John Easum caught for White Swan's City league team long before Gunny joined the roster. Behind the plate, Easum was good, sometimes great. Easum's soft spot showed only when runners tried to steal second. He could not throw to second base. Gunny matched Easum behind the plate and at bat, playing a number of games in his stead and consistently nailing second base with strike zone tag outs. A week before the league tiebreaker against Pritchard, coach John Cassidy took Gunny off the starting lineup and substituted Easum as catcher. Cassidy's mind was made, which meant Gunny would warm the bench in Whistler before hundreds of fans at Martin diamond. While any Twilight or Central league catcher gladly would have traded places with Gunny in a heartbeat, Gunny made City league by playing, not by babysitting a bench.

After stewing for a day, Gunny shocked his team and surprised opponents. He quit White Swan cold, walking out on coach Cassidy. But an even bigger surprise came when Pritchard signed up Gunny before Pritchard's Sunday playoff game against White Swan. Gunny took some satisfaction telling coach Cassidy, who questioned the parentage of Pritchard's coaches and wished them all a swift trip to hell. Catching for Pritchard, though, had its share of wrinkles. Pritchard's Buck Lewis owned the most notorious knuckleball in Mobile County. Nobody on White Swan could hit it, but Gunny needed a tub to catch it. Buck's pitch broke unpredictably, dropping in front of the plate, sliding into the strike zone, or jumping right over Gunny's mitt. Pritchard's new catcher seemed lost behind the plate, snatching at balls that weren't there. Buck pitched six impressive hitless innings, for the most part unmindful of the excitement. Between innings fans attended Buck's needs. When Buck asked for cold drinks, they furnished chilled homebrew. Buck liked good homebrews and swilled more than a few while Pritchard batted. Once White Swan retired the sides, Buck resumed the mound. Gunny sensed a difference. The infamous knuckleball did not break or wobble anymore. And Buck's fast ball lost some of its zip. Suddenly, Gunny was catching changeups that neither zipped nor skipped. He no longer needed a tub. From the seventh on, Gunny rarely needed a mitt. White Swan just waited and popped the ball out of sight. Homebrew took the knuckle out of Buck and gave White Swan a round of batting practice. Pritchard blew the game and lost Gunny in the process. Gunny's flirtation with Pritchard quickly withered. Quitting White Swan stirred a few ripples, but dropping two City league teams in one month made news. Good players fought and weaseled their way into City league, and once there could not be pried out with a church key.

By 1931, a game could be had every day of the week and several times on Sunday. A few diamonds even featured lights for night games. At the corner of Broad and Texas, teams played indoor ball. The size and stitching of the indoor ball suggested post-surgical cantaloupe. However solidly a batter whacked an indoor ball, it just floated lazily into the outfield. Across the street from the indoor ball diamond, Ursulene ran a stand, selling peanuts, drinks and candy during games. For the better part of four hours a night, fans and livestock milled about the intersection at Broad like sugar ants at a picnic. Ursulene did well off the games, but the best deal in town did not even get going until much later. Just a block or so from the indoor ball diamond, Peg waited on his front porch for the hooting and hollering to end and the field lights to shut off. Like Crip Bonham, Peg came by his name honestly, balancing on a leg and a peg. Peg never seemed to think much about it. His day began when ball players wandered over to while away the night. For just a dime they could chase shrimp and pretzels with homebrew.

Gunny played for Zoghby clothing store. When Zoghby won, Gunny got free pants and shoes right off the shelf. Zoghby and other team sponsors promoted their wares through gifts to players. The publicity of a winning ball club generated enough business to cover the costs, and sometimes more. No one kicked up much of a fuss about Zoghby's handouts. It made good business sense for a clothing store team to dress decently, and it attracted better players who might have signed up with Leader and Kalifeh, Zoghby's clothing rivals. Players received no part of a game's receipts. Paying cash would turn the team professional and ruin its amateur standing. Zoghby wanted no part of that. The shame of Jim Thorpe was not about to rear its ugly head in Mobile, at least not on Zoghby's account.

While Gunny played ball in every league that mattered, Al and Rip studied at McGill Institute where Al became one of the best third basemen in high school baseball. School had its place, of course, but Al's passion for the classroom never approached his passion for the ball diamond. And high school baseball did not hold a candle to the excitement of league play. When Al and Rip graduated in May of 1932, Al left for Daphne across the bay. He stayed near Yulle's Wharf and found a spot on the roster with an eastern shore baseball team. Much to Al's delight, Gunny went along, too. Aunt Juanite asked Gunny to keep baby brother Al company for the summer. Memories of waiting outside Grandma Sin's house on an empty belly still stuck in Gunny's craw. Grandpa Joe passed away over five years ago, but some memories did not fade. Gunny thought it odd that Al's sister would ask her nephew to watch over her brother. Except, of course, that no one more street smart came to mind.

For the summer of 1932, Al and Gunny played ball in Daphne. Teammates saw the two as look-alike cousins with play-alike talent. Since Daphne's game rarely measured up to Mobile's level of play, and never approached City league ball, the Gonzales boys had a field day. August Renteria, another Whippet standout, came over to Daphne to horse around with Gunny and play ball. Ellis Ollinger already knew of Gunny and August. As a playground director, Ellis knew hundreds of boys. He watched the Whippets capture State in one brilliant season. Now Ollinger was into his second year at Spring Hill Prep teaching high school history, bookkeeping, and football. Over the summer, Ellis took up coaching in

Baldwin County near Daphne, and got some close-up looks at Gunny and Renteria. Coach Ollinger sensed the difference between athletic experience and instinct. These boys had both, but Ellis bided his time.

Come the 4th of July, Gunny, Al and August found themselves at a dance on Yulle's Wharf. Ellis showed up. Coach Ollinger made his move. "Gunny, I see you and August have been having an easy time of it on the diamond over here. You fellas play good ball, but you already know that. Hell, you could probably coach over here." Gunny and August basked in the unaccustomed flattery. Coach Ollinger was not just anybody. He gave them their due. "Now, I suppose you fellas will probably play league ball next year. You'll both make City league for sure. They'd be damn fools not to take you." Ellis felt it was now or never. "But I was wondering if y'all might give some thought to doing something else."

"Like what?" Both wondered. "What's better than City league? Pro?"

"Can't argue with that, you know. Y'all could go right on to Southern League ball at this rate. So maybe what I'm thinking sounds kinda crazy." Ellis looked them in the eye. "I want you fellas to quit league ball. You can play prep ball in the spring, but only for me. How about you two playing football for me at Spring Hill Prep?" Ellis might as well be speaking Greek.

"Coach, I ain't never played football on a real team. We fool around over at Galvez a lot, but that's just pick up stuff. I like football, but I'm good at baseball. Least, that's what I'm told." Gunny did not rush to accept Ellis' proposal. "Just who are we supposed to play for?"

"The prep school out at Spring Hill wants to put together a team. It's not what you'd call a coach's dream, Gunny. There's all of 90 kids in the high school there, half foreign, and damn few play football. Out of what's left we've got to field a team against McGill Institute, University Military School, and Murphy High School. We're outnumbered and outclassed. You boys would make the difference. What do you think?"

"How are we gonna do that?" August was puzzled. "We'd be up against varsity types. They'd make us look silly. We'd be lucky they don't wipe the field with our asses and trash us on the way out." August spoke respectfully, all things considered.

"And I ain't got the money to go to Spring Hill." Gunny got to the point.

Ellis knew his audience. "You fellas are diamonds in the rough. You know what I mean? I need fast feet and good hands. You've got both. If you can catch knuckleballs, you can handle footballs. And I don't know of anyone at McGill, UMS or Murphy who can outrun you, Gunny. All you have to do is get past the scrimmage line. The ball will be there. The rest is pretty easy to figure out. And, Gunny, don't worry about money. I'm willing to offer you a four-year athletic scholarship. Play ball and go to school free. That's a heap better than playing baseball for ice cream and socks. What'll it be?" Coach Ollinger showed all his cards.

So did Gunny. "I need to eat. I can't go all the way out to Spring Hill every day and not eat. They're gonna have to feed me." Gunny nearly felt embarrassed.

Ellis stared at the dance floor. "We'll work something out I'm sure. You won't go hungry, okay?" Ellis went out on a limb. A scholarship covering the $50 semester tuition for day students did not include free board.

Before the deal could be sealed, Gunny balked again. "I don't have a way to get to school and back, Coach. Uncle Charlie doesn't let me touch his Plymouth, and the trolley ain't free." A bystander might think Gunny wanted to turn down the offer, but Ellis knew better. The crash of 1929 brought people of means to their penniless knees and shamed them to talk about it. Bad as it was, the Depression could not do much more harm to folks around Galvez who had so little to lose anyway. Ellis marveled how gifted athletes rose from such poverty. Unless Coach Ollinger chauffeured Gunny or put him up on campus, Spring Hill would lose Mobile's best walk-on end. A good season, not even a winning season, would be worth all the hassle of getting this kid from Galvez to play football.

"If we can't work out a ride or something, I'll come by for you myself." Coach Ollinger reached out to settle with a handshake. Spring Hill now had two sprinting targets for Mike Donahue and Jimmy McDonald to hit. That would set McGill Institute and Brother Martin on their heels.

CHAPTER 13

All City

From her front porch on Franklin Street, Aunt Nettie watched Gunny climb into the back seat of the black sedan. She wallowed in thick pride as he left for school. It did not matter that he looked straight ahead, not even waving good-bye. She savored the moment, fearing only that this dream would end too soon. Her hand-me-down nephew was going to the Spring Hill Prep School, getting out of south side Gritney to study with the Jesuits. After a stop on south Georgia Avenue to pick up Jimmy McDonald, the sedan crossed Dauphin and turned west to Spring Hill. Under the oak canopy on the oldest college campus in Alabama, the Society of Jesus welcomed Gunny to the most elite high school in Mobile. Ellis Ollinger savored the rich irony he had fashioned by wooing the Galvez baseball star into a purple and white Badger uniform. A baseball dropout became a football walk-on. The Sacred Heart Brothers at McGill could have picked up Gunny by waiving the small tuition that he could not afford. Instead, the Jesuits at Spring Hill paid market value.

Ellis met the car at the foot of the steps to the main building. "Practice starts in one hour. Come with me." Coach led Gunny into the high ceiling office of Mr. Marlowe, from whose purse flowed the funds that sustained needy roomers and boarders. "Mr. Marlowe, this is Gunny Gonzales, the Galvez boy that played with the 1930 Whippets. He starts school today, and he's gonna play football for us. There's not an ounce more than 135 pounds on his bones. Might be okay for a baseball catcher, but it won't do against Murphy's running backs. Make sure the boy doesn't go hungry, okay?" Ellis led Gunny away when Marlowe's face finally coughed up a knowing grin. Spring Hill fed Gunny.

Father James Whelan served as the high school principal more through sheer force of personality than any noble virtue. A humbler priest no doubt would have drowned in the quagmire of administrative and managerial frustration. It wasn't that Father Whelan thrived on it, but thrived despite it. Outside of his spiritual life, Father Whalen found meaning on the gridiron with his Badgers. He and Coach Ollinger were of a singular mind about amateur athletic competition. If it cannot be done well, it is not worth doing. Ellis had recruited Gunny and August with the good Jesuit's prayer that Spring Hill might climb out of the competitive cellar just long enough to stand tall against McGill Institute's fearsome Yellowjackets. Of course, that might also help reverse declining enrollment at the Hill.

Spring Hill expected its gridiron squad to play offense and defense with inspiration. With only thirteen players, any performance short of inspirational would be disastrous. To Father Whelan's satisfaction, Ellis had assembled a scrappy roster for the 1932 fall season that shifted to adrenaline whenever inspiration wore thin, usually in the third quarter. Class president Mike Donahue called the plays as quarterback and covered the secondary on defense. In the offensive backfield stood fullback Bobby Leftwich and halfbacks Bill Camp, Jimmy McDonald, and August Renteria. Captain Maurice Ignatius "Mo" Roy and Charlie Perez centered to Donahue on offense and then switched to nose tackle on defense. In the trenches on the scrimmage line were tackles Jimmie Miller and Henry Stephen "Bubba" Norden and guards Martin Aloysius "Cooty" Norden and Hardy Demeranville. Balancing the line was Bill Capps at left end and Gunny Gonzales at right end.

Spring Hill's defense played offense when they got the ball. Offense played defense when the offense scored or lost possession. None of the Badger's positions enjoyed what Murphy and UMS coaches called depth. Even when everyone dressed out, only a couple of relievers watched from the sideline. Substitution, something of an inside joke, also meant sitting out the rest of the quarter. For the better part of all 4 twelve-minute quarters, Gunny and his starting teammates grudgingly contested each yard offensively and defensively.

In their debut at Hartwell Field on September 24, 1932, the Badgers quickly moved the ball to the Flomaton eleven yard line. After three unsuccessful running plays, right halfback Jimmy McDonald rifled a pass to Gunny in a crowded end zone for the only touchdown of the first quarter. Moe Roy converted the extra point. In the second quarter, the Badgers gave up lots of real estate, letting Flomaton drive to Spring Hill's 33 yard line. Going for the touchdown, Flomaton put the ball up, but Gunny snatched the interception and hustled through 67 yards of open field tacklers to make the score 13 to 0. When Flomaton's pass defense stiffened before halftime, Spring Hill kept the ball on the ground. Jimmy McDonald and Bobby Leftwich executed the running game with the poise of seasoned players. Weaving and charging through the line, the Badgers ground out over 200 yards from scrimmage. McDonald and Leftwich alone averaged five yards per carry. But Spring Hill's next score came from its talented defense. McDonald stepped in front of another Flomaton pass and galloped down the field to set up the Badgers' third touchdown.

The last score of the half turned Moe Roy into something of a legend. Kicking off to Flomaton following his third point after touchdown, Moe booted the ball straight through the goal line uprights into the end zone. In awe, Flomaton's kick off return receiver and most of Hartwell Field stared with disbelief. But tackle Jimmie Miller never broke stride, sprinting down field and falling on the unguarded end zone ball for a touch down. Spring Hill had never played an opening half with such execution.

Both squads stiffened their defenses after halftime, resulting in a scoreless third quarter. Flomaton could not recover, though, from the effects of the first half. No matter what Flomaton tried, the Badger defense closed ranks. When Bobby Leftwich and Bill Camp punched the ball in for two more touchdowns in the fourth quarter, amazement filled the stadium crowd. Spring Hill Prep gave Mobile notice it had come to play football.

Subsequent opponents prepared more seriously for their dates with the Badgers. No one shrugged off Spring Hill after reading accounts of the thrashing Flomaton took. Coach Ollinger's team predictably ran into more wary defensive lines and lost the next four games, the last one being a particularly painful defeat on October 22 at the hands of UMS. Hope of clinching the all important City championship lay in doubt, especially with Murphy and McGill coming up back to back at season's end.

As the largest public high school in Mobile, Murphy dominated the gridiron with extra layers of outstanding athletes. UMS, a private prep school sporting a Citadel motif, also fielded a solid football squad. The other two high schools, Spring Hill and McGill, emphasized Catholic education above football. One usually did not attend either school to nurture a promising football career. So when Spring Hill took on Murphy, the game took on a more allegorical meaning. The Catholics of Spring Hill and the Protestants of Murphy could grapple and fall together on the gridiron, spilling blood and sweat before God and neighbor, but not worship in common or marry across denominational lines without the archbishop's consent. Any decent showing by the Jesuit Badgers against the Murphy Panthers would bring honor to Spring Hill and chagrin to Murphy. For the Badgers to expect victory, however, presumed too much upon divine intervention.

Murphy enjoyed an undefeated record when its Panthers battled the Badgers on October 29. However, the first half defensive struggle left the Panthers with only seven points to show for all their talent and depth. Gunny had little to catch and missed a desperately wide fourth down end zone pass from McDonald. On defense though, the story read differently. Gunny made more than half the tackles for Spring Hill and recovered two of Murphy's fumbles. The partisan crowd at Murphy's home field could not help but admire the Badgers' spunk. Leftwich, Donahue and Renteria punched their way through the Panthers' defense to set up several scoring opportunities that disappeared with interceptions. Murphy's secondary simply excelled, and by the third quarter the Badgers began to wear thin. While Murphy rotated fresh troops into the fray, Spring Hill's scrappy starters huddled up without relief. Any Badger getting hurt could stay in for more action or limp off the field and leave a gap in the line. Fans began to wonder when fatigue would overcome the bruised Spring Hill eleven. Even to Coach Ollinger's surprise, the Badgers' defense hardened after halftime and shut Murphy down in the third quarter. Instead of a quarter to quarter romp by the Panthers, Spring Hill treated its fans to a gritty toss-up into the opening moments of the fourth quarter. After three quarters of non-stop hammering by Panther reserves, though, the Badgers' defense ran out of gas and gave up points. Murphy walked away with an unexpectedly difficult win.

Spring Hill's vicious scrap with Murphy came only a week before the season's ultimate religious experience with McGill's Yellowjackets. Practices took on a sense of urgency, for little time remained to mend before the great battle. McGill turned the season into a one game playoff no matter what Spring Hill's record might be. The hope of whipping the Yellowjackets and avenging last season's miserable 6 to 0 loss motivated the Badgers to regroup. Even the Jesuits girded themselves for battle, launching their own preemptive attack. Father Whelan formally challenged the eligibility of two key McGill players. By midweek, the Alabama High School Athletic Association had disqualified Yellowjacket center Sue Donnelly. Brother Martin, McGill's principal, stewed in his own juices at this public affront. Not intimidated in the least by the wily Jesuits, Brother Martin chalked out a bold counterattack.

On Friday morning, November 4, the Badgers trickled into the locker room to gear up for their final practice before Saturday's showdown. Gunny laced his shoes tightly over bruised ankles and then squeezed into the snug casing of high-waist pants. Strapping on a hard leather helmet, he started for the field. Gunny played mental gymnastics, cutting, blocking, and sprinting against McGill's secondary. He imagined staring across the line of scrimmage into the face of former Galvez teammates. He would give no quarter and ask none in return. Then, the nightmare began.

Coach Ollinger stormed into the locker room and ended Gunny's daydream. "Gonzales! Where's Gonzales?" Gunny stared mute at his visibly excited coach. "Don't just stand there, come with me." Gunny followed Ellis outside to Coach's car. "This morning McGill filed a protest against you and Renteria. That's 20 percent of the team." Ellis grinned wryly despite the circumstances. "August shouldn't play for Spring Hill because he transferred from McGill to some school in Philadelphia, but never attended. When August came back to Mobile, he should have played for McGill or else waited a semester before playing for us. Brother Martin complains that August transferred from McGill directly to Spring Hill just to play football. Can't do that you know. This afternoon, Father Whelan is going to present Spring Hill's side to the High School Athletic Association."

"Why does McGill say I'm ineligible?" Gunny had no idea where Coach Ollinger's story was going.

"Well, I guess McGill's had a pretty rough week of it, what with that Sue Donnelly stuff and all. Brother Martin claims you're a ringer, a professional. He's raising a ripe stink over you. Claims you took part in some boxing matches a while back under the ring name of Young Paglina, or something like that. Can't imagine where he dug up that old skeleton." Ellis let on very little.

Gunny thought a second or two. "Rip Repoll and me used to box down in Oakdale near St. Matthew's. I managed Rip, but he never went in the ring for money. I boxed a couple of times on a card down at the old plate shop near the dry docks. I was still in St. Vincent's at the time. Rip knew I boxed on the card. It was no big deal. Rip probably talked about it over at McGill."

"How much did you get for fighting, Gunny?" Ellis pressed for a number.

"Eight bucks in all, I think. Got four dollars a fight." Gunny hazily remembered getting the third degree from Aunt Nettie. "Does that mean I don't play tomorrow?"

"We'll see." Ellis pulled up to Tommy Littleton's gym on Conti between Claiborne and Joachim. Tommy Littleton had a name in boxing, and for fun headed the local chapter of the Amateur Athletic Union. Gunny followed Coach Ollinger inside, still wondering about the game. While Coach and Tommy carried on in a hush, Tommy studied the football player, nodding often as the Coach spoke. Coach Ollinger turned to Gunny with a jaundiced eye. "Gunny, amateur athletes do not take money for boxing. You made a mistake. You can't keep the money. You have to give it back to Tommy here. If you don't, well you won't be able to play tomorrow. You understand, don't you son?" The AAU ritual had to be observed.

Given those options, the answer stood out like an ugly wart. "Yes sir, I understand." But Gunny had no idea where he'd come up with eight bucks between now and kick off at 2:30 tomorrow. Eight dollars was a king's ransom south of Canal Street.

Tommy and Coach Ollinger already had reached a meeting of the minds. Ellis pulled out his wallet, counted $8, and put nearly a week's pay into Tommy's palm. "Tommy, Gunny is happy to give back what he got for a couple of amateur boxing exhibitions." Tommy excused himself and returned with an AAU jacket, welcoming Gunny back into the ranks of amateur football.

Coach Ollinger picked up Tommy's phone to return an earlier call from *The Mobile Register*. "That's right, Gonzales has been reinstated by the AAU. He took part a long time ago on a couple of fight cards as an amateur boxer. Yes, you can print that. Gunny's been inactive for over a year now and is eligible for reinstatement as an amateur. Yes, I'm sure he'll be playing McGill tomorrow. Yeah, y'all come on out for the game. Bye." Ellis looked up at Spring Hill's reinstated football star in the AAU jacket. "Come on, you're late for practice."

The Mobile Register headlined McGill's showdown with Spring Hill:

McGill Files Counter Protest Against Spring Hill High

Prep Schools to Play Today Despite Row Over Players

Gonzales and Renteria Under Fire on Badger Team;
Professionalism Charged

McGill and Spring Hill hung their dirty linen out to dry in public. But for the free publicity and surge in attendance, Father Whelan and Brother Martin might have preferred settling their differences privately by the lake at Spring Hill. Now that the Catholics had brawled openly, winning carried twice the honor and losing twice the shame. Moments before kickoff at Hartwell Field, Brother Martin announced that McGill would play the game under protest. Alabama's High School Athletic Association had not yet ruled on Renteria and Gonzales, thickening the drama.

Early in the first quarter the Yellowjackets' defense stung quickly. Bobby Leftwich fumbled the ball from center, losing yardage back to the Badgers' five. To make matters worse, Mike Donahue then dropped behind his goal line to punt, but netted only four yards on a shanked kick. McGill's celebrated fullback Henry McKeough promptly crashed through Spring Hill's goal line stand, dragging Badger defenders into the end zone with him. But McGill missed the point after touchdown.

For most of the second quarter, the crowd enjoyed a terrific defensive struggle back and forth across midfield. In the closing minutes of the first half, McKeough dropped back to punt from McGill's 40 yard line. The Badgers surged through the Yellowjacket defense, blocking the kick. Starting from the 40, Leftwich and Camp worked around McGill's end and pushed up the middle until Camp stumbled in on a three yard touchdown run. Donahue's effort for the extra point also failed, leaving the halftime score a frustrating 6 to 6 tie.

Momentum seemed to slowly turn in the Badgers' favor during the third quarter. Spring Hill's defense gave up real estate to McKeough's savage runs, but held McGill scoreless. Then, starting on the Badgers' own 40, Camp and McDonald ran 60 yards in seven plays for Spring Hill's second touchdown. This time Donahue successfully converted the point after touchdown for an unexpected 13 to 6 lead at the opening of the last quarter.

Neither offense had its way in the fourth quarter. Both squads played grudging defensive ball until the undisputed best play of the game. Having been held by Spring Hill for three downs, McGill's

McKeough punted deep to the Badgers' 25. Quarterback Donahue grabbed the punt, rolled off to the sideline and galloped 75 yards untouched into the Yellowjackets' end zone. Then Donahue missed an easy extra point, taking some gloss off his dazzling run.

McGill's powerful backfield quickly ground out its second touchdown, trailing only 12 to 19 in the fourth quarter. The Yellowjackets surged and gained momentum. Then the spark plug of McGill's offense, fullback McKeough, collapsed on the field from exhaustion. Spring Hill's stubborn line, Mo Roy, Cooty Norden and Jimmie Miller took credit for wearing him down. Both stands stood to tip their hats as McKeough was carried off the gridiron. The Yellowjackets surprisingly rose to the occasion, despite McKeough's loss. Starting from McGill's 45 yard line, quarterback Charles Sweeney went to Steiner, Emile Perez and Kearney by air, moving the pigskin down to Spring Hill's 25. Exhausted, numb, and running on fumes, the Badgers gathered to fend off a final assault by the revived Yellowjackets. But before McGill could get off another snap, the clock ran out. Spring Hill's scrappy eleven handled the Yellowjackets for four quarters and left the field under their own power. Father Whelan had lived for this day. He now was ready to go should the good Lord choose to call.

Despite McGill's challenges, Mobile took only three weeks to put Gunny in proper perspective. On the day after his 19th birthday, the Sunday *Mobile Press Register* featured its All-City Prep School Selection for 1932. Charles Joullian made much ado of his nephew's portrait on the sports section front page. He looked varsity. The eleven member mythical team included a disproportionately high showing by the Spring Hill Prep School Badgers. Bobby Leftwich, the powerful offensive runner and solid defensive secondary tackler, secured fullback honors. Jimmie Miller, the anchor in the Badger's defensive line, won the right tackle position. Competition among the ends proved more rigorous. Despite terrific performances by Edwards of Murphy and UMS' Henry Lee McKenzie, the Galvez Spaniard won out at right end for consistent excellence. The sports writers boiled Gunny's first high school football season down to the nuggets: "Gonzales is a spectacular defensive player, a phenomenal tackler and adept in recovering fumbles." Gunny's speed made him an ideal match against the dominating Panthers. To stand shoulder to shoulder with Murphy's potent offensive back field came as no small compliment.

Of the remaining eight City All Stars, Murphy boasted four, and the UMS Cadets walked off with three. Conspicuously, none of McGill's Yellowjackets made the team. Coach Ollinger and Father Whelan beamed with delight that a quarter of Spring Hill's squad won such high athletic honors. That two more Badgers made the All-City Second Team, quarterback Mike Donahue and halfback Jimmy McDonald, added icing to the Jesuits' cake. The 1932 Badgers fully earned their varsity letters just by surviving the season. Playing offense and defense the whole game against UMS, Murphy, and McGill over three consecutive weeks left none of Ellis Ollinger's team lacking for respect. When Gunny brought home his varsity letter, a large script *S* with a small *P*, Aunt Nettie bubbled with pride. But Nettie sensed that something was missing. Without a sweater jacket, the varsity letter looked anemic. Her Manuel had a trophy but no place to show it. Nettie would have none of that. Ten per cent of her pay went to Thoss Sporting Goods until Gunny got that sweater jacket. He was varsity stuff, and Nettie wanted Mobile to know.

29. Spring Hill Prep High School Football Badgers: (top, l-r) asst. coach John Gafford, Henry Stephen (Bubba) Norden (20), unidentified (10), unidentified (15), Hardy Demeranville (5), unidentified (8), Richard Jones (12), Fred Revere (6), Jimmie Miller (21), coach Ellis Ollinger; (middle, l-r) unidentified (17), Emanuel Joseph (Gunny) Gonzales (1), unidentified (2), John Mills Capps, Jr. (22), Martin Aloysius (Cooy) Norden (11), Charlie Perez (9), unidentified; (bottom, l-r) James C. (Jimmy) McDonald (19), Michael (Mike) Donahue, Jr. (16), Maurice Ignatius (Moe) Roy (18), Robert C. (Bobby) Leftwich (13), William (Bill) Camp (14), Spring Hill College, Mobile (Erik Overbey, Mobile), 1932.

30. Spring Hill Prep High School Football Badgers (right end Gunny Gonzales at far left), practice scrimmage south lawn, High School Administration Building, Spring Hill College, Mobile (Erik Overbey, Mobile), 1932.

31. *Spring Hill Prep High School Varsity Football and Baseball letter, awarded to Gunny Gonzales, 1932-1933.*

CHAPTER 14

Pass Christian Overnight

At nineteen, Gunny seldom let on to Irish Ma about his doings and whereabouts. What she managed to piece together painted only half the picture. When Gunny and Pat Healey mentioned going to visit Pat's people in New Orleans, Irish Ma imagined the boys poking along highway 90 in Pat's old Essex, riding a street car out to Audubon Park, and maybe sharing a foot long poboy.

Pat's Essex ran like a bat out of hell when put together. Most of the time, though, it lay scattered in parts and pieces. Irish Ma heard next to nothing about their adventures in the Essex, much less that Pat had no driver's license. She also had no inkling when Pat and Gunny hopped into Tommy Mastin's machine one evening in January 1933 for a sprint to New Orleans. Tommy's work with Texaco Oil gave him access to tank cars in the rail yard. Each week Tommy bled off the sump hoses of empty gasoline tankers. Come the weekend, Tommy's topless car was ready for action.

Highway 90 runs southwest from Mobile over a two lane that passes north of Bayou la Batre before plunging through the swamps of the Pascagoula River basin. No more than a few minutes past Theodore, bayou darkness descended over the highway. On the warmed pavement, rabbit and opossum stared into the head lamps of Tommy's car as it hurtled through the wilderness past the weathered marker at

Irvington. Tonight's stroll down the *Vieux Carré*, a platter of blue crabs and oysters, mugs of near-beer, Café du Monde beignets, and other Crescent City delights led them on.

Atop the Pascagoula River bridge, highway 90 hovered briefly above the vast Mississippi Sound. Descending again into the delta darkness covering the Pascagoula's wetlands, Tommy's roadster sped past black bottom marshes. The damp roadbed floated slightly above sea level in good weather. Spring rain, though, soon would saturate the marshes, letting pools rise up to swallow bits and pieces of highway 90. When the Pascagoula overflowed, there was precious little difference between the marsh and the highway.

After bouncing along the delta bottom for quite a piece, highway 90 rolls south to the saltwater shoreline. Along the wide beaches of Gulfport, into Biloxi, and beyond President Jefferson Davis' home at Beauvoir, the boys closed in on New Orleans. The bright lights of road-houses and honky-tonks along the beach lit the night. Bay St. Louis and the inland stretch to Slidell still lay ahead on the far side of Long Beach and Pass Christian.

Just shy of Pass Christian, the road veers north. Tommy nodded drowsily, unaware the highway had turned. Tommy's car cruised on, straight and true into the wilderness. Gunny hurtled from the front seat to the ground below, where he lay in shock after the car pivoted on his left leg. The crunching sound of breaking bone between knee and ankle quietly merged with the crash of Tommy's flying machine. But a flash of pain pinned Gunny's fleet foot to the earth, motionless and non-responsive. Tonight's outing would not include New Orleans after all. Pat and Tommy suffered no serious injury. They carried Gunny to a nearby house, drawn by a light on the front porch. The Williams twins, good old boys in their sixties from Shelbyville, Kentucky, opened the door to an unexpectedly ugly sight. Getting an ambulance for any poor devil from Alabama was no trouble at all. The hospital lay just a way back down the beach in Gulfport.

Come dawn, Tommy and Pat slowly retraced their way to Mobile. But the hospital staff insisted that Gunny remain until his leg stabilized. Within a couple of days, the hospital had its fill and set Gunny free. Skinny O'Brien, Tommy Mastin's uncle, came over to Gulfport in his old Buick, and carried Gunny out the front door. Word of the accident had spread before Gunny reached Mobile. The only word that mattered, though, came from Dr. Hannon, the bone doctor. Dr. Hannon saw Gunny in his office on Spring Hill Avenue at Ann Street, set the broken bone, and wrapped the left leg in a cast. Baseball presented no problem, Dr. Hannon explained, but the break made football too risky. The bone doctor and Coach Ollinger retired Spring Hill's right end after only one stellar season. Ellis might have yanked the athletic scholarship at that point. Instead, he persuaded the gridiron star to catch baseball for the Badgers. Gunny made do behind home plate, despite a crude leg brace. Though the brace and mending bones put him to the test, the Spaniard lettered in both sports.

By the end of the 1933 spring season, Gunny decided to quit school and resume his studies at Galvez. Nearing 20, he had several years on other sophomores and wanted to play real baseball. Mobile leagues now offered the best of both worlds, pay for play. Uncle Charlie also expected his nephew to get a job and help Irish Ma. Though Ellis Ollinger did not want to see Gunny go, hard times rendered high school something of a luxury. Gunny left in 1933. Two years later Spring Hill Prep High School disappeared from the face of Mobile.

CHAPTER 15

Switching Tracks

Sweating bottles of chilled homebrew crowded a long table inside the whitewashed house facing Texas Street. Fresh from another Friday night indoor ball victory, Gunny and his teammates gathered at their nearest watering hole, reliving the game's highlights with neighbors and passersby. Beer-swilling patrons made no effort to speak easy. The better breweries thrived on foot traffic attracted by the rowdies inside. Sheriff Holcombe could have shut them down had he wanted, being easy enough to find and all. Of course, that would have upset the cash economy below Church Street and cost a pile of votes come election time. Since Willie and Bob Holcombe alternated ever so often as sheriff, raiding neighborhood homes made little political sense. More to the point, by September 29, 1933, most states had voted to repeal Prohibition. Come New Year's Day, real taverns would be pouring drafts downtown across from the sheriff's office.

Somewhere into the third round of brews, pounding foot steps coming down Texas Street echoed into the front parlor. The fun continued until a breathless voice pierced the noisy celebration.

"Gunny Gonzales! You in there, Gunny?"

"Who wants to know?" Gunny grinned from the long table, draining another ten cent brew.

"Gunny, your old man got run over by a train down on Commerce Street in the switching yard just north of Canal. Happened around 7.

Cut off both legs at the knee. City Hospital sent an ambulance, but there's not much they could do." The runner breathed deep. "I heard you'd probably be here after the game. Thought you might want to know." Drinkers around the table set their bottles down easy, not knowing what to say. Gunny walked outside into the street. He did not hear the awkward words of sympathy that teammates offered as he left.

Gunny's pace matched the rush of thoughts stirring in his memory. Mixed feelings greeted the sudden news of his father's tragic death. Grandpa Joe had passed away in May, 1927. A year later Lucinda married Manuel Fraguio, a Cuban seven years her junior who worked at People's Ice House and for some time had boarded in Grandpa Joe's house. Gunny saw little of Manuel Joseph or Lucinda these past several years. Even so, Gunny still thought about his southpaw father beaning Frank Soutullo at home plate. Baseball bound both Spaniards with a kindred spirit that blood had not. Gunny also recalled watching his father and Mayor Harry T. Hartwell lead a dusty parade down the middle of Charleston Street 7 years ago during the 1926 campaign. Hartwell pledged to pave the streets of Mobile, starting on the south side. Manuel senior helped put Hartwell in office that year, giving 12 year-old Gunny an appetite for politics.

The presidential campaign of 1928 found Gunny in the midst of a political event remarkable even by Alabama standards. Alongside the Todd Shipbuilding Company at the foot of Texas Street, a festive crowd of 500 milled about a bunting-clad train car. The intense anticipation erupted into noisy enthusiasm when New York's Catholic Governor stepped into the Heart of Dixie campaigning for Alabama's vote. The rowdy crowd paraded north, attracting curious onlookers all the way down Royal, across Government, to Dauphin, and then west to Claiborne. The party delegation, including Gunny's father, led their Yankee guest through the open doors of the Cathedral of the Immaculate Conception to attend Mass. Defying the Klan and conventional political wisdom, Democrat Alfred E. Smith later stood tall on Claiborne asking the South to elect him President. The linkage between Gunny and Manuel senior, often strained and mostly distant, found its strongest moorings in baseball and politics. As Gunny walked in darkness still sporting team pinstripes, he sensed the dormant lure of politics. He was his father's son, after all, if not his father's family.

The L&N Railroad disclaimed liability for killing Manuel Gonzales, suggesting he was asleep on the rails, but eventually offered $500. Though not a handsome sum, Ursulene accepted. Of that, she gave $75 to Gunny, the price of a 1929 Chevrolet. Not since 1923 had Ursulene tendered much of value to her first born. With the gift of a cheap car, she completed Gunny's rite of passage. In the midst of the Depression at age 20 he was on his own. He had plenty of company, though. Long before the bull market died in New York, folks on the south side of town already had learned to do without. Wall Street's financial convulsions caused few ripples south of Madison Street. The Have-Nots around Galvez barely paused as Black Tuesday squandered the future that the Haves took for granted. The fire of 1919 and flood of 1926 already claimed most of the Have-Nots' future. When Gunny stood beside Aunt Nettie on the corner of St. Francis and St. Joseph watching the People's Bank collapse in 1929, it just provided a curious distraction during their routine search for cheap soup bones. Children living around Galvez learned not to bank on Santa Claus long before the country went broke. They stood in line on the corner of Conti and Joachim at Christmas waiting outside the Lyric Theatre for a handout, a toy, food basket, or shirt.

Driving a $75 Chevy in 1933 was one thing, having a job quite another. Even Charlie Joullian still walked to the *Press* each day, hoping for work in the composing room whenever Morgan Fowler volunteered to take a day off. Uncle Charlie's $25 Plymouth remained locked up out back. A car seemed to ease the trip to the poor house.

Whenever they could siphon enough gas to feed the Chevy, Gunny, Rip Repoll, Elmer Guillot, and Pat Healey whiled away the weekends at Monroe Park or out at Spring Hill. Monroe Park boasted outdoor moving pictures, a roller coaster, and dances on Arlington Pier opposite Fort Whiting. When their pockets ran empty, the boys waded into the bay off Beach Street and picked up soft shell crabs for supper.

Driving out to country club tea dances in Spring Hill took a lot more doing. Rip borrowed suits from Vince Thompson, the kind that shrank when Rip fell or got thrown into a swimming pool. But Vince had steady work with an undertaker and had more than one suit. Gunny wore one of Uncle Charlie's old suits to tea dances. Suit or not, Rip managed to have fun, which usually meant joining a fight already in progress or starting one from scratch.

Pat and Elmer did not pretend to be tea dance material, but they never turned down a free ride. Getting there and back was half the adventure, with or without girls. Gunny's Chevy usually had enough gas to get to the Hill, but not always enough for the trip home to Franklin Street. Long into the dance, the boys quietly retired to the parking lot to siphon gas. Pat did the honor of slipping a hose into the tanks of fancy touring cars. After fumbling around until he had a mouthful of gas, Pat started a flow through the hose into a can. One particular touring car unexpectedly moved as the boys squatted quietly in the shadows near the bumper. "What in the hell's goin' on?" A startled voice inside the touring car spooked Gunny into near bladder arrest.

Gunny felt the drumming of a runaway heartbeat. He found a pair of wide eyes staring out the car's rear window. The loosened shirt collar and wrinkled necktie lent a drunken effect to the anxious face peeking through the window. Before another word popped out, a girl suddenly bolted upright from the back seat, wearing most of a dress around her neck. Gunny found his voice again. "I'm gonna get the hell outta here." Pat and Elmer were too stunned to move.

"You can have the gas, just don't take my car." The face in the rear window pleaded, clearly negotiating from a position of weakness.

"All I want to do is get the hell away from here. I don't want your car." Gunny spoke mostly to himself.

"Don't take my car. You can have the gas." The face in the window repeated itself. Pat yanked the hose and the boys scurried into the darkness. The ride back to Galvez took half as long as the drive out to the Hill. Next week they would find another dance.

CHAPTER 16

On the Road Again

Cherry Cornelius, Al Gonzales and Gunny watched evening games at the indoor ball diamond on Broad whenever their teams had a bye. Before the last out, a good slice of south Mobile would wander by to see and be seen. Their evening promenade followed no less a ritual than baseball, outwardly calm and purposeful while inwardly ready for chaos. During a lull between innings, Al caught sight of three familiar figures strutting across Broad. A rush of adrenalin filled Al's predatory veins. He sat tall on the bleacher.

"Gunny, you and Cherry see that guy across the street, the one in the middle?" Al nodded at three men drifting down Broad Street. "See him?" Gunny and Cherry craned for a better look, but homebrew blurred their view. Al's tone darkened. "I've got business with him. You and Cherry don't have to get into this if you don't want to, but I'm gonna kick his ass right now. If those other two jump on me, I might need a little help." Al leapt from the stands and disappeared into the dark before Cherry or Gunny could say anything coherent.

Having Gunny and Cherry nearby gave Al confidence, though Al preferred to do his own fighting. Shrinking from confrontation postponed the inevitable and lost face on the south side. And the risk of losing a brawl seldom stopped Al from starting one when there were accounts to settle. The calliope wagon dances under the Choctaw Park pavilion off Washington Avenue proved no exception. Triggering a fight did not take much. Anything would do, and reasons were less a cause than an excuse. Al liked the dances and the fights. He was a natural scrapper. He feared no one.

Gunny and Cherry mulled over leaving the ball game. Al probably needed no help, even if all three of those guys jumped him. This was Al's fight, after all. As Gunny and Cherry stared at the diamond, Al closed in on his quarry. Near the corner of Broad and Augusta, Al stopped under a street light and called out. Three silhouettes turned, surprised to be challenged by a lone fool under a street lamp. They needed no introduction or explanation. Word of mouth had it that Al Gonzales intended to settle an account for one of his sisters. But they never thought he would come alone. This was not a sporting match by street standards. Despite the odds, Al's honor demanded as much satisfaction as opportunity would allow.

As his prey came within range, Al attacked without another word of warning. All three pounced on Al, but soon let go. Gunny and Cherry joined the fray and took two to task. Left alone again with his prey, Al delivered a message from the family that would long be visible for others to see. The six brawling figures tangled from lamplight into darkness. Their commotion tumbled under the window of a nearby house. Pistol in hand, the police officer inside stepped onto his front porch. Al, Gunny and Cherry were standing, breathless, over three groaning bodies at their feet. They caught sight of the lawman and bolted down Broad toward the ball field. The fight was over. Gunny finally got around to sorting things out. "Al, what exactly the hell was that all about, anyway?" The fog of homebrew started to clear.

Al felt protective of his sister, the one who limped. "He got her pregnant and won't marry her. That's what it's all about." Al had settled accounts.

The brawl, of course, would not likely improve that relationship any, but such was the price of honor. The price also included a broken finger, Gunny's. After weeks of ignoring what only seemed like another dislocation, his throwing hand turned purple and doubled its size. Gunny no longer could stand the pain of writing and delivering customer notices for shipments arriving at the GM&N terminal. That began cutting into Gunny's $9 weekly pay. Worse, he could barely handle the ball behind the plate for GM&N's ball team. Working a day job to play ball at night for the employer's team summed up the pay to play leagues. Manager Joe Cassidy was none too happy when he learned about Gunny's Broad Street shenanigans. Gunny's younger brother Joseph stepped in for a while down at the GM&N station so Gunny could see Doctor Howard Walker. Doctor Walker understood these things, having promoted boxing matches across from Middie' Tavern near the Alabama Machine Shop at Canal and Royal. In short order, the doctor looked at Gunny's badly swollen finger, put his patient under ether, broke the poorly knitted joint, and set it straight again. The fresh break knitted well, but Gunny lost work down at the GM&N and had to sit out several more games. Gunny figured that Al could do his own fighting next time.

Work at the GM&N terminal on Charleston and Royal was good until word started going around in 1934 that some jobs, including Gunny's, would end when the terminal relocated north of St. Louis Street. There was no other work to speak of, including public jobs through city hall. Even Pat Healey's father lost his job, causing the family to return to New Orleans. Gunny watched the unemployed carrying large traps down Water Street as part of civil works programs to rid buildings of rats. For that they got paid all of $1.50 a day, plus a bounty for each dead rat. They considered themselves lucky. Better jobs might be had by knowing somebody. Being in the Klan, being a Mason, or being in politics helped. Rat catchers, Gunny thought, did not know anybody. For that matter, neither did he. If he could no longer support himself, Gunny figured it was time to leave home. Aunt Nettie and Irish Ma had carried him long enough.

After a year of writing delivery notices for GM&N customers, Gunny could get free railroad passage wherever the trains went. Some GM&N rails led west to Texas, to a crossroad about 30 miles north of Longview called Mt. Pleasant. Roy Cooper, the GM&N bookkeeper's boy, spoke of relatives in Mt. Pleasant. Roy and Gunny decided to ride the rails to Texas in early 1935. For Gunny, the road west might be long and winding depending on his fortune, so 14 year-old brother Joseph took over Gunny's job of writing up and delivering customer shipment notices. Despite his age, Joseph could take care of himself on the street as he did in the ring, boxing under the alias "Gunboat Joe."

Then there was the matter of the 1929 Chevy. Gunny also gave that to Joseph before leaving Alabama. The Chevy's fate took an ominous turn for the worse, though. On the way down Cedar Point Road to pick up older sister Dit at a nightclub, Joseph let 10 year-old sister Nonie steer the car into a tree, removing most of the roof and shaking the gear shift and steering wheel off the column. Otherwise, it still ran fine.

Gunny's journey to Mt. Pleasant lasted longer than the stay. He spent one night with Roy's relatives and woke up the next morning with bedbug welts the size of silver dollars. Saying good-bye to Mt. Pleasant and Roy came easy as Gunny boarded the first train for San Antonio. What he saw as the train wound through dusty San Antonio barrios also cut that visit short. After 1000 miles of rails, Gunny found his resting spot on the island city of Galveston, Don Bernardo's name-sake legacy.

Gunny signed up as a shop helper with Kane Boiler Works on an eight month contract making oil field pipe. He had never made pipe before, but Kane fielded a city league baseball team for the 1935 season. That and 40 cents an hour suited Gunny just fine. Owner and team manager Robert Kane played along side Ken Glowaskie, Earl Colvin from Mobile, shop foreman Shorty Davis, Frank Kilgore, Gunny, Don Maynard, and Shorty Williams. The ball season and pipe contract played out about the same time. Gunny found himself unemployed again. As part of President Roosevelt's public works program, a new Post Office building began to rise in Galveston. Gunny hired on at 40 cents an hour checking material into the construction site. When that job wound down in early 1936, he stayed on in Galveston lubricating cars at 35 cents apiece for Dow Motor Company. Being the last of two persons hired to work the lubrication rack meant he would be the first to go when bad times got worse. That happened in the latter part of 1936, leaving Gunny few options but to try his luck elsewhere. He set out with Orville Stone for Houston, where he managed to find a job at $12 a week as a body shop helper with the Dow Motor Chevrolet dealer at the corner of Milan and Walker. It was good work through the first part of 1937 until automobile shop mechanics in Houston walked out on strike. Crossing their picket line never crossed Gunny's mind. With no other work available, the strike put him on the streets far away from Galvez Park.

Irish Ma and Miss Nettie had not seen Gunny since he left for Texas in 1935. Only a few letters gave away his whereabouts. They figured he would come home when times in Houston got worse than those in Mobile. From what they could gather, a lot of water had since passed under Gunny's bridge. At 23, he took stock of himself and returned to Alabama. When the train rolled to a stop at the Royal Street depot in July, 1937, Gunny stepped into Mobile and walked three blocks to Franklin. He was home again on the south side down the street from Galvez Park.

32. *Kane Boiler Works baseball team, 1935 Commercial League Champions, Galveston Texas: (top, l-r) unidentified, Ken Glowaskie, Earl Colvin, unidentified, owner-manager Robert Kane; (middle, l-r) Shorty Davis, unidentified; (bottom, l-r) Frank Kilgore, Gunny Gonzales, Don Maynard, unidentified, Shorty Williams, Don Maynard's son, Galveston, Texas (Verkin, Galveston), 1935.*

33. *Dow Motors Chevrolet, Gunny Gonzales (1st row), Houston, November 30, 1936 (photographer unknown).*

There is nothing more difficult to take in hand, more perilous to conduct, or more uncertain in its success, than to take the lead in the introduction of a new order of things.

—Niccolo Machiavelli

34. Emanuel Joseph (Gunny) Gonzales, 1939 (photographer unknown).

CHAPTER 17

The Ward Heeler

Jobs with Alabama Dry Dock came and went, playing out as fast as they started. Foremen picked day workers each morning from the swelling ranks of skilled hands, throwing jobs around like Mardi Gras favors. Working one day did not guarantee working the next. Sometimes politics made the difference. Being Catholic or Colored did not help, but being a Mason did. Gunny toyed with the notion of joining a Masonic Lodge to get work. Of course, the Church viewed cultic Masonic rituals with a jaundiced eye, threatening excommunication of Catholics who participated in them. However, the Church did not put any food on Irish Ma's table.

Before he had to cross that bridge, Gunny landed a welding job with Alabama Dry Dock & Shipbuilding Company. For $3.20 a day he stitched barges together with a down hand welding rod the size of a Roman candle. Arcing rods six to eight hours each day bleached the body of its strength. Deep inside the hull, though, welders often did themselves more harm than hard work ever could. When time came to flip up the hood shield and replace a burnt rod, an unexpected flash from the torch of a nearby welder often scorched the unguarded eye. Gunny stumbled home many a night squinting into the dusk. He fought pain and sleepless nights by smearing Vicks Mentholatum on burning eyeballs, trying to smother the sting. Welders swore by the stuff, even though their so-called cure seemed worse than the burn itself. In time,

Gunny put faith in the healing power of raw potato shavings to cool the coals under his eyelids. By the time he grew calloused to flash blindness and potato peels, welding work with ADDSCO died out.

Gunny's layoff wore heavily on Irish Ma, who no longer could handle a full-time job. She had come to depend on the $5 Gunny put in her hand each week when he had work. Her grandson carried the load for them both. The pinch had yet to turn ugly, though, when bad fortune turned better as Aluminum Ore Company broke ground for a new plant. Gunny hired on as a crane oiler at $3.20 a day, then moved up to the blacksmith shop while doubling as a pipe fitting welder. There appeared to be enough work through the middle of 1938.

Meanwhile, a couple of blocks west of Franklin, Ursulene served shrimp and poured dime bottles of real beer in her tavern on the east side of Lawrence Street. Some 15 years earlier, in 1922, Ollie and Alfred Delchamps opened their first grocery on the wedge where Madison and Canal converged and Ursulene's tavern now stood. Once business outgrew its walls, Delchamps moved into a larger store across Lawrence. Ursulene's tavern opened for business in 1936 even though women running bars had not yet caught the drinking man's fancy. It did not take long for business to pick up at Gunny's Tavern, as her place came to be known. Alone at 48, Ursulene tended the till, cooked food, popped beer bottles, nudged pinball machines, fed the music box, and kept the regulars happy. She allowed no gambling, until Gunny and his brother Joseph began exploring such business opportunities. They built out the back and improved the tavern, prompting a rent increase. After a spell, Gunny and Joseph sold baseball and football game cards through runners at the shipyard. Runners took 10% or played the card's point spread on the house. The tavern made money until so many winning cards showed up to collect that it broke the bank and put the would-be bookies out of business. Charlie Joullian bailed out his nephews, who went back to pouring beer and serving shrimp.

After returning to Mobile from Texas, Gunny walked over to the Board of Registrars in the County Court House to register to vote. For most of his life, Gunny had lived within a mile of his birth near Galvez.

The Whippet and Badger hero of Mobile's south side already had made a name for himself in the newspapers, albeit a sometimes controversial one. Gunny was no stranger in Mobile when he confidently strolled in to register. Not one white eye batted when registrars rejected Coloreds and vagrants. The registrars saw to it that democracy not be casually entrusted to just anyone. Gunny carefully completed his application.

"Gunny, we can't accept your application." One of the registrars spoke up.

Gunny did not take that well. "What do you mean?"

"No need to make a fuss, now. But you just can't expect to come in here without a witness to vouch for you." The registrar spoke as though this were common knowledge, the natural order of things in Alabama's universe.

"Why do I need a witness? Who says I have to have a witness?" Gunny was only a lash short of getting riled.

"How do we know what you say is true? Anybody can come in and say god knows what. We can't let that happen. Voting is too important." The registrar neared the limit of his patience.

"Well now, fellas, I suppose Gunny should come back with a voter to vouch for his application, but I've known his family for years." Willie Conrad spoke up, recognizing the folly of standing on ceremony in this instance. "They all live in the south part of town. Gunny could be back in the blink of an eye with any number of folks to vouch for him. There's really no need for that. Why don't I just vouch for him now." By the good grace of Willie Conrad, Gunny became a voter in the State of Alabama. Gunny left quietly, galled that someone had to vouch for him because his word alone was not good enough.

Once registered, Gunny cut his political teeth on the 1937 city election. His Democratic Party ward heeling career began in Ward 6, on the northeast corner of Canal and Warren, when position number three on the City Commission came up for election. Three at-large commissioners had governed Mobile for years from the comfort of staggered terms. Whichever of the three happened to be running for re-election took credit for every windfall accomplishment during the past two years. The incumbent candidate could count on the support of his two brother commissioners, especially if they planned on him scratching their backs during the next election. A remarkable spirit of mutual admiration prevailed at City Hall during these campaigns.

Four candidates, including former Mayor Harry T. Hartwell, had tossed their hats into the race for Place 3. Harry had lost his commissioner seat and now sought to regain it. His political fortune depended much upon the collective wit of his ward heelers, including Gunny and Paul Bonham, whose only purpose was to carry the voting box. Harry had known Gunny's family for years, and counted on Gunny carrying Ward 6 even if Harry lost every other ward in town. A good ward heeler managed to carry the vote, somehow, some way.

If ever a man was loyal, Harry Hartwell was loyal. Harry also meant what he said and spoke plainly. Hartwell had not endeared himself among the silk stocking crowd. He turned to folks in the street and his ward heelers for help. Harry was more dependable than the voting system. For the most part, winning an election depended on who had the ballots last. Stealing an election was no idle expression in 1937. Supply and demand set the value of every vote. With only a few thousand registered voters, the cost of victory depended on the number of live and willing voters. A week's wage of $10 made a big impression in the pocket of folks on the south side. The ward heeler's first job was to get voters to the polls. Gunny made sure of that. The ward heeler's other job was to swing votes, which took a bit more doing.

A ward heeler was a neighbor, not always a politician. On the southeast corner of Charleston and Warren streets, Will Hanlon ran a grocery. Hanlon was not an appointed or elected ward heeler. Hanlon never hung around the polls on election day pressing the flesh for some candidate or other. He was either behind the glass counter at the store or across the street on his front porch. But politicians and three of every five voters in Ward 6, the largest in the city, wanted to know how Hanlon would vote.

During the Depression the people of Ward 6 struggled to make ends meet. Even folks who could not pay still got groceries at Hanlon's.

In the middle of winter, their stoves went cold for lack of coal or creosote blocks. No questions were asked when Hanlon and Jim Martin dumped a quarter ton of coal into the yard. Hanlon answered their prayer without holding their honor hostage. There was no talk of payment. If payment at some time could be made, that was okay. There was no shame in having no money. But shame would run deep for Whites or Coloreds who did not return Hanlon his honor. When they voted with Hanlon, they gave him honor and kept their own. Will was a ward heeler by right.

South side voters relished close elections and the extra attention of ward heelers. Voters expected cash up front. Ward heelers expected votes up front. It was a mating dance that required mutual trust. Soon after the polls opened, the ward heeler obtained his own ballot, marking it for his candidates. Instead of putting it in the ballot box, though, he would slip the ballot into his pocket and walk out of the poll. He now is ready to do business, watching with anticipation as a voter declares himself and picks up a blank ballot. Before the voter marks the blank ballot, the ward heeler approaches, shakes hands, shares a thoughtful word about the family, and walks off. The voter ponders a moment longer, returns to the box, casts the ward heeler's marked ballot, and leaves with the $5 bill taken in trade for the blank ballot. The ward heeler marks the fresh ballot and waits to do business again. Rewarding folks for their civic duty made sense. Should anyone profit from an election, the system seemed to favor the voter over the candidate, who likely would profit once elected.

The 1937 City Commission election was hotly contested, even by a ward heeler's standard. Of 7,500 registered voters, only about 2,000 were expected to appear at polling places. Most of the others resided out of town or in Magnolia Cemetery. At 6 p.m. on election night, Ward 6 closed its polls to count ballots. Supporters of Harry Hartwell were among those charged to certify the tally. The lights blinked off while Ward 6 officials did their duty. Nothing seemed amiss that Harry should carry the ward, or that he already had by the time the lights blinked on again. Electrical problems haunted a number of polls that night, casting a shroud of darkness over ballot boxes throughout the city. Miss Nellie Cammack, one of the sheriff's able poll watchers, found herself holding a box of returns when the light went out. Instinctively, she sat on top of the ballots, prepared to fend off any daring hands that came groping in the dark. Nellie Cammack retained the ballots and her virtue, much to the chagrin of fellows standing nearby as the lights came back on. When the ballots of all the boxes citywide were tallied the next morning, Harry lacked by only 57 the number of votes needed to win outright without a runoff. And that shortcoming could not be blamed on Harry's ward heelers. It seems that many of Magnolia Cemetery's residents had risen to vote against Hartwell, sending an especially disturbing message to the would-be mayor. Though politicians accepted the resurrection as an article of faith, grand juries grew increasingly concerned about Magnolia's deceased casting ballots in the runoff. Harry Hartwell figured that his opponents had hired vagrants, circus types, and other ne'er-do-wells to impersonate the dead, a mite cheaper than rewarding live voters. By carefully limiting the number of living voters, the board of registrars placed a bounty on Mobile's dead voters.

Hartwell reluctantly asked the Mobile County Circuit Court to referee this delicate dispute, fully convinced that some of the courthouse crowd deserved credit for the fine Magnolia turnout. Judge Francis Hare of Birmingham presided over the matter. Flexing its judicial authority, the Court impounded all 36 tin ballot boxes. Ballots cast from this and the next world were placed under 24-hour guard in City Hall itself. Harry's supporters guarded the room where the courthouse custodian guarded the boxes. In the midst of trial, the custodian mysteriously died and the boxes disappeared, ballots and all. Word on the street had it that rats ate the ballot boxes. Rats in City Hall had acquired that sort of reputation over the years. Some supposed the custodian had died of fright, given the nature of that spectacle. Although ballot boxes later surfaced from time to time, the ballots disappeared without a trace. Without evidence of voting irregularities, Harry lost his day in court. Next time, Ward 6 would canvass the dead as well as the living.

CHAPTER 18

Vote Early,
Vote Often

Come July 1938, Gunny left the aluminum plant and weekly $16 take-home pay he pocketed for nearly a year. Only once before had he quit a job cold turkey, walking out of Ibsen's seed store with nothing to show for it. This time he whistled a different tune, pulling down better than twice the pay in his new job as first-class welder on Waterman Steamship's outfitting dock. It was nothing to get uppity about, of course, but few crafts paid more. More importantly, Irish Ma need no longer fret about getting up in age and all. She could stay at home and turn leftovers into bread pudding.

As soon as Gunny landed work with Waterman, he decided to dip into Mobile's political stew again. Only one party machine carried much of any clout in 1938, the Mobile County Democratic Executive Committee. Though Republicans ran for office, they drew more curiosity than votes. Mobile had not yet forgotten the scourge of Republican Reconstruction. Practically speaking, the Democratic Party provided the only political game, players, and chips in town. As an autumn moth seeks the warmth of an evening porch light, Gunny felt drawn into the core of Mobile's body politic. When time came, he announced his intention to leave Ward 6 and run for committeeman of Ward 5 at Conception and Madison. Gunny set out to capture the south side of town.

As it turned out, boss Bob Johnson wanted to keep Ward 5 for himself and, being no stranger to the blue smoke of politics, expected nothing less. Johnson's public and private financial dealings south of Madison had flourished over the years. The south side leader had both name and money. Gunny had neither. Oddly enough, Gunny admired Bob Johnson, but not so much that he could not pull off an upset. Defeating his formidable foe surprised the Old Guard, and did not set too well with Johnson either. Johnson walked down to the foot of Conception Street at Turner Terminal. Dropping his clothes in a pile, Johnson apparently stepped off the dock right into the muddy Mobile River, snuffing out his political career. Despite the ripples left by Johnson's departure, Gunny's political career looked bright.

Ward heeling between elections called for something more than ballot box politicking. Gunny set out to find folks jobs, clothes, and food, whatever Mobile's south side needed, which was just about everything. Ward 5 and its new Democratic Executive Committeeman became alter egos, one depending on the other. Even matters of small importance drew Gunny's attention. For 15 years, old man Joe Rooney had tended Galvez Park, minding the children and keeping the grounds. Getting along in age, Mr. Rooney was losing a constant battle against the push mower, heat, and humidity. Neighbors around Galvez could not abide the shame any longer. It was time Rooney got some help before he dropped dead all at once in right field during baseball practice. Gunny went to see City Commissioner Charlie Baumhauer, the upshot of which resulted in Magnolia Cemetery's keeper trimming the grounds at Galvez. That kept Joe Rooney out of his own plot at Magnolia an extra year or so. Word got around that Ward 5 took care of its own.

Elections remained the grist of a ward boss' political mill. Mastering the ward but fumbling the ballot box lost the game. Close did not count at the polls. Ever so often, though, political free enterprise had a way of strangling the democratic sapling, and needed pruning for its own sake. Striking a blow against disappearing ballot boxes and graveyard constituencies, City Hall acquired fancy voting machines, but old habits did not easily die. Politically correct votes still carried a high premium, voting machine or not. Ward heelers willing to pay the fare had to get past the curtain and inside the booth to see the ballot being cast. Trust had little currency where money came in to play, and newfangled technology could not match the wiliness of seasoned politicians.

Rules allowed no one to accompany a voter behind closed curtains and prevented balloting unless the curtains were securely closed. Of course, not all voters fancied the mechanical beast that replaced the simple ballot box, and some seemed unimpressed by the secrecy of closed curtains. Ever sensitive to signs of confusion and frustration, election inspectors were quick to assist with the machine's operation. Voters interested in doing business with their ward heeler simply summoned an inspector to the curtain for guidance. Never crossing the plane of the parted curtain, the apparently disinterested inspector noted whether the levers favored the inspector's candidates and observed the vote recorded. Precious few words passed between the voter and the ward heeler's inspector. With the ballot safely tallied, the curtains opened and the voter quietly left. Nonchalantly, the inspector tended other matters, clenching a pencil between his teeth. No pencil meant no thank you, and no money. A pencil in the teeth telegraphed politically correct choices and authorized positive reinforcement, usually cash. Machine or not, the ward heeler took care of his own.

CHAPTER 19

Rally Around the Cattle

Mobile next prepared to go to the polls on September 3, 1940. Marching smartly into the new decade, city elders and civic swells came out in favor of the proposed Stock Law referendum, as it was known. Livestock still roamed at will throughout the city, playing havoc with traffic by day and sleeping on warm roadbeds at night. Highbrows found it fashionable to speak of the south side as Goat Town and Gritney. Conventional wisdom felt it was high time to put the cows, pigs, and goats in their place, pastures, or butcher paper. The press hailed the Stock Law as a milestone for civilization in southern Alabama, confident that anyone of common intelligence would agree.

Only fellows who raised livestock seemed to be of a contrary mind, which surprised no one. Farmers and cattlemen, already on the down and out, bristled at the notion of fencing in their heavily mortgaged acreage because of a few stray cows. The threat of landing in Sheriff Willie Holcombe's jail for letting strays wander about caused bile to rise in their gullet. Better to let beasts run wild, they figured, than submit to the know-it-alls downtown. That sort of thinking played well in Saraland and Theodore, but downtown ballots usually outnumbered rural votes two to one. Without some city voters in the bag, cattlemen faced certain defeat before the fight even began. Unless someone within Mobile's political structure openly opposed the Stock Law referendum, farmers and ranchers would take it on the chin.

Saying one thing and doing another is the politician's way of stroking voters and staying in office. Willie Holcombe, good Sheriff that he was, opposed the Stock Law, but had a large city constituency to consider. Getting on the wrong side of the press and other political forces would not bode well come election time. Willie Holcombe had friends, though, not the least of which included Leroy Stevens, Walter Boltin, and cattle king Ben Deakle. Some 10 years earlier, nephew Earl Holcombe and Gunny starred as teammates with the State Champion Whippets. Earl and his father, Sheriff Bob, counted Gunny as a friend, meaning that Gunny was also Willie's friend. By the summer of 1940, Gunny enjoyed a reputation as the can-do committeeman of Ward 5. Willie and his cattlemen friends needed a favor, so they turned to Gunny. If necessary, the south side Spaniard would stand all alone, knee-deep in cow pies, defying the powers at city hall.

In the world of politics, opposing the Stock Law would tighten Gunny's relations with Mobile's sheriffs and county commissioners and boost business for Gunny's Tavern, even if Ward 5 followed the stampede against critters at large. Gunny might have taken the more cautious political path by merely expressing concern that the law would harm hard-pressed farmers. However the vote went, Gunny would have served his constituency's interest and still helped his friends. Even that small gesture would have distinguished Ward 5 from other precincts, for no one else on the Mobile County Democratic Executive Committee openly championed the cattlemen's cause. Gunny, however, went the whole nine yards for his friends.

Ward 5 threw the biggest and only campaign rally for dumb animals in Mobile County. Thanks to Leroy Stevens, piles of steaming boiled shrimp welcomed voters to Gunny's Tavern the night of August 22, 1940. Free beer cheered the crowd inside while free music, a band no less, entertained neighbors in the middle of Lawrence Street. Once the fun started, Gunny rose to the occasion, urging his people to let poor dumb animals live free. Then he yielded the floor to Ben Deakle of the Livestock Owners Progressive Association to say a few words.

Being a man of few words, that's all Deakle could say. The cattle baron thanked all the boys for showing up and wished everyone a good time. Politicking was not Ben Deakle's strong suit.

Two days later, the *Register* vented its wrath on Ward 5's political boss:

> **Cattlemen Hold Antistock Law Rally Down in Gunny's Barroom**
> **Free Shrimp and Beer Offered as Bait to Catch**
> **The "Sucker Vote" in Absence of Logical Arguments**
>
> It was down in "Gunny" Gonzales' barroom. It was there in Mobile's Fifth Ward, Thursday night, that the anti-stock law crowd gave a demonstration of old-fashioned politics.
>
> "Gunny," the little Fifth Ward vote hustler, got up and introduced Ben Deakle, the big cattle owner. Cattle King Deakle upped and thanked the boys for turning out and expressed the hope they were enjoying themselves.
>
> What kind of poor fish do the cattlemen take city-voters to be, seeking to entice them to vote against their best interests with bait of shrimp and beer? Gullible Guppies? Such tactics may convert some of the Royal Street "intellectuals" and bar flies to the cattlemen's cause, but all intelligent voters we feel will resent this insult to their intelligence.

The *Register*'s editorial might have thought better of calling folks down in Ward 5 gullible bar flies. These were voters of uncommon intelligence. They knew which side their bread came buttered. They lived with the kind of animals the law wanted to corral. They liked shrimp, beer, and music. They also trusted Gunny more than the newspaper editor. As most poll watchers predicted, the Stock Law passed by a handsome margin of nearly two to one. Of the city's 11 wards and 25 boxes, 9 wards and 22 boxes voted overwhelmingly to get the beasts off the street. Ward 5, however, voted convincingly to let the critters run wild. Despite the disapproving glare of the press, the leader of Ward 5 had delivered with a plate of old fashioned politics. More importantly, the powers that be recognized that Gunny and his Fifth Ward did not follow the party line. The press' indignation and backlash reflected concern about future challenges that might disturb more important established interests.

CHAPTER 20

War in the Hold

Murphy Justin Carter Hassett and his 17 year-old wife, Frances Lockler, struggled three months to name their firstborn. Murphy wanted a boy. His genetic lottery produced a girl. Murphy took disappointment hard. After emerging from an extended period of denial in November 1910, he finally agreed to "Myrtle." A more androgynous name appropriate for either gender would have better suited his daughter. Despite a remarkably sweet disposition, baby Myrtle quietly despised her name from the moment she first pronounced it. When Murphy Hassett's other child also turned out to be a daughter, he coped with his frustration more reasonably.

Myrtle and younger sister Marion grew up between Selma and Elmira at 610 south Conception near the GM&N rail yard where Murphy worked. Their simple house faced Conception and backed up to the Colored houses on Our Alley. The Hassett girls often traipsed the length of Texas from Conception to Broad, day and night, visiting aunts and uncles halfway across town. They never crossed paths with a Gonzales or Joullian, though. Gunny spent a year at Maryshell School on the corner of Augusta and Franklin while expelled from St. Vincent's. He and Myrtle often walked part of the way to school amid the same herd of neighborhood kids, but had nothing in common. Come 1922 Myrtle moved on to Yerby School behind Barton Academy for the next two years before going across town to attend Murphy High School.

Not long out of Murphy High School and on the eve of Wall Street's 1929 crash, Myrtle Hassett had the fortune to find employment as a secretary with the law firm of Gessner T. McCorvey, a prominent attorney and state Democratic Party leader. The dapper McCorvey fancied bow ties to complement his large oval face and full jowls, cropped hair, high forehead, and narrow thin-lipped mouth. Through the darkest hours of Mobile's economic blight, 19 year-old Myrtle waited on her porch each morning for a lawyer to stop curbside and chauffeur her to work. With upper crust attorneys offering escort service, Myrtle felt no need to drive a car. She also found Gessner fully conscious of his powerful station in Alabama's white society, while equally at home offering colored workers a ride to work. McCorvey's graciousness, though, did not abide any notions of racial equality. He embraced the beatitudes of state's rights and White supremacy. Myrtle accepted Gessner's kindness, worked with Mobile's political elite, and discreetly voted against them on election day. Though increasingly embarrassed over the years by the humbling blight of her south side origins, Myrtle's unpretentious Episcopalian spirit remained largely unaffected from years of supping with the mighty.

Myrtle left the south side in 1930 when Murphy and Frances moved out to 26 Westwood Avenue past the Loop. Charles Joullian met Myrtle not long after Gunny left Mobile in 1935 for Galveston, the same year that a railcar crushed Murphy Hassett to death at work. Only once in their five-year courtship did Charles invite Myrtle home to 407 Franklin, an obligatory introduction to Irish Ma and Miss Nettie. Charles' inherently private nature and chagrin over Irish Ma's modest circumstances channeled his relationship with Myrtle elsewhere. As means allowed, Charles and Myrtle took the backwoods byway down to Mary's Place for fried soft-shell crabs and strolled among pines overlooking Gulf Shores. Charles turned Sunday outings into moments that lightened the growing burden of caring for a mother in failing health and an increasingly unpredictable Miss Nettie. But for those two women in his life, Charles would have considered marriage earlier. As it was, marriage afforded Charles none of the freedom sister Clarice gained back in 1923. He could not abandon the yoke of familial commitment so easily.

Charles finally proposed marriage with vintage Joullian pragmatism. Shorn of romantic frills, Myrtle was offered the option to marry the entire Joullian household, Charles, Irish Ma, and Miss Nettie, or none at all. The bride-to-be felt overcome with mixed emotions. In testament to Charles' character, certainly not his salesmanship, Myrtle Hassett consented. The notion of living with Charles and two old women set in their ways tested the depths of Myrtle's devotion. Actually, Charles failed to mention that Myrtle might be joining a family of four. During their long engagement, Charles built a home in a farm patch next door to Myrtle's parents at 24 Westwood Avenue. Gunny moved in with Uncle Charlie in 1939 when the new house was finished. Charlie Joullian darkly joked that this penitential marriage would atone for all their earthly vices.

Declining the traditional fanfare of center aisle Episcopalian nuptials, Charles and Myrtle met privately with Father John McGonegle to exchange vows on January 20, 1940 in the parlor of St. Vincent's rectory. Holy Mother Church would not allow Myrtle, though a baptized Episcopalian, to wed Charles at the Catholic altar, an unfortunate legacy of Sixteenth Century Counter-reformation. Soft-spoken Myrtle Hassett graciously endured the slight. As the bride and her subdued wedding party gathered in the parlor, Father McGonegle fumbled nervously through the rites. Chagrined, the priest apologized for his ineptitude. "I'm sorry folks, but I've actually never done this before."

Charles' wit relished the irony. "That's okay, we've never done this before either!" Myrtle declined to become Catholic for many years and, when she did, Gunny stood godparent.

The newlyweds planned to escape the south side, but for Irish Ma and Miss Nettie the south side would always be home. Already in poor health, Leona Joullian's world on Franklin finally came to a halt. She and Nettie Pocase packed up their memories and bid good-bye to Mrs. Hamilton, Mrs. Brabner and friends who weathered the years with them. Irish Ma's family became Charles Joullian's family. The child became the parent, and the parent the child. Two months later Irish Ma gave up the ghost at age 69 on March 27, 1940. Miss Nettie watched her best friend descend into the darkness below Magnolia Cemetery to live among the dead. Nettie now had a room all to herself, more than she needed. She bloomed amid all the attention and began to speak her mind with graphic clarity, as though she had grown weary of Southern gentility.

Germany's invasion of France four months later sent urgent ripples of activity through Mobile's shipyards. Gunny left Waterman Steamship for the Alabama Dry Dock shipyards across the Mobile River when an order of 37 steel barges came in. Though the country was not yet at war, thoughts of war infected everyone. John Davis and some of the Galvez crowd joined the Army, hoping to be assigned the same unit. When Gunny got wind of that he went to Ward Faulk, a banker who happened to recruit for Davis' unit, to join up with John and the gang. Ward had bad news. John Davis' unit was filled. Worse, Gunny was a first-class welder in a Gulf Coast shipyard far from U-boat threats. The country and its European friends needed a fleet of boats that shipyards in Mobile, Pascagoula and Galveston began stitching together. Uncle Sam figured on keeping welders where they could do the most damage to the Nazis. Gunny would do battle down in the hold, torching steel in the dark.

Joseph N. Langan served in the Alabama National Guard, an officer with the 31st Division at Fort Whiting. Until his unit was called up to active duty with the Army in 1940, Langan spent much of his time in Montgomery as one of Mobile's state representatives. Not long after John Davis and the maintenance guys had enlisted, Joe Langan bumped into Gunny at the courthouse. He sold Gunny on the idea of coming out to Fort Whiting and drilling with Joe's unit. Getting paid all of $5 a month just for showing up at a couple of meetings sweetened the deal. Gunny figured joining the National Guard might get him into John Davis' unit, so he decided to enlist.

Gunny barely got inside the National Guard hall when the zoo-like clamor of weapons, boots, and commands snatched away his breath. "Hey Gunny, welcome aboard." The quartermaster warmed up to every recruit, at least for the first meeting. "Here're your boots, uniforms, and rifle. About the time you get changed, we'll be ready to drill." Gunny began having second thoughts. The rifle seemed all of 14 feet long without a bayonet. "By next meeting," the First Sergeant confided, "you'll know how to take this weapon apart and put it back together again, blindfolded."

The Galvez ward heeler stared in disbelief. Welding in a dark hold was one thing, welding blind another, but this took the cake. "You must be crazy. I couldn't do that even if I was starin' right at it!" The First Shirt grinned and let Gunny sort things out. The Guard's newest recruit laced stiff leather boots half way to his waist, and suited up as if this were a Badger football scrimmage.

"All right men, fall in!" The First Sergeant barked loud enough to wake the dead. Then came cadence commands, which might as well have been Greek as far as Gunny was concerned. "Ahh-tennnn-hutt" drew sharp responses from all but two of the boots in the outfit. Even had Gunny understood the command, he did not know what it meant. Nobody on the Gonzales side of the family had soldiered in recent memory. He checked out the fellows nearby, searching for a role model.

"Fahh-wahd, harch" started almost everyone out on the same step, which should have been the left foot. Gunny studied the other boots, trying to stay in step and keep cadence at the same time. "Hutt, hutt, hutt, two-tree-foah, hutt, hutt, hutt," the First Sergeant bellowed monotonously to the troops. Gunny strained to understand the words. "To the reee-aaaah, shift!" In a smooth fluid motion, the platoon reversed, pivoting on the left foot and smartly arcing its shouldered rifles about face. It was Gunny's maiden experience with a full cadence reverse shift. The barrel near his nose disappeared as fast as the rifle's butt appeared, causing Gunny to hesitate just long enough for the barrel behind him to smash sharply against the right side of his head. Gunny's marching element remained out of step the rest of the drill.

By the end of the drill meeting, Gunny decided to cut his losses. "Now fellows, you'll probably say I'm gonna do just fine and all, but I've got a feeling I don't belong here. You can have these boots, this uniform, the backpack, everything, the bazooka too. It's all yours. And keep your $5. Can't say I really earned it. Sorry, but this just ain't for me." With that, Gunny discharged himself from the Alabama National Guard and returned to shipyard duty.

Though most of the world seemed headed straight to hell in warmongering handbaskets, good times began to roll on the south side. Claude Betbeze's Plaza dance club off Cedar Point Road drew John George and Gunny's shipyard buddies down the bay. John George had arranged a dinner at the Plaza with Anne Bosarge and her girlfriend. He asked Gunny to join them. Anne worked at City Hospital and lived in the nursing school dorm near Broad and St. Anthony while studying at Spring Hill College. Under the firm hand of the Sisters of Mercy, Anne worked Colored pediatrics and obstetrics, training to be a registered nurse. Her home lay south of Mobile amid the bayous from Carl's Creek to Mississippi Sound. John George introduced Anne Bosarge to Gunny. Several dates later, Gunny and Anne started going together. Anne and Gunny married in Gulfport, Mississippi on July 14, 1941. When they returned to Mobile, Anne resumed nursing school at City Hospital.

Necessities of war changed life in the Heart of Dixie. Gunny found himself supervising 45 welders on the outfitting dock, working overtime seven days a week, and taking home more pay each week than he had ever seen in a month. Alabama Dry Dock & Shipbuilding Company hired every male and female Tom, Dick, and Harry that could follow instructions. Below the surface of this employment boom brewed tensions poised to explode. Gunny had his own way of keeping tensions under control, often working past the shift through dinner when crews on board broke into floating craps games. Steady overtime pay sweetened otherwise small wagers into lucrative pots. Once a crowd of twenty or so huddled to bet on the point, a week's salary could be at stake. Craps lacked the studied pace and crafty illusions that made poker a more elegant way to lose money. There were no restraints against sky-is-the-limit side wagers. Guys would bet their eyeballs and anyone else's if they could. Better yet, odds in craps stayed pretty much the same no matter how badly the dice rolled. Calculating the likelihood of drawing an inside straight, a flush, or a full house did not trouble the feverish minds hovering over craps games. Everyone understood numbers, and everything was right out there in the open. No aces and surprises lay concealed in the hole.

The only way to improve odds in craps is to shave the dice. Marked dice tended to show patterns, especially when weighted for a roll of 7, 11, or particular point combination. Playing trick dice with a crowd of two dozen ship builders also presented notable physical hazards should the ruse fail. Still, Gunny sent off for a set of three marked dice. Two players had to work the dice during a game, multiplying the number of known point combinations so as to camouflage obvious patterns. Once Gunny rolled and got a spot, his man in the crowd picked up the dice, substituting the third die for the next roll. Over the course of a fifteen minute run, nobody caught on, except once. A dock laborer happened to glimpse a third die in Gunny's hand as a game folded. With no bets on the line, none of laborer's money actually traded hands. But three dice in the roller's hand raised a question or two. As the losers milled about, the sharp-eyed dock laborer walked up to Gunny and discreetly introduced himself. No one wanted to kill the golden goose, and no one did. Gambling did not disturb Mobile's war effort on either side of the river.

Vince Noletto, Jr. and the south part of town banked heavily on the war boom to pay bills at the end of the month. Noletto wore his Alabama National Guard uniform on weekends, and during the week built Liberty ships. After the Great Fire, Vince senior operated a shoe shop at the northwest corner of Charleston and Our Alley near Irish Ma's house. The Noletto's and Joullian's were about as tight as peas in a pod. Vince senior lost his business to the Depression. Vince junior survived to weld boats and carry weapons.

The majority of ADDSCO dockworkers came from areas around Mobile and Pascagoula. Until May, 1943 Whites occupied all the better paying welding, shipfitting, and skilled dry dock positions. The War Manpower Commission provided a welding school for Coloreds near Mobile's water front, provoking opposition from white laborers who wanted to climb out of the cellar of poverty and who also took offense at the notion of commingling the races and sexes in close working quarters. Once ADDSCO began building federally funded Liberty ships and transport vessels, the federal Fair Employment Practices Commission acquired an interest in who built those ships. Shortly before midnight on May 25 a dozen colored welders trying to clock in at the Pinto Island dry docks were run off by white dockworkers clocking out.

The dock provided separate but equal restrooms, water fountains, break areas, and pay windows for Whites and Coloreds. However, both sexes were thrown together onto outfitting docks and into welding holds without the guiding hand of cultural convention. White women filled the labor vacuum left by boot camping white men. Under protective glass and steel hoods, welding recognized no distinction based on gender. When the hoods came off, though, white women would not suffer unwelcome familiarities from Coloreds. White men, of course, took an even dimmer view of Coloreds who crossed social boundaries with white girls. Some things the war had not changed.

Gunny supervised welders on the day shift. Over the next few days colored welders clocked in for day shift work. At 3:30 p.m., the shipyard whistle called in the day shift. One time clock serviced the outfitting dock, around which a large crowd of Coloreds, Whites, and women gathered. A thinner stream of clocked-out workers led to the barge waiting to ferry the day shift across the river. In the midst of the crowd clocking out, a small melee erupted over what appeared to be undue familiarity between one of the colored dockworkers and a white woman. The slightest racial impropriety under the circumstances was enough to trigger a brawl. One shipyard official, a big white fellow who played football at Tuscaloosa, boldly stepped into the middle of things to put a lid on the pot before it boiled out of control. He miscalculated, though, by speaking up for the Colored. A more narrow-minded fellow from Mississippi took exception to anyone defending a Colored at the expense of a white woman. He voiced graphic objections and promptly hoisted a two-by-four shoulder level, delivering a lightning swift blow against the head of the former Alabama lineman. When the Tide went down, all hell broke loose. Sensing the climate may have turned ripe for a lynching, some colored dockworkers skipped the barge and hit the river running. By morning, Vince Noletto and the National Guard patrolled the shipyard, ready to do some head-cracking of their own. Any more brawling would be with soldiers armed for combat. The good old boys, Coloreds, and white girls picked up their torches, put on welding hoods, and returned to front line duty down in the hold.

The National Guard found it easier to keep rednecks out of fights than take the fight out of rednecks. Saturday was payday across the river. Crews gathered on the southwest corner of Canal and Royal at Middie's Tavern before riding the barge over to the shipyard. During the week, Middie's put on lunch for the dayshift. Saturday crowds gathered to drink and then get paid, in that order. Gunny met at Middie's with other welders before crossing the river for paychecks. Gunny wore a dark sweater of long mohair to ward off the damp chill. Woody Woods manned the paymaster trailer each Saturday. Any nonsense near the paymaster could result in prompt and permanent loss of work. As Gunny neared the pay window, a co-worker by the name of Moseley made fun of Gunny's mohair sweater. About the size of a fat telephone pole, Moseley had just come from Middie's and one too many rounds of beer.

"Hey fella, I'd like to sign you up to fight Joe Louis. What do you say? You and that monkey ought to feel right at home in the ring hugging together." Moseley taunted Gunny in front of everyone, suggesting he looked like a Colored.

Gunny bristled at the public insult, but did nothing at first, fearful that a brawl was a sure ticket to losing his paycheck and job. Being compared to Joe Louis, though, did not offend *Young Joe Pagaline*. Gunny admired Joe Louis as a great boxer. Moseley blundered by making fun of Gunny's taste in sweaters. The former street fighter leaned over to the paymaster's window: "Now Woody, if he says that again, I'm gonna hit him." Woody looked up from the trailer window, stared briefly at Moseley, and went back to the pay roster, convinced that the little Spaniard would not dare lay a finger on anyone twice his size. Moseley grinned to the crowd.

"Hey little fella, I really do think you're just right to get in the ring with that other monkey. You two would be a perfect match." Moseley had bellowed for the last time. Before Woody could look up again, Gunny hammered Moseley with a solid right cross, dropping the bigger fellow unconscious into a stack of rusty steel drums. The fight started and ended with one punch.

Moseley did not get up. Gunny turned to Woody. "Now how about giving me my check. I'm gonna get out of here before they fire me."

Woody studied Moseley's bleeding scalp. "Hell, you ain't gonna get fired. Hit him again if you have to." Moseley did not stir.

Gunny looked around into the faces of a hundred witnesses. "All these people saw what happened. I'm going before I get fired." Gunny left, still convinced he would be fired for fighting on the dock. Instead, he got promoted. Following the riots, superintendent Willard Peer left the shipyards for Brunswick, Georgia. The new superintendent from Texas stood tall under a ten gallon hat, and went by the name of Tex, of course. Tex wanted Gunny to oversee all Liberty ship hull construction in the upper yard. From there, hulls floated down river to Pinto Island for outfitting. Gunny only had to say yes and the whole night shift in the upper yard was his. But Gunny's regular white welding crew balked. Lots of Coloreds worked the upper yard night shift in segregated crews, too many for comfort so soon after the outfitting dock riots. Few white welders on Gunny's day crew took a shine to working at night upriver with colored crews. They figured that if Gunny wanted to be chief inspector of the upper yard, he and the Coloreds could have the place. Gunny thought it over, said no thanks, got on the barge, and left the dry docks.

Gunny found himself out of work during wartime. Uncle Sam would give him a job in the infantry real quick if nothing else came along. So he met with Police Chief Dudley McFayden about getting on the force. At that point in the war, the police force lacked recruits because young men went straight from high school into military service. Chief McFayden told Gunny the job started at $150 a month, less than half what a first class welding inspector earned. Gunny joined the force, took up fingerprinting, and began patrolling the streets of Mobile. Just 15 years earlier, the Galvez boys kept an eye open for Officer Dumas and the scout car. Now one of their own, the ward heeler himself, patrolled the south part of town. After a year of wearing a uniform on the force, Ingalls Shipyard asked Gunny to inspect hull welds in Pascagoula. The pay was too good to turn down, even though it meant losing touch with ward politics. Gunny, Anne, and baby Joseph Anthony packed up, sold the house on Ryders Lane, and moved to Pascagoula. Building ships for the government gradually phased out after about a year, leaving Gunny with nothing but a layoff notice to show for it. Before leaving Ingalls, the U. S. Maritime Commission hired Gunny as a Liberty ship hull inspector on the Chickasaw Bogue waterway north of Mobile. Anne and Gunny found a small guest apartment on Palmetto Street near Roper about four blocks west of Washington Park.

The hassles of driving every day up to Chickasaw paled in comparison to those awaiting his next Liberty ship inspection assignment at the Waterman docks in Mobile. Gunny knew Liberty ship welds inside and out, including tough spots only a first class welder could handle. He typically snooped around the refrigeration section for spots that the average welder could weld on the inside but not on the backside. In order to seal the weld on both sides, Gunny called on a good welder to link three rods together and reach into the outside crevice missed during construction. Because an outside weld burns the inside surface, the crust first has to be chipped clean for the inside weld to take. Gunny reported the bad welds, setting off an embarrassing flurry of name-calling. None of this set too well with the maritime boss who wanted Gunny off the dock for good. But the outfitting job panned out anyway. As hostilities in Europe and the Pacific came to an end in 1945, the demand for shipbuilding collapsed, ending Gunny's hull inspection career. His war in the hold was over.

35. Myrtle Hassett and Marion Hassett in their fenced backyard next to Colored dwellings along Our Alley between Conception and Franklin streets, 610 Conception Street, Mobile, c. 1919 (photographer unknown).

36. *Leona Pond Joullian (Irish Ma), Our Alley and Nettie G. Pocase's charcoal grill in the backyard at 407 S. Franklin, Mobile, 1938 (photographer unknown).*

CHAPTER 21

Boswell's Genie

In the wake of a collapsed Confederacy, Reconstruction Congresses extended constitutional rights to people of color, forbidding any state to deny the right to vote on account of race. In 1901, Alabama amended its Constitution to allow Whites and Coloreds alike to register to vote if they were gainfully employed and could read and write any part of the United States Constitution. By the close of World War II, Alabama's 44 year-old Constitution had outlived an era when many Whites and most Coloreds neither read nor voted. Post-war Coloreds in Mobile County could read and write. Just as many also had jobs of one sort or another. Nearly everyone qualified to vote. Alabama's state Democratic Party leadership recognized the troubling implications of this problem. The indiscriminate registration of Coloreds and uneducated Whites threatened Alabama's social and political order.

Mobile's Gessner T. McCorvey and State Representative E. C. "Bud" Boswell of Geneva rose to the occasion, guiding Alabama's 1946 legislature to amend the 1901 Constitution with deceptively attractive voter registration requirements. If ratified by the public, the amendment referendum would require a voting applicant to "understand and explain any article of the Constitution of the United States," ensuring that only "those who are of good character and who understand the duties and obligations of good citizenship under a republican form of government" would vote. Christened in honor of Geneva's esteemed legislator, the Boswell Amendment made no distinction based on race.

It emphasized that the vote should be entrusted only to responsible citizens. However, the Boswell Amendment fully intended to secure the means to preserve the supremacy of Alabama's White heritage.

Ratifying the Boswell Amendment in 1946 assumed a level of crucial importance to Alabama's future. Reflecting a collective sense of urgency within the Party, Chairman Gessner T. McCorvey grimly warned members of his State Democratic Executive Committee:

> We are going to see our poll lists flooded with thousands of voters who have not yet fitted themselves to participate in our government. There are any number of counties in Alabama's Black Belt where, unless we do something to tighten up our registration laws, we will very likely, in a few years, have only Colored county officials, as in many of these Black Belt counties, the Negroes outnumber the white people from five to one to ten to one.

The Party's chairman put it all in sharp perspective, sharing his vision so that others might see. Together, McCorvey and Boswell intended that White Supremacy become and remain a reality during and beyond their lifetime. It mattered little what the state Republican Party thought about this, not that Alabama Republicans differed, but the political offspring of carpetbagging Reconstructionists still received short shrift in the Heart of Dixie. Members of the state Republican Party left the strong impression that national party patronage opportunities influenced their politics more than concerns about civil rights.

By August, 1946, McCorvey had polled all 72 members of the state Democratic Executive Committee, persuading an overwhelming majority to use Party funds to support the Amendment. Only 7 state committeemen objected, not only to using Party funds but also to supporting the Amendment itself. Of those mavericks, James Faulkner of Bay Minette, John Caddell of Decatur, and Dewitt Carmichael of Anniston took the somewhat more risky step of publicly denouncing McCorvey's scheme as a ruse to convert suffrage rights into a Party issue. Chairman Gessner did not blink. He proudly noted that the Party should be involved because its *White Supremacy* motto appeared on the ballot. McCorvey saw no reason to shrink from the broader issue confronting Alabama: "It is generally accepted that adoption of the amendment would make it far more difficult for Colored persons to vote." He and Boswell had drawn an unambiguous political Rubicon, a White Supremacy lightning rod, a constitutional litmus test to prevent Coloreds and nearly as many Whites from voting. Those opposed to the Boswell Amendment risked appearing in favor of Coloreds taking over city hall, running White schools, policing White neighborhoods, and taking White jobs. McCorvey and Gessner conjured up shades of neo-Reconstruction, exploiting a volatile wedge issue that presented a political kiss of death for more politically moderate Whites throughout the state. In some counties, Coloreds substantially outnumbered Whites. A good number of the Party's 72 white state committeemen owed their office to minority white constituencies and planned to preserve that tradition.

McCorvey put the state Party on record in favor of the Boswell Amendment, placing the loyalty of Democratic candidates under scrutiny. Few dared to dissent publicly, but James "Big Jim" Folsom, a gubernatorial long shot, did not cotton to the idea of keeping folks of any race from voting. Whatever his shortcomings, that was not among them. Against conventional wisdom, Big Jim publicly denounced the Boswell Amendment and, by implication, McCorvey, Boswell, the State Democratic Executive Committee, and the Alabama State Legislature. No one ever accused the folksy Folsom of being timid. Folsom's attack against Party leaders provided good reason for Mobile's Party establishment to put its money on Lt. Governor Handy Ellis to win the Democratic primary. Whoever won the Democratic primary won the general election as well. It was not good form that Folsom from upstate crossroad Cullman would backhand a prominent good old boy from Mobile like Gessner. Folsom would have a hard row to hoe if he hoped to carry Mobile County, much less the state.

CHAPTER 22

Big Jim
& Little Joe

Stretching south from the L&N tracks at Oakdale to the old Lartigue Cemetery off Cedar Point Road, Brookley Field symbolized the force that crushed tyranny abroad and overcame economic depression at home. In the wake of VJ Day, veterans returned from foreign fronts with unbridled expectations, seeking the fruits of victory, a piece of the pie. A whole generation of Mobile's sons had been plucked from antebellum roots and thrust into the upper branches of the Twentieth Century. However, their descent after a warm homecoming proved bumpy. Not all the winds of change unleashed by war found favor at home. In the corridors of power along Government Street, Mobile's political home guard also saw the influx of Coloreds, veterans and common laborers as a challenge to the traditional order. Within the Party's political food chain, some feared that indiscriminate registration would allow unqualified masses to vote, diluting the value of each ballot, undermining the influence of traditional economic and political powers, and rendering the outcome of elections unmanageable. More ominously, Party elders also saw the specter of a Colored genie about to escape the confines of its White bottle.

President Roosevelt's war boom sprouted housing clusters from Hartwell Field to Brookley Field. In the shadow of Brookley Field's north viaduct along Michigan Avenue spread Birdville's whimsical array of loops, circles, and open fields. Around egg-shaped Cardinal flocked neighborhood circles on Albatross, Bobolink, Oriole, Pelican, Jay, and Warbler. Birdville boasted single, duplex, and two-story triplex frame units with middle-class yards and sidewalks, a nesting ground for Mobile's south side emigrates. Gunny went to see public housing board members Bill Roberts and Frank Boykin. They had the last say about who could live in Birdville, and Gunny wanted in. In 1946 Gunny, Anne, and Joseph Anthony set up house in a two-bedroom at 1508 Bobolink Drive. Despite the move, Gunny still kept a change of clothes in Ursulene's closet at 156 south Hamilton Street. Home for the ward committeeman was where his clothes hung, and Gunny's hung in his ward.

Come January 1946, Alabama's Democratic gubernatorial candidates announced their campaigns. The weight of opinion within Mobile's political house strongly favored Lt. Governor Handy Ellis to lead the primary. Dark horses like Big Jim Folsom were treated with indifference. Big Jim's career highlights included graduating from Elba High School in 1927, a year at Birmingham's Howard College and another in Tuscaloosa at the University of Alabama, a public speaking class at George Washington University, becoming Marshall County administrator, losing a debut political race in 1936 against State Representative Henry Steagall, and then losing a 1942 bid for governor to Chauncey Sparks. Party elders did not consider two-time loser Folsom much to write home about.

Folsom's best hope was that Chauncey Sparks could not succeed himself in 1946. Despite Big Jim's underwhelming track record, he appealed to Gunny as the common man's friend. The colorful populist differed from other political figures in notable ways, singing his own tune on the campaign trail. Although Democrats all ran under the Party's White Supremacy banner, Jim Folsom never mounted the pulpit to preach the politics of race. In private he spoke of sailing oceans with men of color, eating, working, and sleeping together as equals. That kind of talk went down hard in 1946 Alabama.

Big Jim had good reason to write off Mobile. Given the swell of support for Handy Ellis, especially from local Party leader McCorvey, Gunny might have sat out the governor's race instead of bucking headwinds. Despite conventional wisdom and long odds, Gunny and a splinter group of Mobile County Democratic Party committeemen cast their lots against Handy Ellis and the powers that be. They placed themselves in political peril should Folsom lose, and constant criticism should he win. In the winter of 1946, they met Folsom at the Jung Hotel in Montgomery to plot strategy through the primary.

Jim Folsom delivered his folksy message from a flat-bed truck at farmers markets, county fairs, and town squares. As the *Strawberry Pickers* picked guitar and plucked banjo, Big Jim preached his political gospel to the tune of "Ya'll Come." Crossroad towns felt flattered when a grinning Folsom came to their neck of the woods asking for votes. Swinging a broom in one hand and a bucket in the other, Folsom asked common people to help him clean house in Montgomery. Big Jim expected little from the good old boys, but figured he would net more votes by showing folks a good time, shaking hands, kissing ladies, and singing a little off key. Cultivating grassroots could make the difference. Big Jim needed to carry wards and precincts, one at a time. Gunny knew how to do just that.

Joseph N. Langan always pictured himself in public office, indulging in politics as opportunities rose. After high school, he apprenticed in law, gaining admission to the bar in 1936 without attending the University of Alabama or any college for that matter. The self-tutored attorney pursued a modest practice and part-time career in the National Guard, a prudent hedge against an electorate's whimsical moods. Langan's earliest venture into the murky waters of Mobile's political cistern propelled him into the state House of Representatives in 1939. Once there, he tried to distance himself from Alabama's more infamous political traditions. Prior to the advent of voting machines, numbered paper ballots provided a clearly marked trail for incumbents to reward loyalty with jobs and punish opposition with pink slips. Getting city jobs meant picking the right candidate to win, and those already in office enjoyed better than even odds. Reducing the spoils of office also reduced the winner's obligation to reward allies, all of which served Langan's preference to accept support but hover above the fray of patronage. As state representative, Langan sponsored bills to place most city jobs under civil service, arguing such reform should improve the quality of Mobile's municipal workforce. If civil service also weakened the incumbent's political base, so much the better.

Langan would have failed the art of ward heeling, which often determined the outcome of precinct voting. Because the system carefully controlled the number of voters, 400 ballots could swing an election. Acquiring votes was the stock in trade of ward heeling, and the market price per vote merely reflected the consequences of a closed political system. What loose change trickled down into the open palms of Mobile's south side on election day was only a table crumb to politicians who feasted on power. For elders within the established order to cry foul about vote buying was no less than the pot calling the kettle black. Still, reports of money changing hands among registered voters blemished the system's integrity, mocking the notion that carefully screened voters ensured a more responsible democracy.

Langan supported replacing venerable ballot boxes with mechanical voting machines. Aside from Hartwell's notorious 1937 mayoral primary, Langan lamented voters sitting on the fence at Russell School until money persuaded them to cast their ballots. Voting machines promised to remedy ballot marking and petty payoffs without disturbing the underlying scheme of controlled registration. Even so, no sooner did voting machines appear than voters reported loss of eyesight, requiring help behind the curtain from attentive polling inspectors. When that trend passed, illnesses of epidemic proportions seemed to strike statewide on election day, triggering thousands of absentee ballots. Election reforms met with mixed if not begrudging reaction among the Party's grassroots. Corrective legislation eventually cured widespread absentee voting, once again stifling garden variety attempts to exploit a politically closed system.

Representative Langan's National Guard unit, called up in 1940, was but two weeks shy of completing its tour when Admiral Yamamoto attacked Pearl Harbor, interrupting Langan's budding legislative career. He planned to be a U. S. congressman or senator someday, but first he had to test state political waters upon returning from the Pacific in 1945.

As expected, Mobile State Senator Vince Kilborn announced for re-election in 1946, confident of support from financially powerful groups. Langan could count on help only from veterans groups, being commander of the local VFW post and all, but doubted he could oust Kilborn, a formidable figure. Losing to Kilborn would sideline Langan politically and could weaken his appeal in the next election. Without money, organization, and publicity, Langan expected certain defeat.

Equally troublesome, Jim Folsom had just lambasted the proposed Boswell Amendment referendum, carving a sharp political Rubicon into the state party's White Supremacy turf. Folsom did not have a racist bone in his body and had the courage to say so. Few politicians could match the likeable populist's daring for fear of suffering a humbling rout at the polls. But Big Jim, a flamboyant campaigner, offered a new face in Alabama politics, a different approach. His charisma overshadowed even the roots of institutional segregation. People believed that the big lanky fellow, swinging a suds bucket and mop off flatbed trucks, actually could clean up the state capital.

Though Langan personally admired Folsom's style, chances of pushing Big Jim's agenda through a rural pro-Boswell legislature ranged from little to none. Worse, Folsom's thunderous attack against the Boswell Amendment threatened party unity, imperiling the political careers of Langan and others who publicly aligned with Folsom. Langan chose to tread lightly at a safe distance. State Democratic Party Chairman Gessner McCorvey campaigned aggressively for the Boswell Amendment and against Folsom. For Langan to challenge Kilborn would be tough enough without also taking on McCorvey and the Mobile Democratic Party.

Despite the odds, Gunny urged Langan to take on Kilborn, pledging support in currency that mattered most. Gunny's minority faction on the Executive Committee would deliver votes, precincts, and wards. If dumb animals could carry Gunny's south side, so could Langan. Veterans had reason to support Langan, and others had reason to oppose Kilborn. In any given election, a third of the ballots reflected frustration and anger. Langan's lengthy Pacific tour kept him out of

Mobile's political stew for nearly six years, leaving the public little reason for resentment. If Langan ever wanted to capitalize on his circumstances, 1946 provided the most favorable opportunity. Langan threw his hat into the ring and challenged State Senator Kilborn.

Gunny, Tunker Tew, Ralph Lock, Bill Collin, and Mike Marsell hit the campaign trail. Gunny's redrawn Fourth Ward focused on Folsom, Langan, and the Boswell Amendment. Bill Collin and Mike Marsell marketed the election with one slogan: *BIG JIM for Governor, LITTLE JOE for Senator.* One handshake at a time, thousands of *BIG JIM LITTLE JOE* cards saturated wards throughout Mobile County. Marsella Cowan, one of Langan's confidants, supported Handy Ellis. Gunny's campaign strategy made it look as though Folsom and Langan were running on the same ticket, one boosting the other. This drew the ire of Ellis forces, and the risk of a pro-Boswell backlash. Langan called Gunny, Tunker Tew, and Marsella in for a powwow, anxious that Gunny's campaign for Folsom and against the Boswell Amendment might harm Langan's bid for senator.

Gunny took exception. "Let's get this straight, Joe. We are for you, but if you don't want us to be for you we won't. We also are for Jim Folsom whether or not we are for you. If you want, we'll take your name off the damn card." Langan appeared to want it both ways, but could not afford to send Gunny and Tunker packing, at least not before the election. His race was too tight to call without Gunny's Fourth Ward. *LITTLE JOE* stayed on the card and rode the coattails of *BIG JIM.*

CHAPTER 23

Mobile's Most Controversial Figure

Not all the good old boys on the Mobile County Democratic Executive Committee saw eye to eye with Gessner McCorvey and the courthouse crowd. The Fourth Ward, a spin-off from the 1945 redrafting of Ward 5, saw things a whole lot differently. Come November 5, 1946, the polls of Ward 4 at Palmetto and Conception hummed with ward heeling efficiency. Inspector Marvin Thompson, chief clerk M. H. Sellers, first assistant clerk James W. Fowler, and second assistant clerk Joseph V. Gonzales manned Box 1. McCorvey did not find any of these names on his list of trusted poll watchers. Box 2 had a similar troubling ring to it: inspector Emanuel J. Gonzales, chief clerk Joe Calametti, first assistant clerk E. F. Frederickson, and second assistant clerk Claude E. Lomers. Gunny vouched for all of them, which especially bothered McCorvey. Except for the nearly blind Calametti, none of Gunny's officials had been designated by the Democratic Executive Committee's election appointing board. As circumstances would have it, Gunny's troops happened to step in when polling officials designated by the appointing board mysteriously failed to show up.

McCorvey's poll watchers did not like what they saw as Fourth Ward voters came and went, eventually drawing an angry demand by McCorvey that the sheriff be dispatched to the scene immediately. Sheriff Willie Holcombe, a man who took elections very seriously, instructed two utterly trustworthy deputies to observe but not interfere with what all was going on down in Gunny's ward. From 3:10 p.m. until the polls closed at 6 p.m., deputies Medric Eubanks and Charles Ebert observed 31 machine ballots cast, in addition to the 203 cast earlier in the day. Nothing seemed particularly odd to the sheriff's deputies, at least not by Ward 4 standards.

The official tally carried on for 3 days until Friday, November 8. Boswell's Amendment passed state wide, becoming the law of Alabama. State Democratic Party Chairman McCorvey had reason to be pleased. Instead, he was fit to be tied. Mobile County, his own stomping grounds, had repudiated the Boswell Amendment despite McCorvey's financial and political clout. Most of the city's 19 wards split closely over the Amendment's controversial plan to restrict voter registration, the results at 7 polls being decided by 10 votes or less. Conspicuously lopsided by comparison, Ward 4 bashed the Boswell Amendment more than 10 to 1. McCorvey's party machine refused to write that off to an exceptional demonstration of racial tolerance. They wanted to see heads roll, one by one, starting with Gunny's. Nothing less than a grand jury probe would satisfy their protests of voting fraud.

In January 1947, the Mobile County grand jury ordered Sheriff Willie Holcombe to find out what happened down in Ward 4. When it came to investigating, Willie Holcombe stood in no one's shadow. His people tracked down nearly half the names who voted on November 5 in Ward 4. As word leaked out about the investigation, the *Press Register* sought out the Fourth Ward's political leader. Gunny prudently declined comment during Sheriff Holcombe's ongoing investigation, noting that two experienced deputy sheriffs personally stood guard during balloting in Ward 4. They, not he, should be questioned. Willie Holcombe was flattered.

Twenty-eight of those voters interviewed either lived elsewhere or denied ever having voted in Ward 4, fueling suspicion that impostors had assumed the identities of qualified voters. Four of those who voted were dead and unavailable for interview. Relatives insisted their deceased kin missed the election. Modern voting machines were supposed to have eliminated the sort of graveyard opposition that bedeviled Harry Hartwell ten years ago. Not so, the sheriff discovered.

On Friday, April 11, 1947 the grand jury issued its report, indicting no one. However, the grand jury found it curious that there were, in one instance, 12 consecutive ballots cast in names beginning with the same letter of the alphabet, in another 13, and in still another 16. Whatever the probability of such coincidences, statistics did not explain how dead folks kept voting. In a round about way, attention began to focus on the Mobile County Board of Registrars, which retained dead and missing persons on active voting lists. Unwittingly or otherwise, the registrars had set the stage for much of the mischief down in Ward 4. The grand jury suspected that voter lists in every ward deserved a lot more scrutiny than registrars had been giving. The bad-mouthing might have stopped right there, but this grand jury had a mind of its own. It condemned Alabama's election laws, called on Mobile's legislators to straighten out the mess, and for good measure took potshots at the registrars' registration process.

What lesson McCorvey's machine hoped to give the bush-leaguers in Ward 4 somehow backfired into an unexpectedly nasty indictment of the system itself. Sheriff Holcombe and the grand jurors gracefully turned the tables on the crowd that ran the system. Mobile's State Registrars Milton Schnell, Frank McConnell, and C. C. Crutcher were quite happy muddling along without all this attention, and now groped for a way to avoid getting dragged further into the fray. Serving as the Board's stalking horse, clerk Dorothy Blatchford publicly defended Chairman Schnell and the other registrars, suggesting Sheriff Holcombe's criticism rested on erroneous information. Willie Holcombe responded politely:

> Our report was made to the April grand jury which made its own comments and recommendations without suggestions or advice from me. All of the members of the board of registrars are in my opinion men of unquestionable integrity and honor and I have the highest regard for them.

As for how the registrars did their homework, well, that was no matter of concern to the sheriff. For all Willie Holcombe knew, Schnell's crowd did no more or less than what the powers in Montgomery expected. Personally taking on state appointed registrars would pit a county sheriff against the movers and shakers who ran Alabama, including the governor, state auditor, and agriculture commissioner. That match had little appeal to and no payoff for the good sheriff. Willie adhered to a well-established rule in political circles against getting into pissing contests with skunks.

Chairman Schnell reluctantly felt obliged to publicize the Board's painstaking efforts to purge the dead and missing from voter lists. Schnell noted how the Board had discovered 25 persons more than 100 years old still registered to vote. The Board marveled that so many people had lived so long in Mobile County. Schnell was quick to add, however, that the Board could not simply delete the dead from voting lists until the Board of Health confirmed that they were indeed dead, which would take years.

Passing the buck deflected some of the heat, but did not quite explain what the registrars had been doing during the past eight years under Schnell's leadership. The Chairman wrapped up his apologia by appealing for public support, urging newspaper readers to call in with any helpful tips. Now the public would have itself, not Schnell, to blame if folks failed to report dead and missing voters before the next election. The registrars had artfully dodged the grand jury's bullet. Everybody and nobody was responsible for voting abuses in Mobile.

In response to the grand jury's call for reform, newly elected Senator Langan drafted a bill requiring verification of voting machine results and, for good measure, upping the daily pay of election officials from $3 to $5. Those measures scratched the surface and left the core of the problem unscathed. Once the hullabaloo blew over, Mobile County quietly returned to politics as usual.

Underdog Jim Folsom also carried Ward 4, defeating Handy Ellis in McCorvey's own backyard. When Governor Folsom took office two months later, he sent Henry Sweet down to Mobile to run the State

Docks. Before accepting the directorship, Sweet came to town and looked things over. Big Jim told Henry to be sure to look up a good friend of his down in Mobile. Henry rolled into town in a beat up old car and called on Gunny, who insisted that Henry come over for some hospitality and dinner fresh from the creek.

Three Mile Creek wanders easterly from a bog between Spring Hill and Mississippi, across town past Grandpa Joe's grave at Catholic Cemetery, and then north beyond Conception Street where, swelling into a snake infested bogue, it feeds the Mobile River. Long stretches of its densely overgrown banks harbored generations of bellowing bullfrogs, swarming mosquitoes, and deadly moccasins. Drunks, fools, and children sloshed through these infested thickets by day, but drunks and children knew to get out by dusk. Under the pitch dark blanket of night, vines and moccasins all looked and sounded very much alike, shadowy and silent. In the numbing black haze, even the deaf could pick up the telltale of an encroaching alligator, its eyes glowing brightly just above the murky surface. Snakes, though, always played their strong suit, wriggling in the creek, slithering along the banks, slinking across lily pads, and dangling from branches.

Gunny and Chick Bourgot stopped just the other side of the Conception Street bridge, attached calcium carbide lights to their hard hats, slipped jute sacks and gigs into a flat bottom skiff, and slid into the water. They entered the food chain of Three Mile Creek, hunting for the same bullfrogs that snakes and alligators stalked for a living. Poling ever further away from the bridge, Gunny and Chick soon found a group of large croakers squatting on leafy pads. Quickly, they grabbed the stunned bullfrogs, slinging the kicking critters into wet sacks. Deeper into the overhanging growth the boat followed paths of light cast by the lanterns. Depths of 3 to 20 feet all looked the same, dark and ominously threatening. At any moment, reaching out over floating lily pads, the frog catchers half-expected something nasty to break the surface and convert the predators into prey. Grabbing a loud mouthed bullfrog soon became a heart pounding dare. The fear of reaching into an alligator's snout, of something biting back, grew as the night wore on. They did not have long to wait for a close brush with cardiac arrest. Fully focused on a cluster of squatting frogs, they neither saw nor heard a snake drop from the thick overhang straight down into the water between the dazed bullfrogs and the equally dazed hunters. The splash, followed by a rush of leaping bullfrogs, confirmed that the wriggling airborne attack was no vision. Before Gunny's pulse regained a normal rhythm, another snake flashed into and out of sight, hitting the water in a spiral. Looking up, the lamps saw other figures dangling head first over the creek bed, ready to plunge. Gunny neither planned to leap from the boat nor share it with snakes. With nearly 50 croakers in the bag, the snakes could have the rest. On that note, the skiff reversed stream and made straight away for the bridge. All the way down Conception toward town, the din of bellowing frogs convinced Gunny this was his last outing on Three Mile Creek. He would look for fun elsewhere and pay cash the next time frog legs popped up on the menu.

Anne was still awake when Gunny dragged 50 bullfrogs through the door on Bobolink Drive. Nearly eight months pregnant, Anne hesitated when Gunny pulled a magnificent specimen, round as a plate and over a foot long, from a churning wet jute sack. Growing up on Aunt Maggie's place in the bayou left little to the imagination. Catching, killing, and cleaning critters for dinner came with the territory. The best fried chicken usually followed a round of fierce neck-wringing, plucking, and quartering. So Anne bellied up to the sink, watching closely how to handle the squirming beasts, ready to lend a hand. Gunny firmly gripped the first bullfrog, stretched its great webbed legs out straight, and quickly chopped them off. A legless stump of a frog struggled to escape further attack. Dressing and quartering a freshly killed chicken suddenly seemed child's play to mutilating a bug-eyed croaking frog. Fighting back an irresistible urge to heave her own supper onto what would be Henry Sweet's dinner, Anne fled the frogs, leaving Gunny in charge of the kitchen and 49 bellowing entrées. She resolved as well to stay clear of the stove the next evening for fear that the amputated legs would leap out of the frying pan at her. Gunny could have all the honors of cooking the frogs. Anne would have nothing to do with them.

In the spring of 1947 Anne had another boy. For the first time in four generations, a baby bore a family name other than Joseph. They christened him James Joullian in honor of Governor James Folsom, Irish Ma and Charlie Joullian. State Senator Joe Langan agreed to be godfather. Lucille Tew, Tunker's wife, stood in as godmother.

Henry Sweet shared with Governor Folsom a nearly mythical account of his dinner with Gunny. It was just the sort of stuff that Big Jim relished. Anybody that would punt up and down a creek bed in Mobile County at night, dodging tree snakes and snatching bull frogs just to feed the Governor's friend, had to be a straight shooter or crazy as a bed bug. Either way, Gunny was okay with the Governor. After Henry Sweet became State Docks Director, Gunny accepted a supervisory job overseeing workers at the Docks. Later that same summer, the Governor sent for his Mobile ward boss. This was no invitation to drop by the mansion and pass some time over good whiskey. Not that Gunny had not already been asked up to Montgomery for some back-slapping and all. This time, however, Alabama's highway patrol had orders to bring Gunny in. Squad cars escorted Gunny from one county line to the next until, some 200 miles upstate, they pulled up to the Governor's mansion.

From the outset in 1946, Gunny and Jim Folsom spoke plainly to each other as friends. Both knew the score and neither put on airs. Gunny's minority faction on the Mobile County Democratic Executive Committee soundly beat Handy Ellis' political machine in Mobile. Jim Folsom needed no reminders. After paying respects to the family and sharing a few laughs, the Governor turned serious. "Tell me, Gunny, what do you know about insurance or real estate, stuff like that?" Money and power went hand in hand with those who regulated these fields.

Gunny did not see where Big Jim was heading. The Governor wanted to make things right for a trusted ally. It was that simple. If Gunny could carry the load, he had the job, but Gunny knew not to grab beyond his reach. Gunny had played against the odds when he cast lots for Jim Folsom in 1946, and had nearly lost it all by taking on Gessner McCorvey and the Boswell Amendment. Walking out of the governor's mansion with a plum in his pocket would pay the rent and leave Gunny sitting pretty for some time to come. Some folks got fat off politics, slopping at the public troughs. Gunny turned the plums down, though. He knew nothing about insurance or real estate, and said so.

"Course, the State Patrol's always in need of good people, Gunny. I'd be happy to put you on the force down in Mobile." Despite the obvious attraction of good pay and all that went with the job, the Governor sensed he had misjudged the situation. Gunny grinned uncomfortably, knowing he could handle patrol work and wanting to show appreciation for the Governor's generosity. Somewhat sheepishly, Gunny thanked his friend and mumbled a reason or two why he should decline the offer.

Governor Folsom's big frame leaned back, taking stock of this unassuming ally who remained unmoved by gestures of patronage. Despite Folsom's momentary popularity, his fame would someday wither under the Old Guard's steady attack. Cleaning house in Montgomery ran well as a campaign slogan, but not with rural legislators whose fiefdoms were at stake. Though a majority of voters had put Folsom in office, a majority of Alabamians had no vote. A powerful white rural minority controlled the system. Folsom's chances of implementing reapportionment and education reforms were mostly stillborn, and likely would remain so until the choke hold on registration could be broken.

Big Jim had no peer when it came to jawboning, but the Governor could not register even one voter. The state party machine, all but immune to external attack, was vulnerable only from within. Even then, a skilled insider defying conventional wisdom and party tradition could just as easily bring the house down on himself and the Governor, destroying personal careers and whatever else either might hope to achieve. Making matters worse, the Boswell Amendment now lent constitutional legitimacy to practices that had long frustrated voter registration for both Coloreds and Whites. Big Jim needed a reliable insider whose political instincts and determination could undermine a system that the Governor had sworn to maintain. The Governor saw in Gunny a kindred spirit willing to joust at the windmills of Alabama's political castles. As a member of the State Appointing Board, Folsom had yet to name his designee to the Mobile County Board of Registrars. Though not a particularly attractive financial plum, the registrar seat offered the only way to undermine the system from within.

"You know, Gunny, some of the union folks are pretty high on you. They've let it be known they want you on the board of registrars. If you want to be my man on the board, just say the word and it's yours."

Sitting on the board would barely pay for Gunny's time and trouble. Getting rich was out of the question. Mobile's south side ward master had scraped for what he had, which did not amount to much. But knowing where the next meal was coming from did not take a pile of money, and making friends who could open the right doors once Gunny left the board seemed remote. Those kinds of friends were content with business as usual. Mobile's current registrars had made those kinds of friends. Gunny figured he would make more enemies than friends, powerful political enemies at that. But politics as usual stuck in Gunny's craw. Gunny could not abide how the McCorvey's and Boswell's manipulated the system as White supremacists to benefit the Haves at the expense of the Have-Nots.

"Jim, if I got on the board, what would you want me to do? You know where I stand with the Boswell crowd. I'm for letting people vote. That alone would cure half of what's wrong with Mobile. Hell, it's easier for the dead to rise up and go to the polls than for a veteran to vote. That ain't right. If I'm on the board, there could be a stink for sure 'cause I'm gonna register people, Negroes too."

The Governor warmly eyed his friend. This could be the turning point Folsom needed to unravel the political stranglehold that gripped Alabama. "Gunny, if they're qualified, you go right ahead and let them vote. That's what I expect. Fair enough?"

"Fair enough."

"O. H., you out there?" Governor Folsom had O. H. Finney, Jr., his executive aide, join them. "O. H., put Gunny on the Board of Registrars." O. H. smiled at Gunny and left the room. That was it. "What else can I do for you, Gunny?"

"Not a thing, Jim, not a thing." Gunny rose to shake the Governor's huge hand.

"Ya'll come see me sometime, you hear?" Big Jim grinned, fully expecting to be hearing from or about his registrar most anytime. Gunny joked with O. H. on the way out, and headed directly for Mobile. "O. H., see if you can get Joe Langan on the phone for me." As Mobile's only state senator, Langan enjoyed senatorial courtesy. Before announcing Gunny's appointment, the Governor privately notified Senator Langan, expecting no objection. The die was cast. Indeed, Joe Langan would benefit from a political stalking horse, a Party maverick who was willing to stand toe-to-toe with McCorvey's state machine, fight the Boswell Amendment, and shake up the system but good. The surest way to clear the chicken coop was to let in a fox. Gunny was Jim Folsom's fox.

On August 28, 1947, Mobile's Negro Voters and Veterans Association announced plans to register its 8,000 members in time for upcoming elections. In the past ten months, few Coloreds had even attempted to register, and most of those who did were teachers and professionals. The sheer thought of 8,000 Negroes flooding the polls shook Mobile's political foundation. Since passage of the Boswell Amendment, the Negro Association had sponsored classes in Atmore, Thomasville, Montevallo, and Mobile, using college graduates and professionals to teach Coloreds about the United States Constitution. White working people had no need or time to be off sitting in class studying the Constitution. Sponsors of the Boswell Amendment made no secret of their aim to prevent mass voting by Coloreds in Democratic primaries. It mattered very little if Whites neither understood nor explained what the Constitution meant.

A couple of days later Chairman Milton Schnell announced that Mobile's Registrars would sit in session at 109 St. Emanuel Street for 5 hours between 9 a.m. and 4 p.m. on Tuesday, September 2 and again on Monday, September 15 because of upcoming city elections. Schnell cautioned that anyone, veteran or not, must bring a registered voter to vouch for the applicant. That afternoon, political speculation spread around town that changes in the Board of Registrars were coming. The expiring term of registrars Schnell, Frank H. McConnell, and C. C. Crutcher, led the *Press Register* and courthouse insiders to wonder who might be appointed:

> Three state officials - Gov. James E. Folsom, State Auditor Dan Thomas, and Agriculture Commissioner Haygood Paterson — will make one appointment each to the new board. New appointees will serve four-year terms.
>
> Among those mentioned at the courthouse as under consideration for the board of registrars were E. J. "Gunny" Gonzales, Democratic executive committee man from Ward 4, and C. H. Applewhite, president of the Mobile Central Trades Council (AFL). Gonzales is the leader of a minority faction in the Mobile County Democratic Executive Committee.

The new board would have to deal with the inevitable collision between the Boswell Amendment and the Negro Voters and Veterans Association. It did not anticipate a similar collision with Gunny.

On October 24, 1947 Governor Folsom appointed E. J. Gonzales as a member of the Mobile County Board of Registrars. Commissioner Paterson re-appointed Schnell to his third four-year term and Auditor Thomas appointed Mrs. D. C. (Myrtle Gay) Randle. Five days later, on Wednesday, October 29, Gunny Gonzales stood with fellow registrars Milton Schnell and Myrtle Gay Randle to take the oath of office from Probate Judge Norville R. Leigh, Jr.

Within the week Gunny questioned whether state law required that a voter appear in person to vouch for an applicant. Chairman Schnell assured Gunny it did. Gunny assumed that Milton spoke truthfully. Sitting in session over the next few days, Gunny watched Schnell and Randle reject five out of every six applicants. Turning to several attorney friends, Gunny asked for a copy of Chairman Schnell's law. The lawyers reported that no such law existed. Apparently, Schnell had played fast and loose with the freshman registrar. The law simply authorized a board of registrars to adopt rules which expedite registration. The witness voucher requirement amounted to nothing more than law according to Schnell. A ghost in Gunny's past began to stir. Clearing the air with the Chairman, Gunny demanded abolishing the Board's rule. For the first time in Party memory, the Board split into two factions. Schnell and Randle claimed that the witness rule guarded against registering unqualified and untruthful applicants, presuming applicants would perjure themselves absent vouching witnesses. On the other hand, the Board's rule assumed that vouching witnesses would take time off from work to travel downtown and not facilitate an applicant's presumed fraud through collusion. On November 11, 1947, Gunny publicly broke with the Board's majority, declaring his misgivings about business as usual at 109 St. Emanuel:

> I want the people of Mobile County to know that I am against the voucher system. Of course, we as members have to abide by all laws of Alabama that govern the registrations of applicants, but the law does not specify that the applicant for registration must have a witness or a voucher to swear the applicant is telling the truth. It is a matter left entirely up to the members of the board.

> I hold no ill feeling toward my fellow board members, Mr. Milton Schnell and Mrs. D. C. Randle, because this voucher system is inadequate. I solicit their cooperation to change the present system, so the board shall be praised in the future instead of being criticized as is the case now. Too many citizens are denied the privilege of registering and becoming future voters thus hampering our democratic way of living.

Despite airing differences in public, Schnell and Randle did not budge. Gunny yielded to his boxing instincts, following a sharp jab with a cross to the chin. In another letter to the press, the Governor's registrar announced a credo of public service, causing eyes to roll down at the courthouse:

> I consider myself a servant of the people. You, the taxpayers are paying my salary. Therefore, I want to do all in my power to satisfy you. If I can't do this, I will show you the courtesy to resign my job at once, and let someone else do it. I want you, the citizens of Mobile County, to know that if it requires my services at night in order to register the voters who are unable to lose a day's work, I am ready and at your service. The law

specifies that two members must be present to register an applicant and I assure you that I am willing to be one of the members present.

Gunny's press release had the ring of a campaign speech. The startling offer to resign raised the ante. Neither the Board majority nor some of their political sponsors were any too happy that Gunny's civics lesson might generate unrealistic expectations. Populist sentiments provided the fodder of campaign platforms, but threatened the status quo. White supremacy remained very much a pillar of that status quo, and one not likely to yield ground without casualties.

Gunny's soul baring should have faded after a momentary blip on the screen. A sole registrar, a minority of one, lacked the clout to toss out the old and bring in the new. Any real hope of change depended on enkindling public brush fires without torching himself in the process. Within 24 hours, smoke began rising on the horizon. To Schnell's dismay, veterans joined Gunny's battle cry. On November 12 the Board disclosed that the Veterans Cooperative Home Building Association wanted the registrars to break tradition by providing night registration for Brookley Field veterans who could not afford to go all the way down to 109 St. Emanuel during work hours. Veterans would be better served by registering at Birdville's Thomas James Community Center, just two blocks from Bobolink Drive. One registrar agreed, urging as many night sessions as necessary to get veterans registered. However, Schnell and Randle took a dim view of the whole idea, agreeing only to hold one night session on November 19, and forcing veterans downtown at that.

Crowding his opponents into a corner, Gunny pressed the attack. The weekend before meeting with veterans in the Board's small office downtown, Gunny publicly demanded regular night sessions all over the county. As if that were not enough to drive Schnell to distraction, Gunny again urged abolishing the witness rule. Having to bring a registered voter all the way downtown during work hours meant that two people, not just one, suffered a loss of pay. Employers were not required to let anyone off with or without pay to stand in line indefinitely waiting to register. The Board's witness rule discouraged registering blue collar laborers, including most Coloreds.

Gunny again upped the ante. He chose to play most of his cards, including a legal opinion from his friend State Circuit Solicitor Carl M. Booth. Booth concluded that the Board can register an applicant without requiring a witness. Schnell knew that state law did not require witnesses, but let applicants think otherwise. Carl Booth disclosed that Alabama's Attorney General addressed a similar ruling to Schnell eight years ago in 1939 when Schnell first became board chairman. Schnell had ignored the Attorney General's advice. On Saturday November 15, Schnell and Randle voted, over Gunny's objection, to continue requiring witnesses to vouch for applicants. The charade of following state law collapsed. Still, Schnell persisted:

> The board recognizes this provision as all-important in that it protects the vote of the qualified elector against that of the registered applicant who, without qualified witnesses, could, and in a great number of cases, probably would be registered on false information.

> It has been brought to this board's attention in recent months by certain applicants for registration that in order to be able to hold their jobs, they are required to become voters, and in quite a number of instances these applicants, not having the necessary qualifications, put themselves under extreme legal hazards in attempting to register. Without witnesses who put themselves in jeopardy of perjury and upon conviction a term in the penitentiary, the applicant would be hard put in proving the required qualifications he does not have.

> The board sees no reason for eliminating this provision of requiring witnesses in the registering of applicants just for the sake of a little more facility on the part of the applicant.

Chairman Schnell could not identify anyone at Kilby Prison doing time for registering to vote, and could not show that workers had falsified information absent a witness.

Ordinarily, the Board only registered 3 to 12 voters a day, less than two per hour. Nearly 100 veterans unexpectedly crammed into 109 St. Emanuel the evening of November 19, prompting Gunny's renewed proposal for weekly night sessions. Schnell and Randle shot that down, but Schnell proudly noted that the Board would be in session Thanksgiving morning for the public's convenience. That he said *Thanksgiving morning* with a straight face attested to Schnell's ability to manipulate the media and stay the course.

John Wills, a reporter with the *Press Register*, came to the Cradle of the Confederacy by way of Michigan. Wills readily admitted he had never seen the likes of Mobile's political in-fighting. Being a Yankee and all, Wills saw Alabama from a somewhat jaded perspective, but enjoyed the commotion down on St. Emanuel Street. He hit it off with Gunny and struck a bargain: if Gunny would write it, Wills would print it. Wills submitted articles exposing Schnell's shenanigans as fast as the newspaper publisher attacked Gunny with editorials. Of course, the *Press Register* did not relish news articles that tainted the Board. The paper regarded the minority registrar as an agitator, a team member who would be captain or not play ball at all. Wills knew better. Gunny fed the reporter's humor. Wills had an inkling of what it was like for Gunny to be closeted with Schnell and Randle in the Board's back room, maintaining the pretense of civility amid clever duplicity. They shared precious few courtesies behind those closed doors, just enough to vote down Gunny's proposals.

Gunny stayed on at the State Docks while serving as the Governor's registrar. His growing list of critics down at the courthouse started a campaign of whispers, suggesting that Mobile's controversial figure improperly drew state salaries for both jobs at the same time. Double-dipping ran afoul of the law. The State Attorney General ruled that Gunny could be paid as a registrar when he was clocked off the job out at the State Docks. To comply with the law, Gunny started off his day at the crack of dawn taking care of business at the State Docks, then clocked out in time to get downtown for the Board's 9 a.m. session. About all Gunny had to show for running back and forth between the State Docks and St. Emanuel Street was $15 a day. That did not cover time off the clock meeting with veterans, union laborers, and even the teaching Brothers at McGill Institute on Government. Gunny went to McGill Institute one night and let all the Brothers fill out registration applications to avoid standing in line for hours with vouching witnesses. Teaching class five days a week at McGill did not leave the Brothers much opportunity for standing in line. That made no difference to Schnell.

Only 6,800 voters, a pathetically small number and all but a handful of them White, paid poll taxes in 1947. From the Party's perspective, however, a manageable voting constituency rendered elections more predictable. Hurdles that discouraged or prevented some Whites from voting were but a small price to pay, a mere inconvenience, especially when the alternative was considered. Eight thousand Coloreds were out there gearing up to register, threatening to equal or exceed the number of active white voters. That was not going to happen on Schnell's watch, unless Gunny's fussing and fuming pulled the roof down on all their heads. Should Whites begin questioning the Board's doings, all bets were off. Few people gave a hoot and holler whether Coloreds got a raw deal, but there would be hell to pay if the Board trifled with Whites. Schnell hoped to stay the course until the storm and Gunny passed over.

Ever so often, John Wills and Gunny whiled away an evening in the back room after Schnell and Randle had adjourned for the day. John sought the low down, some grist to feed his readers, and Gunny sought an audience. They needed each other. "Hell, John, you don't know the half of it. You should have been up here when Schnell showed me his gun. He keeps it in his desk drawer, but I didn't know about it until just the other day. I could have sworn he'd had his fill of me, and I was about to clock out for good. Well, I looked at that damn thing and asked him what's it doing there. Milton gets real serious and says, 'Gunny, you know, you better watch out for these black people.' Now, don't that take the cake! Here's Milton Schnell toting a pistol and telling me to watch out for the Coloreds."

"So when are you going to strap one on, Gunny?" Nothing surprised Wills anymore.

"Hell, you must be crazy. I looked at Milton and told him, 'What do you mean, *me*? *You* better watch out for them black people. You're the one's giving them a screwing!' Milton didn't think too much of that. If he ever goes for that drawer while we're in session, I'm hitting the floor faster than a bat out of Georgia." Gunny leaned back from the table. On the mantel behind them hung a large print of Lt. Colonel George Custer, both a hero and fool in the face of overwhelming odds. It never crossed Gunny's mind that he had much in common with Custer. John Wills grinned to himself, rolling the story over in his mind. Wills could not get his fill. It was the best show in town. The reporter rested his eyes on the ceiling, in time to glimpse Custer catching an incoming breeze and rising off the mantel. The maverick Indian fighter toppled straight to the floor, just behind Gunny's chair, landing with a crash that shook the room. Wills watched Gunny leap into thin air, shocked out of a heartbeat. The reporter rolled onto the floor next to Custer, howling out of control. Unafraid and alone, Gunny had taken on Alabama's white supremacists, but now cringed under attack by the likes of a two-dimensional George Custer.

STATE OF ALABAMA
EXECUTIVE DEPARTMENT
MONTGOMERY

Montgomery, Alabama

October 24, 1947

Mr. E. J. Gonzales
351 South Franklin Street
Mobile, Alabama

Dear Mr. Gonzales:

The Board of Appointment of Registrars has this day appointed you as a member of the Board of Registrars of Mobile County in accordance with Section 21 of Title 17, of the Code of 1940.

This appointment will take effect as soon as you have qualified as prescribed by law. It is necessary that you qualify at once.

Yours very truly,

James E. Bloom,
Governor

Dan Thomas
Auditor

Hayford Paleson
Commissioner of Agriculture
and Industries

cc: Judge of Probate

37. Emanuel Joseph Gonzales Board of Registrars Appointment Letter, October 24, 1947.

38. *State of Alabama Commission of E. J. Gonzales by Governor James E. Folsom as Member of the Board of Registrars of Mobile County, September 10, 1948.*

39. Probate Judge Norville R. Leigh, Jr., Milton Schnell, Mrs. D. C. Randle and E. J. (Gunny) Gonzales, Mobile County Board of Registrars oath of office, October 29, 1947 (Courtesy, Mobile Press, October 30, 1947).

CHAPTER 24

St. Emanuel Uprising

The Mobile Building Trades Council, American Federation of Labor promptly turned Gunny's uphill battle with the Board into a donnybrook. The Carpenters Union, Metal Trades Council, Painters Union, Marine Pipefitters Union, and Sheet Metal Workers Union appeared before Schnell demanding regular night registration sessions. Citing personal inconvenience, Schnell and Randle voted down Gunny's night registration motion. Schnell told the unions that the Board might call for special night sessions, but only "in response to public demand." Unions did not reflect public demands. As best as Schnell could tell, the public accepted the Board keeping banker's hours. For a laborer and his vouching witness to forfeit several hours of pay just to attempt registration was the cost of citizenship according to the Board's majority, and a bargain to boot.

The unions did not buy any of that. The AFL wired Governor Folsom that the trades council intended to register its people even if that meant declaring a legal holiday, a not so veiled threat of a wildcat strike. The unions demanded that the Governor remove Schnell and Randle, objecting to "the dictatorial powers handed to Mr. Schnell to govern the registration of our people." Gunny's challenges had successfully stirred up Mobile's white community, raising expectations more rapidly than Big Jim had anticipated.

Governor Folsom publicly sympathized, but observed that he lacked the power to remove registrars appointed by State Auditor Dan Thomas and Agriculture Commissioner Haygood Paterson. The Governor took the matter under advisement, choosing to issue no further comment. He happily passed the hot potato to Dan Thomas and Haygood Paterson. Commissioner Paterson denied receiving any complaint about Schnell from the unions, and Auditor Thomas insisted that Randle had done nothing unlawful. That Randle did as little as possible did not concern Thomas.

The Mobile Press chose to level a condescending broadside against those trying to register blue-collar Whites:

> Boiled down, the furor over board working hours seems to be much ado about nothing. Union officials have complained that organized labor is being discriminated against by the two board members opposing night sessions. We cannot see how the present daytime hours prevent any union member who really wants to from registering. Most union members in Mobile work a 5-day 40-hour week.
>
> Labor leaders also object to the board's policy of requiring witnesses for new voters, as provided in the state code. What is unreasonable about that requirement? The board is charged with the responsibility of certifying the voting qualifications of applicants. The three members cannot possibly be expected to know every person who wants to register. The requirement that each applicant be accompanied by a witness is a valuable safeguard and is an assurance that the board makes a determined effort to check diligently each applicant's qualifications.
>
> Unless it can be shown that the two board members are violating the law respecting registrars, they should be allowed to hold the positions to which they were appointed. Firing them for refusal to vote for night sessions per se would be improper and undemocratic.

The Mobile Press failed to recognize the irony of its convoluted reasoning. The unions did not. They stormed Montgomery, demanding the resignations of Schnell and Randle for impeding democracy. The *Press* did not seem troubled that the Board's procedures had the calculated effect of denying a majority of white Mobile County the right to vote. The AFL and CIO lectured Governor Folsom, Auditor Thomas, and Commissioner Paterson: "We're never going to be able to combat the Mobile County political machine unless something is done to allow more of our people to become voters." The incipient uprising in Mobile revealed how the systemic effort to deny democracy to Coloreds also denied democracy to Whites. Union leader Scotty Alsup publicly dismissed Randle as little more than a rubber stamp for Schnell, while applauding Gunny's willingness to register at night. Gunny returned Alsup's serve, offering to work whatever hours necessary and belittling the Board for poorly serving a working class that could ill afford to lose a day's pay standing in line.

Gunny then condemned Schnell and Randle for not holding day sessions elsewhere in Mobile County. For years, Schnell ignored a 1943 law requiring county-wide registration sessions. On January 2, 1948 Gunny smoked Schnell out by publishing an opinion of Attorney General Albert Carmichael that justified Gunny's criticism. Schnell decided that the 1943 registration law simply did not apply to Mobile County regardless of the Attorney General's opinion. The Board also determined that implementing the Attorney General's opinion "will be the worst political blow we have ever had." Schnell tried to buy some time and place the teapot on the back burner, assuring the public that he intended to write Montgomery for a copy of Attorney General Carmichael's opinion. Gunny publicly offered to bring his personal copy to the Board so Schnell could read it without further delay. Deprived of political cover and indifferent about the Attorney General's thoughts on the issue, Schnell tried to dismiss the matter as an example of Gunny "merely trying to stir something up." Gunny promptly denied any intent to stir things up, managing to keep the dispute in the headlines all the more:

> I am not trying to stir anything up. I am only trying to straighten out something that has already stirred up. He has been chairman for eight long years under previous administrations, and there is no one better than he that should know what I am about to stir up.

> I believe that the Board should go into each ward and precinct and register the people to vote instead of compelling them always to come to the Court House and stand in line for hours at a time and some of them with small children in their arms. The majority of the board should eliminate the third degree methods and strict regulations that are thrown on an applicant to register to vote, that no other county in this state or any other state that I have ever heard of uses on the *white* applicant.

Gunny's indirect attack on the Boswell Amendment sailed over the Party's bow for all to see. In ominous terms understood from Mobile to Montgomery, Gunny condemned the Board's practice of impeding White registration by using methods designed to impede Colored registration. Gunny understood that Mobile might tolerate schemes preventing most Coloreds from voting. However, Mobile would not likely tolerate Schnell and Randle trifling with white voters. Though not quite throwing down the gauntlet, Gunny's message clearly drew attention to measures that restricted white voter registration.

Schnell and Randle did not have much opportunity to celebrate the passing of 1947. At the onset of 1948, labor leader Scotty Alsup announced that Randle was not even legally registered to vote and not qualified to serve as registrar. During 1946 the only legal registration period was a ten-day window starting January 21. Randle had registered on October 15, 1946, outside the lawful period. Schnell and Randle reacted to Alsup's attack by adjourning the Board's 1948 registration period until Monday, January 19. Gunny agreed to postpone registration, but served notice that he would boycott holding a session on that Monday, it being a legal Alabama holiday. In thoughtful observance of the birthday of General Robert E. Lee, Gunny stayed home.

Alsup's petition to Montgomery drew a cold response from Auditor Dan Thomas, who announced he did not feel disposed to remove Randle or Schnell, as long as they continued performing their duties according to law. Thomas noted that some of Mobile's leading citizens had nominated Randle as a registrar, but disclosed no names. Commissioner Paterson astutely promised to ask the Attorney General to investigate conditions in

Mobile, and pursue grand jury action if it could be shown that registrars were not doing their job. Governor Folsom announced that he was taking the matter under consideration. Big Jim's attention focused on more pressing agendas, one personal and the other national. In the Governor's absence, O. H. Finney privately assured Gunny on January 12, 1948 of Big Jim's support: "You are doing a splendid job on the Board of Registrars in Mobile County, and we want you to know that we are certainly backing you up." Governor Folsom took genuine satisfaction with the pressure Gunny and the unions had put on the State Party machine.

On the Monday following General Robert E. Lee's birthday, W. C. Harrington and his Mobile Painters Union launched their own attack, suing Randle, Schnell, and the State of Alabama. Harrington's unprecedented lawsuit went for the political kneecap, seeking to oust Randle and declare unconstitutional Alabama's registration laws. State circuit court judges Claude A. Grayson, Cecil F. Bates, and David H. Eddington assumed jurisdiction, announcing that Harrington's suit represented one of the most important cases ever brought before their court, politically at least. Schnell took precious little comfort with the judges' sense of history. Chairman Schnell's majority, already under siege from within, now faced legal scrutiny for violating white people's constitutional rights. It was hard to imagine how the carefully crafted plans of McCorvey and Boswell could go so awry so quickly. Most galling of all, the Party's public relations mess with unions and veterans flowed out of the voting rights battle that Gunny launched only a couple of months earlier. Politics as usual took a turn for the strangely unpredictable, and the Colored genie quietly prepared to flee its White bottle.

Randle smarted from reports that she had never registered or voted in Mobile County until 1946. Magnolia Cemetery's residents seemed more politically active than the registrar from Bayou Coden. To make matters worse, the cloud on her registration undermined her standing as a registrar. Harrington's January 26 suit highlighted the irony of entrusting the likes of Randle with the power to reject would-be voters. Her credibility as a registrar, already weakened by Gunny's persistent attacks, wobbled badly.

This time Randle and Schnell let Vince Kilborn, a more than capable counsel, do their talking. Anyone blessed with cash and serious trouble wanted full use of Vince Kilborn's talents. Kilborn quickly persuaded the court to rule on the pleadings without taking any testimony at all. On Wednesday, January 28, Kilborn and William C. Taylor, Harrington's lawyer, wrangled in court over the law and the Constitution.

Beyond Randle's tainted status as a registrar, Taylor argued that Alabama's registration laws violated the Fourteenth Amendment. Almost everyone in Mobile knew that Reconstructionists bequeathed the equal protection amendment to former slaves, not Whites. Taylor claimed, however, that Alabama's voting laws unreasonably restricted white registration. That made little sense to the court, which concluded that Whites and Coloreds suffered the same restrictions, and that the Fourteenth Amendment does not guarantee the right to register just any old time. A ten day general registration period each year seemed fair enough to this court for the thousands wanting to apply. Long lines, short hours, and lengthy interrogations made little difference to the court. Instead of encouraging registration, Kilborn argued that Harrington's complaint would have just the opposite effect. Indeed, Kilborn reasoned that Harrington's suit actually might disenfranchise persons already registered, especially Randle and whomever she had registered. Kilborn portrayed Randle as the victim.

The specter of union types ousting Randle for whatever reason sent tongues wagging. No one holding political office in Mobile missed the message. Removal from office by political opponents could set a disruptive precedent. Much deeper concerns, though, were triggered by the signals this lawsuit sent to Mobile's Coloreds. Claiming that the Board violated Whites' equal protection encouraged and lent credence to a similar attack by Negroes. Harrington's suit, which Gunny welcomed, disturbed traditional political circles. Mobile's circuit court judges quickly disposed of Harrington's far reaching claims, confirming Randle's legal status and the constitutionality of Alabama's voting laws. Through somewhat limber judicial reasoning, the judges agreed that the mutually inconsistent 1935 and 1943 statutes both applied.

The union's lawsuit died within a week, a mere flash in Mobile's political pan. The system survived the attacks from within and without.

As the Board neared the close of its January 1948 general registration period, Gunny hurled charges across the table at Schnell during open session. A curious crowd, snaking its way down the stairs and out the front door onto St. Emanuel, heard the minority registrar accuse Schnell of refusing to register voters. "I'm going to see my lawyer about this," Gunny promised. After nearly three months of legal scrimmaging, each registrar consulted separate legal counsel. Schnell casually shot back over the background buzz that Gonzales was just trying to stir things up again. Fresh on the heels of victory in Mobile's circuit court, Schnell confidently backhanded Gunny's charges. The crowd got an earful while wasting hours in the long slow line. It was, as they had read in the newspaper, never a dull moment between Gunny and Schnell.

Before the controversy could grow cold, the *Mobile Labor Journal* published Gunny's most volatile broadside yet:

> I want no part of Mr. Milton Schnell's Gestapo methods that he uses on the people of Mobile County pertaining to registration. I do admit that the Board of Registrars of each county in Alabama has the authority granted to them by the so-called Boswell Amendment to force upon the people this undemocratic way of registration, but I know of no other county in Alabama that uses this authority to strangle the citizens from registering to vote. I am referring to the *white* citizens of Mobile County.

> If Mr. Schnell really wanted to keep the voting list pure as a white lily, he should have seen to it that when he first became a member of the Board of Registrars eight years ago, that the qualified voting list was kept cleared of all the dead persons' names who have died in the past within the boundaries of Mobile County.

Gunny no longer saw fit to mince words in polite company. It is unclear, though, whether Schnell got the message.

In the midst of growing public turmoil, Gunny received an unusual overture from leaders of Mobile's Colored community. Bishop Smith privately extended to the outspoken minority registrar an invitation to attend a special gathering at Big Zion A. M. E. Church on Bayou Street, across from the Church Street Cemetery and Boyington's oak. Given the political climate, accepting such an invitation carried significant political risks. Any appearance that Gunny overtly served the interests of Mobile's Colored community would provide powerful political ammunition to his opponents. Already up to his hips in political alligators, Gunny still chose to wade deeper into the swamp. Gunny decided not to formally accept the invitation, but to make a discreet unannounced appearance. He took a seat in the back of the church amid the large crowd that already had gathered. Gunny did not want to be recognized, much less applauded or photographed. He sat near an exit where he could listen and leave without drawing attention. Gunny hoped to remain somewhat inconspicuous, an unlikely scenario for a prominent white politician in a Colored congregation. Moments before the evening's special program began, Bishop Smith called the full church to silence. He stood near the pulpit and asked aloud if Mr. E. J. Gunny Gonzales had arrived. Gunny felt obliged to stand and greet the bishop. Bishop Smith promptly asked Gunny to join the guest of honor at the front of the church. The scene ironically suggested a parable from Luke's Gospel about humbly choosing the seat of least honor to avoid embarrassment should the preferred seat be offered to someone of greater honor. Gunny chose the seat of least honor to avoid being noticed, and now felt embarrassed to be honored. The politics that Gunny embraced produced unusual results. Yet the greater irony stood near the pulpit. The NAACP had carefully followed Gunny's unprecedented public stand on behalf of colored veterans, and now believed the time had arrived to challenge the constitutionality of Alabama's Boswell Amendment. The guest of honor that evening was the chief legal counsel of the NAACP. Bishop Smith invited Gunny to come forward and take his place of honor at the front of the church with Thurgood Marshall.

In anticipation of the November 2 general election, Gessner T. McCorvey and other Dixiecrat notables met to attack President Harry Truman's call for federal legislation against segregation, lynching, poll taxes, and job discrimination. Governor Folsom was conspicuously absent from that meeting. In February, 1948 the President had asked Congress to establish a civil rights employment commission, prohibit racial lynching, and protect voting rights. McCorvey attacked the President's civil rights position as a South-hating program that would likely destroy Alabama's civilization and encourage inter-racial marriage. With persuasive fervor, McCorvey justified segregation statutes, denounced the President's proposed Fair Employment Practice Commission, ridiculed anti-lynching legislation as rabble-rousing sentiment, and championed the poll tax. As for the Boswell Amendment, McCorvey addressed the issue with conviction: "This howl against our registration laws is all out of place. Any man who is unable to understand the Constitution under which he lives ought not to be able to take a part in our government. He is better off if he permits the more intelligent citizens to provide a safe and sound government for him."

The Dixiecrats' Southern strategy for the 1948 national election called for Truman's defeat by selecting uncommitted Alabama delegates for the Democratic national convention in Philadelphia, adopting a Southern platform sensitive to Alabama's White Supremacy interests, and casting presidential elector ballots for South Carolina Governor Strom Thurmond. Southern Democrats anguished whether to bolt the party for an independent presidential candidate or crawl under the sheets with Republicans. U. S. Senator John Sparkman reminded his Democratic colleagues of historical anti-Southern sentiment within the Republican Party, dwelling especially on the Reconstructionists' role in keeping Alabama "under the Conquerors' heel" following the War between the States. Senator Sparkman warned his political kin to expect nothing from Republicans.

Strom Thurmond appeared in Mobile at the Alabama State Bar Association's convention in 1948. By design, McCorvey's element within the Bar Association submitted a resolution calling on the State Bar to endorse Strom Thurmond for president and Mississippi Governor Fielding Wright for vice-president. Richard T. Rives dared to openly oppose the emotional surge about to sweep Alabama's legal community into the arms of White Supremacy. He vehemently argued against the resolution, expressing anger that the State Bar would prostitute itself for political purposes. President Truman subsequently appointed Rives to the federal bench.

McCorvey spoke for kindred white supremacists by promising that Alabama's "Presidential electors are going to support a candidate who will stand up like a man and fight for the traditions of the Southland and do everything in their power to see that our civilization is preserved." McCorvey warned that President Truman "can either commit political suicide in the slums of Harlem or on the front doorsteps of the worthwhile white people of the South." McCorvey's rhetoric appealed to popular sentiment in Alabama. For all practical purposes, no one in Alabama - white or colored - would be able to vote in 1948 for the re-election of the President of the United States. It stuck in Folsom's craw that McCorvey and the Dixiecrats were bolting Alabama out the Democratic Party. Big Jim decided to take on the Dixiecrats in Alabama's Supreme Court. He sought injunctive and other extraordinary judicial relief to require Dixiecrat presidential electors to vote for the national Democratic candidate, President Harry Truman, consistent with the popular vote. Dixiecrat electors had promised they would not cast their electoral college ballots for President Truman should he be nominated on a platform pledging enactment of laws to end racial segregation. On December 1, 1948, Alabama's Supreme Court held that the State of Alabama had no legal interest concerning the pledge of Dixiecrat Democratic electors to vote against President Truman. Robert Albritton and other Alabama presidential electors could bolt and vote against their own national party's nominee. Governor Folsom played his hand and lost. He could do nothing more to stem the tide of Alabama's white supremacists.

CHAPTER 25

Day of Reckoning

Tucked between Harrington's lawsuit in January and the Dixiecrats' summit upstate, Chicago attorneys David Landau and George Leighton filed a complaint on February 28, 1948 with Judge John McDuffie in the U. S. District Court, Southern District of Alabama. Their clients, nine colored men and one colored woman, sued Governor James Folsom, State Auditor Dan Thomas, State Commissioner Haygood Paterson, Bud Boswell, Milton Schnell, Emanuel J. Gonzales, and Mrs. D. C. Randle for using the Boswell Amendment to restrict Coloreds from voting.

John McDuffie was not known to kowtow to anyone even before joining the robed majesty of the federal judiciary. When Franklin Roosevelt offered the congressman Mobile's federal bench, McDuffie hesitated until the President agreed to build a new courthouse and provide suitable chambers. Judge McDuffie felt at home on the bench, comfortably dispensing southern-style federal justice to his people. It did not occur to McDuffie, or anyone else for that matter, that he should excuse himself from this particular case. The judge's grandfather, a prominent plantation master, had owned slaves.

A federal judge sitting alone could not adjudge a state law to be unconstitutional. On October 22, 1948, Judge McDuffie convened a three-judge federal court to consider allegations against Alabama's Boswell Amendment. The Fifth Circuit U. S. Court of Appeals in New

Orleans designated Fifth Circuit Judge Leon McCord and Birmingham U. S. District Court Judge Clarence Mullins to preside with Judge McDuffie. These judges would give Alabama, Schnell, Randle, and Gunny their day in court, their day of reckoning.

Hunter Davis, Julius Cook, Ethel Carter, Russell Gaskins, Johnnie Q. Laine, John Daughtry, Monroe Kidd, W. F. Cunningham, Willie Garvin, and Russell July, Jr. complained they had been deprived of their constitutional rights under the 14th and 15th Amendments and post-Civil War civil rights legislation, all of which permitted voting in Alabama without regard to race or color. They argued that any person acting under the Boswell Amendment to deprive Negroes of the right to vote based on color was liable for damages. As to individual defendants, Hunter Davis and his co-plaintiffs alleged that Boswell had used his influence as a state legislator to persuade Alabama voters that his Amendment would prevent Colored citizens from becoming registered voters. By a margin of only 12,320 votes, Boswell had achieved his objective. For the previous 100 years, Alabama had not seen fit to require that its people explain the U. S. Constitution. Julius Cook told the federal court that Schnell, Randle, and Gonzales acted under Alabama law through the Boswell Amendment to deprive Coloreds of the vote by withholding registration.

Two weeks before the Painters Union sued the Board of Registrars, Cook and Hunter had attempted to register. Schnell questioned both of them:

"Now, Julius, how long have you lived in the State of Alabama?"

"Thirty-five years," Julius replied.

"And how long have you lived in Mobile County?" Schnell continued.

"Thirty-five years." Julius had just qualified himself to register. Schnell pressed on. "Are you a veteran?"

"I am." Julius served two years in the service during World War II.

"How much schooling have you had?" Schnell could have guessed that. Few colored people stayed in school if a job could be had.

"I passed the eighth grade." Julius looked over at George Wise, a friend who sat nearby in the Board's registration room listening with unusual interest.

"Okay, Julius, I want you to read the third paragraph of Article I, Section 2 of the Federal Constitution." Schnell chose one of the more peculiar and insulting provisions to throw at a colored person. At the 1787 Constitutional Convention, southern colonies had agreed that direct taxes should be assessed based on population, but objected to including slaves as part of the population because slaves were property. However, the South wanted slaves to be counted as white people for the purpose of apportioning the number of federal representatives based on total population. The Convention delegates compromised: 10 slaves would count as 6 free persons for purposes of taxation and representation. This resolution drew comment from founding father James Madison:

> We must deny the fact that slaves are considered merely as property, and in no respect whatever as persons. The federal Constitution, therefore, decides with great propriety on the case of our slaves, when it views them in the mixed character of persons and of property. This is in fact their true character. It is the character bestowed on them by the laws under which they live. If the laws were to restore the rights which have been taken away, the Negroes could no longer be refused an equal share of representation with the other inhabitants. Let the case of the slaves be considered, as it is in truth, a peculiar one.

The peculiar slave question ceased on December 6, 1865, when the Thirteenth Amendment abolished slavery. By virtue of the Fourteenth Amendment in 1868, representation would be apportioned on the basis of all male citizens, colored and white. In turn, the Fifteenth Amendment assured the right to vote regardless of race or color. Schnell had instructed Julius to read an irrelevant historical footnote, and Julius read as he had been instructed.

"Explain that paragraph, Julius." Schnell set the stage to invoke the Boswell Amendment.

"Yes, Mr. Schnell," Julius responded, "before the Fourteenth Amendment to the Constitution of the United States, a slave was not a citizen, and could not vote, but in figuring how many members a state should have in the House of Representatives, they all agreed that three-fifths of the total number of slaves be added to the number of white citizens to determine the number of representatives a state could have in the House of Representatives." He remembered well what he had been taught. Julius did not learn much about the Constitution in Mobile's segregated schools during the 1930s. What Julius recited came at the hands of Colored church and community groups in 1947. He and other Negroes intended to register despite Boswell and McCorvey. They met at night after work, reading, talking and memorizing the Constitution. Julius might not understand the great political and moral forces that gave birth to Article I, Section 2, paragraph 3, but he could at least remember how to explain it.

Even so, Schnell found Julius lacking. "I'm afraid that just won't do. Your answer ain't satisfactory, Julius." Schnell tried not to sound harsh.

"But Mr. Schnell, I explained it accordin' to my understandin'." Julius dared to stand ground just like he had been taught.

"I can't qualify you to register, Julius." Schnell turned to others awaiting registration, ending the discussion.

Julius Cook said nothing more. While waiting his turn, Julius watched white folks coming upstairs to register. They all qualified. Schnell and Randle did not question white applicants about the Constitution. Schnell did question and reject one other Negro on January 7, 1948, Russell Gaskins, one of the plaintiffs who studied the Constitution with Julius.

Johnnie Q. Laine, 22 years old, was a literate World War II veteran. He walked into the Board of Registrars on Monday, January 19, 1948, Robert E. Lee's birthday, while Schnell and Randle held session without Gunny. Schnell questioned Laine, but the veteran's answers failed to satisfy Schnell. That same day, Schnell also quizzed Russell July, Jr., John Daughtry, Monroe Kidd, and W. F. Cunningham. All four had served honorably in World War II. All four were tasked to explain portions of the Constitution to Schnell's satisfaction. Each failed to do so, and each failed to register.

Unlike some of his co-plaintiffs, Hunter Davis was not a veteran. Hunter had appeared with George Wise before Schnell and Randle on November 7, 1947, to see what might happen. George had tried to register once before, but had no witness. And George knew he could not explain the Constitution any better than Hunter Davis. Hunter had lived all his 35 years in Alabama. He was raised in Whistler. Whistler is as Alabama as Alabama gets.

"How much schooling you got, Hunter?" Schnell asked.

"Well, I got past the sixth grade, I did," Hunter answered.

"Now Hunter, since you've got education you ought to be able to explain the United States Constitution," Schnell continued, "like this here part of Article I, Section 2."

Hunter stared at Section 2 a good while, straining to remember what to say. "The number of representatives and the amount of direct taxes would be determined in each state by its population. Since some states held slaves and slaves were not citizens or voters and could not be counted as such it was agreed three-fifths of the number of slaves be added to the number of citizens to establish the population of a state. The count to be made three years after the meeting of the first Congress, and every ten years after that. But the Fourteenth Amendment changed all that by giving citizenship to the slaves."

Schnell did not ask any more questions of Hunter Davis. For a 35 year-old sixth-grader, Hunter had answered surprisingly well, but not well enough. Schnell figured Hunter just talked a good line. "Hunter, I'm not satisfied with your answer." Schnell explained.

"Didn't I explain it right, Mr. Schnell?" Hunter asked.

"Well, you might have, Hunter, but I'm not satisfied that you understand the Constitution." Schnell finished with Hunter.

The lawsuit did not discourage Schnell. He faithfully discharged his duties to the people of Alabama without hesitation. Even as the Board Chairman prepared for trial, he diligently questioned Coloreds to ensure their understanding of the Constitution. On October 15, 1948 Schnell refused to register Ulysses S. Reed, a colored World War II veteran. Though Schnell found Reed's explanation of the U. S. Constitution to be unsatisfactory, he registered nine Whites that day without any questioning. Boswell's scheme to remedy the Colored problem gave the Board such discretion. The law did not require that a registrar demonstrate an educated grasp of constitutional law. The law required that Coloreds demonstrate their grasp of constitutional law.

Shortly after Hunter Davis filed suit, Gunny threatened to take the Board to the county grand jury. Though law permitted registering anyone who could meet residency requirements at the time of the general election, Schnell and Randle had only registered those who met residency requirements at the time of registering. Within 24 hours, Schnell and Randle reluctantly capitulated. The Chairman pursued another agenda, a damage-control strategy triggered by the *Davis v. Schnell* lawsuit. On Thursday, March 18, Schnell announced in the *Press* that he proposed a non-discriminatory policy of requiring all applicants to explain the Constitution in writing. Gunny had never heard Schnell suggest such a policy. Gunny could have ignored Schnell's ruse, but silence implied agreement. The next day Gunny distanced himself by publicly denying that Schnell ever made such a proposal and by openly opposing any form of Boswell interrogation.

Schnell's prudent window-dressing strategy continued to unfold in response to Gunny's attacks. With unprecedented fanfare, the Chairman announced that the Board had registered 21 Coloreds and 13 Whites on April 4, 1948. Although intended to dispel claims that the Board fostered racial discrimination under the Boswell Amendment, Schnell's bizarre gambit provoked mixed reactions. Those sharing McCorvey's concern about the possibility of colored voting majorities found little comfort with Schnell's news. Those familiar with *Davis v. Schnell* proceedings against the Board smelled a rat. Schnell also boasted that the number of registered voters had reached an all-time high of 28,008, an increase of 2917 in just one year. Of course, that included hundreds of dead and missing that Gunny demanded the Board purge from the rolls. But Schnell and Randle declined, protesting a lack of authority. Instead, Schnell and *The Mobile Register* asked readers to scan the voting list and report anyone suspected of having died. Meanwhile, Schnell said he would obtain the Attorney General's opinion, without pledging to follow it. *The Mobile Register* took Gunny to task for constant upheavals within the Board: "If it's not one thing with the Mobile County Board of Registrars, it's another." That much was true. Pointing an accusing finger of judgment, the

Register portrayed Gunny as afflicted with a "childish display of temperament resembling nothing else so much as a little boy taking his ball and going home because he can't be captain of the team." This much was partially true: Gunny intended to change captain Schnell's rules.

Milton Schnell had served as a registrar for 8 years and clearly understood the importance of his job. Schnell assumed personal responsibility for implementing the Boswell Amendment, especially with Coloreds. Schnell was in his elements, exercising unfettered discretion over whether a Colored's explanation of the Constitution passed muster. As the minority member of the Board, Gunny enjoyed little influence with Schnell and Randle. His public criticism of Schnell and Randle supported daily columns in local newspapers. Gunny represented job security for as many reporters as editors. Schnell knew not to expect Gunny to help screen out Coloreds. That Gunny also called for a grand jury investigation added insult to injury. When *The Mobile Register* defended Schnell and Randle, readers questioned why the newspaper would not endorse an investigation into reports that Whites also were being denied their constitutional rights.

Since passage of the Boswell Amendment, all of 104 Coloreds had been registered to vote in Mobile, for a total of 801 as of May 1948. Coloreds represented less than three percent of registered voters, but constituted a third of Mobile County's population. This fulfilled Gessner McCorvey's prophecy that few Coloreds were fit for civic responsibility, and reassured Mobile's establishment that democratic institutions remained in good hands, for the moment. On July 6, 1948, the Board reported that 67 new voters had been added, but that one colored applicant "was rejected because of failure to give proper answers to qualifying questions." On Monday August 16, 1948 the Board registered 52 new voters from Pritchard, Chickasaw, and Citronelle where municipal elections were scheduled for September. Schnell turned down 4 Coloreds who failed "to give satisfactory answers to questions concerning the United States Constitution." Gunny again called for a grand jury investigation. On August 20, 1948 the *Labor News* observed that "things have come to a mighty pretty pass when the minority member, Gunny Gonzales, has to ask for an investigation of the activities of the Board." On September 3, Gunny again demanded eliminating the witness voucher requirement. In Montgomery, the *People's Forum* published Gunny's criticism of requiring honorably discharged WWII veterans to have vouching witnesses:

> These same veterans fought to preserve the Constitution of this country and it is my belief that the majority members of the Board here are depriving these veterans of their Constitutional Rights to vote, by doubting their honesty. The U.S. Government didn't doubt their honesty when these same men went into the Armed Forces.

Two days later, *The Mobile Register* published a photo of applicants crowding into a special session of the Board. One of the applicants wore a suit and tie, the only Colored in the crowd, and from the photo apparently lacked a witness.

On September 21, 1948 Assistant Attorney General Silas C. Garrett, III filed a brief in Judge McDuffie's federal court defending Alabama's Boswell Amendment against attacks that it barred colored voting registration. Judge McDuffie took Garrett's motion to dismiss under advisement. While the court considered whether to dismiss the complaint without a trial, the October 15 *Labor News* edition reported a dramatic broadside by Gunny against the Board and Boswell's system:

> I charge that this witness system is used as a weapon to keep the majority of the people of this county from registering to vote and also from exercising their Constitutional Rights in local affairs, by being unable to vote.
>
> Since I became a member of this board, I have seen many veterans of World War II deprived of their Constitutional Rights to vote, because they were refused the right to register, when, unknowingly, they had no witness with them at the time they appeared before the board. There are many other citizens who have appeared before the board to register, but were denied their rights, because they had no witness.
>
> However, there are certain local politicians who make it their business to visit the board whenever it's in session to act as a witness for many applicants in order to further their own polit-

ical ambitions. A majority of these type of witnesses have to ask
the applicant the questions in regards to the applicant's qualification, when this witness should know this information in
regards to the applicant's qualifications personally before
acting as a witness. They openly ask the applicant the following questions: 'How long have you resided in Alabama? How
long in Mobile County? What street do you live on and how
long have you lived there?'

Indeed, from October 1947 to September 1948, Pritchard Mayor G.
V. "Red" Dismukes witnessed the applications of 280 people, swearing that
he had known them all at least two years. That substantially increased the
number of tiny Pritchard's active voters. Red Dismukes knew how to get re-
elected. He won by a landslide on September 20, 1948, but most of
Dismukes' knowledge about his 280 new constituents apparently came
from working the stairs at 109 St. Emanuel. When a prominent witness
vouched for obviously unknown applicants, the Board seemed much more
flexible about bending its procedural yardsticks. Even *The Mobile Press* reluctantly expressed concern about the Board's pattern of witness-vouching.

Some viewed Gunny's most recent attack as just another round in his
continuing squabble with Schnell and Randle. McCorvey and *The Mobile
Press* applauded the Board's refusal to register just any one. However,
Assistant Attorney General Garrett saw Gunny's statement through a more
narrowly focused lens. Garrett could hardly afford for the court to con-
clude that the witness rule served as a barrier against Coloreds and a ruse
for the politically connected. In the midst of a lawsuit, defendants are cautioned to avoid statements that may bolster the plaintiffs' case. As a defendant and agent of the State, Registrar Gonzales provided the colored plaintiffs with ammunition every time he publicly attacked Schnell and Randle.
Garrett could not pick up a paper in Mobile without feeling another fresh
wound to his defense. Then, on October 24, white Alabama lawyers added
salt to Garrett's wounds by filing a companion lawsuit, this time in the
name of Ulysses S. Reed. Reed's lawsuit demonstrated a good grasp of constitutional law. It was too late, though, for Schnell to register Reed.

The Veterans of Foreign Wars invited Schnell and Gonzales to
appear before them on Thursday, December 9, 1948. Gunny said

nothing that the VFW had not already seen in the newspaper. But veterans wanted to hear from the minority registrar who spoke up for them. The gloss of VJ Day had worn off over the past three years. Being a veteran did not land a job or win a voice in government. Gunny preached political power to an historically non-political choir. He argued that honorably discharged veterans should not have to vouch for their qualifications to vote. The VFW liked this new gospel and unanimously adopted a resolution joining forces with Gunny:

> Whereas, the privilege of voting is one of the most precious rights and heritages of an American citizen, and Whereas, the American veteran who has fought on foreign soil to protect that right should be deeply interested in the exercise of that right and privilege, and Whereas, the State of Alabama has exempted all veterans from the payment of poll taxes in order to encourage their voting and to show the gratitude of the state, and Whereas, many veterans have never registered or availed themselves of this right and privilege, and Whereas, on certain occasions, veterans have applied for registration and due to not having a legal voter to vouch for them, they have been refused the opportunity to register as voters,
>
> Now, therefore, be it resolved that Robert L. Bullard Post No. 49, Veterans of Foreign Wars of the United States, does hereby urge all veterans to become legal voters and that the Board of Registrars of Mobile County amend their rules to allow any veteran upon the presentation of his honorable discharge to sign his own affidavit, without a supporting affidavit of a legal voter of Mobile County, Alabama, in order that he may become registered to vote.

The confidence of Mobile's white majority, including those who shared Boswell's vision of the future, began to waver under constant front page attacks. For Schnell and Randle to persuade the court that they objectively applied the Boswell Amendment, Garrett would need to show that the Board's policies also restricted white applicants. While this might bolster Garrett's legal defense that Boswell Amendment practices adversely affected Whites and Coloreds alike, he risked antagonizing the political support of white registered voters who sympathized with veterans, especially white veterans.

On December 10, 1948 the *Veterans Journal's* front-page fanned the fire: "GONZALES SAYS DISCHARGE IS SUFFICIENT." Gunny demanded that the Board unconditionally register both white and colored veterans. It was an unspeakable breach of political protocol for a State registrar to suggest that the Board denied white veterans the vote as part of a ruse to deny colored veterans the vote. It was political heresy for a state official to advocate registering Coloreds without regard to the Boswell Amendment's requirements. Pragmatists saw huge risks and little payoff in Gunny's bold demands.

Schnell understood the risk that special treatment of veterans could present during his upcoming trial. Schnell and Si Garrett would argue to the court that the Board of Registrars' rules applied equally to all applicants. Anything less than that would give the colored plaintiffs evidence of unfair treatment. Schnell would not shoot his own foot again. Carefully prepared, Schnell counter-attacked, putting the veterans on the defensive by rhetorically suggesting that they wanted special privileges.

Of course, the VFW and American Legion wanted to avoid the appearance of favoritism. By insinuating that veterans unfairly sought special treatment, Schnell dodged the ulterior agenda behind witness-vouching. Schnell's reply reflected Boswell's gospel that voting is a privilege, not a matter of right. The chairman had outflanked the veterans, but not Gunny. Taking Schnell to task, Gunny ridiculed the Board's refusal to accept a veteran's sworn statement about his own name and residence. If a veteran is untrustworthy, a sworn witness would not make it otherwise. If veterans can deceive, so can witnesses. Requiring a witness, Gunny argued, was simply a device to limit and reject voters.

On December 17, 1948, the United Veterans of World War II and the Jewish War Veterans joined the VFW, demanding that the Board "allow any veteran upon presentation of his honorable discharge to sign his own affidavit" and register. Gunny had successfully enlisted powerful allies in his assault against Mobile's political machine. Yet Schnell could not allow a colored veteran to register unconditionally. If one Colored was exempt from the witness rule, all Coloreds had to be exempt. If one Colored could not be questioned about the

Constitution, none could be questioned. If the Boswell Amendment did not apply to one Colored, it did not apply to any. Gunny put Schnell between a rock and a hard place. In order to control colored voting strength, colored applicants had to be screened, questioned, vouched, and whenever possible, rejected. Veterans made no difference, except that in order to screen colored veterans all veterans had to be screened. Schnell had to be consistent. His trial started in three days. He could not cave in, even to several thousand veterans. Schnell represented Alabama. He had to protect Alabama from those unfit to govern themselves, much less their betters. Schnell also had to protect himself. Despite Gunny's public attacks, Schnell continued to reject Coloreds and veterans.

CHAPTER 26

Evening at the Battle House

The Battle House Hotel lent Mobile a touch of elegance, a vehicle of commerce, and an occasion of sin. It sheltered the wealthy and allowed men of purpose to be important. Its aging halls witnessed both proud and profane moments, and would witness them again.

The unexpected call came late on Sunday night, December 19, 1948. Gunny picked up the receiver, unprepared for the voice at the other end. "Gunny, this is Si Garrett. How're you doing tonight?" Garrett knew how Gunny was doing. He knew how, on the eve of trial, a defendant reacts to a knock at the door, a telephone ring, and the unnatural world of the courtroom. The plaintiffs' damage claims against the Board had placed a price on Gunny's head, and an adverse verdict could put Mobile's minority registrar in the poorhouse. Alabama's Attorney General knew how vulnerable Gunny would be just hours before trial. Garrett's call was smart and effective.

"I've got no complaint." Gunny bluffed, nervously laughing to put himself at ease. It did not help. He still felt awkward. Like it or not, Gunny knew he was tethered to the man on the other end of the line, a lawyer, a politician, a voice that represented the State of Alabama and its registrars. Garrett was nobody's fool, and no one to fool with. Garrett read Gunny's reaction as a good sign.

"Gunny, I know it's late and you probably have other things to do. But I'm down here at the Battle House getting ready for trial tomorrow.

You know, this is a big case Gunny. Folks think it's real important. You understand we've gotta be prepared. I wouldn't bother you on a Sunday night if I wasn't concerned about you. I was hoping you might like to come down and go over things with me." Garrett's voice could be reassuring and persuasive. "You may get called to the stand tomorrow." He gently nudged the universal anxiety zone. Once in the witness chair, a defendant expected to be grilled, slowly at first, flipped over occasionally, and then charcoaled as counsel politely admired the results. Experienced trial lawyers practiced their art with finesse and civility.

Gunny had little time to think. There was nothing to think. This was Silas C. Garrett, III, the Assistant Attorney General of the State of Alabama. He was in Mobile to defend registrar Emanuel J. Gonzales in the United States District Court before three federal judges. Si Garrett wanted to prepare his client. A conscientious trial lawyer carefully plots strategy, rehearses expected testimony, and smoothes out evidentiary wrinkles before walking into court. Lawyers plying their trade in traffic and common pleas courts rarely can afford the luxury of such preparation. Gunny had good reason to question why Alabama's Attorney General chose the eve of trial to prepare Gunny for trial.

Having Governor Folsom as a co-defendant could provide an umbrella of political coverage for Schnell, Gonzales, and Randle. They were just three of many registrars throughout the state. Though Folsom was governor, the state's chief law enforcer, registrars mostly depended on the Attorney General to guide their work. By comparison, registrars seemed like small fry in this constitutional brawl. Big Jim remained a bigger than life populist in whose political shadow they wanted to wage a defense. It also was not lost on Schnell, Randle, and McCorvey that Governor Folsom had appointed Gunny to the Board. However tempted Gunny might be to side with Coloreds against Schnell and Randle, the Party leaders in Montgomery figured Gunny would not pull the house down on himself and the governor just to spite McCorvey, Boswell, and Schnell.

Initially, trial had been set to begin on November 5, 1948. Si Garrett's attempt to dismiss the case on purely legal grounds did not impress this court. Silver-tongued counsel were not going to talk their way out of this one. This case would go to trial. But, instead of an umbrella of protection Governor Folsom, Representative Boswell, and State Party Chairman McCorvey might have provided for their co-defendants, Schnell, Randle, and Gonzales learned that they would stand trial alone. The plaintiffs' attorneys announced that Folsom, Boswell and McCorvey would be voluntarily dismissed from the case. Governor Folsom, not an essential party anyway, could have under-mined the plaintiffs' case simply by his historical opposition to any dis-criminatory application of the Boswell Amendment. His dismissal, however, changed the nature of the case. No glue of mutual interests bound the three registrars to a common defense. The federal tribunal understood that the Board had to revise its strategy in the wake of dis-missing the Governor and other co-defendants. So the court post-poned the trial to December. Governor Folsom would not be there to support his political ally. Gunny would have to go it alone.

Si Garrett still had to defend the Board and State of Alabama before a federal constitutional tribunal. Winging a defense under these circumstances would be monumental folly. Nothing could be taken for granted. Unlike elected or appointed State officials, a federal judge enjoys a lifetime appointment mostly immune from external political and social pressures, and employs an arsenal of powers. A federal judge does not need courage to render an unpopular decision. Courage cor-responds with risks, most of which had been assumed by a rookie State registrar. However, other political stakes now stood high, placing careers and personal ambitions, especially Garrett's, on the line. A win would give Silas a shot at Attorney General Carmichael's office in 1950. Any flaw in his strategy had to be cured by dawn.

"I can be there in about an hour." Gunny committed himself.

"Glad to hear that. Just come on up to my room. See you in a while." Garrett put down the receiver. The later the better.

Gunny paused, staring for a moment at nothing in particular. "That was Si Garrett. He's at the Battle House and wants to talk to me tonight about the trial in the morning." Gunny spoke to himself as much as to Anne. The decision did not come easy. "I've got to go downtown." Joe and Jimmy, listening to a radio serial, were unaware of what was about to happen.

"I want you to drive down with me. I don't know how long this is gonna last, but I smell a skunk. Si Garrett hasn't said a goddamn word to me in months. Why the hell is he calling me now? What do we have to talk about? That sonofabitch knows where I stand. I wouldn't be at all surprised if Schnell and that frozen-face Randle woman are sitting there in the room with him right now. I don't like it. I don't like it one goddamn bit." Gunny was not happy to be drawn into a hopelessly compromising situation. He had chosen the public forum to wage battle. Meeting alone with Garrett put Gunny at a distinct disadvantage. It would be a long ride downtown.

Gunny and Anne still lived on Bobolink Drive in Birdville. Their front porch crouched in the shadow of Brookley Field's great checkerboard water tower, from which slowly spun a lantern warning off circling aircraft. The lantern alternately bathed Bobolink in red and green every few seconds. In the chill of night Anne packed Jimmy and five year-old Joe into the back seat of their black 1939 Ford. Gunny drove north on Michigan Avenue, past the GM&N tracks at Hartwell Field, up to Government Street and then east to Broad. Few cars trafficked Mobile on Sunday night. At Broad he turned north, then east on Dauphin down to Bienville Square, hurriedly passing Dr. Englert's lawyer son on the way. As Gunny neared the Woolworth store on Dauphin, attorney Englert leaned out his car window, calling Gunny a son of a bitch for passing him. Both cars continued on to Royal. Gunny parked directly in front of the Battle House. Englert pulled up next to the nearby Federal Building. Anne and the boys stayed in the car. Gunny walked over to Englert's car, opened the door, and punched Englert in the mouth. The lawyer's cry for help caught the ear of police Lieutenant LaGuire, who turned and recognized the former cop. "Hey Gunny, what's goin' on over there?" LaGuire shouted across the deserted street.

"Not a whole lot right now. I was coming down to see Attorney General Si Garrett at the Battle House and smart-mouth Englert here leans out his car and calls me a sonofabitch in front of my wife and little boys." Gunny waived at the 1939 Ford next to the hotel. "I don't have to take that kinda bullshit off some smart-ass lawyer. I shut his mouth up. And if he opens his mouth again, I'm gonna punch him again." The common law notion that provocative words might excuse a proportionate responsive physical assault still enjoyed some currency in Alabama.

"Well, hell, Gunny," LaGuire sympathized, "in that case you go right ahead." Englert astutely sized up the situation and chose not to press charges.

Instead, Gunny turned and directed his attention toward the Battle House's main entrance. Some 20 years earlier at this same hour, a little fireplug of a barefoot kid hawked early editions of the *Picayune* near the same doorway. Tonight, the Governor's dissident registrar had more serious business at the Battle House.

A well-groomed uniformed doorman solemnly raised his arm and directed Gunny to move his car. "You can't park here. This here area is reserved for guests of the Battle House." The doorman had grown accustomed to speaking with authority, especially to those of no apparent importance.

Gunny turned slightly as he marched through the front door, a reservoir of adrenaline still pumping through his system. "The hell you say I can't. I'm here to see Si Garrett, the Attorney General. While I'm upstairs, I'm parking my car right there. And it had damn well better be there when I see you again." Gunny went into the lobby, leaving the doorman to do whatever he dared. The doorman made it a point to know when anyone of real importance was in town at the hotel. Si Garrett was in town for almost a week. The doorman wanted no trouble with Mr. Garrett or his people coming and going at night. Turning to look at the 1939 Ford, the doorman watched a little boy and toddler get out of the car and circle it slowly, over and over. It was best to let this sleeping dog lie.

Gunny found Garrett's suite and tapped a familiar knock. The Attorney General opened the door. Their eyes sized up one another silently, then broke off to scan the room. Gunny was wrong about

Schnell and Randle. They were not there, but someone else was. The ward heeler knew nearly everyone in Mobile County. He tried to match a name with the face, but he had not met this face before. Si Garrett paused and then introduced Gunny to Bud Boswell, Representative Boswell, Alabama's white supremacy strategist. Gunny was being sued because of this man. Gunny suddenly felt in over his head.

No one offered Gunny a drink. Garrett quickly got to the point, omitting customary pleasantries about the family. The Attorney General removed some papers from his brief case. Garrett did not mention his meeting with Schnell in Montgomery the past few months to prepare for trial. Garrett knew Schnell did not speak for Gunny. Garrett suspected but did not know what Gunny would say in court tomorrow. This could prove to be difficult, but the die was cast. Gunny's response would determine his own fate.

"Gunny, I want you to take these pleadings home tonight and study them. The plaintiffs' allegations are in there. We are denying their allegations. You shouldn't have any problem with that. You know, we just can't have unfit people registering to vote. The Board's got to make sure that doesn't happen. It isn't discrimination to register only qualified voters. It's your duty. If Coloreds are qualified, we register them like anyone else. We are going to show that there are hundreds of colored voters. We don't treat colored folks differently than Whites. We treat everybody the same. But if you can't agree with any of these denials, Gunny, I will have to eliminate you from the defense. Milton and Mrs. Randle already have agreed to everything here." Garrett laid it out directly, in simple terms, just the way he planned.

"I'll take it home and study it. I'll give you my answer in the morning. But I want you to know Mr. Garrett, I'm not gonna lie for you." Gunny had no choice and he knew it. Garrett had planned very well. There would not be time for Gunny to hire his own lawyer. Garrett had cornered the minority registrar on the eve of trial.

"Thanks for coming down, Gunny." Garrett showed Gunny the door. Driving home seemed longer than the ride downtown. Night was short and morning would come fast.

CHAPTER 27

For the Defense

Sunrise on December 20, 1948 came slowly for the masses anxious
to pack Judge McDuffie's courtroom. Coloreds and Whites alike
sensed something important about to happen in Mobile. Clergymen
of both colors mixed in silence, seeking peace in the temple of justice,
awaiting deliverance from one form of evil or another. They expected
something more than a battle of evidence and test of law. The forces of
light and darkness seemed to gather at this time and place to test the
mettle of justice. Yet, whatever power reposed within the robes of these
three white judges likely would remain sheathed absent compelling
reason to act. Ten Colored plaintiffs claimed wrongs suffered at the
hands of three white and presumably honest public servants who were
faithfully discharging their sworn duties. Absent something close to a
smoking gun, those claims compelled nothing.

Under the scrutiny of probing gallery eyes, teams of lawyers stirred
impatiently at the semi-circular counsel table below the judicial altar.
From this sanctuary the lawyers viewed a congregation of mixed color
and creed. In the moments before a gavel announced the tribunal's
majestic entry, the crowd noticed Gunny Gonzales slowly walk up to
the Attorney General and hand Si Garrett some papers. For many
months folks had read colorful front-page stories about Gunny and the
Board. There, in open court, two-dimensional newspaper caricatures
gave way to life-size walking, talking figures. The congregation studied

every move, sensing this drama would affect them all, though not knowing how.

Si Garrett scanned the denials asserted by Schnell and Randle that Gunny reviewed overnight. Gunny had circled several. Alabama's Attorney General looked up. "Well Gunny, what's it gonna be?" Garrett put the challenge in Gunny's lap.

"I cannot agree with the circled denials." Gunny did not fully appreciate the consequences of the moment, but would not crawl in bed with Schnell, Randle, and Boswell. Everyone watched Mobile's most controversial figure confer with Alabama's Attorney General, the power from Montgomery, and then walk the length of Judge McDuffie's courtroom to sit near the court's exit. Defendants by right normally sit inside the rail at counsel's table near the judge. Gunny figured the exit was close enough for him. Garrett anticipated Gunny's response. Garrett's expression remained steady, fully prepared, betraying his thoughts to no one.

A hush fell as three black robes emerged on the high altar and a voice cried that all who sought justice should draw nigh. There was no room to draw anywhere, much less nigh. Presiding Judge McCord surveyed the pit of lawyers crouching below the bench like predators sniffing prey. "Are all parties ready to proceed?"

Attorney General Garrett rose, speaking with a seasoned air of confidence. "Your Honors, before answering ready, I would like to make known to the court that we find it necessary to withdraw our representation of one of the defendants in this case, Mr. E. J. Gonzales. I called the Chairman of the Board of Registrars, Mr. Schnell, and told him we were desirous of having a conference in Montgomery, for the purpose of preparing the Answer in this case, and would like to have him and both other members of the board, if they cared to come to Montgomery for that conference; but, in any event, we would like to have him present as Chairman. He and Mr. Carl Booth, Mobile's circuit solicitor, came. The other two members did not come. We conferred there all one day and most of one night, and, while Mr. Booth and Mr. Schnell were present, we prepared the Answer.

"I have talked to the chairman and secretary of the board, and we agreed upon a conference here of all the parties yesterday afternoon, and I asked that all of the defendants be notified. I am advised by Mr. Booth that they were notified, and all of the defendants together with counsel whom I have mentioned were present for the conference yesterday afternoon at the appointed hour, again with the exception of Mr. Gonzales. We held that conference. I sent for Mr. Gonzales personally, and told him I wanted to see him. He came to see me. After talking with him very briefly, I learned for the first time that it was possible that he might not be able to go along with the other defendants in the defense of this case. I want to say, in fairness to him, that at no time had I discussed the case personally with him since its inception."

It may have seemed gracious to unschooled bystanders that Mr. Garrett displayed such civility and fairness to E. J. Gonzales, despite an evident difference of opinion. In fact, Garrett's opening remarks were calculated to portray unity among all defendants except one, while disclaiming having obtained any privileged attorney-client information from Gunny which might disqualify Garrett from attacking the dissident registrar on cross-examination.

Judge McCord's interest stirred. "Does Mr. Gonzales not want to defend? Is that it?" The Court did not expect a confession of judgment in a case fraught with important constitutional implications.

Garrett had anticipated some initial confusion. "He will have to answer that himself. I am not prepared to state that he does not want to defend, but he tells me that he cannot go along with the other defendants, Mr. Schnell and Mrs. Randle, in their defense. May I call the Court's attention to the fact that Alabama statute requires Mr. Booth to defend the Board of Registrars, and under our statute, the action of a majority of the Board shall be the action of the board. What I would like to do is this. We are prepared to proceed right now, representing the two individual members of the board, Mr. Schnell and Mrs. Randle, and the Board of Registrars."

Judge McCord savored the opening drama. "They constitute a majority."

"That is correct. The only change I would have to make in my Answer is to ask that each and every reference to Mr. Gonzales, both individually and in his official capacity, be stricken." In doing so, Garrett smoothly withdrew the Answer and denials filed on Gunny's behalf, leaving him individually vulnerable to judgment.

Judge McDuffie filtered the music from Garrett's static. At first blush it made little difference whether one lawyer or three talked on behalf of these registrars. "Whatever happens is going to happen to Mr. Gonzales as well as to the rest."

Si Garrett had prepared to take the high road, invoking ethical canons that ennobled the legal profession and permitted him to cut his clients' losses. "I and my associates did not feel that we, in good conscience, could continue to represent this man when we are in disagreement as to the defense to be made."

Judge McCord, hearing enough about Mr. Gonzales, decided to meet him. "Mr. Gonzales is in Court?"

"Yes, sir." In the distant corner of the courtroom near the exit, Gunny stood, unsure exactly what to say or do.

Judge McCord wanted to test the water. "Your name has been brought up. You do not want to defend in this case?"

"I would like to explain my stand. Things have been said that I think are not true." Calling the Attorney General a liar in open court slipped out easier than Gunny thought. "May I defend myself?"

The Court absorbed the thickening plot. "Yes, sir. You will *have* to defend yourself."

"Mr. Garrett, whom I respect very much, said the Board of Registrars was notified of a meeting in Montgomery. I was not." The congregation stirred. Its Attorney General had fibbed.

Silas quickly reacted to defend his slighted integrity. "I said I did not notify you personally."

Judge McCord did not want anyone to lose focus. "Here is the point. Do you want to go along and let your defense go along with the others?"

"Judge, I cannot quite agree with all the allegations. I don't think you or anyone else would agree to something that is not so." Gunny took an even higher road, suggesting the court should read between the lines of Garrett's Answer to the complaint.

The Court was interested to hear whatever Gunny had to say, good or bad, about Mobile's Board of Registrars. "If you want to offer yourself as a witness, you may do so, but the representation of your board is going on in just a minute."

Standing alone before the power of the United States, Gunny turned and pointed at the Attorney General. "He says he does not want to represent me unless I agree to that paper."

Garrett jumped to his feet again. "I don't care whether he agrees or not, but my associates and I cannot continue to defend him if he differs with our way of doing it. We just cannot represent him."

Judge McDuffie was still trying to sort out what might be fueling the verbal sparring. "Mr. Garrett, you represent the board. As to representing individual members of the board as to whom this suit is filed, you say you cannot represent Mr. Gonzales, but your representation is of the board majority by virtue of the fact that two members of the board are in accord with your viewpoint?"

"That is correct."

Judge McCord issued the Court's first ruling. "The court wants to notify you, Mr. Gonzales, that you may represent yourself."

Gunny was not quite sure what it meant to represent himself. "Can I defend myself?"

Judge McCord managed a grin. "Yes, sir, just sit right down. You can defend yourself. You have a right to defend yourself. We are going to protect every right you have." Judge McCord scanned the length of the semi-circular counsel table. "You can sit right here with counsel. Are we ready to proceed?"

Garrett did not look at Gunny. Silas had not considered this option in his game plan. Without a lawyer to protect him, Gunny actually became somewhat less vulnerable to sniping attacks by Garrett and the plaintiffs' attorneys who feared the appearance of unfairly badgering an undefended defendant. The congregation could sense that something important had just happened, but did not quite know what to make of it. Gunny found his place at defense counsel table, near Garrett. He was in the den with tigers that could readily destroy him. They were poised, educated, and shrewd. Gunny remained an unschooled populist. But for now, the former Whippet, football end, ward heeler, and ship welder had been admitted to practice law *pro se* before a federal tribunal in an unprecedented case of constitutional dimensions. It would be 20 years before another Gonzales would appear as counsel in this courtroom. In the meanwhile, Gunny would just have to make do.

With that distraction behind them, Judge McCord ordered the plaintiffs to call their first witness.

Judge McDuffie leaned over to Judge McCord. "You don't want them to state the case?" Then, answering his own question with belated second thoughts, Judge McDuffie expressed some dismay. "I guess they had better not. It would take too much time."

After reflecting a moment, Judge McCord invited an opening statement from plaintiffs' counsel. "Have you something to say before you call the first witness?"

Plaintiffs' attorney George Leighton wanted to take advantage of every break he got. "We want to make an opening statement for the purpose of the record."

Judge McCord knew that trial lawyers lived by the word. "Please make it as brief as possible, Mr. Leighton."

"May it please the Court, Mr. Garrett, Mr. Boswell, and Mr. Booth." Mr. Leighton overlooked Mr. Gonzales. Leighton then began to read from prepared text, just what Judge McDuffie dreaded. "This is an action by ten citizens of the United States, residing in the state of Alabama and in Mobile County. The defendants, E. J. Gonzales, Milton Schnell, who was Chairman of the Board, and Mrs. D. C. Randle, acting under color of law of their office, as members of the Board of Registrars, did deny these plaintiffs the right to register as voters in Mobile County, and in denying them, demanded that these plaintiffs read, write, understand and explain an article of the federal constitution. And after hearing the answers given by these plaintiffs, the defendant Mr. Schnell told these plaintiffs that he was not satisfied with their explanation and understanding of the federal constitution. These particular persons could not tell in advance whether they could qualify because of the vague requirements of the board. Members of the white race were not asked such questions and were allowed to register without any questions about the constitution.

"This board, acting by majority, has been applying and enforcing a policy by which Negro applicants are asked questions concerning the Constitution of the United States, but white applicants are not. Section 181, Constitution of Alabama, as amended in November 1946, vests in the Board unlimited discretion to grant or deny to the plaintiffs and all the other members of this class on whose behalf this suit is brought, the right to register without providing any recognizable standard or test to be applied by defendants to determine the qualifications of plaintiffs in accordance with due process of law." Leighton's speech ended surprisingly soon. The only notable twist seemed to be an implicit admission that minority registrar Gonzales had not violated the plaintiffs' constitutional rights, since everybody including the Court fully understood that Schnell and Randle ran the Board. Leighton had argued nothing more than these 10 Coloreds had to answer questions that Whites never got asked. That could be hard for Leighton to prove and easy for Garrett to finesse.

Judge McCord thought he'd missed something. "That is your whole case?"

Mr. Leighton rambled on. "These plaintiffs are acting on their own and on behalf of a large group of qualified Negro citizens of Mobile County, who at various dates did appear before this board, and who were asked to read, write, understand and explain articles of the federal constitution, and after they read it and gave answers similar to answers given by plaintiffs, they were told by Mr. Schnell, as chairman, that they were not qualified to register and their answers did not satisfy him."

Judge McDuffie honed in on the obvious weakness with plaintiffs' theory. "Is not your problem the class action? Is it your idea that these tests were applied to one class and not to another?" Leighton garbled his response. The Court then invited the Attorney General to make an opening statement.

Garrett half-rose from his chair. "We stand on our answer." Nothing could be gained by saying something that inadvertently might enlighten opposing counsel or provoke Gunny. Anyway, the judges already knew the position of the Board of Registrars from numerous pre-trial motions, briefs, and hearings. Formalities done, the Court wanted to hear testimony.

David Landau, plaintiffs' co-counsel, called Chairman Milton Schnell as an adverse party before putting any of his plaintiff clients on the stand. "Mr. Schnell, do the board of registrars have any rules regarding registration under which you operate?"

"Which board?" Schnell chose to treat an easy opening pitch as a knuckleball.

Even Landau was taken aback. Trickier questions would come later. "The Board of Registrars of Mobile County?"

"I served on three boards. Which board are you speaking of?" The Chairman of the Board could split hairs with the best.

But Judge McDuffie had no patience with clever semantics. "There is not but one board of registrars."

Schnell had been well prepared. "We have a new board every four years."

"Were the rules approved and passed upon by three members of the board?"

Another soft lob over the plate, which Schnell ought to have confronted, but chose instead to be coy. "At least a majority of the board."

Landau sensed that he was going to pull facts out of Chairman Schnell one tooth at a time, but overlaid the moment with slight sarcasm. "You are not sure?"

The Court got a glimpse into what Gunny's life was like at 109 St. Emanuel Street. "At least a majority."

"You are not sure whether it was by a majority of the board or all three members of the board?"

"I am sure it was by a majority." Schnell would not admit the obvious.

Judge McDuffie tired of the play between counsel and witness. "Do you mean they were approved or acted upon by a majority of the board?"

"They were acted upon by all three members of the board." Schnell persisted with semantics.

Landau welcomed prodding from the Court. Schnell's credibility could run aground if he continued to spar over matters of public knowledge. "Did all three members of the board in existence at that time approve the rules?"

"I don't think so." Even when cornered, Schnell would not commit.

"You are not sure?" Landau gently toyed with Schnell's evasive and mysterious responses.

"I am not positive." It seemed that Milton had not been reading the newspaper the last year or so.

"Who do you think didn't approve?"

"I don't think Mr. Gonzales approved of all. He may have approved of some."

"What gives you that idea?" With the possible exception of someone who had not picked up the *Press* or *Press Register* in the past 14 months, most folks in the county would have sworn on their mother's grave that damn few things met with Mr. Gonzales' approval.

"Just remembering."

"Do the rules adopted by the Board of Registrars prescribe a specific manner in which applications for registrations are handled?" Landau decided to move the questioning along.

"In certain particulars, yes, sir." Every answer came wrapped with qualifiers and exceptions, a sign of meticulous preparation by Garrett and Carl Booth that complemented Schnell's disposition.

"In what particulars?" Landau patiently tracked his quarry.

"Well, it's been quite a while since I have seen the regulations we drew up." The Chairman carelessly sought an escape, implying he could not even recall his own rules.

"You don't remember them?"

Schnell regained his faculties. "It prescribes the hours of the board for handling the applications for registration. It stipulates the fact that each applicant shall have a witness, who is a qualified elector of Mobile County, who has known the applicant at least two years."

Landau savored the first decent response of the morning. "All right. Are there any special rules which apply specifically to the handling of Negro applicants?" Emboldened, Landau ventured too quickly into the meat of his examination.

"None whatsoever."

"All right. Are there any which apply specifically to the handling of White applicants?" Landau's technique seemed generously open-ended, nothing that resembled the sort of crisp leading questions expected during the examination of an evasive or adverse witness. However, Landau probably recognized the negative implications of recklessly attacking a white registrar and the State of Alabama without having first established some compelling reason.

"No, there is no difference between the two."

"As far as the rules prescribe, there is no difference in the handling of Negro and White applicants for registration?" Landau finally began to assert himself and lead the witness.

"No difference. No, sir."

"In other words, what duties you have are not prescribed by the rules, but are imposed by statute?" Landau needed to show that the Board's actions were based on statute, not internal housekeeping procedures, in order to attack the Boswell Amendment head-on.

"That is right." Schnell just eliminated local rules as a scapegoat and excuse.

"Explain what would happen if I, as a prospective white voter of Mobile County, came in to register."

Schnell no longer wanted to be coy. This question allowed him to make the State's case, to step up to the plate and hammer the ball. "We ascertain whether or not he has a required qualified witness. We then swear in the witness and the applicant, put them under oath, then they give us information. We want to know from the witness whether he has known the applicant two years, whether he knows where the applicant lives, that he knows the applicant does live in Mobile County, and what part of the county. We ascertain educational qualifications. Generally we can tell. If he is a doctor we don't have to go into educational qualifications. A doctor generally gives

us his title. In some cases where we are in doubt about the educational qualifications, according to Section 181, I ask the applicant just what he has in
the way of education, has he been to school, and has he attended college. If
this white man says he has attended college and has a degree or something
of that sort, we go no further in the investigation of his educational qualifications. We then present him with the application to be filled out and
signed by him and later to be turned back to the board, for the board rec-
ommends as to whether or not he shall be given a certificate."

"Now, you spoke of asking those questions and ascertaining the
educational background of a white person. Do you derive that authority from Section 181 of the Constitution of Alabama?" Landau wanted to firmly link Schnell's actions with the Boswell Amendment.

Schnell saw no risk. "The board derives its authority from all sections in the code pertaining to it."

However, Garrett could foresee problems the longer Schnell wove
a web about his discretionary decisions. "May it please the Court, this
man is not learned in the law. He is a layman. I have with me a copy
of the Constitution of Alabama and also Title 17, Section 33, of the
Code of Alabama. I think they speak for themselves."

Judge McDuffie disagreed. "This witness said he relied upon the code
and that raised the presumption that he knew what sections he relied on,
layman or no layman. I overrule your objection." Garrett sat down.

Landau tightened the loop a little more. "In other words, in determining qualifications under the Boswell Amendment, when you ask a
white man about his educational qualifications and do not ask him any
questions about being able to read, write, understand, and explain the
Constitution of the United States, are you then complying with the law?"

Schnell was still wondering about Garrett's objection. "After the
applicant is put under oath, in a majority of cases we ask them, according to your educational qualifications, do you understand the
Constitution of the United States and can you explain it, and we call
on them to do so." He was not sure how far to commit.

"In a majority of cases, but not in all cases?" Landau took advantage
of the one time that Schnell should not have allowed for any exception.

"In some cases." Schnell changed direction without hesitation.

"In how many cases?" Landau did not particularly care at this point. Any guess would do.

"When we are rushed in the board, each individual member is handling certain applicants, I cannot tell you how many cases." Schnell safely retreated, though already on record that only a minority of applicants were tested about constitutional matters. Landau knew other testimony would show that Schnell took it upon himself to question most of the colored applicants personally. Landau decided to bait the hook.

"Would you say ten percent of the cases?"

"I could not say whether it was in better than fifty percent or less, or whenever necessity arises, that we ask those questions." The chairman took refuge in meaningless babble, protesting ignorance.

A tactical rip in Schnell's legal knickers began to show, though only to the trained eye. "Let me approach it from another angle. You ask every white applicant if he can read, write, understand, and explain the Constitution of the United States, after he has taken the oath and filled out that application form?" At last, Landau seemed willing to testify for Schnell, though not aggressively.

"No, sir."

"All right. Now, when a Negro comes before the board of registrars, is exactly the same procedure followed?"

"Yes, exactly the same procedure is followed." At this point Landau had merely established that neither all Whites nor all Coloreds are questioned.

"Is it not a fact, Mr. Schnell, that when a Negro makes an application before your board, you ask him to read a section of the Constitution and then afterwards ask him what that section means and what his understanding is?"

"In some instances, yes. In some cases, we do." The chairman just confirmed an essential element supporting the plaintiffs' complaint.

"All right. When a Negro makes an application, after you have interrogated him, do you get Mrs. Randle to join you in rejecting or approving that application?"

Schnell saw that one coming. "I do not. I will add to that. I do not get her any more than Mr. Gonzales. It makes no difference." Very deftly, he looped the minority registrar back into the line of fire, a gift Landau accepted.

"Have you ever rejected a Negro application which rejection also was approved by Mr. Gonzales?"

"Yes, sir." Schnell did not suggest any pattern of rejection.

"Does it happen very often?"

"No, it does not happen very often." Schnell implicitly conceded that he and Randle disapproved nearly all Negro applicants.

"You ask a Negro citizen what his education is?"

"Yes, sir."

"You do always?"

"99 chances out of 100 we do, yes, sir, unless we have a doctor or someone of that sort, some person who is a college professor."

"Is it not a fact that you make it your business to handle the applications of a majority of Negroes coming before the board?" Landau revisited his earlier question, locking Schnell into a fast answer.

"When I am in the office, I do."

"You, as a member of the board, would determine to your satisfaction a particular individual's qualifications, regarding his ability to read, write, understand and explain the Constitution of the United States?" Landau needed to explore the Chairman's personal mastery of constitutional issues.

"After the applicant explains it or gives me his interpretation of it, if I don't think it is a proper interpretation, I reject it and pass it on to the next member of the board and see what they want to do with it." Schnell slipped, first by acknowledging that his conclusion might warrant a second opinion, and then by passing the buck to Randle who seldom professed an independent thought.

"What are your educational qualifications, Mr. Schnell?" Landau casually slipped the knife in gently, fully aware of the forthcoming response.

"I am a high school graduate and a University extension student." Milton's response left a pathetically hollow ring in the silent courtroom.

A high school diploma was fairly respectable in Alabama at the time, but not much to crow about when lording over others.

"What background have you had concerning the understanding and interpretation of the Constitution of the United States?"

"Eight years on the board of registrars. Nine years." Schnell answered with pride, the image of a self-taught scholar.

"That is your only qualification?" Landau could barely resist the urge to flavor his tone with incredulity.

Schnell sensed or imagined the mood of the gallery, if not the judges, moving him to pad his underwhelming resume. "Other than the fact that I have read it and studied it at other times prior to the time when I was not on the board." It usually took a public uproar before Schnell would read, much less follow, an opinion of the Attorney General. Newspapers had documented the Board chairman's tendency to dispute or ignore opinions of legal experts. It was simply too much to imagine Schnell studying constitutional law while working at Gill Printing.

Landau had not scored a direct hit by exposing Schnell's overly inflated opinion of himself. Alabama got what it paid for, which sometimes included petty tyrants in the bargain. But Schnell's personal flaws did not necessarily demonstrate intentional discrimination. Landau still needed a smoking gun. And Garrett was not about to cough one up by asking Schnell any questions at this point during the plaintiffs' case. The Attorney General passed the witness. The plaintiffs then called Registrar Myrtle Gay Randle of Coden as an adverse party.

"Was there any reason for differing between colored applicants and white applicants?"

"No." Since Randle was a party defendant, she remained in the courtroom during the testimony of Schnell and other witnesses. The aroma of chairman Schnell's examination still lingered in the air. Randle could better appreciate the importance of her preparation.

"Now, as a member of the board, how do you determine qualifications of prospective white applicants for registration? Suppose somebody comes to you and sits at your table, a white person who wants to register?"

"Well, I treat them as I would a colored person." Both Whites and Coloreds had reason to doubt Randle's answer. "I ask if they have their witness and then their qualifications as to residence, and then sometimes you have your own opinion as to whether you are going to ask about the Constitution. We ask the colored and the white the same questions."

"It is within your discretion whether you ask about the Constitution or not?"

"Some we do and some we do not." Randle essentially admitted the question.

"May I ask your background, what schooling you have had?"

"I am a high school graduate."

"Have you had any special training?"

"No." At least Randle had the good sense not to puff herself up into a fool. Her experience administering the Constitution coincided with her brief experience as a registered voter. Until 1946 she simply kept house in the bayou.

"In regard to the United States Constitution?"

"Well, I have read it." For that matter, so had the Coloreds she and Schnell refused to register. Alabama's Auditor and Agriculture Commissioner had entrusted Randle with Mobile's democratic franchise and the mandate to register only those persons who understand the duties and obligations of good citizenship under a republican form of government. Registrar Randle presented a case study for the transparent agenda behind the Boswell Amendment. But the question before the court concerned unlawful discrimination, not rank incompetence. Si Garrett could stipulate that Randle possessed only a porous understanding of constitutional concepts, and still win the case. The Constitution did not require that common sense or intelligence lubricate the engines of democracy.

"You have read it, but you have had no special education about it?"

"No special education." Randle did not know she was wounded.

"When you propound a question concerning the Constitution, concerning one's ability to read, write, understand, and explain the

Constitution, do you propound such questions equally to white and Negro citizens alike?"

"Yes, sir."

"In other words, you ask them whether they can read, write, understand, and explain the Constitution?"

"Yes."

"That is all?"

"Yes."

"You don't ask citizens anything about answering a specific question about the Constitution?"

"You ask that, and if you decide to have them read, they do, and if you don't decide to have them read it, they don't." What seemed simple to Randle raised the specter of whimsical decisions by registrars.

Judge McDuffie found this exchange intriguing and irresistible. To Landau's delight, His Honor joined the discussion. "What controls your judgment in determining whether or not to ask as to any particular section of the Constitution? When do you decide that, and what controls you?"

"When one says ... yes ... well ..., I think, your Honor ... sometimes you can realize that people can ... you can look at a person ... the way they talk and speak and the way they act." Aside from being nonresponsive, Randle's lack of focus suggested that she could not meet her own ambiguous criteria.

"You have no standard, beyond that?" Landau confidently jumped in.

"No." Randle conceded the Board lacked a common clear basis in deciding whether to question a particular applicant, and what to ask.

"In the course of asking such a question, do you rely on any particular section of the Constitution?"

"Any one that you choose."

"You pick one at random?"

"Any one that you choose."

"After you decide you are going to ask that person a specific question about the Constitution, in what manner do you do it?"

"We have been having them write the answers down on a piece of paper for me to read and I have them explain it orally."

"Was that the process indulged in from October 1947 to this date?"

"It has been."

"Or has it been recently adopted since the filing of this suit?"

"I don't know whether it has or not." Randle's answer seemed befuddled, but sincere. Landau had squeezed all the blood that would drip from this turnip. Predictably, Mr. Garrett rose to advise the Court he had no questions of Randle at this time, but reserved the right to call her later. Prudence dictated that Garrett not run the risk of exposing Randle to any more damaging examination without further preparation.

Leighton then announced that the plaintiffs wanted to call E. J. Gonzales as an adverse party. That these colored veterans tactically chose to call Gunny last belied his importance. Leighton had no reason to expect Schnell and Randle to publicly fall on their sword and admit their tawdry role in Boswell's charade. Landau had established the underwhelming competence of two Board members. However, the Constitution did not require Alabama to govern competently, just not discriminatorily. White supremacists did not promise Alabama better government, just a presumably better educated one. The benchmark set by Schnell and Randle indicated a failure or inability to provide either.

Leighton knew that proving the plaintiffs' case would turn on whether Mobile's most controversial Democrat had the courage to stand ground in open court, despite the political cost. Schnell and Randle had given their accounts, leaving the court to assess their credibility. Schnell and Randle could be recalled to the stand by Garrett to repair damage caused by the minority registrar, though at considerable risk. However, the judges on the panel were not oblivious to Gunny's front-page assaults against Alabama's political icons. From all appearances, there seemed little personal gain for a pillar of the governing Party to pull the Dixiecrats' political temple down on his own head for the sake of registering some veterans and Coloreds. That earned the dissident registrar credibility before the trial even started. When Gunny dismissed the Attorney General in open court, distancing himself further from Schnell, Randle, and the Boswell Amendment at great personal risk, the impact was not lost on the court. It did not matter who chose to call Gunny to the witness stand. The judges figured they had a smoking gun in the courtroom.

Somewhat unexpectedly for a seasoned trial lawyer, the Attorney General turned to Leighton and asked whether Mr. Gonzales was being called under the same rule as Schnell and Randle had been called as an adverse witness. Opposing sides may treat one another as adverse and hostile witnesses, allowing unrestricted cross-examination with leading questions. Si Garrett's question seemed unusual because Gunny remained a named defendant, a party adverse to plaintiffs. But Garrett wanted to argue otherwise, that Gunny shared interests in common with plaintiffs and adverse to the State of Alabama. That would deny Leighton the freedom to lead Gunny through potentially collusive questioning, and yet allow Garrett to aggressively cross-examine his former client, the dissident registrar. Portraying Gunny as the plaintiffs' witness also would expose Gonzales to public ridicule for conspiring with Coloreds and outside agitators, a prospect Garrett clearly relished.

Judge Mullins abruptly cut Garrett off before his strategy developed. "Put him on. I don't think it makes any difference how he calls him." Judge Mullins did not intend to entrust the examination of Gunny Gonzales to Leighton or Garrett anyway.

After an initial battery of background questions, Leighton carefully tested the water with Mr. Gonzales. "What is the procedure you take, as a member of that board, acting for the board, when an applicant for registration as elector comes before that board?"

"The first thing I do, when a white person comes down, he sits down, the witness is with him, I ask his name, he gives me his name, I ask his witness' name, I tell them to raise their hands and take the oath, and I give the applicant the application blank." The court and Leighton detected no evasiveness.

"After he fills out that, do you ask any questions about educational qualifications?"

"I don't make a practice of it." Gunny quickly distinguished himself from his estranged co-defendants.

"Do you ask him any questions, if he is a white man, about understanding or explaining the Constitution of the United States?" Leighton might have been chided for tossing soft pitches to the pivotal witness. Leighton all but let go of the steering wheel, hoping that Gunny would take charge of his own examination.

"Very few. I have not made a practice of it. It has not been the practice of the board up until lately." Gunny volunteered more than Garrett or Leighton had expected at that point, establishing that the Board had treated Coloreds differently than Whites prior to the lawsuit. Leighton hesitated, not sure how to best exploit the growing anticipation in the courtroom. Leighton hesitated too long.

Judge Mullins leaned forward, studying the maverick registrar that both the Attorney General and the plaintiffs' lawyers regarded with apprehension. The judge mentally reviewed waffling accounts by Schnell and Randle on that same point, recalling that Gunny had refused to go along with Garrett's defense of the case. "You say it has not been the practice of the board up until lately?"

"Up until this case started."

That's what the judge thought he heard. Taking over the questioning from Mr. Leighton, Judge Mullins pressed Registrar Gonzales. "My second question is this. When a colored applicant for registration comes before you, as a member of the board, what happens?"

"Well, he sits down with his witness. I take his name. I take his witness' name. The same procedure is followed with the witness. I ask the applicant how much schooling he has had and he tells me. I ask him, 'Can you read, write, understand, and explain any article of the United States Constitution?' "

Leighton could not take credit for the question or the answer. Gunny was chatting directly with the court. Judge Mullins continued. "As to that, except in rare instances, you *never* ask that question of white applicants?" The court recalled how difficult chairman Schnell found these same questions.

"That is right." Gunny did not hesitate. Benches throughout the temple squeaked as weight shifted forward under bodies straining to catch every word between the judge and Mr. Gonzales.

"In the case of colored applicants, you ask if they can read, write, understand, and explain an article of the Constitution?"

"That is the procedure of the Board."

"You are following the procedure of the board?" The Court wanted confirmation.

"Yes, sir."

"What is the authority for such procedure?"

"I don't know. It is the policy of the board. I follow the policy of the board."

"How did you learn about this policy?" Judge Mullins' curiosity sounded spontaneous, not methodical.

"You see, this law was enacted in 1946. It was the procedure before we went on the board, I assume. Mr. Schnell was on the board before I was on the board, and that policy continued after I got on the board." Gunny had been preaching that to *The Mobile Press* for over a year now. This was no news flash to anyone who read newspapers.

"Now, when you ask a colored applicant whether he can understand and explain the Constitution, how do you ask him to show you his qualifications on that question?" Neither plaintiffs nor the court had to lead Mr. Gonzales through rigorous cross-examination.

"Well, I pick out any article in the Constitution and ask him to read it. When he tells me that he understands it, I give him a little piece of paper and let him write what he read."

"You have never received any instructions from any source as to what constitutes a test of the accuracy of the answer to that question?"

"No, sir." Gunny sank one more nail into Boswell's legislative coffin.

"Is there a certain policy that one member handles all Negro applicants and the others handle the white applicants?"

"When all of us are there, it has been the practice of the board for Mr. Schnell to handle all colored applicants." The gallery heard another nail go in.

"Now, from your experience and observation as a member of this board, are the applicants for registration who are White persons handled in the same manner that applicants who are Colored are handled by that board?" Judge Mullins posed the ultimate issue before the court.

"No." Gunny's admission as a member of the Board and representative of the State of Alabama bound the Board, Boswell, and McCorvey.

"In what manner does the procedure or processing of application made by colored applicants for registration differ from the processing of applications made by white applicants? In what manner does it differ?"

"During my presence on the board, I have never seen where a white person was required to read and write an article of the Constitution. I have objected to that locally and publicly." The dissident registrar stood his ground. There were few nails left for Gunny to drive home.

"So, if the policy were adopted whereby a white person were asked to read, write, understand and explain the Constitution, you would have seen it, would you not?"

"Again, I answer my own way. You asked me the same question over. We can ask whites that question. It has been the policy of taking their word. But insofar as actually writing it, no. And insofar as explaining it, no whites have explained it to me." It must have amused the other members of the panel to hear an unrepresented defendant rebuke Judge Mullins for asking repetitive questions.

Judge McDuffie elbowed his way into the free for all. "You mean the majority of the white people are not asked to write, understand or explain the Constitution, whereas the majority of the colored people are?" The slave owner's grandson lobbed a key question over the middle of the plate.

The former Whippet hammered it. "That is right."

The case seemed to spiral out of control before Attorney General Garrett presented any evidence. Judge Mullins refused to yield the floor. "That is the policy of the board? That is the way that all three of you handled it? Is that right?"

"I tell you frankly I don't make it a habit of asking white people. I have several times, but I don't make it a habit."

Judge Mullins continued chatting with Gunny, altogether ignoring Mr. Leighton who wisely remained quiet. "As I understand you, the practice is that you don't even ask the white people and the other members of the board don't ask white people about the Constitution?"

"Sometimes they do."

"That is the policy of your board?"

"Yes."

Judge Mullins wanted to tie down each loose end, once and for all. "Would you say it is rather an exception when the board does ask a white person about the Constitution?"

"Yes, sir." Leighton had little reason to ask another question even if given an opportunity.

Judge Mullins wanted to tie down each loose end more than once. "You don't require white people to read, write, understand and explain the Constitution or any part of it?"

"No, sir." Gunny confirmed the Boswell Amendment, at least as applied, to be a sham.

The judge wanted to hear it again. "With the colored applicants, you not only ask them but require them to write it and explain it?"

"They used to explain it, but they write it now."

"Do all the members of the board have them write it now?"

"Yes, sir. Up to the time this suit was filed, they used to explain it, but now they write it, so we keep a record."

Leighton sat down several questions earlier, willing to be left somewhat out of the loop. Gunny and the judges seemed to be doing just fine without his help. Garrett, on the other hand, could only watch with dismay. There was no diplomatic way for the Attorney General to object to questions posed by a panel of federal judges. And each critical question drew an astonishingly candid admission, fueling even more questions. Finally satisfied that all the elements of the plaintiffs' case had been repeatedly confirmed by Registrar Gonzales, the judges leaned back. Leighton chose not to muddy the water with further questions. The court invited Alabama's Attorney General to question the witness, which placed Garrett in the peculiar role of cross-examining a representative of the State of Alabama as an adverse party.

"Mr. Gonzales, how long has it been the policy of this board to take written answers from either white or colored applicants for registration, in regard to their ability to understand and explain any section of the Constitution?"

"To my personal knowledge, since this suit began."

Most of Mobile could have answered that. Garrett tried to quibble with the court's smoking gun. "Since on or about March 1, 1948?"

"Since this suit began." Gunny declined the bait.

"Is it a fact that shortly after the three of you became members of the Board of Registrars of Mobile County, it was not mutually agreed among the three of you, because of the fact that Mr. Schnell had eight years of experience on the board in registering persons, white and colored, and had some experience since the passage of the Boswell Amendment, and you and Mrs. Randle had none, that if he was present when a Negro applicant came in before the board, that, as the usual practice, he would handle the processing of his application?" The Attorney General recited his defense of the case and resorted to leading his former client.

"No, because I have the ability to do it." Though unschooled and uncoached, Garrett's adversary would not bite.

"I didn't ask about your ability." The Attorney General foolishly quarreled over the words he tried to put into Gunny's mouth, indicating the lawyer could not control the witness. Garrett should have known better.

"No."

"You did not mutually agree to that procedure?"

"No."

Garrett seemed unable to shake loose of Gunny's damaging admissions. The substantial rift between the Attorney General and the Board's registrar clearly undermined the Board's defense.

"Did you not testify that you had never seen a white man who applied for registration required to read or write the Constitution or make an attempt to explain any article of the Constitution?"

"In my personal presence, no."

Judge Mullins heard this before, but the answer seemed more credible and damaging under Garrett's cross-examination. Garrett's next question underscored one of the reasons he could not represent the dissident Registrar. "I will ask you if it is not a fact that you, as a member of the board, have participated in the denial of registration to white applicants because they could not read, write, understand and explain the Constitution of the United States to your satisfaction?"

"No."

Garrett kept finding Gunny's foot in the Attorney General's mouth. "Mr. Gonzales, you testified that you have been present on numerous occasions when Negro applications were before the board, is that right?"

"Yes, sir. That is right."

"Did Mr. Schnell always process their applications when he was there?"

"Always, when he was there, yes, sir."

"Have you ever been present and seen Negro applicants come before the board and seen the board register them without asking them any question whatsoever concerning the Constitution?"

"Yes sir."

"You have?" Garrett fumbled in disbelief, momentarily surprised and off guard. On that note, he should have quit. But Garrett persisted, like a moth clinging to a porch lamp on a rainy night.

"Yes sir, school teachers and doctors."

Garrett felt encouraged. "You have seen the same as to white applicants?"

"Yes sir."

That narrow concession allowed Garrett to argue the absence of discriminatory denial of civil rights. However, his personal animosity towards Gunny obscured a fundamental rule that seasoned trial lawyers normally observe at times like this: sit down. "You say you have never seen a white applicant denied registration because of his inability to read, write, understand and explain the Constitution?"

"Not in my presence."

The Attorney General seemed to have an infinite capacity for pain, and no evidence to impeach the witness. "You never participated in the denial of a white applicant?"

"Not for that special reason, no."

Garrett eventually gave up and announced to the court that he had no further questions of Mr. Gonzales. Fragments of Garrett's would-be withering cross-examination lay strewn about the floor near the Attorney General's feet. Gunny's simple responses indicted the Board of Registrars and Alabama's Boswell Amendment. Neither plaintiffs nor Garrett, much less three federal judges, expected a white politician, a prominent member of the Party, a representative of the State, to openly break rank in federal court with the powers that be. Garrett's questions to his unrepresented adversary underscored the charade that could have stymied the court had Gunny submitted to Montgomery's wishes.

Though no less a defendant than Schnell and Randle, Registrar Gonzales found common ground with colored veterans who sought the right to vote. Without benefit of counsel, Gunny engaged three federal judges and defied the white supremacists that had hijacked Alabama's Democratic Party and state legislature. Having said his piece, Gunny stood down from the witness chair. Neither the plaintiffs nor the State of Alabama wanted to recall Mr. Gonzales to the stand. He walked the length of a silent courtroom and left the U. S. District Court house on Monday, December 20, 1948. The minority registrar told it like it was.

CHAPTER 28

Stroke of Midnight

The *Mobile Press* solemnly reported on January 7, 1949 what many suspected the moment E. J. Gonzales stepped down from his witness chair. Writing for the federal tribunal, Judge Mullins began by noting that Schnell and Randle answered the complaint for the Board of Registrars, denying the Boswell Amendment is either unconstitutional or that registration laws are applied differently as to Negroes. The court observed that "E. J. Gonzales declined to join in the Board's answer, stating that he could not join in all of the denials contained in their answer. He filed no formal answer, but testified and represented himself on the trial of the case."

The court put to rest any doubt about what had been going on over at 109 St. Emanuel, finding that the Board required Negroes to explain the Constitution without exacting a similar requirement of Whites. Negroes were refused registration because of their race even upon interpreting the Constitution, and during the 4 months preceding the lawsuit the Board had registered 2800 Whites but only 104 Negroes in a county of 230,000 of which one-third was Colored.

Judge Mullins concluded that the Boswell Amendment repealed objective standards in Alabama's 1901 Constitution by introducing an exceedingly unreasonable and arbitrary burden to understand constitutional articles about which even federal judges routinely disagree. Shamelessly compounding this impossible hurdle, few members of

Alabama's poorly educated boards of registrars possessed a competent, or even correct, grasp of the Constitution. The moving force behind the Boswell Amendment, the State Democratic Executive Committee, had expended funds as an official arm of the State and secured adoption of the Amendment in its endeavor "to make the Democratic party in Alabama the White Man's Party." Judge Mullins noted that Gessner McCorvey had originated the Amendment, advising Alabama's legislature how to maintain the fight for white supremacy. No less distinguished a source than the *Alabama Lawyer*, an official arm of the Alabama State Bar, carried testimonials by reputable attorneys that "the people of our State are expected to adopt this Amendment in order to give the Registrars arbitrary power to exclude Negroes from voting." Rejecting Garrett's argument that the Boswell Amendment was not racist in purpose or effect, as written or applied, the court found that circumstances and history showed otherwise. The principal object was to restrict Colored voting through ambiguous standards that purposefully granted arbitrary power to registrars. The court found that "the administration of the Boswell Amendment by the defendant board demonstrates that the ambiguous standard prescribed has, in fact, been arbitrarily used for the purpose of excluding Negro applicants." Both in its purpose and implementation, Boswell's Amendment offended the Constitution:

> While it is true that there is no mention of race or color in the Boswell Amendment, this does not save it. The Fifteenth Amendment nullifies sophisticated as well as simple-minded modes of discrimination and prohibits onerous procedural requirements which effectively handicap exercise of the franchise by the colored race although the abstract right to vote may remain unrestricted as to race. We cannot ignore the impact of the Boswell Amendment upon Negro citizens because it avoids mention of race or color. To do so would be to shut our eyes to what all others than we can see and understand.

The court permanently enjoined Alabama's Boswell Amendment.

Assistant Attorney General Garrett, back in Montgomery, declined to comment on the decision. Garrett appealed to the United States

Supreme Court on February 4, 1949. Alabama argued that states have a right to prescribe literacy tests, noting that the high court had already upheld Mississippi's requirement that voters be able to reasonably interpret the state constitution. Only in desperation did Alabama offer Mississippi as a role model. Giving short shrift to Garrett's appeal, on March 28 the United States Supreme Court sustained the federal tribunal's order, striking down the last significant barrier to Colored voting rights and mortally wounding white supremacy in Alabama.

During the month after Judge McDuffie's tribunal threw out the Boswell Amendment, nearly 1200 Coloreds registered in Mobile County compared to the 39 who registered between November 1946 and March 1948. For the first time in history, the majority of live registered voters in Ward 7 near Raphael Semmes School were Colored. Capitalizing on their fortune, the Mobile Negro Voters and Veterans Association began chartering chapters to advance Colored registration throughout the state. By nullifying the Boswell Amendment, the federal court in Mobile effectively reinstated the provisions of Alabama's 1901 Constitution, requiring only that a voter be able to read or write any article of the Constitution. Alarmed by the disturbing implications of this profound decision, *The Mobile Press* complained that Alabama's constitution could no longer assure an intelligent electorate and prevent mass voting by the unqualified.

In Montgomery, Alabama's House of Representatives paused as the Boswell Amendment died at the hands of federal judges. Even while the matter was on appeal to the Supreme Court, Senate and House members gathered behind closed doors with Gessner McCorvey, fashioning a new law to replace the stricken amendment. Neither McCorvey nor the legislature benefited from experience. On the night of May 11, McCorvey presented another scheme to a joint legislative conference. The Democratic Party Chairman condemned Alabama's 1901 Constitution as a farce. "We need a new voter law to preserve the intelligence of the Alabama electorate," McCorvey announced with a straight face, and to replace "the most ridiculous and biggest fool qualification law of any state." What had suited Alabama 50 years ago at the height of

Jim Crow no longer satisfied Dixiecrat political realities. Too many Coloreds in 1949 satisfied Alabama's 1901 constitutional standards. All twenty-five legislators in attendance, including Mobile representatives George Stone, Jr., Joseph C. Sullivan, and Thomas A. Johnston, supported McCorvey's proposal, thus assuring passage by both houses. *The Mobile Press* enthusiastically embraced McCorvey's bill, proclaiming that it had been closely studied and blessed by none other than Charles Wallace Collins, a Dothan legislator and author of "Whither Solid South?," the Dixiecrats' scripture. Nothing more need be said.

With nearly 70 co-sponsors, Dallas County Representative Walter Givhan introduced McCorvey's solution in the House on May 17. During hearings the next day, only a few voices spoke in opposition. Dorothy Danner Daponte, a Mobile widow, slandered the bill as an undemocratic device to limit voting, giving registrars the power to be arbitrary and promote despotism. Birmingham Representative James Adams, Jr. took strong exception to Daponte's remarks, accusing her of making discriminatory remarks about the character of Alabama's House judiciary committee. Mildred Laurendine, a Brookley Field employee, suggested the time had come for Alabama's Legislature to accept democracy. Montgomery attorney Richard Rives warned that it would be a serious mistake to give registrars arbitrary discretion to deny voting rights, recommending instead an objective literacy test which by 1960 would permit only high school graduates to vote. Ironically, that would have directly addressed the purported concerns of McCorvey and the House judiciary committee about creating, if not preserving, an intelligent electorate. However, there seemed to be little appreciation for the fact that Alabama's Legislature and educational system bore some responsibility for a poorly educated public. Indeed, the notion of linking voting rights with educational achievement in Alabama drew a howl from Etowah Representative E. L. Robers, who complained that Rives' proposal would disenfranchise nearly half the state. Only about 17 per cent of Alabamians had earned a high school diploma. A goodly number of would-be disenfranchised Etowah voters, mostly white ones, came to Robers' mind. Exploiting marginally educated people seemed more consistent with the vision of white supremacy.

Back in Mobile, the white dominated Alabama Federation of Labor repudiated McCorvey's latest scheme. Adopting a resolution sponsored by Colored members, organized labor condemned the bill as a device to deprive white and colored citizens of their rights and demanded endorsement of the National Democratic Party's non-discrimination plank. Speaking on behalf of Governor Folsom, Judge W. C. Taylor urged Alabama's labor movement to register its people, and to remember that Governor Folsom is the best friend laboring people ever had. Alabama's legislature chose to shun common sense while ignoring federal law. On May 26 the judiciary committee enthusiastically adopted McCorvey's bill, amending Alabama's 1901 Constitution to restrict voting to only:

> Those who can read and write any Article of the Constitution of the United States in the English language which may be submitted to them by the Board of Registrars, provided, however, that no persons shall be entitled to register as electors except those who are of good character and who embrace the duties and obligations of citizenship under the Constitution of the United States and under the Constitution of the State of Alabama, and provided further, that in order to aid the Members of the Board of Registrars, who are hereby constituted and declared to be Judicial Officers, to judicially determine if applicants to register have the qualifications hereinabove set out, each applicant shall be furnished by the Board of Registrars a written questionnaire, which shall be uniform in all cases with no discrimination as between applicants.

The committee then deadlocked 6-6 over whether to report the new bill to the floor of the House for a vote. Upstate representatives first wanted to get the blessing of Alabama's Supreme Court, while south Alabama members tried to send the bill to the full House for immediate passage. The committee had good reason to assume that Alabama's Supreme Court would bless McCorvey's latest stratagem. Like its predecessor Boswell Amendment, the new bill contained superficially neutral language. Justices on this Court had long espoused the notion that an act adopted by the Legislature, or a House committee's trial balloon, must be presumed constitutional. Even where a reasonable interpretation would render a statute unconstitutional, the Court felt obliged to embrace an available alternative that would save the legislation. Alabama's judicial branch considered it to be the "recognized duty of the court to sustain the act unless it is clear beyond reasonable doubt" in violation of fundamental law. The Supreme Court afforded the Legislature the highest degree of deference. At the same time the Court demanded that anyone asserting a constitutional violation must satisfy the extraordinary burden of proof traditionally reserved to criminal prosecutions. White supremacists who controlled both the state House and Senate could count on Alabama's justices to extend them the benefit of doubt, even though McCorvey's scheme arrived at the Court under a constitutional cloud.

McCorvey personally assured the committee that the proposed law would not discriminate against anyone. "I am interested in an intelligent electorate," McCorvey insisted. "I have always taken the position that all those qualified to vote should be given the ballot. I do not favor mass voting by the unqualified, either white or colored." For good measure, McCorvey emphasized that the new amendment, by requiring would-be voters to embrace the duties and obligations of citizenship, should prevent communists of any color from voting in Alabama. The constitutional merit of that after-thought had not been explored during the trial in Mobile.

Within 24 hours, the Alabama House of Representatives requested Alabama's Supreme Court to determine whether McCorvey's bill, as written, complied with the Fourteenth and Fifteenth Amendments to the United States Constitution. Four of Alabama's Justices replied on June 3, 1949 that:

> The standard of qualification and accompanying requirements must be of such a character as to furnish a reasonably marked guide for the boards of registrars in a judicial capacity to so act that there will not be in the ordinary course any discrimination in the application of the Fifteenth or Fourteenth Amendment.
>
> On the face of the Amendment as a whole, nothing is manifest of an intention to discriminate against anyone in violation

of the Fifteenth or Fourteenth Amendment, or to abridge any of the freedoms secured by the First and Fourteenth Amendments, or any freedom of citizenship in the United States.

Until the contrary appears, it must be assumed that the board will accord due process. When an applicant has had his claim to register considered by a court having constitutional authority to make a judicial determination of his right, and has been accorded procedural due process, such determination will not be presumed to be influenced by discrimination, and such determination will stand on the same basis as the judgment of any other court. Of course, if in any given proceeding, such discrimination is shown to exist, the constitutional rights of the applicant can be protected through ordinary processes of law.

In so many words, a majority of Alabama's Supreme Court deferentially advised Alabama's House that the proposed amendment was not discriminatory as written, was presumably untainted by any discriminatory intent, and was free of the Boswell Amendment's failure to furnish a reasonable standard to govern registrars in passing on the qualifications of prospective voters. Also, by converting boards of registrars to judicial proceedings, any future denial of voting rights would enjoy the presumption of constitutionality. Under McCorvey's scheme, any subsequent disagreement with the *judicial* decisions by Schnell and Randle would have to be appealed to the learned Alabama Supreme Court itself.

News about McCorvey, Boswell, and their white supremacist agenda apparently had not yet seeped into the sterile chambers of Alabama's Supreme Court. Facially nondiscriminatory language in any bill authored by McCorvey remained inherently suspect. And the presumption that registrars would dispense voting rights without regard to race reflected judicial myopia. The ordinary course of business within Mobile's Board of Registrars had been found constitutionally deficient, though the Boswell Amendment as written bore no evidence of intent to discriminate. Converting registrar Schnell to *magistrate* Schnell reflected a transparent scheme that Alabama's Supreme Court majority willingly embraced.

With nearly apologetic reluctance, Justices Thomas Lawson and Robert Simpson dissented. Justice Lawson cautioned the Alabama

House: "I am of the opinion that the proposed amendment does not meet the objections pointed out in the recent case of *Davis v. Schnell* wherein the so-called 'Boswell Amendment' was held violative of the 14th and 15th Amendments to the Constitution of the United States." Somewhat more diplomatically, Justice Simpson assured the legislature of his great deference and respect, but regretted that the Supreme Court of Alabama lacked authority to construe the proposed amendment's constitutionality under the 14th and 15th Amendments. That, he modestly reminded legislators, remained within the exclusive jurisdiction of federal courts. Though misguided in his analysis, at least Justice Simpson erred on the side of caution. In fact, nothing precluded Alabama's Supreme Court from determining whether McCorvey's bill offended federal constitutional rights. However, Justice Simpson correctly observed that federal judges, not Alabama's, would have the last word. Armed with the moral and legal support of Alabama's Supreme Court, the judiciary committee reported McCorvey's amendment to the full House within a week, where it handily passed by a 77 to 6 vote.

Chairman Milton Schnell, suddenly hospitalized in Biloxi following a heart attack, was not available for comment. However, Schnell's absence had little if any calming effect on sessions at 109 St. Emanuel Street. State Auditor Dan Thomas appeared at the July 5 session, sparking a row with Gunny and allied veteran groups. The dispute erupted when Gunny and Ralph Britain, commander of the Disabled American Veterans, demanded that Thomas exercise his State Appointing Board authority to permit honorably discharged war veterans to register without need of witnesses. Thomas, at whose pleasure Randle served as a registrar, still refused to change how Randle conducted business. Commander Britain publicly scolded Thomas, accusing the State Auditor of being unfit to hold public office. Sensing why Thomas had attended the session, Gunny cut to the quick:

> Dan Thomas appealed for veteran support in 1946 as State Auditor. Now, he has turned his back on the veterans. He has refused to assist the veterans of Mobile County in lifting restrictions of current registration procedures and has no interest in the common citizen. I appeal to all veterans in this

county and this state to vote against Dan Thomas for whatever office he may seek in the 1950 election.

The Governor's Registrar crossed another political Rubicon, condemning Thomas and urging that politicians like Thomas get off the fence or be voted out of office. Nearly 9 months after Gunny began crusading for veterans to register without witnesses, State Senator Joseph Langan announced on July 8 that he would support such legislation.

From his Mississippi hospital bed on July 13, Schnell cosigned with Randle a letter asking that Governor Folsom withdraw his support for Gonzales' demand to throw out witness requirements for war veterans. Employing skillfully distorted logic, Schnell and Randle tried to assume a high moral ground:

> To require a non-veteran to have a witness and eliminate this requirement for veterans is purely and simply discrimination, undemocratic and in violation of the registration laws of this state. If this practice were put into effect, each member of this board would be violating his or her oath of office and the trust placed in us by the people.
>
> If we abandon the practice of requiring a witness, anyone who found a veteran's lost discharge papers could come to our office and register, placing us in the position of registering persons who are not entitled to register. We hope that upon considering this matter, you will realize that the requirement of at least one witness to identify or vouch for an applicant to register is a proper and fair requirement and that it prevents much fraudulence in any attempted padding of our registration lists.

Except for the dead who still cluttered the Board's voting rolls, the risk of imposter veterans padding voting lists was too small to measure. From McCorvey down to Schnell, the message read loud and clear. There would be no mass registration of a presumed unintelligent citizenry, which McCorvey estimated to be nearly 83 per cent of Alabama's adult population. Those fortunate to survive combat in the nation's defense did not necessarily possess the intelligence to vote, or so the white supremacists reasoned. McCorvey, Schnell, and Randle apparently felt it was more democratic to deny voting rights than to give veterans the benefit of doubt. Neither the irony nor insult was lost on Gunny.

The guardian of Mobile's public interest did little to improve matters. On July 11 the *Mobile Press Register* accused Gunny of causing confusion and trouble, refusing to cooperate with other registrars, and failing to register applicants. It appeared that the newspaper's right hand did not know what its left was doing. For the better part of two years, a veritable political upheaval in Mobile kept most newspaper reporters and editors fully occupied. At the core of the skirmish over states' rights, voting rights, and civil rights, powerful forces mobilized for battle. Catalysts catapulted fundamental beliefs into broad confrontations. Big Jim Folsom and Gunny Gonzales served as catalysts, the front lines of forces opposing McCorvey and Boswell. Folsom and Gonzales waged a battle by, against, for, and within Alabama's own political order. At the end of the day, the high tide of Alabama's white supremacists had been turned.

The editorial conscience of the press observed events without recognizing history, reporting skirmishes without understanding the battle. While Alabama's political and governmental institutions scrambled to preserve White Supremacy with skillful but deceptive rhetoric, the newspaper's editor belittled those who repudiated the sham. It made no more sense to blame the lightning rod for attracting storms than to chide Gunny for opposing Boswell, McCorvey, Schnell, Randle, and Thomas. It was their common fate to join battle. The call for Gunny to cooperate with Schnell and Randle constituted a coded demand to collaborate. No party to this struggle could yield without also denying its nature. Compromising fundamental principles, like peeling onions, leaves no core identity or being.

One might forgive a small town newspaper for failing to grasp the larger drama unfolding before its own eyes. But suggesting that Gunny had refused to register applicants cannot be kindly attributed to editorial discretion. The insinuation misled the public. Data available to the *Mobile Press* and *Press Register* showed that the rate of voting registration had increased five-fold and the number of all white and colored voters expanded 20 per cent since Gunny assumed office. More dramatic, though, was the pace of colored registration during that same period. It had exploded beyond comprehension, posing for the first time the prospect that Coloreds would become a significant political force. This disturbed the *Press* and unnerved powerful white supremacists throughout the state, especially in the legislature. Folsom's attempt to reapportion the state based on the notion of one man, one vote now presented an even more sinister threat to the established order. Mobile's controversial figure had changed everything.

That did not trouble the Governor or Gunny. Just two days after Schnell publicly defended the registration witness rule, Governor Folsom appeared on Mobile's bay causeway to sign a multi-state fishery compact. Seizing the opportunity to clear the air, the Governor casually backhanded Dan Thomas and Milton Schnell by openly supporting Gunny: "The veteran's discharge papers should be sufficient proof of his right to register" without need of witnesses. Again taking the lead, Gunny publicly scourged Schnell and Randle for refusing to register WW II colored and white veterans, prompting enthusiastic VFW and American Legion endorsements. Choosing to play this one safely from the side lines, *The Mobile Press'* lead editorial of August 11, 1949 achieved an unenviable place in the annals of southern journalism:

> But here again there arises the question as to whether war service alone qualifies a person as a voter. There are many who will say yes. There are many, including veterans, who will say no.

No editorial signature took credit for this underwhelming display of conviction. But it was no secret that McCorvey's political and economic allies opposed change that might disturb their exercise of power. To McCorvey zealots, principle dictated the crusade. Financial interests responded to more basic instincts. If changes occurred, if masses of people voted, many surely would start demanding rights, benefits, and power. This would mean sharing power, raising taxes, surrendering control and distributing wealth. Somebody had to pay. Someone's ox always gets gored.

Within the week, the Mobile Central Trades Council publicly commended Gunny for his progressive stand on behalf of veterans and laborers. The AFL delivered its sentiments to Governor Folsom, Mobile's legislative delegation, and the *Press Register*. Three weeks later, State Senator Langan introduced a local bill to permit Mobile's veterans to register without the need of a vouching witness. As a local bill having no effect elsewhere in Alabama, Langan's measure could easily become law if Mobile's legislative delegation wanted it so. Gunny and the Veterans Council endorsed Langan's bill, mustering public support and pressure for passage. However, *The Mobile Press'* editorial all but sanctioned the defeat of Langan's bill. Sure enough, on August 23, 1949, Mobile state representatives Tom Johnston, III, George E. Stone, Jr., and Joseph Sullivan unanimously killed the legislative proposal to register war veterans without sworn witnesses. The machine was alive and well, refusing to share democracy with those who fought to preserve it.

In the waning days of the 1949 legislative session, McCorvey's forces moved to push his new legislation through the state Senate. Within six days of adjournment, Governor Folsom maneuvered to the floor a controversial reapportionment bill, a move expected to provoke bitter opposition and prolong debate. Alabama's 1901 Constitution required the Legislature after each national census to reapportion the state Senate and House into districts of equal populations. However, the Legislature had refused to reapportion and redistrict itself since 1901. Rural districts representing about 25 percent of Alabama's population controlled both the House and Senate. It could be said without derision that cattle in numerous counties enjoyed more voting power than did people in Mobile and Birmingham. In order to wield such disproportionate power and control, rural legislators and white supremacists allied to resist reapportionment and impede voter registration. As long as a deferential Alabama Supreme Court chose not to intervene, the Legislature methodically diluted and distorted voting rights secured by Alabama's own Constitution. Gunny's public dissent illustrated how legislative schemes designed to deny Coloreds access to political rights also served to deny Whites similar access. Declaring the

Boswell Amendment unconstitutional relieved Coloreds as well as Whites from a stranglehold by which rural and white supremacy interests exercised control. The House's urgency to adopt a successor to the Boswell Amendment was matched only by its resolve to avoid reapportionment at all costs. Governor Folsom reasonably expected his reapportionment proposal to be greeted with hostility.

Folsom had all but abandoned hope of his remaining agenda surviving either house, prompting him to marshal senatorial allies in a determined effort to derail McCorvey's amendment. Big Jim outlined his strategy with a small cadre of only six senators, hatching plans to filibuster Boswell's successor to death. The Governor cagily waited until the last moment to play his hole card. Big Jim was fond of telling friends not to wipe off mud slung by opponents, but to gently flick it off after the mud had dried. With only two working days of the legislative session remaining, the *Press Register* and other McCorvey allies warned that Alabama would be the real loser if the amendment died in meaningless debates over Folsom's proposed reforms.

According to plan, Langan introduced an alternative to McCorvey's amendment, gutting all but the minimal "read and write" provision from McCorvey's bill, and rendering it comparable to Alabama's 1901 Constitution. That prompted condescending criticism from the *Press Register*:

> The fact is, of course, Senator Langan is more interested in blocking adoption of an amendment to replace the patently inadequate qualifications provided in the present law, than he is in putting through his substitute bill. In fact, by offering a substitute, he will be delaying Senate action on the bill. As it is, the Senate would do well to kill the substitute and adopt the House-approved bill in its original form.

Two years would pass before the next legislative session convened. McCorvey's amendment, if killed, could not rise from its grave until at least 1951, late into the term of Folsom's successor. Gunny had inflicted a terminal wound into the underbelly of Alabama's white supremacists. Governor Folsom did not want that wound to heal on his watch.

On the last day of its 1949 session, the Senate convened shortly after midnight, wearily eyeing a logjam of pending bills and benches of bickering colleagues. McCorvey's allies had 23 hours to clear the agenda and pass their amendment. At the sound of Lt. Governor J. C. Inzer's gavel, the filibuster began. Broughton Lamberth of Tallapoosa, Tom Blake Howle of Calhoun, Rankin Fite of Marion, and Joe Langan took turns eating up the clock, trying to keep McCorvey's bill off the floor and off the books. As the hours swept by, dozens of measures withered on the vine. Langan annoyed his opponents with endless readings from Father James Keller's *You Can Change The World!*. In a vain attempt at compromise, Crenshaw's Verne Summerlin suggested a truce under which both Folsom's reapportionment amendment and McCorvey's voter amendment could be brought to a vote. That dog did not hunt. The Governor faced certain defeat on both measures. Deep into the evening's groggy hours, the filibustering quartet began to smell victory. Lt. Governor Inzer, no ally of Folsom on the amendment, suddenly yielded his gavel to Etowah's James Allen, an exceptionally skilled parliamentarian, to break the filibuster. On a question from Allen, the Senate voted 15-15 that none of the four filibusterers could speak again in opposition to McCorvey's bill. Passage of the amendment itself suddenly came up for consideration when, to Allen's chagrin, Lafayette's Fuller Kimbrell and C. B. Harvey of Blount County unexpectedly counterattacked, jump-starting the filibuster anew as Folsom's strategy unfolded.

The Senate clock showed less than 60 minutes remaining before the session would automatically expire at midnight. Senators lacked the power to legislate even one second beyond that witching hour. But Alabama senators enjoyed the means to make time stand still. Upon unanimous consent, Alabama's senators simply ordered the clock to stop, and it would. This elegant tradition found its roots in the last minute rush to pass pending bills, convey them to the Governor's desk for signature, and ensure their return to the legislature for closing business prior to the session's midnight adjournment. By law the legislature had to adjourn, *sine die*, after so many days, but occasionally found it necessary to turn back the clock. The number of statutes passed after legislative authority had expired is anyone's guess. Of course, if a gentleman senator objected to unanimous consent, time moved on. However, no one could recall that ever happening.

As midnight approached, the second-hand sweep of the chamber's clock stopped cold. Lt. Governor Inzer ruled that he, the chair, would keep time but issued no call for consent to stop the clock. Mysteriously, the chamber's clock sputtered back to life, only to die again moments later. When the clock neared 11:30 p.m., McCorvey's forces sought consent to stop the clock. That took some gumption, considering that these same gentlemen had resorted to sharp tactics earlier in the evening to silence senate colleagues from whom they now sought consent. Yet consent was regarded as a courtesy, a civility to be conveyed regardless of controversy. It came as a rude shock when Folsom's filibusterers refused to stop the clock. Hollering on personal levels erupted between the snarling groups. Senator Henderson indignantly protested, refusing to accept this unpardonable ambush. Gentlemen senators simply could not do this. Lt. Governor Inzer ticked off the minutes, slowly, methodically, amid verbal potshots and bickering, until both time and McCorvey's amendment expired after 23 grueling hours, on the stroke of midnight, September 9, 1949.

In its flagship editorial the following Sunday, Mobile's *Press Register* beat the dirge of defeat, lamenting the death of McCorvey's amendment and finding blood on the culprits' hands:

> A minority in the State Senate killed a proposed voter qualification law that would have met Alabama's needs. A small group of senators prevented the people of Alabama from voting on a constitutional amendment designed to strengthen our voter qualification laws. This is regrettable. Only time will tell the extent of the damage.

No one needed to wait very long to count casualties. Within the week, Gessner T. McCorvey announced that he would not seek re-election to the State Party chairmanship. McCorvey's nemesis, Big Jim Folsom, announced that he would support a good Democrat to succeed McCorvey. Two days later the Governor publicly applauded those six senators whose marathon filibuster killed McCorvey's attempt to replace the Boswell Amendment: "Here we are preaching the franchise all over the world, and trying to take it away from our people at home. It's just not consistent." Among Folsom's accomplishments during the 1947-1949 legislative session, this ranked as the most important.

The high-water mark of 20th Century white supremacy crested in Alabama in November 1946 and began receding in 1949. Governor Folsom and his allies undermined the Boswell Amendment and broke the grip of McCorvey's political machine. Down in Mobile on St. Emanuel Street, Gunny put thousands of voters on the rolls as fast as possible. Half of those were Colored. Gunny rejected no one, cranking the voter floodgates wide open. Still hospitalized in Biloxi, Schnell could do little to close the political sluice through which a steady stream of laborers, veterans, Whites and Coloreds rapidly poured. Above the din and sometimes violent resistance that arose over the next 15 years under the banner of states' rights and segregation, the slow death rattle of white supremacy could be heard.

CHAPTER 29

Politics as Usual

Joseph Mitternight's election to the Mobile City Commission on September 12, 1949 left one vacant seat on the County Commission of Roads and Revenues. Gunny's turbulent life as a registrar would be over once Jim Folsom's term ended. The ward heeling registrar had not pleased McCorvey and other white supremacists who still controlled the state Party. Folsom's successor would want nothing to do with Mobile's most controversial figure and, for that matter, neither would Gunny's political bedfellows.

Gunny went to see the Governor about being appointed to fill Mitternight's vacancy. Big Jim warmed up to Gunny's proposal and explained that Joe Langan, as Mobile's senator, had to approve appointing Gunny to the County Commission. Wondering whether a rift might have soured Langan toward Folsom, Gunny asked Big Jim how he was with Mobile's senator. The Governor's large shoulders shrugged. Big Jim figured he and Joe Langan were friends.

After the close of the 1949 legislative session, Gunny paid Joe Langan a visit about filling Mitternight's vacancy. To Gunny's surprise, Langan hesitated, unwilling to make any commitment. Gunny listened as Joe Langan spoke about druggist Jimmy Redding wanting the job and Jimmy Stein also asking to be considered. Langan expressed concern that he might make enemies by appointing Gunny county commissioner. Gunny recalled Langan talking this way before when

would-be senator Langan worried that political ties with Big Jim could
be risky. Never mind that Gunny would have been a credit to the
county commission. Talk of making enemies tripped Gunny's wire, the
unspoken message reducing his relationship with Langan to a cost-
benefit equation.

"The hell you would." Gunny rejected Langan's unconvincing excuses. "I am the main one that got you to run. I supported you from the
start." Gunny felt that Senator Langan wanted the best of all worlds, readily accepting a helping hand but reluctant to return one. Gunny did not
buy Langan's concern about Redding and Stein. That had the marking of
a ruse. Another agenda seemed to be brewing. Unknown to Gunny,
Folsom already had spoken with Joe Langan about filling Mitternight's
county commission seat. Exercising senatorial privilege, Langan rejected
the Governor's proposal. Big Jim could do nothing more.

With only a year left to his senatorial term, and no other legislative
session in Montgomery before standing re-election in 1950, Langan
viewed Mitternight's vacancy as an opportunity to strengthen his political base prior to the next election. Appointing Gunny would advance
none of Langan's personal goals. Appointing himself would, which
Langan discreetly arranged with the Governor. On the evening of
October 6, 1949, O. H. Finney announced the appointment in
Mobile. Langan's new $3,000 government job necessitated resigning
from the State Senate. County commissioner Langan announced that
his pay would be donated to the VFW, a calculated effort to deflect
foreseeable criticism. He did not need the money anyway.

On the heels of Langan's self-appointment, Gunny made a trip to
the hospital. Anne gave birth to a daughter. Gunny promptly returned
to unfinished business. Ever since Schnell's heart attack, the Board chairman had not functioned as a registrar. Back in August 1949, Gunny had
asked Attorney General Carmichael whether Schnell should be replaced,
permanently or otherwise, because of chronic absence. Even after returning to work at Gill Printing & Stationery, Schnell avoided 109 St.
Emanuel. Replacing Schnell, with whom Gunny hardly saw eye-to-eye
about anything, also might improve Gunny's chances of killing the wit-

ness rule. As of December 1949, Attorney General Carmichael still had
not responded about Schnell. With Gunny's blessing, Mobile's Central
Trades Council and the United Veterans started pushing political but-
tons, demanding that Randle change her ways. Randle refused, continuing the stalemate. Trades Council president Morris Alpert then asked
Governor Folsom to direct Schnell to do his job or find a replacement.
On January 9, 1950, Carmichael ruled that the state appointing board
had to replace Schnell. Three months later, Randle resigned. That
squared just fine with the Governor's agenda. Folsom had recently
appointed a blue-ribbon panel of veterans and like-minded allies to
investigate how Alabama's registration practices discouraged veterans
from voting. Big Jim echoed Gunny's charges: "With a small electorate,
a minority clique could control this state and maneuver the government
to its own petty whims." Both the Governor and his registrar in Mobile
had reason to beware the Dixiecrats' power. A voting bloc of veterans,
laborers and Coloreds provided the best available antidote. Expanding
the rolls also would plant the seeds for the Governor's re-election bid in
1954. Jim Folsom planned to leave the pot boiling as his term expired in
January, 1951.

Gessner McCorvey had other plans. On January 12, 1950 the
State Democratic Executive Committee announced that the Party
would disqualify from its May primary any candidate who had openly opposed McCorvey and other Dixiecrat presidential electors in
1948. Of course, nearly everyone in Alabama knew that Governor
Folsom had led the opposition, trying to stop Dixiecrat electors from
embarrassing President Truman. Though McCorvey's ax had Folsom's
name on it, Big Jim could not succeed himself as governor in 1951
anyway. McCorvey's strategy required Democratic hopefuls to sign a
loyalty oath, swearing they had not opposed the State's Rights slate that
bolted for Strom Thurmond's Dixiecrat ticket. Those who supported
Truman's civil rights platform would, by their own admission, cast
themselves into political oblivion. That included nearly everyone allied
with Folsom's administration. McCorvey cast his mission in heroic
though somewhat delusional dimensions: "Alabama and three of her sis-

ter Southern states won the admiration and respect of the nation in the fight which we made in 1948 for a return to constitutional government, for local self-government and home rule, rather than centering all of our government in Washington." Such rhetoric suggested that Alabama's white supremacists offered America its best hope of preserving constitutional democracy. When the 1948 Democratic convention boldly adopted a civil rights plank on live television, former Lt. Governor Handy Ellis staged a walk-out with half of Alabama's delegates, brandishing William Jennings Bryan's rhetoric into a warning that "The South shall not be crucified on the cross of civil rights." Contemptuous of Truman's commitment to civil rights, McCorvey and his segregationist allies led their flock into the desert under the banner of states' rights. They talked a good game but, once all the rhetorical dust settled, came up short on substance. Alabama's Dixiecrats demanded freedom for state party segregationists to dissent from national party civil rights, yet tolerated no similar freedom for Alabama's Democrats to dissent from the Dixiecrats' white supremacy dogma. Demagogues have no shame. McCorvey's forces wanted to entrust self-government only to themselves and their kind. Chanting the chorus of states' rights, Dixiecrats rekindled sentiments sacred to the memory of Civil War heroes. Ironically, this same tune also provided cover under which Alabama's Dixiecrats could openly consort with Republicans. An Alabama Republican still remained something of an oxymoron in 1950. Within most political circles, except perhaps in Alabama's Free State of Winston County, Republicans squirmed under the glare of a jaundiced Democratic eye. With relative impunity, Dixiecrats could flirt with Republicans while defending segregation under the flag of state rights. Only an occasional voice warned Alabama's Dixiecrats that McCorvey was selling the Democratic Party downriver to Republicans.

With the May 1950 primary just four months away, Democrats began declaring for office. Whoever won the Democratic primary won the general election as well. County Commissioner Joe Langan announced he would run for state senator. Mobile State Representative Tom Johnston, who supported McCorvey and wanted veterans to have vouching witnesses to register to vote, lined up as Langan's sole opponent. On February 10, 1950, Gunny declared his candidacy for the County Board of Revenue and Road Commissioners' seat being vacated by Langan. Serving as county commissioner provided political stepping stones for Joe Mitternight, Joe Langan, and Charlie Hackmeyer. That's how Gunny saw his future. Unlike Langan, though, Gunny had to defeat ten opponents, including druggist James Redding.

Joe Langan marketed his strong points, emphasizing service as a state representative, state senator, Mobile County Commissioner, Alabama National Guard battalion commander, and Chickasaw City Attorney. Of his legislative record, Langan boasted implementing voting and election reforms and establishing the Mobile County Merit System. Though practicing law and teaching part-time at Spring Hill College, Langan had not yet completed college. His opponent, a University of Alabama graduate and attorney, had served in the State House since 1942. Tom Johnston also saw eye-to-eye with rigidly conservative positions advocated by Mobile's newspapers. Langan lost. The race was not even close. By a decisive 3 to 2 margin, Tom Johnston soundly defeated Joe Langan in city and county returns. Mobile did not reward Langan for filibustering in Montgomery against McCorvey's plan to preserve Alabama's culture. Appointing himself to Mitternight's seat gained little for Langan, whose quiet aspirations for Congress expired with his brief tenure as county commissioner. None of that mattered. Within the year, Truman called up Langan's National Guard battalion for action in Korea.

Gunny's uphill battle did not enjoy the financial support and organization of Langan's campaign. Gunny drove and walked the campaign trail from one side of Mobile County to the other, shaking hands and passing out cards one by one. His paid spots in the *Press Register* tended to be modest, noting his faithful service on the Board of Registrars. He suffered no illusions about the number of enemies his public service had generated, including hostile opposition within the press and his own party. When the returns were tallied, though, Gunny led the field with 5,216 votes out of nearly 22,000 cast, not enough to avoid a runoff against second-place George Toulmin's 4,537 votes. That so many had voted could be credited to the surge in registered voters and the publicity generated by Registrar Gonzales. Turnout in the city alone nearly tripled since 1945.

Prior to the May 30 runoff against Toulmin, Gunny thanked those who had voted for him, acknowledged the endorsements offered by unsuccessful candidates, billed himself *A Man Of The People, For The People*, and pledged progressive government during the next four years. George Toulmin, a contractor with 15 years employment among different federal, state and county agencies, reflected the financial interests of construction businesses but otherwise stood for nothing in particular. He enjoyed a prominent family name and town namesake of Toulminville. In a runoff, however, Toulmin attracted those who disliked Gunny, including the McCorvey crowd, the press, and significant financial interests. Those who voted for Gunny would support him again. They agreed with what he had done, but that would not prove to be enough. Toulmin rode into office on 9490 votes to Gunny's 6523, a bitter pill for Mobile's populist to swallow. In that same election, Silas Garrett won his bid to become Alabama's Attorney General. In a somewhat unexpected twist, though, Democrats loyal to President Truman regained control from Dixiecrats of the State Democratic Committee.

In the wake of defeat, Gunny prepared for the end of his tenure with the State Docks and Mobile County Board of Registrars. His first priority in 1951 was moving the family from Bobolink to a three-bedroom house at the top of Albatross Drive. Until the next election or something better came along, he marketed goods for Toomey Dry Goods on a route through Bayou la Batre, Coden, Heron Bay, and Mon Luis Island. Come December, 1952 Gunny and Anne bid goodbye to Birdville, moving south to Hemley Road on the eastern outskirts of Bayou la Batre. The kids did not see much of Aunt Nettie again. Gunny continued making rounds for Toomey, netting a meager $65 per week. He had no access to larger department stores, and smaller shop owners often resented Gunny marketing to their competitors. The days of circuit riding salesmen seemed numbered, but moving to

Bayou la Batre had more to do with politics than peddling dry goods. Somewhere an idea hatched that Bayou la Batre's Seafarers International Union would make Gunny its head. Few political figures in Mobile County more closely identified with the blue-collar crowd. Gunny developed close ties with Mayor Jiggs Nelson. Jiggs and his wife Nattie operated an inn populated with stuffed wildlife. Uncle Jiggs, as the boys grew to regard him, had an engaging wit and sense of humor. As fate would have it, though, the union's overture to Gunny backfired. A disgruntled faction complained to Toomey that Gunny was stirring up trouble with the union. No longer managed by Gunny's longtime friends Jack and Billy Toomey, the Dry Goods company took a dim view of Gunny's union activity. Gunny would have to go, and that was that. The next day Gunny walked down Water Street into Gulf Dry Goods store, and temporarily signed on with Toomey's competitor.

More importantly, he also began laying plans to return to Mobile for the next election. Come July, 1953 Gunny left Bayou la Batre. From their $600 savings, Gunny and Anne put money down on a house at 1660 Ogburn Avenue south of Brookley Field. The pace of political life picked up. After Sunday Mass, Gunny would take the boys on a weekly pilgrimage downtown to Dauphin and Royal for political shoptalk at the Van Antwerp Building. They drove through Birdville up Michigan Avenue to Virginia, east to Conception, and then turned north. Within sight of St. Vincent's steeple at Canal, Gunny jabbed his left arm out the open window, reminding the boys: "That's Galvez Park. I used to play ball there." He spoke in a distant voice, as though Galvez were alive instead of a weathered plot amid the aging debris of Mobile's south side.

Van Antwerp's drugstore lobby boasted a gleaming soda fountain along its Royal Street side, complete with spinning barstools and full-length mirror, and one of the city's finest cigar stands. Though the lobby welcomed any foot traffic that might stray in on a quiet Sunday morning, it regularly catered to a backslapping huddle of serious-minded men by the soda fountain. A seamless web of grown-up talk about Mobile's political landscape might have bored Joe and Jimmy as the hours drifted from morning to afternoon. But the boys whiled away their time chumming with the cigar stand lady and collecting empty boxes to store baseball cards, marbles, and allowances. As old men sized up the political fortunes shared by Gunny and other potential candidates, Joe and Jimmy nursed cherry colas atop spinning barstools. Ever so often the chatter stopped to welcome another grayhair into the huddle, pausing for ritual handshakes that included introducing new faces to Gunny's two boys. Van Antwerp's political insiders politely greeted the young offspring of Mobile's most controversial figure. Then, without loss of rhythm, baritone conversations resumed in mid-sentence as though speaking from script.

While Gunny talked shop with Dr. Howard Walker, Charlie Barrett, and George Meyers, Joe and Jimmy made their way down Royal Street to the newsstand. Each Sunday the boys lingered over new comic book issues, peeking under slick covers before choosing two at ten cents each. Then they were off to Bienville Square, where pigeons foraged under sprawling oaks for popcorn handouts and goldfish circled the large fountain. With so much to do, the boys did not quite figure out why Gunny just stood around in Van Antwerp's lobby talking politics. For all its glamour, Van Antwerp's lobby could not hold a candle to the adventure, odds and ends, toys, popcorn machine, and squeaky wood floors that Woolworth and Kress offered. These and other prominent downtown stores also featured water fountains, some even refrigerated, bearing *White Only* and *Colored Only* designations. Such public notices in segregated Alabama conveyed an unambiguous directive somewhat more emphatic than that of a traffic stop sign. Both Coloreds and Whites were expected to comply. Violating the law often produced swift and sometimes peculiar consequences, especially from the uncomplicated perspective of a child. Unrelenting summer heat persuaded downtown visitors to linger where fountains and ceiling fans provided momentary relief. July and August had a notably direct impact on the length of water fountain waiting lines. Youngsters frequently gathered about these watering holes while accompanying their mothers during back to school shopping. No one openly questioned the wisdom of waiting in line for a White Only fountain just two feet away from an otherwise available Colored Only fountain. Though youngsters might disregard some social taboos without consequence, there were limitations. Instead of waiting in the White Only water fountain line on a particularly hot day, Jimmy walked right up to the Colored Only fountain and turned the handle. Before attempting the first swallow, the young scofflaw was quickly intercepted. A tall white man, one of the store attendants, pointed to the large Colored Only sign and directed the youngster to the White Only water fountain. The white faces waiting in line watched the attendant and boy with silent understanding and approval.

September brought with it another round of city elections, for the first time putting all three city commission seats up for grab at once. Mayor Charles Baumhauer and commissioners Ernest Megginson and Joseph Mitternight faced vigorous opposition, including challenges from Joseph Langan, Henry Luscher, and Charles Hackmeyer. Seeking re-election, the mayor claimed credit for restoring the city's fiscal integrity following its near bankruptcy 20 years earlier, and considered himself responsible for bringing Brookley Air Force Base to Mobile. Commissioner Megginson boasted of Mobile's park and recreation program, claiming the city had made more progress in the 12 years of his administration than in the previous 200. Jousting with Mayor Baumhauer, Langan reminded voters of his own experience in office, called for expanded park facilities, promised to work full-time on the job, and pledged not to pursue private business while in office, something which Langan chided the long-term mayor for doing. For his part, Luscher made much ado of costs related to a couple of minor city land purchases, suggesting that Commissioner Megginson either slept at the wheel or lacked sound business judgment. Transparently thin innuendo of cozy arrangements with land brokers netted Luscher a lot of unearned mileage at Megginson's expense.

Substantive issues did not dominate the campaign; personalities did. Joe Langan mimicked Big Jim Folsom's campaign style, hosting rallies in city parks off the back of flatbed trucks, passing around his

Army knapsack for dollar donations, and using a large empty chair to taunt the absent Baumhauer. One of his first successful rallies turned into a near circus in the park on Washington Avenue across the street from St. Matthew's, where the Klan had demonstrated a few years earlier. Blaring loudspeakers, music, and barbecue energized the large nighttime turnout. Putting aside bruised memories from the last election, Gunny worked the crowd for Langan while Anne and the kids mingled with friends. But the campaign's biggest crowd pleaser was George Meyers, who ran around town with three brooms sticking out of his car urging "Let's Sweep The Bums Out."

Against this carnival backdrop Baumhauer and Langan managed some serious exchanges. One of Baumhauer's ardent supporters, attorney M. A. Marsal, charged that Langan had appealed to prejudice in an attempt to attract a Negro bloc vote. Four years earlier, an insinuation of that sort would be inconceivable as the number of Negro voters hardly mattered, but the flood gates of registration had turned that around. Now it was possible for white politicians to play the race card as circumstance and public opinion allowed. However, for a politician to patronize Coloreds to win their racial bloc vote come election day did not set well with Whites. Langan bristled at Marsal's accusation. Langan reassured Mobile that he had never attended any political meetings with Coloreds and had never solicited their votes.

Marsal also scratched another nerve, challenging Langan's position on interracial marriage and citing comments the former state senator made on the floor of the State Senate. A circular making the rounds of political rallies included a reprint of *The Mobile Register*'s September 10, 1949 story that captured Langan's verbal skirmish in Montgomery. While filibustering against McCorvey's second generation version of the Boswell Amendment, Langan took a question from Senator T. B. Perry of Marengo, who asked whether Langan believed in "inter-racial marriage between the white and colored races." Langan parried the attack, responding: "It is a person's privilege to marry anyone he wants." Picking up the scent, Senator Dave Patton of Limestone challenged Langan to affirm his belief in the segregation of the races, to which Langan replied: "I'll wait until I get to Heaven or elsewhere and see if God believes in it."

Langan may have cleverly thwarted senatorial adversaries in 1949, but recognized the insidious effect those comments could have on his campaign. He announced that he opposed intermarriage of the races and supported state laws prohibiting racially mixed marriages. He protested that Marsal had taken out of context Langan's Senate floor statements, which "was to the effect that I was sure that no Southern women would choose to marry members of other races. I worked in the Army to dissuade our American boys from marrying members of Asiatic and other races. I have always fought this sort of thing, and I always will."

But the race card would not go away. The Non-Partisan Voters League, a Colored organization, asked whether candidates favored employing Negroes on the police force for law enforcement purposes, and if so, would they be assigned only to Negro neighborhoods and only to arrest Negro violators. The question begged the broader social convention that would not tolerate Negro police officers arresting and manhandling Whites, much less their women. Baumhauer sidestepped that political quicksand, noting that he did not want to do anything that might disrupt the genuine harmony and good will prevailing among the races in Mobile. Langan responded more assertively:

> I would not be in favor of any general employment of them that would change the scope of the personnel picture that now exists. I believe special colored officers could be hired to handle enforcement in their own areas or at their own events, such as athletic contests. Possibly, colored officers could be hired to look after colored prisoners down at the jail. But there definitely would be no contact whatsoever with white persons. Any we did have would be confined to watching over colored activities and would not do any general police work. They would never be any place except where colored persons are under the procedure I have outlined.

Langan's response dodged the bullet and reasonably distanced himself from politically insidious suggestions that he supported integration.

When asked about employing Negroes in the city fire department and maintaining separate fire stations for Negro units, the mayor replied that: "The Creole Fire Department is one of the oldest volunteer fire departments in Mobile's history. This department has continued to function and is now a part of our fire department. I am in favor of continuing the fire department on its present basis in this respect." Joe Langan agreed: "We've got one station now. I'm in favor of continuing the present policy as far as the fire department goes." Asked whether any of the candidates favored employing Negro clerks or stenographers in City Hall offices, Baumhauer favored continuing the present policy set up by city government. Challenger Langan answered with equal candor: "I would not be in favor of employing them in those offices where I was the appointing authority." Langan knew that civil service, not patronage, filled most city jobs. Lingering concern that Langan harbored notions hostile to segregation was mostly repudiated by the candidate on the eve of election. Whatever chemistry moved voters in the privacy of their automatic voting booths, Luscher beat Megginson and Hackmeyer ousted Joe Mitternight. It was not quite a clean sweep, though. Langan led but did not defeat Mayor Baumhauer in the primary, throwing the two of them into a runoff. The mayor subsequently chose to forego the political risk of a runoff defeat, gracefully conceding the contest to Langan.

Within 6 months, the 1954 general election primary began to heat up. George Toulmin left the county road commission for greener pastures, having been appointed by Governor Gordon Persons to fill the better paying vacant License Commissioner position. Toulmin announced for re-election, relatively assured of victory as the incumbent over an unknown opponent. Charlie Dumas and others, though, could not abide Toulmin. At the last moment, they turned to Gunny, offering to pony up the $100 filing fee and some modest campaign funds. For the second time, Gunny went toe to toe against Toulmin, crisscrossing the county's backroads. People expected somebody who wanted their vote to ask for it. Gunny asked. Joe or Jimmy usually tagged along for the ride.

On one of those late afternoon drives from Coden to meet with Fritz and Evelyn Thompson's clan in Heron Bay, Gunny and Jimmy pulled up behind a pickup on the two-lane blacktop. The truck seemed to have a mind of its own, wandering across the yellow line and then onto the narrow shoulder several feet above the marsh below. The truck straightened out, the passenger door sprung open, and a woman flew out onto the gravel shoulder and rolled down the bank. The truck paused in the middle of the road, then pulled over. The driver waited patiently until the bloodied woman crawled up to the blacktop and climbed into the truck cab. Campaigning the backwoods proved anything but dull. At night it also could turn scary. Crossing the long plank bridge over Fowl River was unsettling even in broad daylight without oncoming traffic. But at midnight, during a blinding squall, visibility on the unlit bridge dropped to less than twenty feet. When the windshield wipers failed during a storm while crossing the river from Mon Luis Island, only a blurry image of the two-by-four wooden guardrail appeared in the headlights. In the middle of the river, where the bridge sharply peaked to allow for passing ship masts, sheets of rain caught the headlights and even the guardrail disappeared. That was get-right-with-the-Lord scary.

In the heat of the campaign, Gunny left one afternoon for Bayou Coden, past Bayou la Batre to the southern tip of Irvington Road. Jimmy went along for the ride. Plans called for a stop at Henry Royal's place, followed by other visits nearby. Henry ran a junkyard, owned a bit of property, and had a bunch of kids. Henry knew lots of folks, lots of voters. More importantly, Henry had influence among Negroes. He was Colored. Gunny and Henry had known each other for some time, so driving up to Henry's front porch at night caused no stir inside the house. Jimmy had never been inside a colored family's house. While Gunny and Henry talked politics at the dinner table, Jimmy nodded off to sleep on a stuffed chair in the living room. Gunny went on to other meetings, leaving Jimmy asleep in Henry's home. He intended to return before Jimmy awoke, but that did not work out as planned. When Jimmy's eyes opened Gunny was still gone. Henry and one of his boys sat at the table watching the little white boy look around for his dad. Nothing but anxiety showed on their faces.

"You know how to play dominoes?" One of Henry's boys broke the tension.

"No."

"Want to play? I can show you how." Henry's boy lifted a box of dominoes. Jimmy got up and sat at the table. "All you gotta do is match the number on this here domino with one of the ones in your hand. Here, watch." Jimmy watched. He had never seen dominoes before, but the game was on. Jimmy forgot about Gunny and being alone in someone else's house, a stranger's house, a Colored's house. Odd things happened on a campaign trip, like playing dominoes with Henry Royal's boy at night in segregated Coden, Alabama. On the way back to Mobile that night Gunny barely spoke about the visit at Henry's house.

In the closing hours on election eve, May 3, 1954, Gunny ran a live spot on WKAB-TV, featuring the whole family. Beforehand he talked with Jimmy, explaining what to do when the large camera rolled in for a close up shot. "Remember now, there's nothing to be scared of. It's just a big camera. Now, what are you going to say to the camera?" Gunny rehearsed the scene.

"Please vote for my daddy." Jimmy practiced his sound bite.

The TV studio seemed odd, so unlike what little TV the youngster had seen. Men suddenly were talking, counting time by seconds, until a huge camera zoomed in on Gunny for a moment and then found Jimmy, grinning in awe at the strange contraption with blinking red lights. There was a pause, a long silence in the room, and then the camera moved on. Without a cue, a question, a signal of some kind, Jimmy just grinned and blew his line. Before the sun dawned, though, Jimmy knew from radio election returns that Gunny made the runoff. Gunny's poorly funded eleventh-hour campaign polled a surprising 9,700 votes to Toulmin's 12,000.

The June 1, 1954 runoff turnout for License Commissioner set a record of nearly 30,000 votes. Gunny's bid failed by 3,500 votes, a remarkable showing against an incumbent given the lack of money, publicity, and organization. But even the disappointment of that defeat would soon be overshadowed by infamy. Albert Patterson of Phenix City won the Democratic nomination for attorney general in the June 1 runoff and certain victory come the November general election. By general consensus, Phenix City was the moral cesspool of Alabama's Bible Belt. It pandered to gambling and prostitution, marketed loaded dice and marked cards, and boasted the only advertised safecracking school in Alabama. Patterson had pledged to clean out corruption. Charges of voter fraud, as common in Phenix City as clay, cropped up immediately following Patterson's victory. Like most everything else about Phenix City, even voter fraud had a bizarre twist. The original runoff tabulation sheets seemed to find their way into the hands of none other than Gunny's old adversary, Attorney General Silas Garrett. Under very questionable circumstances, official tally entries appeared to have been changed, from 3's to 8's and 1's to 7's, in favor of Gadsden's Red Porter, Patterson's runoff opponent. As of June 18, a Birmingham grand jury still had the whole mess under investigation. But that night, a Russell County deputy sheriff assassinated Patterson in a Phenix City alley. Russell County circuit solicitor Arch Ferrell, seen fleeing the shooting, also was charged with murder. Garrett appeared before the Birmingham grand jury for ten hours, and later was report-ed to have checked into a mental institution somewhere near Galveston. Governor Gordon Persons eventually declared martial law and sent in the Alabama National Guard.

It seemed anti-climatic that Big Jim Folsom won his second term as governor. Soon after Governor Folsom took office in January 1955, Gunny accepted a foreman's job at the State Docks grain elevator. There was little else except politics for Gunny to fall back on, and he now found himself out of the turbulent political mainstream. For the populist ward heeler and Truman Democrat, this political winter would be long and hard. Having a minority voice on Mobile's Democratic Executive Committee was better than having no voice at all, but he could only grit his teeth as demagogues splintered the Party statewide. Gunny worked local campaigns. Langan won re-election in 1957 to a second term on the City Commission, soundly defeating

Charles Baumhauer and E. C. Barnard, self-proclaimed Imperial Wizard of the Gulf Ku Klux Klan. On January 23, 1958, the Admiral Semmes Hotel hosted Mobile's political leaders to present the 1957 *Mobilian of the Year* award. City Commissioner Henry Luscher did the honors. Gunny, Anne and Jimmy attended as the Bienville Placque was awarded to Langan in "gratitude for splendid and devoted services to the community and to the cause of moral, social, and civic betterment." In part, the award implicitly recognized Mobile's peaceful dismantling of racial barriers following the Boswell Amendment trial, compared to the public chaos and boycott in Montgomery following the arrest of Rosa Parks on December 1, 1955. Mobile quietly staged controlled arrests for the strategic purpose of having presiding judges strike down similar segregationist bus and lunch counter ordinances. Mobile did not share Montgomery's experience.

40. *Mobile County Board of Registrars registration session, 109 St. Emanuel Street, Mobile (Courtesy, Mobile Press staff photo) c. 1949.*

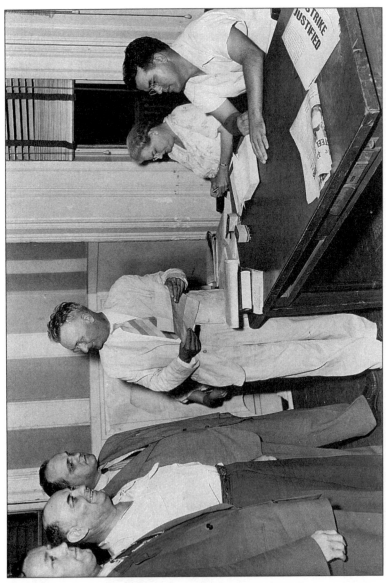

41. Mobile County Board of Registrars registration session, 109 St. Emanuel street, Mobile (Courtesy, Mobile Press staff photo) c. 1949.

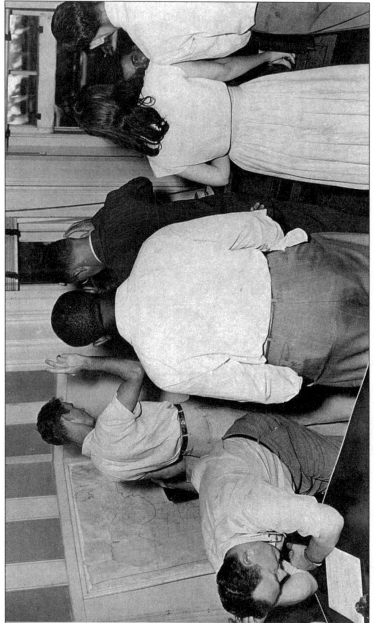

42. *Mobile County Board of Registrars registration session, 109 St. Emanuel street, Mobile (Courtesy, Mobile Press staff photo) c. 1949.*

43. Campaign photograph, E. J. (Gunny) Gonzales, Mobile County Road &
Revenue Commission Democratic primary, c. 1950 (photographer unknown).

CHAPTER 30

Reflections

B etween Reconstruction and 1954, politicians had no race card of any consequence to play in Alabama. By controlling the voting franchise and ensuring that white voters far outnumbered colored voters, it mattered very little whether Coloreds voted at all. As long as the ruse of restricting ballots to the better educated served the demagogic purposes of white supremacists, the impact of colored voting remained largely hypothetical. For much the same reason, open political hostility against Coloreds reflected an unnecessary and reckless appetite for racial confrontation. State parties had nothing to gain by pandering to or belittling the handful of colored voters who made no difference anyway. Prior to the 1950's, candidates had little reason to solicit Negro voters and dared not do so after 1949. Inconsequential colored endorsements of white candidates that once signaled racial harmony within the established order now provided the springboard for white political backlash.

In an ironic historical footnote, the fall of the Boswell Amendment undermined the pillars of white supremacy while bolstering segregationist campaign rhetoric. That block-voting Coloreds could put their white candidate into office after 1950 sent tremors through the political marketplace. Gunny had staked his fortune with disenfranchised veterans, laborers, and Negroes. He gave voice and power to Coloreds and Whites alike, for which a political ransom would be exacted by opponents. Winning primaries with the colored vote made any candidate vulnerable to attack in a runoff once an opponent alerted white voters that Coloreds were about to put their man in office.

Gunny's election campaigns ran into increasingly righteous, manipulative, and effective segregationist propaganda. In the 1954 runoffs, election campaigns began to play the race card, alerting Whites of Negro voting patterns, stirring fears of racial bloc voting, and damning with faint praise whomever Coloreds supported in the primary. As the 1958 election approached, race-baiting matured into a tactical art. During the May 1958 run-off campaign for the state legislature, candidates felt obliged to vigorously repudiate any ties to Negro voting groups. At a Battle House forum sponsored by the Young Democrats of Alabama, state senatorial candidate John M. Tyson charged that some women on the west side of town "carried out a vicious house-to-house rumor campaign accusing me of being tied up with the NAACP." Tyson assured Mobile that his "segregation record is perfect," that he "shall be for segregation" as long as he lives, and that he is firmly against Negro bloc votes. Tyson and State Senator Garet Van Antwerp III happened to be endorsed in the primary by the Negro Non-Partisan Voters League. Somewhat embarrassingly, Tyson led in predominantly colored Ward 10. Representative John A. Murphy, also endorsed by the same group, announced that he would do all he could "to maintain segregation" and was "the only person in this race who didn't go out and seek" the Negro vote. Bogus sample ballots appeared in the newspaper purportedly endorsing candidates "most favorable to the colored race." In the same daily edition, candidates felt obliged to campaign for segregation and publish the number of colored votes received by opponents. Front page news accounts in *The Mobile Register* tracked Negro "pink ticket" ballot guide endorsements along with the primary voting returns for those candidates supported by Coloreds. In order to temper radical race-baiting, even moderate candidates had to demonstrate a reassuring commitment to segregation.

Before Governor Folsom's second term came to a close in January 1959, the writing on the wall galvanized segregationists throughout the state. Within a year of taking office in 1955, Big Jim entertained flamboyant colored New York Congressman Adam Clayton Powell at the mansion in Montgomery. Powell bragged of sipping Scotch with Alabama's Governor, while Big Jim admitted only to having the congressman over for a beer. That alone ruffled social taboos, although it was all quite consistent with Big Jim's unconventional flair. Then came the enrollment of Autherine Lucy on February 1, 1956 at the University in Tuscaloosa, the first Colored to cross segregated school lines. The campus rioting that followed came as no great surprise. Whites well understood that if one Colored entered the campus, separate but equal segregation would not survive. Defiance and resistance initially appeared to turn away the storm of integration. But segregationists were just spitting into the eye of a hurricane. State legislators seemed poorly equipped to address the demise of segregation, passing a bill that same month purporting to nullify federal court desegregation orders. Never at a loss for words, Folsom observed that Alabama's legislature acted more and more like a hound dog baying at the moon and then claiming the moon's been treed. He had witnessed similarly desperate and radical legislative behavior in 1949. History had a way of repeating itself.

Democratic hopefuls eager to fill Folsom's gubernatorial shoes in January 1959 included Attorney General John Patterson and state circuit judge George Corley Wallace. Wallace previously served in the state legislature during Governor Folsom's 1947-1951 term, having campaigned in Mobile for Big Jim's election in 1946 and later for passage of Folsom's populist programs in the legislature. During the 1958 gubernatorial primary, Wallace embraced a moderate segregationist agenda, trying to appeal to growing numbers of colored voters. He even sat as trustee of colored Tuskegee Institute.

John Patterson had good reason not to bank on the colored vote long before the 1958 primary. As Attorney General, Patterson persuaded state courts to ban the NAACP from Alabama for illegally boycotting Montgomery's buses in 1956 following the arrest of Rosa Parks. Patterson so shrewdly targeted his white constituency that he even drew criticism from Wallace, who condemned Patterson for sounding like the Klan. Wallace lost by a stunning margin, in part reflecting

Patterson's ability to stoke segregationist frustrations with social unrest and "activist" federal judges. The little fighting judge, as Wallace fancied himself, infamously conceded the power of race-baiting politics: "John Patterson out-niggered me. Boys, I'm not going to be out-niggered again." Capturing the governor's mansion became an exercise in unabashed race-baiting as the death rattle of white supremacy echoed from Mobile Bay to Birmingham. The 1958 campaign demonstrated the strategic value of capturing votes by beguiling Whites with false promises of permanent segregation. Gunny's political fortune fell prey to those who pretended to stuff Alabama's colored genie back into its shattered white bottle.

The 1962 Democratic primary for governor fielded candidates who whetted every political appetite: populist Jim Folsom, ambitious Attorney General McDonald Gallion, moderate State Senator Ryan deGraffenreid, notorious Birmingham police commissioner Bull Connor, and little fighting judge George Wallace. The sight of Ku Klux Klan Grand Dragon Shelton on the campaign trail with Wallace left little room for anyone, in the little fighting judge's words, to "out-nigger" George Wallace into the governor's mansion. Setting the campaign's tone, Wallace chose to joust against the windmills of federal marshals, federal judges and federal law. The striking image of an Alabama state judge fearlessly snapping at the heels of outside agitators and federal court judges transformed an ambitious opportunist into a self-anointed savior. Understandably, the pink sheet Guide Ballot of the Colored Non-Partisan Voters League endorsed deGraffenried.

As Wallace's political star rose on the Southern horizon, Big Jim Folsom's sank into obscurity. Folsom left Alabama better off than he found her, and for that he might have been re-elected a third time. However, even his loyal followers gasped at the television in disbelief when their two-term populist candidate plucked out his false teeth and waved them at campaign cameras. Some suggested that opponents had plied Big Jim with liquor, maybe even drugs, while others simply saw a man wallowing in his cups. Whatever the truth, Governor Folsom's colorful career had come to an equally colorful end.

Despite the odds and Wallace's popularity, Gunny campaigned for deGraffenreid. Alabama rewarded Wallace with a 45,000 vote margin over runner-up deGraffenreid. It hardly mattered whether Wallace personally loathed Coloreds. The would-be governor's rhetoric pandered to those who did. Eight months after Wallace's racially charged inauguration in January 1963, promising "segregation now, segregation tomorrow, segregation forever," radical segregationists bombed the Sixteenth Street Baptist Church in Birmingham, killing four colored girls. Alabama's race-baiting agenda came home to roost.

The 1962 gubernatorial contest clearly stretched the contours of Alabama's political landscape. However, the corresponding congressional election that year secured an equally bizarre place in history. Credit for what happened goes to Alabama's Legislature. Consistent with well-established practice, the state Senate defeated reapportionment proposals introduced in 1956 during Governor Folsom's second term, and again in 1959 and 1961 during Governor John Patterson's term. As of 1960, state senators represented disproportionately populated districts ranging from 15,000 to 630,000 while House members represented districts as small as 6,700 and as large as 104,000. Although Alabama's Supreme Court previously found that the Legislature had failed to comply with State Constitution reapportionment requirements, the Court felt obliged not to interfere. Between the 1962 primary and general election, three United States District judges including George Wallace's law school classmate, Frank M. Johnson, ordered that Alabama's Legislature be reapportioned based on population, not livestock or trees. The United States District Court ultimately exercised the judicial responsibility that Alabama's Supreme Court chose to avoid.

Although Alabama needed to decrease its congressional delegation from 9 to 8 seats following the 1960 census, the Legislature also refused to reapportion congressional districts. Instead, the Legislature crafted a scheme under which 8 party nominees chosen in a statewide run-off from the 9 existing congressional districts would then stand a statewide general election for the 8 congressional seats. Under this "9-8 plan" each at-large congressman represented the same statewide district. As of November 1962, Mobile no longer had a congressman; it had 8. Kenneth A. Roberts, a New Deal congressman from upstate Calhoun County, survived being shot by Puerto Rican separatists in 1954 on the floor of the House of Representatives and later survived Alabama's 1962 marathon statewide congressional election. In 1964 Congressman Roberts nominated a senior from McGill Institute in Mobile to attend the U. S. Air Force Academy. That same year, the United States District Court in Mobile declared Alabama's statewide at-large congressional election scheme unconstitutional.

By 1965, the ghosts of 109 St. Emanuel Street were spinning in their graves. As the effective date of the Federal Voting Act approached, Alabama Attorney General Richmond Flowers ordered state boards of registrars to stop using literacy tests and witness requirements. It took 18 years, several federal court judges, and an act of Congress to vindicate Gunny's controversial struggle against Alabama's tide of white supremacy. On December 13, 1965, Alabama's Legislature officially repealed the Boswell Amendment.

Some 20 years after Big Jim's fall from grace, Gunny traveled with Mobile's Knights of Columbus to a convention in Bessemer. Governor Folsom was at a Baptist hospital in nearby Birmingham. Gunny had long planned to pay the Governor a visit, even taking along the registrar certificate Folsom gave Gunny in 1948. Pushing open the door of Big Jim's hospital room, Gunny saw Folsom's daughter Ruby and her brother James Folsom, Jr. Big Jim sat in a chair eating a banana. The Governor could not see Gunny. Big Jim was blind. Gunny motioned for Ruby and Jim not to let on about who had come to visit.

Jim turned to his father, the Governor. "You've got a friend here."

Big Jim tilted his head, scanning the silence. "Who is it?"

Gunny spoke up. "It's me, Jim."

Despite the passage of many years, the Governor cackled at the sound of Gunny's voice. "I know who it is now," smacked the large grinning face. Turning to his son, Big Jim shared one of his own bittersweet memories. "This is the only man that ever came to me and thanked me for what I'd done for him." Gunny did not see the Governor again. Big Jim Folsom died in 1987, six years before Alabama convicted and removed from office its first admittedly Republican governor since Reconstruction. Democratic Lieutenant Governor James E. Folsom, Jr. became Alabama's 52nd governor.

Gunny retired in 1976, but his political life with the Mobile County Democratic Executive Committee opened a new chapter. After 43 years, the minority Mobile Democratic committeeman became party chairman in 1981, providing a new generation of reporters with column fodder. Ten interesting years later on July 12, 1986, Chairman Gunny Gonzales announced the time had come to step down at age 72 and entrust Mobile County's Democratic Party to somewhat younger blood. As might be expected, he struggled over what to say after so many years of breathing politics. Giving up the fight did not come easy. Quitting politics meant quitting life. Ultimately, Gunny turned to his close confidant to find the right words. Gunny chose to leave politics much as he had lived politics, with a parting shot over the bow:

NEWS RELEASE

With great pride, I have served the people of Mobile County and the Democratic Party for more than forty-five years. I became a member of the Mobile County Democratic Executive Committee in 1938. Since then I have maintained an active interest in matters which concern the public good. What concerns the public good, of course, is not always free of controversy. However, a difference of opinion and belief is healthy, and a controversy or two serves the interest and humor of the people.

What the people do not need are public representatives who ignore or violate the people's trust. Also, we do not need anything less than a vigorous and meaningful two-party system. Not only must each party clearly represent its own convictions, but those elected to public office under the banner of that party must represent such beliefs. Whether Democrat or Republican, public representatives discredit themselves when they belong to a party only to gain endorsement and contributions. Yet we all know those who are conveniently Democrat in name but who avoid being Democrat in office.

Perhaps they fear losing their Republican or Independent voting constituency more than they feel obligated to remember their Democratic one. The result seems to produce representatives most loyal to themselves. Loyalty to party is not always evident among Democrats, although it is known to be a virtue among Republicans.

Something has been lost in politics in this county. It is not that there are not differences between the parties. In part it is because a good number of our elected representatives forget or ignore such differences, and leave us to guess at what stripes they wear. Instead of just two parties, we have as many parties as there are politicians. Speeches, beliefs, and political unity are not as important today as one's personal image and public relations. Current political strategy seems to avoid commitment and positions. We should not be surprised then that some of those elected are long on form and short on substance.

Since 1981, I have been Chairman of the Mobile County Democratic Executive Committee. I am proud of the Democratic Party. I cannot always say the same about some of our local elected Democratic officials. I can remember when elected Democratic officials in Mobile County showed unity, courage, and conviction as leaders of the Party. How much leadership, unity, and courage do we see today? Indeed, it is a rare event for some of our locally elected Democrats to publicly endorse Democratic candidates in the general elections. This lack of vision threatens the identity and dependability of the Party within the community.

I chose to share these parting thoughts with all Democrats to encourage renewal and commitment within the Party. This will be my last year of service as Chairman. Although I will continue to support and participate in Committee and Party activities, I will not seek re-election to the Chairmanship. Once I have surrendered my responsibilities as Chairman, I will begin a project that should be equally interesting. I plan to write memoirs about politics and events in Mobile County during the past fifty years.

Already I can hear the phone ringing.

E. J. (GUNNY) GONZALES, Chairman
Mobile County Democratic Executive Committee

The phone did start ringing. Republicans called to wish Gunny well.

44. *William Green administering to E. J. (Gunny) Gonzales oath of office as Chairman, Mobile County Democratic Executive Committee, January 27, 1981 (Courtesy, Mobile Register, photographer Roy McAuley, January 28, 1981).*

PART FOUR

Politics are almost

as exciting as war,

and quite as dangerous.

In war you can

only be killed once,

but in politics

many times.

—Winston Churchill

45. *Gunny Gonzales, granddaughter Kimberly Gonzales and J. B. (Red) Foster (Chief Slacabamorinico), Joe Cain People's Parade, Mardi Gras, Mobile, February 21, 1982 (Copyright © 2007 James J. Gonzales).*

CHAPTER 31

Magnolia Rest

Under the watchful eye of a warm April sun, the small cortege of cars slipped through Magnolia Cemetery's Ann Street gate. Other early risers already out and about tended tiny plots in the vast tombstone garden, weeding, planting and nurturing memories which lend meaning to life and hope beyond death. Amid the landscape of fading marble monuments, robins stalked earth worms and thickly scented azaleas seduced bees. Spring's rite of renewal held court even within the city of the dead.

The cortege traveled a geometric grid of narrow lanes through crowded monochromatic neighborhoods. Bleached white shells on the roadbed broke the morning's peaceful spell, groaning under the slowly rolling hearse, and announced to the departed that their sister had completed her long pilgrimage in this world. On April 10, 1955, Nettie Pocase died just shy of turning 85.

The caravan pulled over, parking on a narrow sloping shoulder. Smells of freshly mown grass and turned soil led the family down a path past a faithful cocker spaniel keeping watch over a child's grave. Gathering around the open grave near Irish Ma's headstone, they waited to bid Aunt Nettie goodbye. Surrogate nieces and nephews had come to commend her soul to God and renew their faith in the Resurrection. Ritual prayers, polished through the centuries, reminded the Father of His endless mercy, recalled His Son compassionately raising

Lazarus from the dead, and asked that His light shine forever upon Nettie Pocase until the last day, when she would rise again and see His face.

This was powerful stuff for young minds, inscribing bright images on their primitive theological horizons. For adults, the familiar ritual brought the message of mortality closer to home. They came to honor Nettie, as she had once honored them, and so in turn they honored themselves. With that, Miss Nettie took her leave, retreating slowly into Magnolia's open womb. The moment splintered into pockets of familiar but sometimes clumsy grown-up chatter. Meanwhile, unattended cousins romped through rows of ancient markers, stood solemnly atop nameless graves, and dared the nether world to say boo. Curiosity overcame their fears, for the ambiguities of life had not yet befuddled their simplicity. Near the lane where the path and grassy shoulder met, Jimmy balanced atop a narrow concrete wall enclosing a neighboring plot. Child's play could be had in the here and now no matter what went on in the hereafter.

"James Joullian!" A familiar raspy voice called out, summoning her grandson's attention. Ursulene Joullian's tone suggested no impatience or reprimand, as might be the case when Anne addressed her son formally. Aunts, uncles, and grandparents invoked the christened name of their nieces, nephews and grandchildren mostly to avoid confusion.

James Joullian recognized his Nannie's summons. He paused and answered: "Ma'am?"

Nannie came closer. "James Joullian, do you know where your Aunt Nettie is now?"

"Yes ma'am. I know."

"Where do you suppose she's gone?" Nannie pressed on, serious and straight-faced. To her eight year-old grandson, she sounded worried, as though she had misplaced something. Grown-ups, he thought, should know where grown-ups go. That Nannie did not know bothered Jimmy. He knew his Aunt Nettie. He had hunted Easter eggs with her in Birdville. He wondered what Nannie knew about Aunt Nettie. He knew that Aunt Nettie was not really in the casket in the ground.

She was somewhere else, heaven, hell, or purgatory, but not Mobile. Nannie could have figured it out by herself. She was a grown-up.

James Joullian looked squarely into Nannie's wide sagging face. "Aunt Nettie's in heaven, with God. That's where she's gone." Nannie paused, pulling away wearing a satisfied look, and released her grandson with a nod. Jimmy wandered off to the car, ready to go home and get out of his starched clothes and stiff shoes. Aunt Nettie's funeral etched an indelible image in his mind.

CHAPTER 32

Galvez University

Mobile sacrificed Galvez Park and most of the south side on the altar of urban renewal in the 1960's. Forty years earlier, a great inferno reduced the south side to rubble from which Galvez Square arose. What survived disaster, depression, and war fell prey to asphalt, parking lots, and interstate concrete. Despite Galvez Park's passing, Pat Healey's house on Canal, Grandpa Joe's place on St. Emanuel, and St. Vincent's Church somehow endured.

Galvez Park's sandbox now lies buried below the parking apron south of the Municipal Auditorium just off the west shoulder of Claiborne Street. On the narrow spit of grass between Claiborne and where Jackson ducks under the Interstate 10 overpass, Galvez's water fountain stood on the spot where Gunny was born. Home runs once dropped into left field under what is now Claiborne and the auditorium's parking lot. But Galvez Park's spirit still waits under an open sky to be stirred again. On the grassy mall midway between Interstate 10's east-bound and westbound lanes, some 40 feet north of present Canal Street's center line, the 1930 Whippet Athletic Club took batting practice at home plate. From there, the third base line ran westerly along Canal.

Today, Mobile drives by, over and around Galvez Park. There are no chalk baselines, bags, or home plate to remind Mobile that on this obscure grassy mall an unlikely gaggle of street-wise kids defied the odds and played the best game of baseball in Alabama. Yet, Galvez meant more than baseball, truant officers, and the Whippets. This modest baseball diamond produced many of Mobile's finest athletes, a number of which turned professional and semi-pro. It also drew upon the salt of the earth and yielded a generation that did Mobile proud combating fascist aggression abroad and political oppression at home. Galvez Park symbolized an uncommon deposit of character shared by its alumni.

Despite five turbulent decades, the bonds that Galvez Park formed with its offspring drew them back together. In 1976, a most improbable array of alumni gathered at Gunny's instigation to induct kindred spirits into the *Galvez University Hall Of Fame*. Gunny entered the Hall of Fame the following year with Red Foster, his friend from the Great Fire of 1919 who later masqueraded as legendary Chief Slacabamorinico during the Joe Cain Mardi Gras parade. Dennis Smitherman, Sports Editor of the *Mobile Press* who as a youngster lived across from Galvez on Canal, served as master of ceremonies and reported the annual Hall of Fame inductions. Eleven rowdy reunions between 1976 and 1986, occasionally blessed by Archbishop Oscar Lipscomb, Jr., inducted 122 surviving spirits before they faded into the history of Mobile's south side.

GALVEZ UNIVERSITY HALL OF FAME

Reynolds Alonzo

Frank J. Andrade, Jr.

Joseph H. Andrade

Colden A. Aubert

Bubba Barnes

J. B. Barnes

Ronnie Barrett

Frank W. Barter

F. H. (Peanut) Bell

Stanley Bell

Joseph D. Bemis

Clarence Berg

Donald Billie

James Bonham, Jr.

James (Crip) Bonham

Paul P. Bonham

Albert E. (Chick) Bourgot

Martin J. Brabner, Sr.

William E. Brabner

W. T. (Ty) Brabner

Eugene Bradley

Lewis Bradley

Joseph Bresewitz

Manuel Brown

Johnny Browning

Charles L. Byrd

C. (Shrimp) Calhoun

Dorothy M. Campbell

Harry T. Campbell

John W. Carey

Joe Casey

Emile L. Chaillot

Gabe Chamblin

Tincy Chamblin

Jimmy Chambliss

Bert Chappell

J. F. (Jimmy) Charest

Buster Collier

Edward T. Conniff

William (Willie) Conniff

Leo Cool

George M. Cox

Jack D. Cox

Peter V. Crolich, Jr.

Alexander M. (Mac) Crow

J. Kenny Crow

Cecil R. Dana

George A. (Tweet) Davis, Jr.

John C. Davis

Hazel (Rice) Dees

I. D. Denny

Jack Donald

J. P. Donoghue

Sue Donnelly

Maurice (Casey) Downing

John Robert Doyle

Dreaper F. Dumas, Sr.

Dot (Sweeney) Durant

Clyde Fail

Johnny Fath

Edward Ferniany

George Ferniany

Dorothy M. Fleming

Emmett R. Foster

J. B. (Red) Foster

Jimmy Foster

James T. (Sammy) Francis

Louis L. Francis

Patrick J. Francis

Adolph Freeman

Shaw Freeman

Earl E. Garner

Alphonse C. (Al) Gonzales

E. J. (Gunny) Gonzales, Jr.

Joseph Alfred Gonzales

Joseph V. Gonzales

Luthia (Dit) Gonzales

M. C. (Connie) Gonzales

George Green

Johnny Green

Richard Green

Elmer Guillot

A. V. Hall

Preston Hall

Robert Hamby

Charlie Hanwick

Leo Hanwick

Bernard M. Harrison

William J. Harrison

Donald Hawie

Francis Healy

George Healy, Jr.

Pat Healy

Bernard Hite

Percy Hubbard

Hilton Jackson

Aubrey Jernigan

Gene Jernigan

Pat A. Jernigan

R. A. (Buddy) Jernigan

Henry L. Johnson

J. Melvin Johnson, Jr.

Bookie Kollins

John A. Kramer

LaLa Kramer

D. R. (Nick) Kunz

John P. Kunz

Chester A. Lewis

Hortense L. Lewis

Claude E. Lomers, Jr.

Victor T. Lomers

Joe Lose, Sr.

Joseph C. Lose

Robert C. Lose

W. P. Manders, Jr.

James B. (Bernie) Martin

Joseph (Joe) Martin

J. R. (Scrappy) Martin

Thomas P. (Tom) Martin

William (Bill) Martin

Harry Mattei

Emmett A. McAtee

Harold J. McAtee

LeRoy McAtee

Marion F. McAtee

Mary A. McAtee

Max B. McGill, Sr.

Charlie Meyers

Chubby Meyers

Simon T. Miller

William M. (Billy) Mingus

Frank E. Moore

Benedict Morrison

G. (Giggy) Morrison

Joe Morrison

Leon Morrison

Bill (Honey) Murphy

Roy Newell

Vincent A. Noletto

William F. Noletto

Robert C. Norris

Marie J. O'Brien

Sam Oliver

Naomi H. Phillips

Homer L. Pippin

J. (Cotton) Quinn

R. (Dick) Quinn

Norma R. Reese

John A. (Rip) Repoll

Rowland Riel

Sheldon E. Robinson

Joe Rooney

Cliff Schaffer

George (Bo-Bo) Schaffer

Harry F. Schilling

Nonie Schuler

Robert Schuler
T. (Forbes) Sciple
Clifford A. Shields
Delroy Scott
W. D. (Buck) Scott
William (Bill) Scott
Harold A. Sherman
Richard Shields
Dennis G. Smitherman
Ross Smitherman
Johnny Soutullo
Paul David Stewart
Alice A. Stokes
Fred L. Stokes, Sr.
Jack Stokes
Gary P. Sullivan
W. A. (Willie) Taylor

James L. (Tunker) Tew
J. Trachy Tew
Robert (Spud) Thompson
Eugene (Gene) Tillman
Victor G. Valdez
Jimmy Wall
John R. Wallace
Harry Ward
Roy F. Ward
Artemus (Arty) Watson
Elmore H. Wentworth
William J. Westbrook
Teddie White
Clarence Wooten
John E. Yockers, Sr.
Joseph R. Yockers
William (Billy) Yost

46. Galvez Park baseball diamond home plate site, Canal Street at I-10, Mobile, 1994 (Copyright © 2007 James J. Gonzales).

CHAPTER 33

The Eulogy

I drove Gunny downtown to Wintzell's Oyster House for dinner on December 20, 2005. At 92 he still craved a platter of fried oysters. Gunny knew cigar-chomping Oliver Wintzell since the oyster bar opened in 1938, when a buffalo head nickel fetched a nice size oyster on the shell. Spanning the west wall, the oyster bar still provided no nonsense satisfaction for the curious tourist and seasoned shucker alike. Gunny shucked with the best, sober and otherwise. After my commissioning from the Academy in June 1969, we visited Nolan Ladnier's place just south of the bridge on Dauphin Island, and picked up a tub of Mississippi Sound oysters off the morning boat. By mid-afternoon, under the shade tree in the front yard, we had polished off most of the tub, hot sauce, crackers, and two six-packs without any notable injury.

Hurricane Katrina's August assault on oyster reefs seemed to have little impact on the menu that night. As Gunny finished off his platter, a young waitress wandered over. When I asked for the tab, Gunny leaned across the table and confided that the bread pudding here was "okay." Not disposed to exaggeration, Gunny placed great stock in whatever he deemed *okay*. Translated, he wasn't leaving Wintzell's just yet. Among few genuinely fond memories of eating that survived his youth, bread pudding never lost its appeal. He might sample banana or rice puddings, but those were mere substitutes. The waitress grinned and disappeared. For someone who checked his blood sugar twice daily, an okay bread pudding probably posed more risks than did raw oysters.

Gunny wandered off into his memories, then returned with a surprising anecdote. "Mama used to make bread pudding and sell it to Oliver Wintzell for the restaurant here." He paused. "That was a long time ago." When the waitress reappeared with the pudding, I asked to speak with the manager. She did not hesitate. A relatively young assistant stepped over with an uncertain look, perhaps expecting some complaint about the potato salad, fried okra, or whatever. I complimented him for having a celebrity in the house. His expression changed. I introduced Gunny and shared the story of Ursulene supplying Wintzell's with bread pudding long before the assistant manager's time. He seemed intrigued, visited awhile, and left bemused.

Gunny nudged toward me what little remained of obscenely good pudding. His eyes scanned the chaotic array of Oliver's folk wisdom and salty humor covering the walls. It seemed a fitting close to our bittersweet afternoon, visiting Anne bedside at the hospital, passing Callahan's Irish pub on Charleston, circling Washington Park, and recalling infant Joe atop the bronze deer some 60 years ago. We paused at Palmetto and Roper streets near Oakleigh Plantation. Gunny reminded me of Joe tossing bread from a window of their WWII apartment and then giggling as rats swarmed over the crumbs.

We finally bid Wintzell's oyster bar goodnight and returned to his apartment. Gunny sat silently in his rocker for a while. Thinking took more time and effort for him these days. I waited and watched. His expression looked familiar; something I had seen before. He seemed anxious to float an idea. Gunny was thinking about visiting Julie and me. This would prove no small feat for a man of 92 years who dreaded flying. His last trip to Colorado turned into a two-day adventure through train depots from New Orleans to Denver via Chicago. But Gunny enjoyed riding rails, whether by boxcar or coach. He arrived at Union Station with a bounce in his step and fresh tales for the cabooses, as he called the grandkids. Travel by air, though, required a brew or two, especially when connecting through Atlanta. His arrival at Denver's Stapleton Airport provided great spectacle as the children watched their Papa G step through the boarding gate door and, amid the milling crowd, gratefully kneel to kiss the concourse floor. No matter how smooth the flight, Gunny focused on the inevitable: sooner or later, the airplane would hit the ground.

Gunny's affection for the Wild West led us to one of the most colorful square miles in Colorado's mining and gambling history. We left Denver one spring morning in 1985 for Central City. Near the turnoff to Buffalo Bill's grave, feathery snowflakes started drifting out of the mountains. Having just left Mobile's balmy heat, he marveled at the snow. We pulled into Central City's deserted streets and parked near the Teller House. Gunny stepped up to the saloon door, adjusted his hat and jeans, and flashed a gold constable's badge. I followed Constable Gonzales into the bar where he ordered beer and rested a foot on the brass rail. He fit right in, like an extra in a grade B western movie. After absorbing the atmosphere and beer, Gunny paused at the painting of Madeline's face on the barroom floor and then strode into the street. He ascended Colorado's mountains and entered his childhood fantasy.

Gunny's air and rail adventures ended long before December 2005. Even so, he now imagined passing time in Denver again, with Julie in particular. His spirit brightened when she visited or telephoned. They hit it off in June 1969 when Julie visited Mobile after graduation. At first meeting, though, Gunny reserved judgment because Julie's Texas Panhandle twang sounded suspiciously Yankee to his ear. He seemed reassured to learn she was born in Galveston near Texas City about the time harbor ships blew up in 1947, and grew up in Amarillo. She also proved herself a good sport, helping Gunny lug crab traps and tubs over Dauphin Island's sand dunes to reach the south pier by dawn. Gunny's hospitality nearly backfired, though. He unexpectedly invited Julie to sit at the head of the table one afternoon where he placed crackers, hot sauce, a fork, a saucer and, curiously, a knife. Julie seemed flattered by all the fuss until Gunny filled the empty saucer with a raw oyster the size of an omelet. Julie paled. She sensed I could do nothing but witness her maiden experience. Yielding to her Texan instincts, Julie snapped up the knife and cut the oyster down to bite size, disemboweling the naked critter of its greenish viscera.

Gunny seemed stunned. I could not recall him ever questioning a guest's table manners, but then I could not recall anything quite like this. Even when my classmates from Guam and Westport Washington smothered one plate of grits and eggs with ketchup and the other with milk and sugar, Gunny pretended not to notice. Still, the etiquette of slurping raw oysters, however minimal, does not abide surgery on the dining table. Gunny let Julie know in typically blunt terms that this simply was not done in polite company, much less in his. He quickly removed the knife, saucer and mangled oyster. Julie apologized to no avail. Before she could escape, Gunny replaced the saucer and served up another trophy specimen. Julie glared at the oyster, wondering how to gracefully dispose of it. Gunny tried to be encouraging: "Honey, you can tie a string around it and pull it back up to chew some more if you can't swallow it the first time."

Julie looked ill. My mind wandered back to June 1968, sitting in the jungle near Nakhon Phanom, Thailand, birthplace of Ho Chi Minh. I had volunteered to accompany an unarmed Air Force civic action team delivering medical care to remote villages. Four female Thai soldiers in royal blue jumpsuits provided armed security. In a gesture of hospitality, the village chief placed fresh jungle fruit on a wooden chopping block, grasped a machete, and surgically prepared the offering. Women and children squatted at the edge of the open-sided hut, watching with anticipation. I sat nearby on the ground under a thatched roof. Without pause, the chief turned and stepped closer, presenting me first choice of unrecognizable fruit. The villagers understood this honor. They grinned with pride and amusement, the same expression I noticed on Gunny's face. Our pre-mission briefing included a vague directive: eat whatever you may be offered. I smiled politely at the chief and hesitated, like a rabbit staring at approaching headlights. The pre-mission briefing also warned about parasitic gastrointestinal nightmares. From my ground level perspective, I reviewed the situation: a machete dangling from the chief's hand, 45-calibre side arms bulging from the hips of my bodyguards, dozens of toothy grins, and the medic team NCO's anxious stare. My choice seemed clear: graciously eat nameless fruit, ignore lurking parasites, and preserve relations with Thailand. The look on Julie's face betrayed a similar quandary. She silently reviewed the situation. Determined that this too shall pass, she drowned the oyster in hot sauce and shoved the whole thing in on a cracker. Her eyes watered but the oyster stayed down. Gunny beamed with admiration. Julie proved her mettle, but never ate another.

The long day wore thin on Gunny. We finally called it a night, knowing I would leave for Denver the next day. After tending to some distasteful family business in the morning, I visited Gunny again on December 21. The frailties of his aged worn body frustrated and confused the restless soul within. He yearned to drive a car again. He spoke of getting a job, as though he were young and robust. I tried to comfort him with what he treasured most. We spent time wandering through his memories of the 40's, which is where I left him. Two months later, my brother Joe called with news that Gunny took ill and entered the hospital. I arranged a flight to Mobile for Sunday March 5. A couple days later from his bed Gunny spoke of "Jimmy on the airplane," which Joe took as a request to see me. After four days of deposing government investigators, I prepared to leave for Mobile. At 7 p.m. on Friday March 3, Joe called from the hospital, his voice unsteady: "Dad is gone."

I drove directly from the airport to the funeral home in Mobile where Joe waited with the staff to discuss arrangements for the wake, for which Gunny left no instructions. Before the days of elegantly appointed funeral parlors, Gunny attended neighborhood wakes in modest south side homes where friends toasted the deceased and occasionally blessed the open casket with good whiskey. For this occasion I hand-carried a bundle of memories. At many a Mardi Gras, Gunny suited up in white tie and tails for the Mystic Stripers Society Ball. Gunny managed the blackcoats, as members in white tie and tails were known, during callouts of the king's court and maskers. He left floats, throws and costumes to others. When not on the ballroom floor guiding a retinue of younger blackcoats, Gunny patronized the party rooms, reveling with his friends into the morning hours. After his last

Mystic Stripers Mardi Gras ball, Gunny kept the white tie and tails under wrap in his closet. When Gunny and Anne moved to a retirement home, they left most everything in the house. Furnishings and clothes were given away, except for the white tie and tails that accompanied me to Colorado to await Gunny's final callout.

Gunny would attend his wake dressed for the Ball. However, an open-casket wake in Catholic Mobile observed certain social and religious traditions. Anyone viewing an open casket expected to find the deceased piously holding rosary beads, as though deeply in prayer. Gunny probably last touched a rosary in the 1920's, shortly before being expelled from St. Vincent's school. It seemed more becoming that Gunny have Mardi Gras beads in his hands, if not around his neck. Initially that notion generated enthusiasm, despite the funeral parlor director's subdued response. True, those who knelt beside the casket to pray for the salvation of his soul might find Mardi Gras beads distracting. There also remained a remote chance of the archbishop appearing at the wake to pay his respects and bless Gunny. And, of course, family and friends traditionally prayed the rosary during the wake. Tradition played a strong hand at times like this.

Ordinarily, a wake occurs within three days. We pushed the date out another four days for grandchildren and Aunt Nonie to arrive from Seattle, Cincinnati, Jacksonville, Denver, and Atlanta. Gunny's baby sister and only surviving sibling, Nonie looked and talked remarkably like Gunny, although their salty candor seemed more startling when coming from her. I last saw Aunt Nonie in 1988 at Gunny's 75th birthday bash. Some of the grandchildren had yet to discover their grand Aunt Nonie.

Friday morning dawned on mixed emotions that too brief a span of time had not yet sorted out. The Thursday edition of the *Mobile Register* ran the obituary with a befitting photograph of Gunny I took during the 1978 Mardi Gras. Writing the obituary came easily, as though I had prepared many years for this. A reporter from the *Mobile Register* asked me late Thursday afternoon to "Describe your father." My arms could not wrap around that question. I invited her to imagine the soda fountain counter and cigar stand that once graced the Van Antwerp building's lobby some 50 years ago. Gunny met there on Sundays with political leaders, and usually wanted Joe or me to accompany him. One Sunday, while I sipped cola at the counter, a well-dressed man leaned over and asked, "Young man, do you know who your father is?" I remember giving a predictably simple answer: "He is my dad." The man paused and said, "he is the most controversial man in Mobile." I continued sipping the cherry cola, but could not forget what he said, though it made little sense at the time. The March 10, 2006 edition of the *Mobile Register* featured an article about Mobile's former Democratic Party chief and the Sunday political caucus at Van Antwerp's.

Gunny's granddaughter Katy and her older brother Brian planned to honor their Papa G in song during Saturday's funeral Mass. Katy and younger brother Michael drove into Mobile from Ohio late Thursday. Neither had ever attended a wake. Michael would serve as one of his grandfather's pallbearers, another experience of first impression. Michael left Dayton and the university without dress shirt or shoes. Katy and husband Mike Kristoffersen carefully packed dark dresses and suits which, after stepping out of the car in Mobile, they remembered leaving in a closet in Cincinnati. Come Thursday evening I had hoped to escape the commotion of events and quietly prepare the eulogy. Some things, though, are not meant to be. Instead, we crawled the mall, threaded a madding crowd, selected suits, tried on shoes, matched ties, picked shirts and rummaged dress racks, exceeding my collective mall experiences for all of 2005. Fifteen minutes prior to closing, Katy gave up in desperation and left the mall empty handed. My feet refused to walk any further, for any reason, anywhere. Betting against odds, I crossed Airport Boulevard and stopped in front of the last store in the north mall. "Katy, you have 10 minutes to find a dress." I tried to sound encouraging and optimistic, but hedged my bets and turned to Mike. "Get a suit for Katy if she can't find a dress!" My son-in-law grinned. Katy scooted into the store. I found a dark spot in the middle of the parking lot to think in peace. Twelve minutes later two silhouettes with bags approached the car. Katy's grin said it all. My stress returned to normal.

Anne would not be attending Gunny's wake or funeral. Her condition did not allow for either. She would remain under care at the nursing home. After breakfast Friday morning, Kim, Katy and Michael planned to pick up their brother Brian in Gulfport and view some of Katrina's devastation. The hurricane's summer swipe at Mobile clobbered the bay's western shore, ruining Joe and Betty's home. However, the grandchildren's day of grief began by visiting their Mama G at the nursing home. One by one they whispered in her ear, but the grandmother who always comforted them did not respond.

Family traditionally gathered in the funeral parlor before guests arrived. Joe and Betty assembled a display of photographs and memorabilia highlighting Gunny's life. Much as he did with Julie, Gunny had taken a shine to his daughter-in-law Betty. Initially, the mood in the parlor remained subdued. The family quietly mingled: Joe and Betty; their children Misty, Tony and Kerri and son-in-law Dennis Wilson; and Julie and I with Kimberly, Brian, Michael, and Katy and her husband Mike Kristoffersen. The stately parlor absorbed whatever whispers it heard. While adult grandchildren slowly came to terms with their Papa G nearby, Misty's toddler Ashton adjusted quickly, wandering into the flower sprays, playing on the prayer kneeler, peeking into the mirror, and hiding under the wall table.

Before guests arrived, I paused at the casket. Gunny's white tie and tails matched the parlor's elegance, lent character to the occasion, and left no doubt about the guest of honor. His right lapel sported a brass Mystic Stripers emblem, his left lapel a Friendly Sons of St. Patrick leprechaun. Under a green felt derby, Gunny faithfully had paraded for years with the Friendly Sons of St. Patrick on March 17 from the Cathedral down Government past the archbishop's residence into the nearest pub, usually Callahan's Irish Social Club, then the next nearest pub, and so on until March 18.

Uncle Joe's only son, who the family knew more as Butch than by his given name Joseph, walked into the parlor alone. I last saw Butch at our 1965 high school graduation. Gunny's funeral somehow renewed the glue that tethered the family. I turned to watch Aunt

Nonie reluctantly enter the parlor with the help of husband Robert Schuler and my cousins, Dottie, Robbie and Bobbie. She and Jean Gonzales, Uncle Al's widow, joined family on the sofas. I sat down next to Nonie. The wake visibly troubled her. Only three years ago her other brother, Joseph, passed away in Mobile. At 82, Nonie was family legacy. She gripped my hand while I humored her in an irreverent Gonzales fashion. "You're bad." Aunt Nonie grinned in mock disbelief, clasping my arm. I teased and scandalized Nonie into laughter until she was nearly beside herself. "You're really bad!" Nonie protested. "You should go to confession." Nonie all but shouted, still holding my hand.

I looked up to see Brian, Katy and Michael staring at Nonie. "Dad, why haven't you introduced us? We didn't know Papa G had a sister!"

They had discovered their grand Aunt Nonie, and their faces betrayed their thoughts. "Well, the longer I keep her away from y'all, the fewer stories she can tell about me."

Brian shamelessly begged Nonie. "Tell us something about Dad." Just as I figured. They wanted to gather the goods on me.

Nonie glanced at me, then back to Brian. "I'm not saying anything!" Aunt Nonie scrunched her mouth shut, as though something might slip out. It seemed safe to leave her alone with my brood.

At 5 o'clock, the parlor doors opened for guests. Joe stood near the foot of the casket, greeting friends and accepting condolences on behalf of the family. My eye caught a black suit and pectoral gold chain crossing the room in our direction. Oscar Lipscomb, Jr., Archbishop of Mobile, came to pay his respects. I looked over my shoulder into the casket. Gunny piously gripped a rosary. Archbishop Lipscomb paused in prayer at the casket and extended his blessing to Gunny. Oscar Lipscomb, Sr. had played baseball in the 1930's with Gunny. I shared with Archbishop Lipscomb that Gunny often spoke of Oscar Lipscomb, Sr. and other ball players who grew up on Mobile's old south side. We spoke of Gunny's amazing knack for remembering hundreds of family trees. I mentioned how Gunny often questioned me about the families of girls I dated during high school. The archbishop chuckled. Mobile and ancient Greece shared a similar culture, he jested: both are deeply religious and both worship their ancestors. The archbishop left as he arrived, graciously and without fanfare. After hours of stirring emotions and memories, the gathering took its breath in growing pockets of silence. Deacon Gordon Kenny, a seasoned man of modest stature and uncomplicated convictions, stood apart, patiently waiting to lead the faithful in the mysteries of the rosary. Gunny's wake closed with the traditional chant of ancient prayers.

Saturday morning arrived too early. In the pre-dawn hours, I found a quiet nook in the hotel lobby to collect some thoughts. Driving alone to Our Lady of Lourdes Church, I pulled up behind the white hearse and focused on the lonely silver casket. Inside the church Brian and Katy played through some musical selections and traded vocal segments. It seemed less a rehearsal and more an arrangement. At a younger age, their notion of a piano duet meant sharing some of the bench but none of the keyboard. They played intuitively. I began to drift along with fragments of songs, but the eulogy kept pulling me back. I sat alone before the church filled, then walked outside. Across the parking lot beyond the hearse stood Aunt Nonie flanked by Robert, Dottie and her husband Melvin Barnett, Robbie, and Bobbie. I walked past the hearse and hugged Aunt Nonie. She looked somber: "I don't know if I can get through this." She did not seem willing or able to move past the hearse.

I took her by the arm. "Nonie, you and I are going in together. I want you to sit up front with family." She slowly walked with me around the hearse into the church up the aisle near the altar, and then began to cry.

By tradition, immediate family gathers at the entrance and places a linen, Bible and crucifix on the casket. To the dirge of pipes, Joe and I followed as the closed casket moved to the altar. Family occupied the front two rows to the right of the casket and pallbearers sat to the left in front of Aunt Nonie. Forty minutes into the liturgy, Katy and Brian honored their Papa G with a mesmerizing New Orleans rendition of an essential jazz spiritual, *Just a Closer Walk with Thee*. As the final note faded, nothing more need or should be said. A remarkable peace spoke eloquently enough. I wanted the spell to linger, but the time for eulogy had come. I stood in the aisle, placed a hand on his casket, stepped up to the altar, and looked into their faces:

At some moment in life we probably wonder whether what we do matters. At some point, we might even ask if we matter at all. We gather today to recognize a man who mattered. What honor is greater for a son than to share the story of a father who mattered?

As sad as this occasion may be, remember that Gunny always felt at ease attending a funeral. He preferred that to a wedding. He would be sitting today in the last row to my right, next to the door. That is where he sat in this church. As a young boy, I recall talking with Gunny about funerals. I once asked him: "Do you think you'll go to heaven?" Now, Gunny believed in heaven and hell. His answer tried to reassure and humor me. Without hesitating, Gunny said: "I don't really know, but don't worry. I've got plenty of friends in both places."

In 1988, on the occasion of his 75th birthday, as family gathered to celebrate, I asked Gunny what we should put on his tombstone. He had become accustomed by then to my many questions. He paused and said "Tell it like it is." That is probably what Gunny did best. For nearly 30 years I have researched and written about Gunny's history in sports, politics, WWII, and the south part of town. Gunny had something to say about most everyone who once lived on Mobile's old south side. He often asked that I not publish the book until, in his words, he was six feet under. He did not want to embarrass his friends. Well, he outlived most of his friends. I began to think he would outlive us as well.

Gunny took great pride in his family. He worked hard to be a parent, but he was not raised by his own parents. At 5 years old he stood in the middle of Franklin Street, watching his home and most of Mobile burn to the ground. For much of his youth Gunny was raised by his Irish Ma, Leona Joullian, Uncle Charlie Joullian, and a woman of no particular kinship by the name of Nettie Pocase. Aunt Nettie, a 90-pound spinster, somehow managed to make Gunny toe the line. Together, they survived the Depression, making ends meet as a family.

Religion centered around old St. Vincent Church. When raising his own children, religion still centered around St. Vincent Church. Gunny took time from work when I was in first grade to pick me up at Maryvale School each week and drive across town to study catechism at St. Vincent and prepare for First Communion. On Mother's Day, 1954, Gunny stood with Uncle Charlie, his mother Ursulene, sisters Nonie – who is with us here today – and Dit, and brother Joseph to watch a new generation of cousins, Dottie, Butch and me, enter the church together. This was a special moment for Gunny, but not because he was a pious man. Seldom did Gunny speak piously. He spoke plainly, and did not suffer fools gladly. Gunny attended St. Vincent's School 28 years earlier. His name usually appeared on the chalkboard. The names of students who had not paid tuition were written on the chalkboard for all to see. There was no money for Gunny's tuition. This was the Depression. Gunny was a humble but proud man. He valued education. Gunny resolved this would not happen to his children.

As much as Gunny loved politics, politics could be cruel. Success and failure came and went. Politics took away as much as it gave. As I rode with Gunny to meet on Sunday with politicians in the lobby of the Van Antwerp building, he often said: "Get your education. No one can take that away from you." Gunny knew what it meant to do without. This led him to be compassionate, to help others help themselves. Gunny served as a Party ward heeler on Mobile's desperately poor south side. A ward heeler took care of his people, seeing they had coal in winter and food to eat. He sometimes had one meal a day when growing up. As a young boy, Gunny knew neighbors who could not afford milk for their babies. This is something that you do not know. Gunny would follow the milk wagon at dawn as it delivered to those who could pay. When the milkman left two bottles on someone's doorstep, Gunny would take one bottle and leave it on the porch of a family that could not pay for the milk. He did not dare tell Irish Ma or Aunt Nettie about this. That would not have gone over well. We don't know how the missing milk bottles were ever sorted out.

Gunny knew people. He had a knack for faces and names. He knew half of Mobile at one time, and told me that most of the others are probably related. As a child walking with Gunny from one downtown block to another, it was normal to stop several times to visit with folks he recognized. It took a while to get anywhere. But when I started dating in high school, it got worse. Gunny questioned me about the family tree of girls I dated. He knew most of the families. As I was going out one Friday night, after the routine questioning Gunny stopped me and said: "Jimmy, you know, you're dating your cousin." Now, exactly how are you supposed to deal with that?

We read about people hoping to have 15 minutes of fame in the newspaper, on TV, or winning a lottery. Fame did not affect Gunny, and he had his share. For three years State Registrar Gunny was on the front page in Mobile. Some of that fame was not friendly. He told me he did not worry that folks were talking about him. The time to worry, he said, is when they make up their minds and stop talking. Gunny was most proud, though, of his 1930 Alabama American Legion baseball championship with the Whippets. This team grew up around Galvez Park on the south side. Gunny and his team proved themselves, despite where they came from.

Segregation was the law during Gunny's years as a State Registrar. Yet he managed to earn the respect of Mobile's Colored community. On one occasion Gunny received a personal invitation from a Colored pastor to attend an event at the A. M. E. church on Bayou Street next to the Church Street Cemetery. This event was at night during the uproar over the Board of Registrars denying Colored veterans the right to vote. The Colored community wanted Gunny to meet a special guest speaker. Gunny chose to attend. Predictably, he took a seat in the back of the church, preferring to remain inconspicuous. Of course, his white face was surrounded by darker ones. Shortly before the program started, the pastor asked the audience if Gunny Gonzales had arrived. One should think that finding Gunny in the audience would have been easy. Gunny stood and greeted the pastor, who then asked Gunny to join the guest of honor near the pulpit. The guest speaker was Thurgood Marshall, an attorney who subsequently became the first black U.S. Supreme Court Justice.

As a young boy, I accompanied Gunny one evening to Bayou Coden during a political campaign. Gunny stopped first at the home of Henry Royal. I had not previously visited a Colored family's home. I fell asleep in a chair while Gunny and Henry talked politics. When I awoke, Gunny was nowhere to be seen. The look on my face probably mirrored the concern on their faces. Henry explained that Gunny would be back soon. That did not help very much. One of Henry's sons, playing at the table, asked if I knew how to play dominoes. I didn't, but I learned. When Gunny returned later that night, I was still playing dominoes. What happened that night was significant in segregated Alabama, but Gunny did not say much about it on the long drive back to Mobile.

As many of you know, Anne is not able to be here today. She is ill. When Gunny retired in 1986 as Chairman of the Mobile

> County Democratic Party, Anne wrote to our children about their grandfather. This is what she had to say: "He is a loving person, honest, and always there for his children and grandchildren. He is independent and stubborn, full of pride, and has accomplished much. He had no father to help him, and a mother who worked to rear four children. He was never rich, but his life has been full, with room for many friends and family."

I stepped down from the altar, patted Gunny's casket, and sat. When the liturgy ended, the pallbearers rose. Tony, Michael, Dennis, Robbie, Budda and Melvin escorted Gunny to the hearse, accompanied by the bagpipe. Joe and I, family and friends followed the hearse under sheriff escort to Pinecrest Cemetery. On the way, folks pulled to the curb or stopped mid-lane, paying their respects. Family, Mystic Stripers and Friendly Sons of St. Patrick carried Gunny the last few steps of his long pilgrimage. At graveside in the shade of a tall pine, we bade Gunny farewell and the Church commended his soul to eternal rest.

The family's public mourning ended by mid-afternoon. Black dresses and suits returned to the closet. Just a short walk from Washington Park east down Charleston, the quiet south side neighborhood around Callahan's pub soon stirred with commotion. Here Gunny often celebrated with fellow Mystic Stripers and Friendly Sons of St. Patrick. Here on the east wall still hang snapshots of history, vintage scenes of Gunny's baseball and football era. Here on the south side of town there was more reason to celebrate Gunny's life than mourn our loss. Here the family raised its glass and left grieving for another day.

47. Gunny and Anne Gonzales, Mystic Stripers Ball, Mardi Gras, Mobile, February 11, 1988 (photographer unknown).

48. Gunny Gonzales, Nonie Gonzales Schuler, and Joseph V. Gonzales, Bay Front Road, Mobile, November 26, 1988 (Copyright © 2007 James J. Gonzales).

49. *Gunny Gonzales, south lawn, Administration Building, Spring Hill College, Mobile, October 16, 2005 (Copyright © 2007 James J. Gonzales).*

CHAPTER 34

Mama G

G rief soon demanded its due. I took the call in Boise on the eve of trial. Anne Marie Bosarge Gonzales died on April 18, 2006. Despite the certainty that this day would arrive, the departure of a family's nurturing spirit casts a heavy pall. Anne left quietly, even predictably, within seven weeks of Gunny's abrupt passing. The levee that keeps emotional tides at bay gave way, sending me adrift among memories of distant times.

In a small kerosene-lit room on May 5, 1920 Sadie Powell Bosarge labored to deliver her third baby in three years. Her humble frame house on Little River Road offered basic bayou comforts. Through an open window the room's muggy heat mingled with fresh air. Electricity had not yet reached Bayou la Batre, making it easy to do without motorized fans no one could afford anyway. Decorated with church readings and pictures, cardboard hand fans worked well under most circumstances, birthing excepted. Plumbing also had not yet disturbed the way of life down Little River Road. Bucket drawn water simmered next to a coffeepot on the wood fed iron stove in the kitchen. The closest thing to running water was the well out back.

Sadie knew first hand the hurricanes of '06 and '16, and the sight of bodies and boats dangling from trees, houses resting on one another, and animals floating in the bayou. Sadie knew about living hand to mouth among destitute people. She now labored in a clean bed under a tight roof, a far cry from many yesterdays of doing without. Raised on Dauphin Island among the Collier's and some Greeks who took the name Powell, Sadie married into the Bosarge family in 1915. She was 15 and Baptist. William Eugene Bosarge was 18 and Catholic. Between fall harvests, Sadie sewed and took in neighbors' laundry. Between winters and birthing, she tended cows, chickens, pigs and vegetables. Following the tradition of his French ancestry, Willie chose the boundless stretch of Mississippi Sound over narrow field furrows, preferring life as a fisherman, for which he earned the nickname *Pecheur*. They ate what Willie caught off the boat and Sadie grew in the field. Other than coffee, tobacco and kerosene, they had little use, time, or money for store bought goods.

The Bosarge's possessed land and lineage that predated Alabama and most of its wars. Following Don Bernardo de Galvez's conquest of Mobile, Joseph Bousage of Portiers, France and his wife Louisa Baudreau settled their family near a remote marshy bayou several hours by horse southwest of Mobile. Catherine Louise Baudreau descended from Jean Baptiste Baudreau, a Cat Island Acadian, and Catherine Vinconot. Long before Don Bernardo defeated the English, Louisa's father got mixed up with mutinous Swiss mercenaries assigned to Cat Island who slaughtered French garrison commandant Duroux. Governor Kerlerec took strong exception to mutineers and those who lent them aid. The Swiss took Baudreau to guarantee their escape to Georgia, relying on his fluency and trust among the Creek and other Indian nations. Jean Baptiste returned to Mobile where he was arrested by Mobile Commandant DeVille. Baudreau pleaded that he went along as an unwilling hostage all the way to Georgia, where the Swiss set him free. Skeptical Governor Kerlerec thought otherwise. Louisa later fished her father's body from the Mobile River following his fatal bout with the rack. Two captured Swiss mutineers were convicted, placed alive into wood coffins, and, in the manner befitting condemned mutineers, cross-sawed in half.

In 1786, at age 60, Joseph Bousage mustered all his wit, nerve, and shame to petition his Catholic Majesty Carlos III, King of Spain, and sovereign of Louisiana and Mobile's bayous, for an understated favor.

In what might mark the high tide of Bosarge eloquence and bayou literature, William Eugene's great great grandfather dared address the world power that ruled much of the Americas.

To his Excellency Stephen Miro, Colonel of the Royal Armies of his Catholic Majesty and Governor General of the Province of Louisiana etc., etc., etc.

Joseph Bouzage, an inhabitant of the Jurisdiction of Mobile, has the honor to represent to your Excellency that he has been compelled in consequence of the State of his misery to retire with his wife and children on a piece of land situated on Bayou Battree, bounded on the East by Lisloy and on the West by Pine Point, which makes a distance of one league in front, for the purpose of fishing and planting some corn for the support and maintenance of his family. He further represents that the said land has never been claimed by any person, only some prisoners who were living on it without title, possession or right to the same, and who have abandoned it short time afterwards, and by Barthelemy Grelot better than eighteen months ago, who then moved to Bay Saint Louis. Wherefore your petitioner dares to hope that his unfortunate situation will exercise the sense of your Excellency's feelings, and will be pleased to grant him the said tract of land, in order that he may live thereon undisturbed, and to conceal from the Eyes of the World a Poor father of family having seven children, who is in trouble and his wife sickly, and lastly, this desolated family in stretching their arms towards your Excellency, humbly entreats your Excellency to grant them your honor's protection. In acknowledgement of which, they will not cease in offering the most passionate promises to God our Lord for the preservation of your Excellency's health and prolongation of your days, and of all those who are dear to your Excellency.

I remain with profound respect and entire submissions, Excellent Sir, Your most obedient and humble servants, Mobile this Sixth day of October, one thousand seven hundred and eighty six.

Joseph Bouzage

Mobile's Military Commandant attested to most of Joseph's petition before submitting it for approval to Spain's Governor General in New Orleans.

Peter Favrot, Captain of the Regiment of Louisiana Infantry, Political and Military Commandant ad-interim of the Town of Mobile and its District, etc.,

Do hereby certify that the land described in the preceding Memorial was formerly owned by the said Barthelemy Grelot, who abandoned it better than eighteen months ago, and moved at Bay Saint Louis with all his effects. In testimony whereof, and at the request of the said Barthelemy Grelot, I grant these presents at the aforesaid Town of Mobile this the twenty third day of October one thousand seven hundred and eighty six.

Peter Favrot

Joseph's financial circumstances and business acquaintances already were known to Mobile's Military Commandant. Some years back, Joseph Bousage's family inhabited a modest house on the outskirts of the Town of Mobile. Under the rule of his prior sovereign, England's George III, to whose majesty the town of Mobile had pledged allegiance, Joseph bartered all his cattle for a plot of John Favre's tract to house Joseph's family.

This Indenture, made the Eleventh day of April in the year of our Lord, one thousand seven hundred and seventy and in the tenth year of the Reign of our Sovereign Lord George the third by the grace of God of Great Britain, France and Ireland King Defender of the Faith, and so forth;

Between John Favre of the one part and Joseph Bousage of the other part, both of the Town of Mobile in Charlotte County in the Province of West Florida, Witnesseth;

That the said John Favre for and in consideration of the sum of two hundred dollars, value in horned Cattle to him in hand paid by the said Joseph Bousage, . . . John Favre doth hereby acknowledge and hath granted, bargained and sold, aliened, and confirmed . . . unto the said Joseph Bousage his heirs and assigns forever: all that lot of land, messuage, and tenement situate and lying in the Town of Mobile in the Province and County aforesaid, bounded on the Streets to the North and East and by the lot in the possession of Peter Insan and Henriette Liroy, and also, all houses, out houses, lands, trees, woods, underwoods, titles, commons, common of Pastures, profits, commodities, advantages, hereditaments, ways, waters, and appurtenances whatsoever . . . And the said John Favre for him and his heirs, and against all and every other person and persons whatsoever, to the said Joseph Bousage, his heirs and assigns, shall and will warrant and forever defend by these presents. In witness whereof the said John Favre hath hereunto signed and sealed these presents the day and year above written.

John Favre

Signed, sealed and delivered in the presence of us who have hereunder subscribed our names. McGrauts   R. Roi

I, the undersigned Marguerit Wiltz, wife of John Favre, Do hereby certify that I have given and granted full power and authority to the above named John Favre, my husband, to sell and dispose of the house and lot which we have acquired of McGillivray, and in virtue thereof, I ratify and confirm and by these presents do ratify and confirm the sale and transfer which he has made in favor of Joseph Bousage of the premises aforementioned. Done at Pearl River in the presence of witnesses there being no Notary on the twelfth day of November, one thousand seven hundred and seventy one.

Marguerit Wiltz

Witness — LaBrike   Ls. Blaudeau.

Joseph's circumstances did not noticeably improve and the value of his property did not appreciate. Three years later Joseph and Louisa sold out for no more than the price they had paid.

On this day the Sixteenth of February in the year of our Lord, one thousand seven hundred and seventy three, I, the undersigned Joseph Bouzage, and Mary Louisa, my wife, in the presence of witnesses, have granted, bargained and sold forever, unto Lewis Maroteaux, a certain lot of ground together with all the buildings thereon, situate lying and being in the Town of Mobile, under the same dimensions and boundaries as it was conveyed to us by Mr. Favre, bounded on one side by Mr. Insan's lot, and on the other covering on the Street, for and in consideration of the sum of two hundred Dollars, which sum, I, the said Joseph Bouzage, do hereby acknowledge to have received cash in hand, and myself therewith fully satisfied and contented, warranted free of all encumbrances on my part, as well as my heirs, executors, administrators and assigns. Done and passed in the Town of Mobile on the day, date, and year above

written, having hereunder signed our names before the undersigned witnesses in proof of the execution thereof.

Joseph Bouzage

Mark *X* of his wife

Witnesses — Barthelemy Grelot Orieu

However, by 1773 Joseph and Barthelemy Grelot had become well acquainted, a most fortunate and profitable event for the Bousage's. Joseph's acquaintance with Barthelemy Grelot and John Favre reveals how the Bousage's found their way to Bayou Battree. Favre held a Spanish grant that extended from the mainland shore west of Pinto Island south of Canal to Government, and enjoyed favor with British and Spanish governors. Favre's wife attested that the house sold to Bousage had belonged to McGillivray, a name instantly associated with the prominent John McGillivray and Colonel Alexander McGillivray of the Creek-Scottish trading family that wielded enormous political influence with British, Spanish, and American governments throughout West Florida from Pensacola to New Orleans. After the April 11, 1770 sale to Bousage, Favre traveled on to Pearl River, beyond Bay St. Louis. Barthelemy Grelot, who witnessed the Bousage's 1773 sale, reportedly moved to Bay Saint Louis after a lengthy stay at Bayou Battree. Joseph Bousage departed the relative comforts of Mobile long before 1786 to homestead the remote bayou where Grelot conducted business. Though impoverished, Joseph Bousage enjoyed the benefits of befriending influential forces. Bousage's 1786 petition reflects first hand knowledge concerning the described tract and those who occupied it with Bousage for several years. Once the prisoners, Grelot, and other inhabitants abandoned the area, Bousage could legitimize his discreet but unauthorized stake in Bayou Battree. In remarkably swift fashion, the Governor General issued an order to Captain Favrot:

New Orleans, Seventh of November, one thousand seven hundred and eighty six. The commandant of Mobile, Pedro Favrot, shall permit the petitioner to establish himself on the tract of land which he solicits, situated on River Batree, bounded on the East by Ocas Island and on the West by Pine Point.

Stephen Miro

By such simple order Joseph Bousage gained dominion over the mosquitoes, snakes, alligators, marshes, and tillable lands within a tract 40 *arpents* (7000 feet) wide that ran the length of Bayou Batterie's left bank to the Gulf of Mexico. For the next nine years the Bousage's prudently kept to themselves, fishing and farming. When Joseph died in 1795, however, Louisa found her interests in the land threatened by an opportunistic competing claim that exploited a latent flaw in the grant's legal description. Despite her insignificant state in life, Joseph's widow petitioned Mobile's Spanish Commandant to measure the 40 *arpents* not from where bayou met marsh, as custom required, but from where marsh met land.

To his honor the Commandant.

Louisa Bousage, who is an inhabitant of this district, with the greatest respect presents herself before your Honor, and says that sometime in the year of our Lord one thousand seven hundred and eighty six her deceased husband (Joseph Bousage) petitioned for and obtained a grant from his Excellency the Governor General of these provinces, for a tract of land situated lying and being on Bayou Batterie and bounded on the East by the Island Aloye or De Ocas, and on the West by Pine Point, with the ordinary depth, as will more fully appear by reference to a copy of the said grant which accompanies this memorial and petition. And your petitioner further very respectfully makes known to your Honor that from the Sea shores which was considered the front point of the land granted to her deceased husband and running on a line for the purpose of ascertaining the depth of said land from North to South on the left bank of said Bayou Batterie, and near on a parallel line with the whole of the said tract of land, there is nearly thirty arpens of marshy swamp land which is not susceptible of tillage, as the same is always overflowed. In consequence of which, although it was stated in the said grant that the same should be bounded on the east by the island Aloye or De Ocas and Bayou Batterie, and on the West by Pine Point, her said deceased husband did not believe that he was bound to commence the measure of forty arpens in depth, which is the regular quantity usually granted, at any other point than that at which the land would admit of cultivation. My husband therefore, made his settlement on the said left bank of Bayou Batterie, at the most suitable and convenient spot for dwelling, and at not great distance from a bayou known by the name of Bayou Dupon, or Sacales, and on the other side of which he planted his crop of corn and other cultivation for nearly nine years. Your petitioner and her family together with her deceased husband during his life, have been in quiet and peaceable possession of the said tract of land; but they now find themselves on the eve of being turned out of possession, in consequence of a petition which is about to be made for a grant of the said tract of land by a certain Mr. Triseran, which if granted will without doubt reduce your petitioner and her children to the wretched condition of perishing by want and hunger, that is, should they be deprived of the fruits of the industry of her said deceased husband in the improvements of the said land, which industry and labor were intended mainly for the support and maintenance of his family. Your petitioner therefore most humbly prays, that it may be ordered by his Excellency the Governor General that the depth of the said tract of land may begin and be established, and counted from the place where the tillable land joins the aforesaid marsh, extending back to the Bayou called Sweet Water, which will include with, but a small difference the forty arpens in depth, to which she is entitled according to the grant made to the deceased husband. This favor she humbly hopes to receive from the known goodness and equity of your honor. Mobile, the twenty third day of July, in the year of our Lord one thousand seven hundred and ninety five.

Louisa Bousage

Louisa prudently omitted mention that she was the offspring of Jean Baptiste Baudreau. Instead she offered the testimony of Pedro Olivier, who confirmed that measuring the grant of 40 *arpents* from the bayou's edge would reduce Louisa to tilling swamp.

To his Excellency the Governor General of these provinces,
From the information which I have received from respectable inhabitants of this district, who are well acquainted with the situation and quality of the land described in the above petition and memorial, it is satisfactorily proved, that either through mistake or from the ignorance of the person who obtained a grant for said land in the year 1786 he found that he had received a grant for land which was utterly useless, if the said grant should be so construed as to confine him to the land specifically designated in the said grant, inasmuch as almost the whole distance in depth of the land so granted was found to be altogether unfit for cultivation, for the reasons assigned in the petition and memorial herewith transmitted to your Excellency. If, therefore, your Excellency should be pleased

to order that the sides and bounds of the said grant should be allowed according to the prayer of the said petition and memorial, the petitioner will be essentially benefited and no person in any way injured as Your Excellency may seem just and right. Given at Mobile the twenty seventh day of July in the year of our Lord one thousand seven hundred and ninety five.

Pedro Olivier

Governor General Baron de Carondelet found it befitting to do equity, grant the widow's petition, amend the 1786 tract description, and quiet title in Louisa Bousage.

In consideration of the representations made by the petitioner, and of the information herein contained from his Honor the Commandant, it is hereby ordered that the time referred to in the above petition which bounds the depth of the tract of land which was granted by my predecessor in this Government, his Excellency Don Stephen Miro, on the seventh day of November in the year of our Lord one thousand seven hundred and eighty six, situated on the Bayou Baterie, and bounded on the East by the Bayou de Ocas and on the West by Pine Point, shall be so altered as to begin at and be estimated from the place at which the low and marshy land joins the land that is tillable and habitable, and the said line shall run straight back to the Bayou called Sweet Water.

El Baron de Carondelet
New Orleans the 19th of August, An.Dom.1795.

Louisa Bousage's tract of 1250 acres became the cornerstone of Bayou la Batre and secured the Bousage's a future. Louisa's son John Joseph and daughter-in-law Jacqueline Chest secured the Bosarge lineage with offspring Joseph, Dennis, Pauline, Francis, Isalea, and Edward Eugene, Willie's grandfather. Edward Eugene's wife, Lucinda Goulmin, subsequently gave birth to Edward, Rodney, Cecilia, and Henry, Willie's father. Aunt Cecilia married into the Rabby's before the War between the States. Alabama seceded to join the Confederacy on January 11, 1861 and by October 1861 the Rabby's and Bosarge's volunteered. As dirt poor farmers and fishermen, they had little reason to become combatants other than pride and a contentious disposition. Jacob M. Rabby, a captain at 28, commanded Rabby's Coast Guard Company No. 1,

Alabama Volunteers. Eugene Bosarge at age 38 and 18 year old son Edward served under Captain Rabby's command. The Bosarge's survived the War but Reconstruction took its toll in property taxes. Parcels of Louisa's Tract had to be sold at depressed Reconstruction prices to quiet the tax collectors. On August 13, 1869 the heirs of Joseph and Louisa Bousage quitclaimed to Delsie Brown for $200 their land grant title to that part of the south half of Louisa Bousage's Tract from the bayou to the Little River. Dennis and Adaline Bosarge, Francis Bosarge, Pauline Bosarge Clarke and husband Thomas Clarke, Isalea Bosarge Gurlotte and husband John Gurlotte, and Eugene Bosarge each marked a distinctive "X" to quitclaim their property interests. They also quitclaimed to George W. Perrine for only $160 another parcel of acreage from the same south half of Louisa's Tract.

What one sovereign granted the Bosarge's in the wake of the Revolutionary War, another sovereign taxed away in the shadow of the Civil War. When 21 year old Henry Bosarge married 16 year old Florence Augusta Greene on March 14, 1876 at the end of Reconstruction, the Bosarge's had more lineage than acreage and more debt than dollars. Exercising few remaining options, Henry and Florence invested much of their energy to generating offspring. Within 42 weeks Florence Augusta gave birth to Anna Cecilia, named in honor of Florence's mother and Henry's sister. Florence then gave birth to Mary Ella in 1879, Ida Rose (after Florence's sister Ida Greene) in 1882, Margaret Gertrude in 1884, William Eugene (after Henry's father) in 1886, Maude Augusta in 1889, Henry Maurice in 1892, Joseph Homer in 1895, and Arthur Edward (after Henry's brother) in 1898. Between the Bosarge's, Powell's, Collier's, Greene's and Gurlotte's, Sadie and Willie were related one way or another to most folks from Dauphin Island to Bayou la Batre.

Florence Augusta Bosarge watched daughter-in-law Sadie yield to a woman's primal instinct to push. The head crowned, then emerged. Another push expelled a baby into the skillful hands of its 60 year old grandmother. Florence Bosarge and Sadie's mother Alice Collier Powell helped birth most babies in Bayou La Batre, Bayou Coden, Heron Bay and Dauphin Island. The look on Florence Augusta's face explained the room's ominous silence. Sadie had birthed a blue baby girl that did not breathe and soon would die. Alice Powell attended to her daughter Sadie. Family comforted Sadie's loss, but she already had two children, Henry Maurice and Florence Augusta, named after Willie's father and mother. No doubt young Sadie would bear more. Family thought it better that Sadie tend the children who are than grieve over one who isn't.

Grandmother Bosarge said little. She snipped the umbilical cord and quickly removed the limp blue body. While family busied itself with Sadie, Florence the midwife stepped out of the bedroom. She cleared the small mouth and dangled the lifeless form upside down to drain. The lungs did not respond. Florence then placed her mouth over lips and nose. Faith could not explain the loss of Sadie's baby, and nature did not share all its mysteries with a midwife. A resigned hope in God's obscure will helped family cope with what they could not control or understand. Those who survived today's malady might be taken away by tomorrow's hurricane.

Florence breathed slowly into the still body. A barely detectable reflex grew into a chest spasm, a desperate struggle for air, and finally a weak cry. Florence brought her granddaughter to life, at least for the moment. Florence knew well enough that bringing back a blue baby had its risks. Star-crossed babies did not always fare well and required many days of care. Still, Florence the grandmother claimed naming rights. She invoked the blessing of her mother Anna Marie Fraser Stevens of Carolina, who married Augustus Bush Greene. Grandmother Bosarge named the child Anne Marie, and called her Anna.

Before entering school, Anne Marie already grasped some of life's fundamentals. Sadie continued bearing babies with remarkable regularity, eventually adding Maude, Wilhelmena (Mena), Sadie Mae, Mildred, William Eugene, and Robert to her brood. The cycle of pregnancy and birthing in the close quarters of a small two-bedroom house left little to a child's imagination. Anne, brother HM, and sister Florence customarily tended younger siblings, more so in the fall after canning vegetables and fruit preserves for winter. With Willie off on a boat during all but the coldest weather, Sadie expected the older kids to keep house when she took in laundry or cleaned shrimp at the packing house. Sharing the burden at home also meant HM and Florence missed a good bit of school each month. That did not much trouble Sadie, who skipped high school altogether. Schooling had not put food on the table, fish on the boat, clothes on the children, or roof over the bed. Children born into poverty first study survival, a lesson Sadie learned quite well. However, indifference to schooling did not stop at the end of Little River Road, but ebbed and flowed along the bayou like a tide.

Sadie's kids shared some hand-me-down shoes, but rarely wore them. Few occasions required a lap or yard child to wear shoes. The oddest of those few occasions occurred in 1924 when all the children came down with measles. Shoes stayed on the kids' feet until the measles ran its course. When the croup struck, shoes did not matter. The children crowded the fireplace for warmth and heated wet towels against the hot bricks. Folk remedies were mostly an art that relied on some assurance of prior success. If the child survived, something must have worked.

Summers found Anne picking vegetables, figs, pears, and blackberries, collecting eggs, and tending animals. Come fall, she gathered pecans under 22 trees for days on end. The fruit of certain trees, though, was forbidden. HM and Anne caused a stir by climbing the fence to eat their Aunt Maude's figs. Aunt Maude did not especially care for the figs, which usually fell and rotted on the ground. But Maude cared even less for Willie's kids to graze off her trees. Maude had words with Willie, but he saw things differently and dismissed his sister's concern. Maude did not take too well to that. In a burst of odd logic, she resolved the matter by chopping down every fig tree in her yard, leaving the kids little reason to return. Maude did not think she might be cutting off her nose to spite her face. Her Bosarge temperament just saw things differently. But Aunt Maude got what she wanted. Her nephews and nieces left her alone for years.

Of all Anne's many chores, drawing well water appealed least. Too much water in the bucket proved too heavy to handle, and too little water meant more trips to the well. All the water that went into the house and animals came out of the well in a bucket. On top of that, at least once a week, usually Saturday night, Sadie had HM, Florence and Anne warm enough water on the wood stove to fill a number 3 galvanized tub several times over. One by one the children bathed in the tub, then threw the dirty water off the porch. Drawing enough water to bathe everyone on Saturday night was one thing. At least Anne got a bath out of that bargain. But drawing water because of cats seemed penitential. The small benefit that cats offered depended on their being hungry and clever enough to kill mice. Otherwise, they proved to be useless at best and more often a nuisance. Curiosity, cats, and water wells did not mix. When a cat found itself stranded in a pecan tree, it stayed there or jumped. When a cat found itself at the bottom of the water well, the cat and the water had to go. Anne spent however long it took, bucket by bucket, to drain the well and get the cat out as fast as possible, dead or alive.

When weather proved agreeable, Anne and sister Florence washed the clothes in the creek near Little River. Until the clothes dried on the line, the girls had to keep the cows from eating the laundry. Anne and Florence only had dresses, no pants or shorts to mention. Even so, they took nearly the whole day to iron clothes each week. The girls used one triangular flatiron while two more flatirons warmed up on the wood fired stove. Ironing day in the summer kept the house plenty warm and humid. It ranked right down there with drawing well water.

Play mainly meant spending the summer with Grandmother Powell. Each June, Willie took Anne and sister Florence by boat to Dauphin Island. When midwife Alice Powell traipsed across the island to deliver babies, Anne tagged along. Cows, billy goats and wild boars proved more troublesome than delivering babies, often chasing Anne and Grandmother Powell up and down the trail. If close enough, Alice and her granddaughter took refuge inside the cemetery fence. If not, they just ran until the beast tired. For her services, Alice Powell received payment in vegetables, chickens, and fish. Come September, Willie returned to the island to reclaim the girls for another fall harvest.

Play did not mean toys. Anne had no toys to speak of. Christmas gifts came in different sizes and colors, but mostly clothes and something homemade. When the Baptist Church gave away trees at Christmas, Sadie and the girls dragged one right down the middle of Little River Road into the house. Otherwise, Sadie did not throw away good money on a dead tree. Play meant cousins, swarms of them. There were no neighbors other than cousins. In the summer that Anne turned six, a gaggle of 25 cousins gathered to horse around and play pop the whip. Being one of the smallest cousins, Anne grabbed onto the tip of the whip, which popped her into a palmetto bush. A couple of days later, ugly black spots broke out all over and Anne fell seriously ill. In a rare visit with Dr. McCall the pediatrician, Sadie learned that Anne might live only to 30, assuming she recovered at all. The illness remained something of a mystery, but Anne subsequently shied away from palmetto palms and popping the whip with cousins. She also did not start school that September. Sadie kept her home until the following year.

St. Margaret Catholic Church hosted a major community event in Bayou la Batre to celebrate opening its elementary school. Sadie, Willie and their children walked south down Irvington Road, crossed the bridge, toured the new school, met the nuns, and enjoyed the occasion. The Bosarge's did not ride anywhere, as they had no horse, buggy, or car. At the end of the day they walked back to Little River Road. Between the large live oak in the front yard and the outhouse in the back, an ugly pile of white ashes and scorched boards spewed smoke into an empty sky. While the Bosarge's visited at school, their house burned to the ground. The hurricane of 1916 left Sadie and Willie empty-handed some ten years earlier. The fire left them with a hen house and passel of children. Sadie farmed out her kids until Willie built another house.

Not long after Sadie and the kids settled into their new house, a visitor unexpectedly showed up in the night, pounding on the screen door and calling for his uncle Willie. Few relatives and fewer neighbors paid social visits down Little River Road after dark. Anything worth saying would keep until daylight. Walking through the pitch black of night could be spooky. Snakes and wild four-legged critters enjoyed curling up on the warm clay roadbed, especially during a cold spell. Stepping on or over one of them carried some risks. Cows also favored the road at night. Despite its size, a sleeping cow remained fairly well camouflaged absent a full moon. Falling onto startled cows in the dark had trouble written all over it.

The commotion at the door stirred the children, but only Willie got out of bed. One of Willie's nephews stood at the door bearing bad news, which did not come as much of a surprise. The boy had just walked barefoot without a lantern from Davenport Lane over Carl's Creek, across Irvington Road and down Little River Road. Willie's older sister, Margaret Gertrude, had fallen very ill. She sent a nephew to ask for help. Margaret wanted to borrow one of Willie's children for a spell, as long as it took to get back on her feet.

Aunt Maggie lived only a mile away, but she might as well be living in Georgia. She resembled Willie, which meant tall, lanky, and homely. Maggie married Green Verneuille of Mobile in September 1906, two weeks before hurricanes flooded the bayou. She never had children of her own, and seemed to get along just fine without any. For the most part she also managed to do well without Green, a career fireman and doorman at Gayfer's department store, who spent one weekend at home for every two weeks in Mobile. Maggie plowed and tended a large garden, kept cows and pigs, and raised chickens. In season she labored at the packinghouse, picking crab and heading shrimp. Maggie did not socialize much with Willie and Sadie. Green did not socialize much with any of the Bosarge's, and hardly anyone else for that matter.

They did not expect Green back from Mobile for another week, and Maggie could barely take care of her self. Sick or not, someone had to tend the animals each day, milk the cows, collect eggs, feed the chickens and pigs, draw water, stoke the fireplace, and tend the stove. Willie knew Maggie would not send for help if given half a choice. Willie turned to his older children, HM and Florence, hoping either might be willing to stay with Aunt Maggie. Both already were in bed, and both said no. Willie knew better than to sour the situation by dragging one of the kids over to Maggie's. Willie did not bother to ask Anne, who only was 7 at the time. Anne heard Willie talking at the door with her cousin, and then with HM and Florence. Most of the children slept in the same room. Anne did not know much about Aunt Maggie or Uncle Green, but everyone knew Aunt Maggie sewed First Communion dresses for all her nieces. She also pretty much lived alone. Anne sat up in bed and looked at Willie. "I will go." Willie eyed Anne for a moment and sized up the situation. He nodded, fixed up a lantern, and walked his daughter down the dark road over Carl's Creek to stay for awhile with Maggie.

Maggie's whitewashed house sat back on the north side of the narrow lane, obscured by mimosa trees and camellias. A screened-in porch swing looked south over a fence crawling with honeysuckle vines. Under a stand of pecan trees, the chicken yard and hen house took up the southeast corner. Maggie's garden filled out the northeast corner. Two doors led inside off the front porch. The west door opened into a parlor where Maggie kept a cylinder Victrola. Maggie had little formal education, but collected books and operas. On the far side of the parlor another door led to Maggie's bedroom and a large brick fireplace that dominated the north wall. In the kitchen, just east of Maggie's bedroom, a cast iron wood stove provided the only other source of heat. Keeping the fireplace stoked meant keeping warm. Even so, potted plants in the parlor often froze and died during cold snaps.

Anne stayed with Aunt Maggie by day, and returned home at night. Aunt Maggie recovered as might be expected, leaving Anne to come and go as she pleased. What pleased Anne surprised her aunt and left her parents at somewhat of a loss. Despite the circumstances, Aunt Maggie and Anne grew on each other. Maggie never left any doubt what she expected of Anne. What little Aunt Maggie had did not come easy, a message Anne heard more than once. Maggie worked the garden twelve months a year, planting, raising, and canning everything they ate. She kept cows, chickens, pigs, turkeys, ducks, cats and dogs, and butchered most of the animals she cooked. When the shrimp boats came in from trawling, Maggie left at 2 or 3 in the morning for the packinghouse. She mostly got paid in tokens accepted by the grocery and dry goods store. Real money could be had shucking oysters, but the knife wounds that plagued shuckers rendered shrimp peeling unbearably painful. Still, Maggie let it be known she wanted to get the first oyster call, and the 15 cents that came with it.

Maggie expected her niece to rise by 4:30 every morning, Sundays included, milk the cows, feed the chickens, calves and dogs, and clean the house. Before supper, Anne cut firewood for the stove and tended kerosene lamps for the night. The day began early and ended late, but the hardship seemed normal. However firm Maggie's expectations, they seemed to have a purpose. Though Anne spent little time with her family and cousins anymore, she did not miss home or feel lonely. In the span of only a few weeks, Maggie had nimbly affected her niece. Maggie spoke plainly, without the nurturing voice of a young mother. She wasted words on no one, but spoke with the breeding of a literate woman. Anne marveled at the collection of books and operas, but not because she understood any of them. The books and operas made Aunt Maggie different than anyone else in or out of the family, a distinction Maggie owed to her mother. As circumstance allowed, Florence Augusta gave her children books for Christmas. Maggie acquired her mother's disposition. Her shelves also gathered books originally inscribed for her younger brother, including Edward's 1889 *Life of Kit Carson* "from Mother" and 1899 *The Rifle Rangers* "from Sister Margaret."

Maggie shared what she valued. Sewing white First Communion dresses for nieces, who got along fine every day in hand-me-down gingham, took an unseemly amount of effort and resources for just one morning's wear. Aunt Maggie seldom saw her nieces, except at church, but her hand-sown dresses spoke a lot about her and something about them. Maggie let it be known early and often that when the time came, Anne would be in school every day, no matter what. Maggie Verneuille did not abide ignorance, which was common as pig tracks in parts of the bayou. It would have to thrive without her niece. Though Maggie might again fall ill and need help did not mean Anne could miss class. It meant Anne would rise before dawn to tend animals, fix breakfast, cross the bridge, and arrive on time. It also meant no lollygagging after school. Homework and firewood came first and before supper. Anne grasped enough of her aunt's meaning to chew on it at night in a communal bed with her brothers and sisters on Little River Road.

Once Maggie fully recovered her strength, everyone expected Anne to go back home for good. Any contrary notion certainly never occurred to Willie or his older sister. Anne did go back home, but kept returning. As weeks grew into months, neither Willie nor Maggie made much ado of it. Months grew into years. At the end of May 1931 Anne finished the third grade. She had just turned 11. Daylight began to linger into the evening hours as summer settled once again over the bayou. Anne did not visit with Grandmother Powell that summer. She showed up on Davenport Lane at dawn. Maggie's niece decided the time had come to choose a home. Aunt Maggie and Uncle Green had prepared for this as best they could, which was not near enough. Much to their surprise, Anne went to bed that night on Davenport Lane. She no longer thought of Little River Road as home. She planned to sleep under Aunt Maggie's roof from then on. Anne clung to the childlike notion that no one would notice, or much care. Maggie honored her niece's druthers, but saw in the bargain the seed of a nasty feud. She and Green figured they would cross that bridge when they got to it.

Mobile firemen collected and repaired toys for Christmas. Uncle Green saw to it that Anne had a toy under the Christmas tree. Despite a generally deserved reputation as aloof, if not cold, Green also managed to have an Easter basket on the table for the girl of the house. No one accused Green Verneuille of doting, but for him this came close. Because he traveled Irvington Road every other week, Green enjoyed the distinction and envy of having an automobile. On July 4 and other holidays he crammed the car with nieces and nephews for picnics. Anne seemed to give Uncle Green an excuse to play.

Maggie did not take religion lightly. She knew the Bible and had no qualms sharing the Gospel. Questioning whether Adam and Eve existed would draw a pained look of amazement that shamed the upbringing of any poor soul who needed to ask. Maggie celebrated the baptisms and First Communions of her nieces and nephews. She attended church regularly, and made a fuss over Mass on Easter and Christmas Eve. Whatever hand-me-down Anne wore any other time of the year simply would not do on high holy days. Maggie's elegant long fingers sewed Anne new outfits for Easter and Christmas, which had to last until next year's outfit. Even gussied up, though, Maggie's niece did not always make it to midnight Mass Christmas Eve without tumbling over sleeping cows on Davenport Lane. On Christmas Day Anne dressed up again to visit her parents and Grandmother Bosarge. After Anne went to live with Aunt Maggie, Willie and Sadie never gave their daughter another gift. Maggie figured that Willie still had his nose out of joint. Even so, Maggie insisted that Anne take Sadie and Willie a gift of preserves or something. Aunt Maggie would not cotton to trashy behavior, especially on Christmas. That was that, no if's, and's, or but's about it.

Anne walked to school barefoot. Her brothers, sisters and cousins went to school barefoot. It simply cost too much to shoe a child's growing foot. Their feet did not seem to mind the summer asphalt, road gravel, or metal bridge grating. During barefoot weather, nobody paid much attention. Once the weather turned cold, most feet found some kind of shoe to wear. Hand-me-down shoes did not always fit, though, and often came off with the next warm spell. Each afternoon a stream of kids migrated out of St. Margaret School northbound across the bayou. Three of Anne's fifth grade classmates, Rosemary, Helen, and Monique, made fun of Anne and her sisters for not wearing shoes. Anne had reached the top of the bridge's walkway one afternoon when Rosemary publicly shamed Anne with catty ridicule. Anne turned, slapped Rosemary back down the bridge's walkway above the bayou, and yelled for all to hear that if it weren't for Rosemary's father taking Willie's money for moonshine, Anne and her sisters would have shoes. The main difference between what adults knew and what children knew was that children talked about it in public. Anne spoke nothing of this to Aunt Maggie that night at supper.

When Anne got to school the next morning, Sister Regina told the still barefoot fifth grader to hold out her hands. The good nun intended to impose punishment for what Anne said about Rosemary's father. Rosemary and supportive witnesses had reported the high bridge brawl. Sister Regina exercised unchallenged authority to discipline student misbehavior. However, she underestimated an unusually indignant 12 year-old that morning who showed no remorse and expressed no regret. Anne's spunk matched the nun's determination. "No, you aren't going to punish me. You are supposed to help me get shoes, not whip me for not having shoes and fighting for what I thought was right."

Sister Regina sent the uppity Bosarge girl home. No nun would brook such back talk, especially in front of on-lookers. Anne went home and told Aunt Maggie the whole story, expecting the worse. Aunt Maggie was not disposed to outbursts, but started spitting cotton once they got to school. Maggie demanded justice. Fighting might not be the right answer, but making fun of Anne and her sisters for not having things they needed in life simply would not do. Maggie demanded that Anne be returned to school without punishment. The nun's jurisdiction to police the children's behavior on the bridge had never been questioned. Maggie challenged the nun's judgment and values, something entirely more threatening to the exercise of moral authority. The pastor reluctantly ended up mediating the impasse between the two strong-willed women, an unenviable task with unattractive consequences. The priest could cripple Sister Regina's authority and earn the nun's enmity by yielding to Maggie's demands, or he could quietly boot Margaret Bosarge Verneuille and her niece out the door and risk alienating half the parish and local fire department. Seminary training provided limited guidance about management and politics. Nuns worked for next to nothing. They ran the school as they saw fit, or not at all. The pastor found himself between a rock and a hard place. He eventually opted for what appeared to be the lesser of two evils and reluctantly overruled Sister Regina, sending a seismic ripple through the school. No one mocked the Bosarge's bare feet again.

However, the nuns sent Anne home once more. Anne Bosarge's name most always stayed on the blackboard because Aunt Maggie could not keep up with tuition. Maggie promptly marched her niece back to school. This time the nuns had shamed them both. Margaret Verneuille entered St. Margaret's school downright mad, jaws clenched and eyes narrowed. She was not naturally disposed to do bodily harm; she just looked that way. Maggie shared a piece of her mind, and then walked back home. Anne returned to class. When Anne finished the eighth grade and left St. Margaret's for good, she considered that day the happiest of her life.

As might be expected, relations between Willie and Maggie headed south after 1930. Christmas and Easter pilgrimages by Maggie and Anne down Little River Road did not heal the wounds. Pride certainly played a role. Marrying off at 15 was one thing among Bosarge's, but no one could recall any 10 year-old having the gumption to leave home without so much as a hello, goodbye, or thank you. When Maggie displayed Anne at Christmas and Easter all gussied up, it salted the wound. Willie and Sadie were still figuring how to make ends meet, what with their latest arrivals. Grandmother Bosarge, always pleased to see daughter Maggie and granddaughter Anne Marie, left Willie without much moral support within the family. That Maggie would feed and clothe one of his children initially found Willie indifferent. As Anne's older brother HM and sister Florence left home, though, Willie's mood changed. Understandably, Sadie needed help around the house and she let Willie know about it. Willie then let Maggie know about it. Maggie told Green. Green thought on it, and then left for Mobile. When Willie sensed that he was getting nowhere, he called the law. More than once a sheriff's deputy went down Davenport Lane to have a word with Maggie and deliver Anne to Willie's doorstep. Once the deputy left, though, Anne walked through her parents' house, out the kitchen door, and over the back fence north of the hen house. She was back at Aunt Maggie's place before the deputy reached Mobile. That prompted Willie to have the sheriff arrest Green and Maggie for keeping Anne. The threat of having to leave Aunt Maggie's for good lingered over Anne day and night. The sheriff got tired of driving down to Bayou la Batre looking for one of Willie Bosarge's daughters. Once

Anne turned 14 in May 1934, she, Aunt Maggie and Uncle Green took a ride to Mobile. Anne filed a petition appointing them her guardians, ending the tug of war between Little River Road and Davenport Lane.

Carl's Creek flowed south for miles, emptying into the bayou halfway between Maggie's house and Irvington Road. Although mostly non-navigable upstream, the creek spanned about 50 feet where the Davenport Lane bridge crossed. Anne acquired her swimming skills off this bridge before entering the first grade. Willie considered swimming a bayou necessity, not a pastime or sport. Willie taught Anne to swim, not how to swim. He tossed her off the bridge into the deepest point of the creek where it seemed less likely to contact underwater roots and stumps or disturb snakes and alligators in the shallows. Anne practiced arm strokes before testing them out in the creek. She splashed about a bit before going under. Willie pulled her out for a second go at it. She went under the second time. Willie pulled her out again. After a few moments catching her breath, Anne climbed back up on the bridge. Willie's teaching style emphasized survival, not technique. Sooner or later Anne would figure out how to reach the bank before drowning. HM and Florence did. Anne felt tired and did not relish going under again. She did not think about what lived underwater or in the shallows. After hitting the water a third time, she bobbed up to the surface and clawed, kicked, and splashed to the nearest bank. Willie's work was done.

Living with Aunt Maggie meant crossing Carl's Creek at least twice a day, rain or shine. A rainstorm never kept Anne home from school. Without any shoes or raincoat to speak of, she usually arrived at the creek already drenched head to toe. When a heavy downpour or squall hit, the creek often rose and the bridge disappeared underwater. By the time the water crested and receded to its banks, a day or two might pass. Anne could not stand around in the rain waiting for the creek to go down. She either went back home or she swam to school. One way or another she arrived somewhere dripping wet. Anne swam a flooded Carl's Creek and arrived at school dripping wet. Aunt Maggie seldom ever seemed troubled by this. She allowed Anne to swim the creek in good weather, provided her niece wore a dress. Maggie did not think much of swimsuits. Otherwise, as long as Anne got to school, swimming Carl's Creek hardly mattered to Aunt Maggie.

Maggie took a somewhat dimmer view when storms threatened to flood Carl's Creek at night. Hemmed in by the bayou on the south and by the creek on the west, Maggie and her neighbors saw the wooden bridge as their only means of escape. At her age, Maggie preferred to flee over the bridge than into the creek. Treading a swollen creek by day was one thing. Drifting through darkness into a flooded bayou, marsh, or swamp critter was another matter. As a storm bore down, Aunt Maggie sent Anne down the lane ever so often with a lantern to eyeball the rising creek throughout the night. If it rose too fast for comfort, they crossed to the other side.

Irma Wilcox and Maggie neighbored on the lane long before Anne moved in. Irma packed a fine picnic basket and kept a rowboat for fair weather outings. Early on, Irma took a shine to Maggie's niece. It helped that Anne knew how to handle the boat. Aunt Maggie could hardly say no when Irma asked Anne to row them up Carl's Creek on the high tide for a picnic and some fishing. Maggie counted on Anne to catch enough for dinner and gather some winter firewood on the way back. Once in a blue moon Aunt Maggie even ventured out on the bayou. She and Anne poled a skiff up the long creek to Indian shell mounds. They lunched on Maggie's bread, pickles and some sausage that one of the hogs donated each fall. The business at hand required navigating under low thickets of dangling Spanish moss. Maggie planned to replace their lumpy bedding with fresh moss mattresses. Tearing clumps of moss off branches sometimes exposed startled opossum that played possum after falling to the ground. Anne had no quarrel with opossum as long as none dropped into the skiff.

Guardianship presented Aunt Maggie something of a mixed blessing. Maggie acquired a niece who chose to become a daughter. Both aunt and niece had more than an inkling of what each offered and expected of the other. In the bargain, Maggie discovered a young companion whose spunky differences matched her own. Punting the skiff to a creek's headwaters in search of mattress stuffing became a summer event instead of a lonesome chore. Tending fields and animals allowed Maggie to teach her niece more than what to eat. Sharing dusty books and scratched recordings rekindled memories and moods that withered when left unattended. Maggie also picked up burdens that her niece left on the doorstep. Each Sunday Maggie presented Anne to Grandmother Bosarge, not to Willie and Sadie. Anne traded one set of choices for another, one part of her family for another, when she crossed Irvington Road. Aunt Maggie provided her niece sanctuary, but not escape. Anne still had to account for herself.

Long before Anne entered Alba High School, Aunt Maggie let it be known she would not abide her niece wearing make up, shorts, or swimsuits. And, no matter what the cousins did, which included most everything, Anne would not date. Maggie set her mind on Anne graduating from high school, God willing and the creek don't rise. No boy need bother coming around before then. But Maggie chose not to sit back and wait for the problem to knock on the door. She circled the wagons early. Before Anne's freshman year began, Maggie forbade the Alba High School principal from letting Anne travel out of Bayou la Batre on a school bus, even to see a football game in nearby Grand Bay or Theodore. Anne knew better than put her aunt's will to the test.

By the same token, Maggie knew when not to test her niece's will. From freshman year on, Anne attended Alba's annual prom. Maggie even took it on herself to sew Anne a new outfit each year. In all her finery, Anne walked from the house to the prom and back, over the bridge and past St. Margaret's School, without a date. Anne made do without. She invited Ann Wright from Fowl River to go together to the prom and then stay over night at Aunt Maggie's. Otherwise, Ann Wright lived too far away to attend the prom at all. It set well with Maggie that Ann Wright also went without a date. Except for Sunday afternoons, Anne had little free time to date anyone anyway. After church and visiting Grandmother Bosarge on Sunday, Anne and classmate Helen Ruth would row down the bayou to Mississippi Sound just for fun. Anne could out-fish, out-swim, and out-row most of her friends. She felt proud of herself. Even Saturday night usually was taken. In 1934 Maggie talked Uncle Green into getting a radio. Not many neighbors had a radio. On Saturday night after supper, Maggie and her niece gathered around the radio and listened to the Opry.

Aunt Maggie seldom spoke about the packinghouse. Women stood for hours in front of bins picking crab and heading shrimp without much conscious thought. They did not share the satisfaction of a successful catch, trawling open waters by moonlight and warming in the glow of the cabin's straining engine. The monotonous process of cleaning seafood that the women neither caught nor ate lacked the rewards of tending gardens and raising animals. At the end of a day Maggie took home her pay, along with cracked and cut fingers. She resolved that her niece would never work in the packinghouse. She forbade Anne to set foot in the place, even during the summer. Aunt Maggie did not indulge in subtlety or sarcasm, and attempted humor only on rare occasions. She expected to be taken literally.

Anne accounted very well for herself at Alba. As graduation approached, Aunt Maggie saw her niece's diploma as a passport to opportunities that the bayou did not offer young women. Every day at the packing shed reminded Maggie of that. On her left and right women stood in rubber boots on wet concrete floors, covered with long aprons, bandanas, and soggy gloves. They broke the silent monotony with idle chatter that seemed to repeat itself from day to day. As might be expected, several turned instinctively when an unexpected commotion disrupted the shed in May 1940. Maggie did not quite believe her eyes or ears. Anne burst into the packing shed waving some papers and calling out to her aunt. Anne had just received a National Honor Society invitation to be recognized at a graduation awards ceremony. She ran all the way across town to the packinghouse unable to contain herself. She had to share the excitement with Aunt Maggie. Anne blurted out the details for all the women to hear. Good news or not, Maggie struggled to control the fury that smoldered within. Maggie could not pause to enjoy this special moment with her niece, particularly in front of the other women. The look on Maggie's face reminded Anne never to set foot in the packinghouse.

Aunt Maggie and Uncle Green dressed up in their Sunday best, took Anne to Alba High School, and watched their ward receive the

NHS pin. They understood how much that meant to Anne. Sadie and Willie did not attend the ceremony. None of Anne's sisters and brothers showed up. Anne invited them all, but they did not see what the fuss was all about. Maggie knew better. She took Anne to Mobile to shop for graduation. They picked out a long white dress embroidered with flowers. Anne happily posed for graduation in her first fancy store-bought dress. Most of the bayou, even Sadie and Willie, showed up for evening commencement ceremonies at Alba High School on Wednesday, May 29, 1940.

Anne's graduation celebration took place under something of a cloud. German troops invaded Denmark and Norway in April and by May 15 seized the Netherlands, Belgium and Luxembourg. Britain bombed German cities the week before Anne's graduation, and British forces fled Dunkirk into the English Channel even as the graduates received diplomas. That night, for the first time in ten years, Aunt Maggie allowed her niece to leave the house and Bayou la Batre with someone else. Anne rode with her English teacher, Mrs. Davis, to a hamburger joint and then a dance in Theodore. Even at 20, Anne had no date.

Aunt Maggie longed to see her niece graduate and leave Bayou la Batre someday, though not necessarily all at once. Just before graduation Uncle Green surprised Anne with a steamer trunk. Spring Hill College had accepted Anne into the School of Nursing on scholarship. She began packing to leave the bayou. Aunt Maggie shopped Speigel's catalogue for a watch, an essential tool for student nurses. Anne had never worn a watch. Maggie bought a nice one for the princely sum of $11. In the few weeks that remained, Anne still tended the animals and chopped firewood. She and Helen Ruth rowed the skiff up and down the bayou, past the packinghouse, out into Mississippi Sound, just for fun. Germany's blitzkrieg seized Paris on June 14 and defeated France a week later.

Uncle Green drove Maggie and Anne to Mobile. Nursing training began July 1 at City Hospital on the corner of Broad and St. Anthony. Aunt Maggie made a point to speak with Sister Laura, the nursing supervisor. Anne managed to get through high school, get into college, and earn a scholarship without so much as one date. Aunt Maggie wanted to keep it that way until Anne completed nursing school. Maggie told Sister Laura that Anne should not fritter her time away on dating. The nun found Mrs. Verneuille's concern perfectly understandable. First year nursing students attended classes and worked wards each day of the week, leaving only every other Sunday afternoon free to do as circumstances allowed. That reduced the likelihood of dating to mere happenstance. Maggie did not find the assurance completely satisfactory, but let it go. Maggie faced a long ride back to the bayou that night. She stood by her niece for 13 years, and Anne did Aunt Maggie proud. Maggie's spunky companion grew up and left home a lady, an educated one at that. Understandably, the light in Maggie's life would dim until Christmas break.

Anne entered college literally without a dollar to her name. She looked forward to Sunday afternoon visits with Uncle Green. He carried pastries from Aunt Maggie and usually left Anne a couple of dollars spending money. Maggie did not travel with Green to Mobile for these brief hellos and difficult good-byes. She counted the days until Anne's Christmas vacation. Maggie longed to hear stories about college and hospital wards, and to show off Anne at church. In the meanwhile Maggie listened to her radio. September 1940 broadcasts brought nothing but bad news. Germany began its daytime bombing attacks on London, Italy invaded Egypt, and President Roosevelt signed the Selective Training & Service Act. The government began drafting boys from Mobile, Theodore, and Bayou la Batre. Before Thanksgiving, Rumania, Hungary and Bulgaria joined the Axis. The growing prospect of war also placed a premium on training more nurses. However, the nursing school continued about its business unaffected by national and worldwide upheavals.

As the summer of 1941 approached, Anne made travel plans. She had seen Theodore and Mobile, and felt little desire to summer again

50. Anne Bosarge, Alba High School Graduation, May 29, 1940 (photographer unknown).

51. Anne Bosarge, City Hospital Nursing School, Mobile, September, 1940 (photographer unknown).

52. City Hospital, Mobile, February 11, 1994 (Copyright © 2007 James J. Gonzales).

53. *Green Verneuille, Anne Bosarge, and Margaret Gertrude Bosarge
Verneuille, Davenport Lane, Bayou la Batre, 1941 (photographer unknown).*

370 GUNNY Memoirs of Mobile's South Side

in Bayou la Batre. Anne fancied visiting her sister in Crowley, Louisiana, just beyond Lafayette. Crowley had little to say for itself in 1941, other than being near Cajun country on one side and an unprecedented gathering of Army tank divisions on the other. None of that mattered as much to Anne as just doing something or going somewhere different. Anne celebrated her 21st birthday at City Hospital. She no longer had guardians, or need of any. At the same age, Sadie already counted three children and another on the way. Anne had yet to be kissed, much less courted, and the likelihood of either remained largely speculative. In May 1941 President Roosevelt proclaimed an unlimited national emergency, asserted America's right to freedom of the seas against Nazi U-boats, commenced a massive ship building program, and announced that "the only thing we have to fear is fear itself." America prepared for war as Anne's freshman year drew to a close.

After her shift on Thursday May 29, Anne asked Sister Laura for permission to have dinner with John George, a shipyard welder recovering from an appendectomy. Anne invited Margie Knight to go with her. They met at Claude Betbeze's Plaza nightclub on Terrell Road. Junior, as Anne called him, brought along another welder, Gunny Gonzales, who proved to be charming and a very good dancer. Anne had no experience with charming dancers. During dinner Gunny asked Anne for a date. Anne told Gunny that she could not date. She worked Colored pediatrics and obstetrics throughout the week and lived in a dorm under the watchful eye of the Sisters of Mercy. Before dinner ended, Gunny bet Junior $5 he could get a date with Anne, despite the nursing school's onerous schedule. Waiting until Anne's next available Sunday afternoon off did not discourage Gunny. He had met an "angel from the country" and already was infatuated. He invited her to go swimming at Gulf Shores. Of course, Anne never had any use for a swimsuit. She always swam Carl's Creek and the bayou in a dress. That could look odd at Gulf Shores, though. Anne shopped for a swimsuit. In just one outing, Anne experienced several firsts: a swimsuit, a beach without snakes and alligators, a date, and a kiss. The experience was mostly agreeable, though Anne dove into the surf still wearing her wristwatch. It never occurred to remove the timepiece. She would need to buy another watch without Aunt Maggie being any the wiser. On the ride back to Mobile, as they drove past Malbis, Gunny asked Anne if she would like to go steady. She promptly said yes.

On Sunday June 22, with but another week of school remaining before summer break, Germany declared war on Russia. While Anne packed for Crowley, Gunny shopped for an engagement ring. The following Sunday Gunny proposed. Anne did not pause to seek the benefit of Aunt Maggie's advice. She said yes, and then left Mobile for Louisiana. Within the week, a letter arrived in Crowley. Gunny asked Anne to meet him in New Orleans. She did. On impulse, they tried to get married in New Orleans, but traditional legal requirements did not allow for that. However, Mississippi did not trifle with such details. Anne wore a red and white dress when they married in Gulfport on July 14, following a courtship of only six weeks. The brisk course of world events seemed to accelerate the traditional pace of social conventions. In a period of less than six weeks, Germany invaded and conquered Belgium, the Netherlands, and France. Within the span of a customary courtship, Nazi Germany captured Europe.

Anne had good reason to fret over breaking the news to Aunt Maggie and Uncle Green. She expected a stew of indignation and disappointment. Eloping deprived Aunt Maggie the pleasure of giving away her favorite niece and surrogate child. Yet, Anne could hardly have shared with Aunt Maggie her desire to marry someone that Anne had no permission to date in the first place. Eloping also failed to satisfy canonical requirements for marriage recognized by the Church. Uncle Green predictably promised to take a shotgun after Gunny at the earliest opportunity. Gunny did not regard Green Verneuille lightly, keeping his distance until the dust settled. Neither Aunt Maggie nor Uncle Green found it easy to warm up to the notion of Anne getting married, much less eloping. They figured she would do better to finish nursing school first, though that meant waiting another two years. By bayou standards a bride of 23 drew gossip. Even Maggie married by 22. None of that mattered much now. For at least the fourth time in memory, Maggie was fit to be tied.

When summer ended, Anne returned to the nursing school dorm. Word eventually slipped out that Anne Bosarge was now Anne Gonzales. The consequences were swift. Sister Laura did not allow nursing school students to marry. Without much ado, the nun forced Anne to leave City Hospital and Spring Hill College shy of completing her nursing degree. That is all there was to it. Appeal to reason or higher authority did not exist. Within two months, though, Sister Laura took note of the world war being waged against Japan and Germany. A dramatic wartime need for nurses, married or otherwise, persuaded the nursing school to reconsider its priorities, but Anne never completed her degree.

Shortly before the United States declared war, Anne moved into her own home two blocks west of Pinecrest Cemetery on Ryders Lane. She became a dentist's assistant, a job she never previously imagined. By August 1942 Anne was pregnant. She gave birth in the spring of 1943 to Joseph Anthony, a notably olive complected child. The demand for trained medical assistants in Mobile remained strong, assuring employment if Anne wanted to continue working. Her choice between staying home with baby Joe or returning to work came easily. Dismissal from nursing school and losing the scholarship deeply anguished Anne. The dream she once shared with Aunt Maggie evaporated overnight, leaving an ache that did not ease with time. Dental assistant work, good as it might be, remained just a job that could not replace a dream. Anne enjoyed keeping house on Ryders Lane with Joseph Anthony. Despite hardships and twisted fate, Anne wanted what little she had, which seemed more than enough. Anne's first born also helped smooth Aunt Maggie's ruffled feathers. For Christmas, Maggie gave her niece a family Bible inscribed: "From Uncle Green & Aunt Margaret to Anne, Gunny, Joseph Anthony. Dec 24th 1943. God Bless your home." Though she abided the familiarity of nicknames and such, Maggie always regarded herself as Margaret and baby Joe as Joseph Anthony. As she approached 60 Maggie took stock of emotions common to grandmothering, but remained true to character. The Bible and her simple blessing reflected basic priorities.

Anne took Joseph Anthony down Little River Road to meet his grandparents. At the birth of their respective first born, Anne was half a lifetime older than Sadie had been. The Bosarge homestead on the north side of Little River Road had weathered a bit. Under the sprawling crown of a massive live oak, most of the front yard remained bare of grass. Sadie's last born, Robert Andrew, was still a lap child, much like Anne's first born. The years had not been kind to Sadie, though, leaving her looking worn half again her age. Anne led Willie and Sadie to the back yard where they posed with Anne's baby brother and son.

With the cost of war-rationed meat being what it was, Gunny decided to grow his own. He went to Bay Minnette and paid $10 for three live goats. They were a bargain at twice the price and, after a little fattening up, would be money on the hoof. Gunny soon learned, though, that goats come by their reputation honestly, eating clothes off the line and tearing up fences to snack in the neighbor's garden. Gunny could only afford two weeks of fattening. So Gunny asked eight brother officers out to the house on Ryders Lane for an old fashioned cookout. The main course was still chewing its cud when guests began arriving. No bundle of shrinking violets, they promptly tackled dinner, slitting throats, skinning hides, and quartering flanks as though hunting upstate. Gunny's backyard looked like a slaughter house. Despite its leathery texture, the barbecue went down just fine on a stream of cold brews. Then out came the dice for a night of friendly craps.

Baby Joe's demand for rationed milk soon prompted Gunny to put a cow out back. He and Aunt Maggie struck a deal for one of her cattle. Anne grew up tending chickens and milking cows for Aunt Maggie and figured it was worth a try. Gunny drove alone to Bayou la Batre, inspected the animal, and forked over $25 to Maggie. When Anne went outside the next morning to milk the cow, she found no teats to speak of. Gunny bought himself a bull. It was barbecue time again.

Raising chickens costs next to nothing and takes no more effort than flinging feed out the back door. In the winter of 1944 Gunny next set out to raise chickens from peepers. When a cold snap struck, he brought the chicks in off the back porch and put them in a tub with a light for

warmth. By morning all but one had broiled on the bare surface of the
scorching light bulb. Again, he turned to Aunt Maggie, taking 50 full-
size chickens off her hands at two bits each for resale. Maggie did not get
rich off Gunny, but never lost money either. All 50 took a liking to the
backyard, huddled just fine under the house in cold weather, and respected the neighbors' property. Then they all came down with the sorehead,
thanks to constant mosquito attacks. Dipping a chicken's head into oil
usually healed sorehead caused by insect bites. If the cure did not take at
first, more dipping followed. But folks would not buy or eat chicken
with signs of sorehead. Either the sorehead had to go or Gunny was out
fifty chickens and another $25. He placed a call to his friend Willard, a
one-time indoor ball pitcher, who ran a poultry place on Dauphin.

"I got a bunch of chickens here Willard, and I've got to get rid of
them. I'm leaving town for a while and thought you could use them.
I've already cut their heads off," Gunny explained.

"Tell you what to do, Gunny, you bring 'em on down and I'll go
clean 'em and sell the damn things." They sold, but Gunny quit the
poultry business after that.

When Ingalls Shipyard offered Gunny better paying welding work,
Gunny also quit the police force. Gunny and Anne packed up and
moved to Pascagoula for about a year. When Gunny returned to Mobile
as a Liberty ship hull inspector at Chickasaw Bogue, Anne and Gunny
found a small guest apartment on Palmetto Street four blocks west of
Washington Park. Joseph Anthony and Anne would stroll down
Palmetto Street for outings in Washington Park. Amid live oaks and blos-
soming azaleas, Joe rode the bronze deer and watched squirrels play. Joe
was big enough to tricycle about in daylight, but foot-long rats owned
the sidewalks after dusk. From the window of his kitchenette apartment,
Gunny tossed bread crumbs into the alley at sunset. He and Joe watched
the rats wrestle for supper. Something had to give before the rats decided to come through the front door and serve themselves.

About the time Joseph Anthony turned two, Anne found herself pregnant again. Within a matter of days Germany surrendered, a good omen
of sorts, but combat in the Pacific raged on. In the summer of 1945 Uncle

Green fell ill. He died at home on August 8 two days after *Enola Gay* destroyed Hiroshima. Amid surging hope that fighting soon would end, someone had to deal with the immediate task of rounding up pallbearers. This proved no small matter. Green grew up in Mobile, had few roots in the bayou, and burned his bridge with the Bosarge's in 1934. Green and Maggie pretty much kept to themselves after Green retired when Anne left Bayou la Batre for nursing school. As it turned out, Green chose wisely not to shoot Gunny four years earlier. Few volunteers in Bayou la Batre seemed willing to haul Green Verneuille out of his parlor on Davenport Lane. The situation in Mobile proved nearly as discouraging, though Green retired as a fire captain. The war had drained the cadre of many fire departments. However, Gunny eventually prevailed on enough brother fire fighters to show up Saturday morning in mid-August, take Green to St. Margaret Church for the funeral Mass, and then escort him to the cemetery. The newspaper reported that Green Verneuille was survived by his wife Margaret Gertrude, brother Frank, and daughter Anne.

Anne gave birth in December 1945 to her second son. John Michael lived and died in but one day, a fate that nearly befell Anne and Charles Joullian under far more primitive conditions. Post-war celebration did not comfort Anne. What she left behind in Bayou la Batre no longer remained. What seemed normal in 1940 now existed only in memories. Within the span of a few months, she lost part of the past, the future, and herself. Burying Uncle Green and John Michael exacted a toll that celebration did not cover.

Anne, Gunny and Joseph Anthony soon left the small apartment on Palmetto Street for 1508 Bobolink Drive in Birdville, a city housing development northwest of Brookley Field. Cardinal Drive looped around Birdville, intersecting Bobolink on the southeast side near Brookley Field and crossing Eagle Drive on the southwest side near Maryvale Elementary School. Their two-bedroom house was sandwiched between the street ellipse on the north and a large open field to the south. Anne's new neighborhood of mostly young families provided playmates for three year-old Joe, an experience quite unlike Davenport Lane. Anne found the change agreeable. Ronnie and Robbie Lamey became some of Joe's close friends. Tragedy unexpectedly returned, though, when Robbie and Ronnie lost their father on April 16, 1947 to the Texas City ship explosions in the harbor near Galveston.

Anne soon was pregnant a third time. Contrary to bayou tradition, no midwife attended her. Just shy of Anne's 27th birthday, Dr. Alexander J. Brown helped her deliver a boy at Providence Hospital. The next day Gunny's mother Ursulene, sister-in-law Helena Gonzales, and Father James Patrick showed up at the hospital to see Anne and pass around a blonde blue-eyed baby Joullian. More remarkable, though, Anne's mother Sadie and sister Mena paid a rare visit to Mobile. Sadie handed Anne an identification bracelet for the newborn. Anne had reason to be content. No other visitor need walk through the door. But no door could keep Gunny's sister Dit and Anne's neighbor Nell Cobb away. That both dropped in on the same day can be understood only in astrological terms. Having no children of her own, Dit felt obliged to mother all her nephews and nieces whether they needed it or not. Cackling aloud, Dit dragged a large high chair through the door, a present for the baby to grow into. Gunny's other sister Nonie, husband Paul Stewart and son Paul David came to check out the baby the next day. Anne let Gunny name the baby after Governor James E. Folsom and Charles Joullian. Three weeks later at the Cathedral, godfather Joseph N. Langan, godmother Lucille Tew, Tunker Tew, Aunt Nettie, Joseph Anthony and Father James Patrick christened James Joullian.

Anne took her boys down to Bayou la Batre and Coden to visit Aunt Maggie and the rest of the Bosarge's, and then to Fairhope across the bay to celebrate the Fourth of July. The boys logged more miles in 1947 than Anne and Gunny did in their first 12 years. Back on Bobolink, Gunny wrapped the front yard with a white knee-high picket fence. For nearly a year, it managed to keep one crawler in and other crawlers out. When all the crawlers reared up on their hind feet, Gunny corralled the house with a goat proof barrier.

Anne and Gunny made up for lost time celebrating the boys' birthdays. In April 1948 they observed Joe's fifth and Jimmy's first with cousins Butch Gonzales, Dottie Stewart, and Paul David Stewart,

54. Anne B. Gonzales, 1946 (photographer unknown).

55. Joe, Jim & Anne Gonzales, 1508 Bobolink Drive, Birdville, Mobile, May, 1948 (E. J. Gunny Gonzales).

neighbor Donnie Cobb, grandmother Ursulene and the family. Ursulene did not care to be called grandmother, much less grandma. She took a shine to "Nannie," a misnomer of sorts. Aunts Dit, Nonie, Myrtle and Helena, uncles Joe Gonzales, Paul Stewart and Charlie Joullian, Nannie, and Aunt Nettie assured Joseph Anthony and James Joullian of an unusually outspoken and colorful extended family. Dit never forgot the boys' birthdays. Anne knew something about eccentric families, and little about normal ones. Anne saw more toys and clothes at that one birthday party than every birthday and Christmas she could remember on Little River Road. Come May of 1949 Anne kept the party simple. Aunt Nonie and Uncle Paul, Uncle Joe and Aunt Helena, Aunt Nettie, Paul David, Dottie and Butch gathered on Bobolink for cake and ice cream. Already three months pregnant, Anne did not ask the neighborhood over.

Anne enrolled Joe in the first grade at Maryvale School in August 1949. Each day a cluster of kids from Bobolink made their way across the field to Eagle Drive and then on to Maryvale, about as far as Anne's walk to St. Margaret School. A couple months later, and nearly eight months pregnant, Anne suddenly wanted to get away to New Orleans. She took the boys out to Audubon Zoo on the St. Charles trolley, ate poboys, and strolled the French Quarter down to Café du Monde. Then Joseph Anthony came down with an aggravated case of chicken pox. Gunny turned to Aunt Nettie. Despite nearly 80 years of wear and tear, Nettie appeared at the doorstep on Bobolink Drive and took charge of Gunny's brood. Five weeks later Anne gave birth by Caesarian section to her last child and only daughter. Anne honored Aunt Maggie by christening her newborn Margaret Kathleen. Aunt Nettie moved in to tend the children. The house on Bobolink suddenly seemed very cramped. Though frail, increasingly addled, and seldom given to humor, Aunt Nettie still got down on all fours to frolic with her rowdy wards. Come Easter Sunday, 1950 she hunted eggs with Joe and Jimmy, often forgetting where she hid the eggs. Later that year Gunny and Anne gathered up the white picket fence and moved north one block to a three bedroom house at 1520 Albatross Drive at the top of the circle. Aunt Nettie returned on Easter Sunday 1951 to hunt eggs for the last time with Manuel's boys on Albatross Drive.

The gaggle of Bosarge cousins that once gathered to play on Little River Road some 25 years earlier reappeared in Birdville in the form of Robbie Lamey, Ronnie Lamey, Donnie Cobb, Chad Jordan, Jimmy Jordan, Billy Barrett, Gary Bean, Jimmy Dunaway, Danny Dunaway, Jane Ward, Connie Stein, Linda Stevens, Peggy Swain, and Warren Barrow. Anne and Gunny invited the neighborhood and cousins to celebrate Joe turning 8 and Jimmy turning 4. About 40 kids showed up on May 29, 1951, nearly half of them girls. Most sported white shoes, dresses, pants, shorts, shirts, and other Sunday go-to-meeting finery. Birdville's post-war baby bumper crop came to party. They shared ice cream and cake, marveled at the presents, and played as though there had been no war, no rationing, and no hardship to speak of. For the kids it was a birthday; for all the parents, a coming out.

Not long after seeing Dit and the Audubon Zoo just a few months earlier, Anne's itch to travel broke out in a rash by late July, 1951. It did not much matter that she picked the hottest time of the year to visit Wichita Falls, already in the midst of a dry spell that drove snakes through sewers into bathroom plumbing looking for water. Anne packed up the kids and rode with her sister Mildred to Sheppard AFB, spending nearly two weeks criss-crossing Texas and Louisiana. After returning to Mobile, Joseph Anthony started the third grade at Maryvale with his Birdville friends. Anne got to know Joe's teachers and attended parent school events. The best parent-attended classroom earned the kids an ice cream party, a lure that converted third graders into naggers with a mission. Unlike her childhood, though, chores did not compete with schooling. By comparison, Joseph Anthony had no chores to speak of, no need to tend animals, draw well water, chop wood, pick fruit, or gather pecans. Doing dishes and finishing homework became routine before running outside to play or turning on the radio.

One block north of Albatross, in the large triangle between Raven, Cardinal, and Eagle, the Thomas James Community Center opened its doors on weekday mornings for pre-school when Maryvale held classes. Older kids had run of the game room, basketball gym, and baseball field in the afternoon. Anne took an interest in the pre-school program, which did not exist in her bayou childhood. Aunt Maggie gave Anne a keen respect for schooling youngsters early. Mrs. Harriet Mayes taught a half-day pre-school class of about 16. At age four they learned songs, played games, shared crayons, usually followed instructions, and discovered confidence, all without doting mothers nearby. At home they showed off seasonal renderings of Halloween goblins, Thanksgiving turkeys, Christmas toys, and Easter eggs. Staying inside lines mattered a lot, more so than technique or color. Anne liked what she saw and packed Jimmy off to school.

Among the pre-school memorabilia Anne treasured most, one event in particular captured her imagination. On the evening of April 18, 1952 dozens of preschoolers from Thomas James, Rickarby, Springhill Avenue, Toulminville, and Baltimore playgrounds flocked to the Springtime Festival of Music and Folk Dances at the Spring Hill Avenue Community Center. Costumed *de rigueur*, they created a spectacular garden of flowers, birds, and bees. For several weeks, the short, jovial, and balding music director Richard DeNeefe, and taller talented piano accompanist Nancy Bennett, rode circuit rehearsing musical numbers with playground preschoolers. A few days before the festival, Anne outfitted Jimmy as a bluebird, convincingly equipped with beak, tail, and thin bare legs. The bluebird's mother managed not to laugh, not out loud at least. Instead she shamelessly persuaded her bluebird to rehearse his garden routine in the front yard for the neighbors. This event and more generally the entire preschool program impressed Anne. She celebrated Jimmy's fifth birthday at Thomas James with Nancy Bennett, Harriet Mayes, and all the preschoolers.

The boys summered at Thomas James and in fields around Albatross. On Saturdays Anne let them walk to the Brookley Theater for a double feature of Gene Autrey, Roy Rogers, Lash LaRue, or Abbot

56. Charles Joullian & Nettie Pocase, Easter Sunday, 24 Westwood Avenue, Mobile, 1949 (photographer unknown).

57. Joe Gonzales, Nettie Pocase, and Jim Gonzales, Easter Sunday, 1508 Bobolink Drive, Birdville, Mobile, April 9, 1950 (Anne Gonzales).

58. *Jim Gonzales, Billy Barnette, Joe Gonzales, Gary Bean, Kathy Gonzales, and Chad, Linda & Jimmy Jordan (l-r), 1520 Albatross Drive, Birdville, Mobile, 1951 (Anne Gonzales).*

59. *Birthday Party, 1520 Albatross Drive, Gunny and Jim Gonzales (center), May 29, 1951 (Anne Gonzales).*

60. Birthday Party, 1520 Albatross Drive, Joe and Jim Gonzales (left of center), May 29, 1951 (Anne Gonzales).

61. Anne, Jim & Kathy Gonzales, 1520 Albatross Drive, Birdville, Mobile, Easter Sunday, April 13, 1952 (Joseph A. Gonzales).

62. Thomas James Recreation Center Spring Festival, bluebird Jim Gonzales, 1520 Albatross Drive, Mobile, April 14, 1952 (Anne Gonzales).

63. *Jim, Joe & Kathy Gonzales, Mississippi Sound at Bayou Coden, Mobile, June 1953 (Anne Gonzales).*

*64. Jim Gonzales, cousin Dottie Stewart, and cousin Joseph (Butch)
Gonzales (l-r), First Communion, St. Vincent Church, Mobile, Mother's
Day, May 9, 1954 (Anne Gonzales).*

and Costello. Joe started the fourth grade at Maryvale in August, but life in Birdville came to an unexpectedly strange end by Christmas, 1952. For reasons that had little to do with Maryvale, Thomas James, Birdville, or Anne, the family pulled up roots and left their neighbors. To most everyone's surprise, especially the Bosarge's, Gunny and Anne moved to Hemley Road on the southeast outskirts of Bayou la Batre.

Joe enrolled at Alba Elementary School over Christmas. However, Anne found no preschool or kindergarten for Jimmy, certainly nothing the likes of Thomas James, and no street circle of playmates. The boys got to know Mrs. McGallager's cows in the pasture on the south side and hogs in the sty to the east. They learned to be mindful as they wandered about the bayou. Any grassy thicket near water likely harbored a snake of some sort. Pulling grass by hand to feed the rabbits sometimes yielded a green snake or worse. Anne saw Aunt Maggie and her family more often, to be sure. She let Willie take a cane pole to the bridge at Carl's Creek on Davenport Lane and teach his grandsons to fish, not swim. He also took them out at night in a skiff to cast for mullet just shy of where the bayou meets Mississippi Sound. In the pitch dark silence Willie listened for fish and anything else that moved about. From the bow he hurled a hand sewn cast net into calm water as black as the moonless sky. Some six feet below the surface Willie felt desperate mullet confused by the closing net. He sensed the difference between fish, snake, and alligator by movement of the net. Jimmy sat still at the stern, providing some ballast for the bow, and Joe amid ship with the flashlight. Neither could see the net, much less whatever moved in the dark. Willie allowed no light until the net came aboard, so as not to frighten off the mullet. He allowed no talking so as to better hear jumping mullet. The boys quietly trusted their grandfather not to haul a water moccasin into the boat, and hoped Willie would not argue with any alligator caught in the net, but tales about *Pecheur* gave cause for doubt. Leaving the skiff was not an attractive option, though, even with a disagreeable predator aboard. More of the same waited underwater. A clock seemed ill-equipped to measure the pace of time in the silent darkness. The number of casts, a change in the wind, or the size of the catch determined when to return upstream. Time did not slow down in the bayou; it just did not matter.

Movies took time finding their way from Mobile to Bayou la Batre. The small theater at the intersection south of the draw bridge did not offer double features or matinees, and often nothing at all. *Miracle of Fatima* starring Roland Gilbert arrived amid much fanfare for a showing in the spring of 1953. Anne agreed to let the boys go see it, provided they wore shoes. The theater floor had an unsettling adhesive feel due to liquid residues of uncertain origin over the years. Most of that stickiness usually wore off on the walk home. More distracting, though, was the herd of rats that raced over bare feet to snatch spilled popcorn and what not. The boys agreed to wear shoes and tote their own grocery sack of popcorn. They liked the miracle, ate the popcorn, sat on their feet, and ignored the rats.

Trading Birdville for Bayou la Batre proved a mistake for most everyone in most every way. As soon as Joe finished the semester at Alba Elementary, Anne packed the family and returned to Mobile in June, 1953. Gunny and Anne put $500 down on a two bedroom house in a pecan orchard on Ogburn Avenue a few blocks south of Brookley Field. On Independence Day, with a basket of fried chicken and butter sandwiches, they picnicked amid tombstones in Pinecrest Cemetery, watching twin-tailed C-119 and C-124 transport planes overhead. At sunset, Gunny placed chicken bones and leftovers in a tree basket for night critters.

Anne quickly befriended Annie and T. B. Ingram, a kind couple who lived next door on the downhill side. Older and childless, the Ingram's somehow managed to remain lifelong friends despite an open yard that the boys trafficked at will. When the kids grazed off pecans from both sides of the line, the Ingram's never shooed them away. When the boys nailed a basketball backboard to a tree and shot hoops on the Ingram's wooded back lot, T. B. watched quietly from his breezeway puffing a pipe. And when one of Annie Ingram's Siamese cats treed itself, she called on the tree climbers next door for help. Sugar, eggs, milk, and what not traded hands with the Ingram's through the door many a morning. As fate would have it, Ruth Dunaway and her boys Jimmy and Danny moved in next door to Anne on the uphill side. Anne found herself surrounded with friends among the few houses dotting the wooded neighborhood. She let the boys explore nearby woods and catch crawfish down in the creek. At summer's end Joe returned to Maryvale School, this time with Jimmy. Mrs. Steelreath, a short heavy-set woman, piloted the school bus from her house on Rosedale Road through the narrow neighborhood streets in a loop back to Fulton Road and on to Maryvale. She ran a tight ship, breaking up most fights with single sharp command but occasionally dangling a determined belligerent from one of her massive arms. Without hesitation, Anne entrusted the boys to Mrs. Steelreath's daily custody. Beneath the woman's stout no-nonsense exterior flowed a deep reservoir of patience that mothers envied.

Anne and Gunny had high regard for first grade teacher Della Smith. Gunny expressed their appreciation with modest gifts of scarves and sacks of produce. Anne found the first grade Thanksgiving projects especially memorable. Della Smith introduced simple but telling poetic insights that a six year-old could grasp:

> Where we walk to school each day
> Indian children used to play
> All about our native land
> Where the shops and houses stand
> Not a church and not a steeple
> Only woods and Indian people.
>
> Thank Thee for the world so sweet
> Thank Thee for the food we eat
> Thank Thee for the birds that sing
> Thank Thee Lord for everything.
>
> Thanksgiving means Give Thanks to God.

As far as Anne was concerned, Della Smith and second grade teacher Elsie Higgins hung the moon.

Having but one older car in the family, Anne mostly stayed home with her three year-old and left payday grocery and other shopping to Gunny. On Sunday mornings Anne was content for the boys to ride with Gunny downtown for Mass at the Cathedral and then on to Van Antwerp's for politics, comic books, and cigar boxes. Near the end of his first grade at Maryvale, Jimmy began preparing for First Communion at St. Vincent School. In April and May, Gunny picked Jimmy up from Della Smith's first grade classroom for the trip across town to St. Vincent's. Only a couple of things had changed in the 26 years since Gunny last sat in the school's iron desks or rummaged through lunch bags in cloak rooms. There were no names on chalkboards for overdue monthly tuition, and there were girls in the desks. Jimmy and other first-graders studied catechism with the Sisters, learning and memorizing mysteries of faith. Somehow the youngsters managed to sort it all out, or at least bluff their way through it.

On Mother's Day, May 9, 1954, five days after Gunny's primary election results, the Gonzales-Joullian clan gathered under the oaks of St. Vincent's. Jimmy and first cousins Dottie Stewart, Nonie's girl, and Butch Gonzales, Joseph's boy, were ready to march into the venerable old church together. Observing such a milestone anywhere else simply never occurred to anyone. Gunny, sisters Nonie and Dit, brother Joseph, Charlie and Myrtle, and Ursulene had returned to their south side roots.

❧

Money did not come easy after Gunny lost his job with Toomey Dry Goods. Anne bought on time at stores and kept an open credit account at the pharmacy for the kids' prescriptions. The boys earned a 25 cent weekly allowance, coincidentally the cost of a Saturday matinee and popcorn at the Brookley Theater. At the end of the school year, Della Smith arranged a round-trip for her class from Mobile's L&N train station to Atmore to learn about trains, see mothballed WWII ships, have lunch, and return. Maryvale opened doors of opportunity, modest though they be. The youngsters often marveled at lengthy freight trains crossing Fulton Road south of Maryvale. Della Smith preferred they marvel about an adventure on the train. The $1.30

roundtrip fare seemed pretty steep, but Anne made it happen. On June 3, 1954, she packed Jimmy off on his first and only Alabama train ride.

Anne let the boys roam farther and longer away from home the following summer. They often toted BB rifles, especially when hunting along the snake-infested creek bed at the foot of Ogburn Avenue. She gave them rein to find pick-up games of football and tireball, usually in Mrs. Steelreath's field or Mrs. Cassie's pasture. Anne only required them to be home for lunch and to ask permission before cutting up someone's broom or garden hose. A cheaper version of baseball, tireball required a solid broom handle, a 6 inch garden hose section, no gloves, no baseball diamond, and only two or more players per team. A solid whack launched a tireball whistling like a roman candle some 50 yards over the pitcher's head. Catching a flying tireball retired the side, but barehanded seasoned fielders avoided line drives. The boys cannibalized most of the neighborhood's worn brooms and hoses in one summer, usually with permission.

At night the boys waded with Gunny into the bay off Bay Front Road at low tide from Brookley Field to Dog River in search of flounder and soft-shell crabs. Due to years of welding, Gunny no longer could see flounder nestled in the mud and could not tell the difference between soft-shells and hard-shells. Mistaking a hard-shell for a molting soft-shell often resulted in a bloody finger or two. He taught Joe to use the gig and tied the tub around Jimmy as they waded into the nighttime darkness far away from shore. The boys hunted in the light of hissing gas lantern mantles. With the cooking skills he picked up from Irish Ma, Gunny converted the hard-shells into black *roux* gumbo and served the fried soft-shells in place of bacon for breakfast. Anne seldom worried about them wandering up and down the bay all hours of the night. They were not likely to run across any bayou predators.

Anne managed to cope with two crazes that struck in 1954 about the time the boys returned to Maryvale. Nearly every male from first to sixth grade started carrying to school a sock full of marbles, shooters, and cat-eyes. They played for keeps, which some teachers and parents found disturbing, a vice akin to gambling. The game also took its toll on socks and knees of good pants, and led to an occasional fistfight around the circle. By and large, Anne expected it all to end once the boys lost their marbles, so to speak. They didn't and it didn't. On top of that came Fess Parker's Davy Crockett coonskin cap rage that Anne also ignored until it mercifully went its way.

By the end of 1954 the boys experienced more serious rages at Maryvale. In a surprisingly well planned exercise, all Maryvale students walked from class to cars surrounding the school, packed into an assigned car, and fled a mock nuclear attack launched by Russia or Red China. The panic-free drill did not explore the fate of several hundred displaced children following an actual attack, but most parents took comfort that someone somewhere had their children. Maryvale also provided parents hope their children would be spared polio. Teachers lined up all the students for Salk vaccine shots, a scene vaguely similar to military draft induction centers.

Anne decided to put her five year-old Kathy into school and go back to work. Unfortunately, Maryvale required a first grader to be six years old. The nuns who operated Our Lady of Lourdes Catholic school proved more flexible about accepting underage children. Joe went on to junior high while Jimmy and his sister attended Our Lady of Lourdes school, about halfway between Ogburn Avenue and the Dog River bridge. Anne first worked as a part-time traffic control officer for Sheriff Ray Bridges at Adelia Williams school on Fulton Road. She then found a part-time position with the City Recreation Department herding an endless stream of swimmers at Baltimore Playground's large competition pool. When the director at Rickarby Park retired in 1957, Anne took the job.

Much smaller than sprawling complexes at Thomas James, Springhill Avenue, Baltimore, Sage Avenue and Lyons, Rickarby covered but one block in the Loop area southeast of Government and Fulton Road. Rickarby featured a modest 75 foot square park house on the northwest corner, a circular wading pool at the southeast corner, and a minimal base-ball diamond on the southwest corner. At first blush Rickarby seemed to provide little more than the shaded comfort of a quiet recreational back-water. It lacked the wherewithal to field football or basketball competi-tion, and limited track events to mostly a sprint around the block between the sidewalk and curb. Despite underwhelming physical assets, though, Rickarby sponsored a two semester pre-school program, weekly summer events including a pet show, amateur show, nature study, citizenship study, doll show, music program, arts and crafts, and hobby show, and city wide tournament competition in Chinese checkers, hop scotch, croquet, paddle tennis, checkers, and horse shoes. Five years earlier Anne stood in awe of programs she now had to deliver with minimal resources in an unfamiliar neighborhood. She turned to her staff, Bill, whose many tal-ents kept up the grounds, wading pool, locks, water fountains, fans, rest-rooms and outdoor equipment. Bill also chased off an occasional stray animal, covered graffiti, and removed wasp nests. Bill happened to be Anne's entire staff, as well as the only Colored person in an all White neighborhood to set foot on Rickarby. Each had a job difficult to do together, and impossible to do alone.

Anne could have been a fine registered nurse, a skilled and nurtur-ing caretaker, and a ward supervisor. She might have affected, even if briefly, the health and well-being of many children. However confident she once felt on the hospital ward, Anne now faced challenges for which she seemed ill-equipped to handle. In a stew thick with irony, Rickarby entrusted its new playground director to provide children with experi-ences her own childhood lacked. Bereft of a common history with the youngsters inhabiting Rickarby, Anne instinctively retreated. She could not simply rely on being the adult in command. At any given moment Rickarby's inmates might dissent, destroy, or simply disappear. Whether by intuition or calculation, Anne chose to be part of the experience she offered these youngsters. Anne did not relive her childhood, such as it was, but fashioned one she would have lived. She befriended her new wards as an aunt might play with nieces and nephews at birthdays.

Anne faced a summer marathon of tournaments and special

events. Girls and boys competed evenly in checkers, Chinese checkers and hopscotch. Boys dominated paddle tennis, croquet and horse shoes. Girls had the doll show all to themselves. In past years, though, the mid-summer doll show drew interest from a fairly narrow field of participants. The smaller size of the park house tended to discourage much of a turnout, offering limited space and minimal security under the same roof with other programs and activities. Anne noticed that categories of doll competition seemed endless with multiple entries per category as well as multiple categories per entry. Anne chose to make up for the absence of dolls in her childhood. Mrs. G, as she came to be called at Rickarby, decided to turn the entire park house into a doll house for the whole week. Guys could visit but not touch. Anne gave the girls their day and the dolls their due. Guys learned to deal with it.

Come December 1957, Anne did not merely introduce seasonal crafts and music to her first pre-school class. She arranged for Santa Claus to appear. Gunny made the most of his masquerade, causing as much stir as four year-olds could stand. Word spread among families around the Loop that Rickarby had connections with Santa Claus. The hundreds of kids who filled pre-school benches over the next ten years returned to Rickarby each summer like swallows.

When Joe entered McGill Institute High School for boys in the fall of 1957, Anne transferred Jimmy and Kathy to a public school near Rickarby. Following Jim Folsom's re-election in 1954 as Alabama's 47th governor, Gunny devoted most of his attention to work at the State Dock grain elevator and cold storage facility. Even so, Gunny kept an eye on how and what the kids did in school, providing encouragement as challenges arose. A glimpse of Gunny's unusual wit emerged over the guise Jimmy should assume for the school's Halloween costume festival. Gunny suggested appearing as the mysterious "Hindu Lu." Anne lent her seamstress skills to the madness of masquerading her son as a well-endowed woman of uncertain ancestry bedecked in a long sleeve floor length gingham dress, replete with painted face, derriere, bandana, gloves, lipstick and earrings. Gunny attached Hindu Lu's name to her generous bosom, dispensing with the need of awkward introductions. When Hindu Lu entered the school hall, teachers regarded her presence with amusement and her silence with curiosity. The ruse survived until teachers eventually gathered contestants by gender for judging. Neither Anne nor Gunny had offered Hindu Lu much guidance beyond keeping quiet. Hindu Lu had to fend for herself, instinctively opting to stand with the guys. Without warning, a commanding hand led Hindu Lu across the open floor to a dense pack of about 75 fifth and sixth grade girls. Hindu Lu balked midway, drawing attention from both directions. The unappealing notion of competing against girls as a girl forced Hindu Lu to violate her monastic silence. Looking up into the face of a puzzled teacher, Hindu Lu confided: "I'm no girl!" Unaccustomed as she was to fifth grade cross-dressing, the astonished woman stepped back, mouth agape and eyes wide with amazement. She summoned other teachers. Some covered their mouths, others just laughed aloud. Hindu Lu turned her derriere to the teachers and waddled across the open floor as dozens of conflicted male eyes gave the brazen hussy another look over. The guys did not pay close attention to the girls' costume competition. Hindu Lu sensed a confusing surge of mixed emotions when the grinning judge awarded Hindu Lu top prize as the best dressed guy. Though Anne and Gunny were proud to hear about the lasting impression Hindu Lu left on everyone, her public debut and finale ended that evening .

For reasons unrelated to Hindu Lu, Gunny enrolled Jimmy and his sister for the next three years in a small Catholic parish school on Fulton Road just north of Maryvale. The pastor of St. Monica Church knew Gunny from their younger days together on Galvez Park. Harold A. Sherman did not excel at baseball, football, or politics. His exit from the south side led through the seminary to the priesthood. Father Sherman also was not particularly blessed with a gregarious personality or knack for enkindling inspiration. However, Gunny contented himself with Galvez brethren of all shapes and stripes, asking nothing more. Ever mindful of life's uncertainties, Gunny admired any south side pal who found a steady job. Beyond that though, Gunny enjoyed the satisfying irony of watching his son the altar boy chanting Latin during Mass with Harold Sherman from Galvez Park.

Mobile's WALA-TV began broadcasting when Joseph Anthony attended Alba Elementary in 1953. By 1957 WALA regularly featured on Saturday morning "Your Playground Reporter," sponsored by the City Recreation Department. Superintendent Martha B. Maitre introduced Rickarby Playground to Mobile on February 22, 1958. Anne presented a mostly fifth and sixth grade neighborhood ensemble of some 40 dancers, singers, and actors performing live. Anything at anytime could go awry within earshot of studio microphones and sight of camera lens. Families, teachers, and friends gathered around television sets to watch, barely knowing what to expect. Just to see a relative, neighbor, or class mate on television provided novel excitement. A talented routine would exceed expectations. Once the camera went live, the kids put on their show. One of the program themes reflected Mobile's fascination with the February snowfall that blanketed the port city. The last notable snow fell in March 1954. The rare appearance of Gulf Coast snowmen soon yielded to a grim meltdown. Rickarby chose to commemorate both, decorating a live Frosty the Snowman to his popular theme song and then promptly melting him down on camera. For the kids, it just couldn't get much better than that.

Something of a social ecosystem evolved at Rickarby over the next three years. The junior high age group in particular gathered at the park house throughout the summer, coming and going from day to day. Scratch ping pong ladders, volleyball skirmishes, and Rook challenges floated from week to week. Marbles were out; wall-ball was in. The shaded north brick park house wall saw steady cut-throat play, banking a hard rubber ball off the sidewalk into the wall for distance without it being caught. On any given day Anne would hear some of the regulars enter the park house, including Peachey, Jerry, or John Ed Henley, Donnie Cobb, Donnie Connick, Kenny Franco, Jimmy McAleer, and Scooter McCarron. Anne hooked the older guys on Rook. Card games began to float among partners from one week to the next. When asked to fill in a four-some at the Rook table, Anne played to win. Challengers jockeyed for turns at the Rook table. The oldest, rowdiest bunch on the park got in their licks trying to beat Mrs. G at

Rook. Lunch did not interrupt the ruthless competition. Someone usually went out for hamburgers and drinks. Over cards Anne also managed to keep current with what all happened among the kids at school and families around the neighborhood.

For the most part, the wading pool in the far corner saw little use, and then only by toddlers with their mothers. Signs warned older kids to stay out. In the dog days of August, when even the shade broke out in sweat, the coming school year and a restless mood could turn the park house crowd a bit more obnoxious than normal. Anne often called time out and shooed the rowdies outside, even though the temperature and humidity both hovered somewhere above 90. She would ask Bill to turn the hose on the worst of the lot. From front porches across the street neighbors watched a crowd of all sizes following Bill from the park house to the pool. Once there, the oldest, tallest, and loudest stepped down into the hot dry concrete basin. Few bothered to run home for swim wear, but hopped in with whatever they had on. Girls and younger kids gathered around to witness the spectacle. Bill grinned as he opened the hydrant until water arced across the pool into the waiting mob. Anne knew how to play this crowd. Rickarby's regulars liked what they saw. Mrs. G was not an overwhelmed adult trying to manage the inmates at Rickarby. She was one of them.

Anne's years at Rickarby slipped by quickly. Her neighborhood kids grew up, got drafted, or went off to college. Come May 1965, Joseph Anthony graduated from Spring Hill College with an Army reserve officer commission and prepared to leave Mobile for law school at the University of Alabama in Tuscaloosa. At the same time, Dottie, Butch and Jimmy graduated high school from McGill Institute and Bishop Toolen High School for girls, another milestone in the family album. They celebrated in procession at the new Municipal Auditorium just north of St. Vincent Church in the old south part of town. A few years back, Mobile leveled Ursulene's Hamilton Street home near Galvez Park, sending her off to Birdville. Nannie could not celebrate with her grandchildren, though. On February 25, 1965, death came for Ursulene Joullian Gonzales. She joined Lena Joullian and Miss Nettie in the Joullian plot at Magnolia Cemetery.

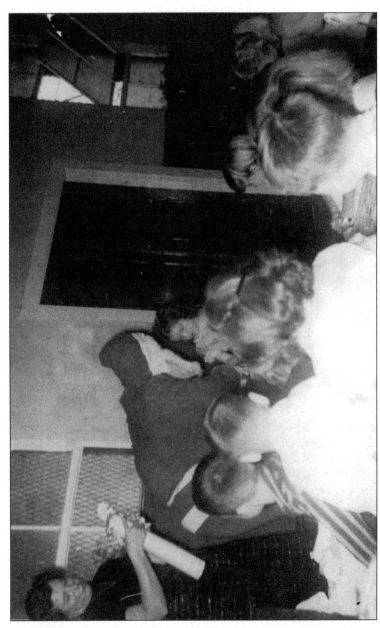

65. *Anne Gonzales and Santa Claus (Gunny Gonzales) with Rickarby Playground preschool class, December 1957 (photographer unknown).*

66. *"Your Playground Reporter" WALA-TV, Mobile City Recreation Department Superintendent Martha B. Maire (center), Frosty the Snowman (Jim Gonzales), Rickarby Playground Director Anne B. Gonzales (right), on the air February 22, 1958 (photographer unknown).*

67. Rickarby Playground Director Anne Gonzales, Recreation Department Spring Festival, April 1961 (photographer unknown).

Anne preferred that both her boys remain close to home after graduation. The conflict in Vietnam began to show signs of insidious escalation. She felt a mother's relief that Joe would be in Tuscaloosa the next three years, and that Jim would attend Spring Hill College in Mobile. Anne bore the news with visibly mixed emotions when Congressman Kenneth Roberts nominated Jim for an appointment to the U.S. Air Force Academy in Colorado. Though she left home at an early age, Anne did not adjust as well as did Gunny about the boys leaving Mobile, especially at the same time. Davenport Lane was just across the highway from Little River Road. Colorado was somewhere across the Mississippi. Gunny decided to observe the moment somewhat as he had years ago by heading for New Orleans, this time with Jim at the wheel, for an evening in the French Quarter, some Dixieland jazz, and a round of hot beignets. No one in the family had yet set foot on an airplane when Gunny and Anne stood on the airport's tarmac in June 1965 to watch Jim climb the steps into a propeller driven Super Constellation.

The day arrived when Anne decided to leave Rickarby and try something different, this time closer to home at Newhouse Park on Rosedale Road. Anne took up ceramics, creating art work and kitchen ware, and crocheted intricate multi-colored afghan spreads. She often combined pastimes, listening at night to her police scanner while weaving afghans. Some of her work went to fundraisers at Our Lady of Lourdes Church, but most went to the children. Anne did not so much retire from what she liked doing as trade her day job for the freedom to do everything else. When not tending flowers, designing afghans, and producing ceramics, Anne traveled the country's highways. She made a point to visit the Air Force Academy in September 1965 for parents' weekend to see her cadet.

Mobile's mayor also paid a visit to the Academy that first year. Joe Langan arranged to have freshman Cadet Gonzales join him on the staff

406 GUNNY Memoirs of Mobile's South Side

tower in Mitchell Hall for lunch and later at the Officer's Club to trade war stories. Joe Langan enjoyed talking about political and military campaigns with his godson. Three years later, Mayor Langan lent a helping hand for senior Cadet Gonzales' political science study of Mobile's government. That same year Joe Langan left City Hall for good.

In June 1969, Anne and Gunny drove across the country to attend graduation ceremonies at the Academy. They dined with all the graduates in Mitchell Hall, and strolled the evening terrazzo with Jim and Julie. They heard President Richard M. Nixon address the Class of 1969. They watched 600 white caps soar above the stadium into a clear blue Colorado sky. They were startled by a well-timed flyby that seemed surprisingly low, but nothing similar to the one in 1968 that pushed Mach 1 and blew the windows off the southern face of Mitchell and Vandenberg Halls. In an unexpected twist of fate, they witnessed Army Captain Joseph A. Gonzales swear in Air Force 2nd Lieutenant James J. Gonzales. This happened to be the only occasion that Anne and Gunny saw Joe and Jim together in uniform as active duty officers. A newly admitted member of the Alabama State Bar, Joe was studying Vietnamese at Fort Bliss in El Paso Texas before rotating into the war zone. Anne avoided talk of tomorrow's uncertainties. She still found it troubling that Jim had parachuted out of perfectly fine airplanes into Alabama swampland during Airborne training at Fort Benning, and then flew off last summer to someplace in Thailand near the Mekong River.

Over the years Anne sent postcards from Canada, Mexico, California, New England, and stops in between. Occasionally, Anne persuaded Gunny to travel with her to visit the grandchildren, driving while Anne navigated directions from one state to another. How they found their way around Washington D.C., Nashville, Dayton, Atlanta, Denver, and elsewhere still remains somewhat a mystery as Anne could not read road maps. They toured the backroads and parts unknown between unfinished interstate highway segments. Nothing short of a miracle explains their unexpected arrival for the first time in Alexandria, Virginia 30 years ago, rapping on the patio door one night

68. *Gunny, Anne and Cadet James J. Gonzales, USAF Academy, June 1, 1969 (Copyright © 2007 Julia Chase Gonzales).*

in a complex of several hundred apartments. Trying the wrong door could have prompted gunplay.

Anne attributed seemingly uncanny or clairvoyant moments to a sixth sense. Before the dawn of cheap long distant telephone service and cell phones, Anne sometimes called unexpectedly under peculiar circumstances for no purpose other than to ask what just happened. She seldom spoke openly about this gift, other than to say she chose not to exploit it. That may be, except when working casino slot machines in Biloxi with her church group. Gunny did not openly question Anne's sixth sense, but pointed impishly at her bottle of Mogen David in the icebox.

Grandmothering filled whatever gaps retirement created. Anne transitioned easily from playground director to grandchild director, as Mama G simply took over where Mrs. G left off. She traveled to the grandchildren's births, baptisms, and graduations. She vacationed with them at the Smithsonian, Yellowstone, Grand Canyon, Niagara Falls, Mesa Verde, and Maroon Bells. Despite advancing age, she took them climbing into cliff dwellings and kivas, trout fishing in the Roaring Fork and Maroon Lake, wading through sand dune drifts, haggling with pueblo Indians over jewelry and pottery, dodging Aspen's mall water spouts, wandering close to the edge of canyons and waterfalls, and waiting on cold curbs at night for Mardi Gras parades. Mama G gathered her little ones in bed for books, scary "Green fits," and tall tales from the bayou. She introduced them to lizards, toads and other critters in her flower garden. They played unruly marathon rounds of dominoes and rummy, grandmother and grandchildren alike claiming victory and challenging shady plays. At her hand they learned to abide by and bend rules with equal skill. Each grandchild renewed Anne's yearning to be with those who needed her most.

The grandchildren journeyed to Mobile from afar to honor their Mama G. Tony and Michael helped shoulder her casket to the altar in

Our Lady of Lourdes church. Anne and Gunny remarried many years ago in the Church and renewed vows on the occasion of their 50th anniversary at this same altar. Misty and Kimberly read to their Mama G from *Ruth* and *Revelation*. Katy and Brian rendered musical reflections of the grandchildren's sentiments. Misty collected the cousins' thoughts and anecdotes to eulogize her Mama G through a grandchild's eye.

We then journeyed quietly to Pinecrest Cemetery. Nearby traces of Gunny's unmarked grave signaled the passing generation that once guided the family. The Church prayed over Anne and commended her soul to eternal rest. Smiling grandchildren posed at graveside around the casket, commemorating their farewell. They honored their Mama G and Papa G, now residing among Mobile's ancestors, and did themselves honor in turn. We left Anne in peace next to Gunny in the shade of tall pines where they once picnicked on the Fourth of July.

May the road rise up to meet you,

may the wind be always at your back,

may the sun shine warm upon your face,

may the rain fall soft upon your fields and,

until we meet again,

may God hold you in the hollow of His hand.

—Old Irish Verse

69. Charles Joullian & great grandniece Kimberly Gonzales, 24 Westwood, Mobile, June 1974 (Copyright © 2007 James J. Gonzales).

70. *Charles & Myrtle Joullian with great grandniece Kimberly Gonzales, 24 Westwood, Mobile, July 1979 (Copyright © 2007 James J. Gonzales).*

71. Sadie Powell Bosarge with Joseph Anthony Gonzales & William Eugene (Pescheur) Bosarge with son Robert Andrew Bosarge, Little River Road, Bayou la Batre, 1944 (Anne Bosarge Gonzales).

72. Grandchildren (l-r) Kimberly Gonzales, Katherine Gonzales Kristoffersen, Tony Gonzales, Misty Gonzales Wilson, Kerri Gonzales, Michael Gonzales, Mike Kristoffersen, Brian Gonzales, and Dennis Wilson with great granddaughter Ashton, April 22, 2006 (Copyright © 2007 James J. Gonzales).

Photographs, Maps & Illustrations

Part One

1. Emanuel Joseph (Gunny) Gonzales, Mobile, 1919 (Brown's Studio).

Chapter 1

2. Joseph Gonzalez family: (1st, l-r) Juanita, Josie, Alphonse, Lucinda Varedo Gonzalez, Pauline, Joseph Gonzalez (Gunny's Grandfather); (2nd, l-r) Frances, Emanuel Joseph (Gunny's father), Amelia, January 3, 1915 (photographer unknown).

3. Sebastian Gonzalez family: (1st, l-r) Manuel Joseph (Nelo), Arthur Sebastian, Leopoldina Perez (Mama Grande & Tia Leo), Marguerita (Peggy), Sebastian Gonzalez; (2nd, l-r) Victor A., Marietta (Cushie), Emilie (Mil), c. 1921 (photographer unknown).

4. Great Fire, Mobile's south side, May 22, 1919 (Courtesy, Erik Overbey Collection, University of South Alabama Archives).

5. Great Fire, Mobile's south side, May 22, 1919 (Courtesy, Erik Overbey Collection, University of South Alabama Archives).

6. Great Fire, Mobile's south side, May 22, 1919 (Courtesy, Erik Overbey Collection, University of South Alabama Archives).

7. Great Fire, Mobile's south side, May 22, 1919 (Courtesy, Erik Overbey Collection, University of South Alabama Archives).

8. Mobile's south side in 1891 from Charleston north to Eslava and from Cedar east to St. Emanuel, showing St. Vincent Church and school, Cunningham's grocery at Madison and Hamilton, Gunny's birthplace on Madison east of the Franklin street trolley, and Grandpa Joe's house on east side of St Emanuel south of Canal, but omitting Our Alley Colored dwellings from Palmetto south to Texas between Conception and Franklin (C. J. Pauli Company, Courtesy, University of South Alabama Archives).

9. Mobile's town center in 1891 showing (l-r) the Cathedral, Bienville Square, and Battle House Hotel (C. J. Pauli Company, Courtesy, University of South Alabama Archives).

10. Gonzales Family, 1924.

Chapter 2

11. Ursulene, Clarice, and Charles H. Joullian, 300 Elmira, Mobile, 1909 (photographer unknown).

12. Clarice and Charles H. Joullian, 300 Elmira, Mobile, 1910 (photographer unknown).

13. Emanuel Joseph (Gunny) Gonzales, Jr., 210 Charleston, Mobile, 1917 (photographer unknown).
14. Gunny Gonzales, First Communion, Mobile, May 7, 1922 (photographer unknown).
15. St. Vincent Church, Lawrence St., Mobile, 1994 (Copyright © 2007 James J. Gonzales).
16. Leona Pond and Charles H. Joullian, 210 Charleston, Mobile, c. 1919 (photographer unknown).
17. Joullian Family, 1924.

CHAPTER 4

18. Gunny Gonzales, Ernest James, Jr., & Mrs. Waldstrom's calf, 408 Charleston, Mobile, 1925 (photographer unknown).
19. St. Vincent School, Charleston Street, Mobile, 1994 (Copyright © 2007 James J. Gonzales).
20. Ursulene Joullian Gonzales, 1928 (photographer unknown).

PART TWO

21. Gunny Gonzales, Leona Pond Joullian (Irish Ma), Nettie Pocase (Aunt Nettie) & Ernest James, Jr., 408 Charleston, Mobile, 1928 (photographer unknown).

CHAPTER 9

22. George Herman (Babe) Ruth, with William H. Armbrecht, Jr., John Paul Wilson, Jr., William Ross Little, Con Roberts Little, Jr., Erwin E. Little, Wilkerson V. Jones, James W. Little, and unidentified youngsters, exhibition game, Mobile (Courtesy, Erik Overbey Collection, University of South Alabama Archives), c. 1923.
23. Mobile south side showing Galvez Park and Our Alley (Sanborn Map Company 1956).
24. Galvez Park sandbox, water fountain, swings, and ball diamond, and Gunny's addresses at 205 Madison, 308 S. Franklin, 210 Charleston, 408 Charleston, and 407 S. Franklin from 1913 to 1939 (Copyright © 2007 James J. Gonzales).
25. Galvez Park, looking southeast across baseball field toward Canal and Claiborne, Mobile, c. 1935 (photographer unknown).
26. Galvez Park, looking northeast toward John Rigas' store at Madison and Claiborne, Mobile, c. 1935 (photographer unknown).

CHAPTER 10

27. Alabama State Champion Whippet Athletic Club: (top, l-r) manager Van Matthews, Leo Reinhart, Johnnie Geary, Earl Holcomb, unidentified, Johnnie Smith, coach Maurice Drain; (middle, l-r) Al Gonzales, Lamar Doyle, Roy Knapp, John (Rip) A. Repoll, Henry Richardson; (bottom, l-r) Jack Stokes, Gunny Gonzales, Hallett McDonough, Charlie Wilcox (Courtesy, Mobile Press Register, Sunday, July 27, 1930).

28. American Legion Alabama State Champion Certificate, awarded to Emanuel Gonzales by Baseball Commissioner Kennesaw Mountain Landis, September 1, 1930.

CHAPTER 13

29. Spring Hill Prep High School Football Badgers: (top, l-r) asst. coach John Gafford, Henry Stephen (Bubba) Norden (20), unidentified (10), unidentified (15), Hardy Demeranville (5), unidentified (8), Richard Jones (12), Fred Revere (6), Jimmie Miller (21), coach Ellis Ollinger; (middle, l-r) unidentified (17), Emanuel Joseph (Gunny) Gonzales (1), unidentified (2), John Mills Capps, Jr. (22), Martin Aloysius (Cooty) Norden (11), Charlie Perez (9), unidentified; (bottom, l-r) James C. (Jimmy) McDonald (19), Michael (Mike) Donahue, Jr. (16), Maurice Ignatius (Moe) Roy (18), Robert C. (Bobby) Leftwich (13), William (Bill) Camp (14), Spring Hill College, Mobile (Erik Overbey, Mobile), 1932.

30. Spring Hill Prep High School Football Badgers (right end Gunny Gonzales at far left), practice scrimmage south lawn, High School Administration Building, Spring Hill College, Mobile (Erik Overbey, Mobile), 1932.

31. Spring Hill Prep High School Varsity Football and Baseball letter, awarded to Gunny Gonzales, 1932-1933.

CHAPTER 16

32. Kane Boiler Works baseball team, 1935 Commercial League Champions, Galveston Texas: (top, l-r) unidentified, Ken Glowaskie, Earl Colvin, unidentified, owner-manager Robert Kane; (middle, l-r) Shorty Davis, unidentified; (bottom, l-r) Frank Kilgore, Gunny Gonzales, Don Maynard, unidentified, Shorty Williams, Don Maynard's son (bat boy), Galveston, Texas (Verkin, Galveston), 1935.

33. Dow Motors Chevrolet, Gunny Gonzales (1st row), Houston, November 30, 1936 (photographer unknown).

PART THREE

34. Emanuel Joseph (Gunny) Gonzales, 1939 (photographer unknown).

CHAPTER 20

35. Myrtle Hassett and Marion Hassett, in their fenced backyard next to Colored dwellings along Our Alley between Conception and Franklin streets, 610 Conception Street, Mobile, c. 1919 (photographer unknown).
36. Leona Pond Joullian (Irish Ma), Our Alley, and Nettie G. Pocase's charcoal grill in the backyard at 407 S. Franklin, Mobile, 1938 (photographer unknown).

CHAPTER 23

37. Emanuel Joseph Gonzales Board of Registrars Appointment Letter, October 24, 1947.
38. State of Alabama Commission of E. J. Gonzales by Governor James E. Folsom as Member of the Board of Registrars of Mobile County, September 10, 1948.
39. Probate Judge Norville R. Leigh, Jr., Milton Schnell, Mrs. D. C. Randle and E. J. (Gunny) Gonzales, Mobile County Board of Registrars oath of office, October 29, 1947 (Courtesy, Mobile Press, October 30, 1947).

CHAPTER 29

40. Mobile County Board of Registrars registration session, 109 St. Emanuel street, Mobile (Courtesy, Mobile Press staff photo) c. 1949.
41. Mobile County Board of Registrars registration session, 109 St. Emanuel street, Mobile (Courtesy, Mobile Press staff photo) c. 1949.
42. Mobile County Board of Registrars registration session, 109 St. Emanuel street, Mobile (Courtesy, Mobile Press staff photo) c. 1949.
43. Campaign photograph, E. J. (Gunny) Gonzales, Mobile County Road & Revenue Commission Democratic primary, 1950.

CHAPTER 30

44. William Green administering to E. J. (Gunny) Gonzales oath of office as Chairman, Mobile County Democratic Executive Committee, January 27, 1981 (Courtesy, Mobile Register, photographer Roy McAuley, January 28, 1981).

PART FOUR

45. Gunny Gonzales, granddaughter Kimberly Gonzales and J. B. (Red) Foster (Chief Slacabamorinico), Joe Cain People's Parade, Mardi Gras, Mobile, Sunday, February 21, 1982 (Copyright © 2007 James J. Gonzales).

CHAPTER 32

46. Galvez Park baseball diamond home plate site, Canal Street at I-10, Mobile, 1994 (Copyright © 2007 James J. Gonzales).

CHAPTER 33

47. Gunny and Anne Gonzales, Mystic Stripers Ball, Mardi Gras, Mobile, February, 1988 (photographer unknown).
48. Gunny Gonzales, Nonie Gonzales Schuler, and Joseph V. Gonzales, Bay Front Road, Mobile, November 26, 1988 (Copyright © 2007 James J. Gonzales).
49. Gunny Gonzales, south lawn, Administration Building, Spring Hill College, Mobile, October 16, 2005 (Copyright © 2007 James J. Gonzales).

CHAPTER 34

50. Anne Bosarge, Alba High School Graduation, May 29, 1940 (photographer unknown).
51. Anne Bosarge, City Hospital Nursing School, Mobile, September, 1940 (photographer unknown).
52. City Hospital, Mobile, February 11, 1994 (Copyright © 2007 James J. Gonzales).
53. Green Verneuille, Anne Bosarge, and Margaret Gertrude Bosarge Verneuille, Davenport Lane, Bayou la Batre, 1941 (photographer unknown).
54. Anne B. Gonzales, 1946 (photographer unknown).
55. Joe, Jim & Anne Gonzales, 1508 Bobolink Drive, Birdville, Mobile, May, 1948 (E. J. Gunny Gonzales).
56. Charles Joullian & Nettie Pocase, Easter Sunday, 24 Westwood Avenue, Mobile, 1949 (photographer unknown).
57. Joe Gonzales, Nettie Pocase, and Jim Gonzales, Easter Sunday, 1508 Bobolink Drive, Birdville, Mobile, April 9, 1950 (Anne Gonzales).
58. Jim Gonzales, Billy Barnette, Joe Gonzales, Gary Bean, Kathy Gonzales, and Chad, Linda & Jimmy Jordan (l-r), 1520 Albatross Drive, Birdville, Mobile, 1951 (Anne Gonzales).
59. Birthday Party, 1520 Albatross Drive, Gunny and Jim (center), May 29, 1951 (Anne Gonzales).
60. Birthday Party, 1520 Albatross Drive, Joe and Jim (left of center), May 29, 1951 (Anne Gonzales).
61. Anne, Jim & Kathy Gonzales, 1520 Albatross Drive, Birdville, Mobile, Easter Sunday, April 13, 1952 (Joseph A. Gonzales).
62. Thomas James Recreation Center Spring Festival, bluebird Jim Gonzales, 1520 Albatross Drive, Mobile, April 14, 1952 (Anne Gonzales).

63. Jim, Joe & Kathy Gonzales, Mississippi Sound at Bayou Coden, Mobile, June 1953 (Anne Gonzales).

64. Jim Gonzales, cousin Dottie Stewart, and cousin Joseph (Butch) Gonzales, First Communion, St. Vincent Church, Mobile, Mother's Day, May 9, 1954 (Anne Gonzales).

65. Anne Gonzales and Santa Claus (Gunny Gonzales) with Rickarby Playground preschool class, December 1957 (photographer unknown).

66. "Your Playground Reporter" WALA-TV, Mobile City Recreation Department Superintendent Martha B. Maitre (center), Frosty the Snowman (Jim Gonzales), Rickarby Playground Director Anne B. Gonzales (right), on the air February 22, 1958 (photographer unknown).

67. Rickarby Playground Director Anne Gonzales, Recreation Department Spring Festival, April 1961 (photographer unknown).

68. Gunny, Anne and Cadet James J. Gonzales, USAF Academy, June 1, 1969 (Copyright © 2007 Julia Chase Gonzales).

69. Charles Joullian & great grandniece Kimberly Gonzales, 24 Westwood, Mobile, June, 1974 (Copyright © 2007 Gonzales James J. Gonzales).

70. Charles H. & Myrtle Hassett Joullian with great grandniece Kimberly Gonzales, 24 Westwood, Mobile, July 1979 (Copyright © 2007 James J. Gonzales).

71. Sadie Powell Bosarge with Joseph Anthony Gonzales & William Eugene (Pescheur) Bosarge with son Robert Andrew Bosarge, Little River Road, Bayou la Batre, 1944 (Anne Bosarge Gonzales).

72. Grandchildren (l-r) Kimberly Gonzales, Katherine Gonzales Kristoffersen, Tony Gonzales, Misty Gonzales Wilson, Kerri Gonzales, Michael Gonzales, Mike Kristoffersen, Brian Gonzales, and Dennis Wilson with great granddaughter Ashton, Mobile, April 22, 2006 (Copyright © 2007 James J. Gonzales).

GONZALES

CARLOS GONZALEZ (Galicia, Spain)
——*married* Luisa Fernandez (Spain)
|
    MANUEL GONZALEZ [b. 3-1838 (Galicia, Spain); d. 7-21-1907 (Mobile)]
      ——*married* Maria Moll de Gonzalez
      [b. 1836 (Menorca, Spain); d. 11-5-1897 (Mobile)]
      |
      Johanna Gonzalez [b. 3-10-1873 (Spain); d. 5-26-1941 (Mobile)]

      Louisa Gonzalez (*married* Antonio Ballardares)
      [b. 12-1-1869 (Spain); d. 6-27-1942 (Mobile)]

      Sebastian Gonzalez (Uncle Sebastian)
      [b. 12-1-1869 (Spain); d. 10-14-1926 (Mobile)]
      ——*married* Leopoldina Perez (Mama Grande, Tia Leo)
      [b. 10-24-1870 (Campeche, Mexico); d. 4-29-1958 (Mobile)]
        |
        Manuel Joseph (Nelo) Gonzales
        [b. 3-3-1893 (Mobile); d. 9-18-1946]

        Marietta (Cushie) Gonzales (Turrentine)
        [b. 7-16-1895 (Mobile); d. 5-20-1956]

        Emilie (Mil) Gonzales (Dekle)
        [b. 3-21-1900 (Mobile); d. 8-30-1982]

        Victor Armand Gonzales (Ella Wheyland)
        [b. 7-1-1904 (Mobile); d. 9-21-1985]

        Arthur Sebastian Gonzales
        [b. 11-24-1912 (Mobile); d. 3-20-1993]

        Margarita (Peggy) Gonzales (John Walsh)
        [b. 5-1-1916 (Mobile); d. 10-21-1981]

JOSEPH GONZALEZ (Grandpa Joe)
[b. 5-25-1851 (Galicia, Spain); d. 5-27-1927 (Mobile)]
——*married* Lucinda Varedo [b. 9-16-1869 (Point Clear); d. 12-4-1947 (Mobile)]
|
    Joseph Gonzales, Jr. [b. 11-23-1902; d. 12-24-1904]

    Juanita Gonzales (*married* Joe Cazalas)

Frances Gonzales (*married* John Donnelly)

Josie Gonzales (*married* Norris Farnell)

Pauline Gonzales (*married* Leroy Brannon) [b. 8-16-1909; d. 11-15-1987]

Amelia Gonzales (*married* George A. Davis)[b.1894; d.12-24-1942]

Alphonse C. Gonzales (Uncle Al) [b. 11-21-1914; d. 4-11-2001]

EMANUEL JOSEPH GONZALES, SR. (Manuel)
[b. 6-6-1892; d. 9-29-1933]
——*married* Ursulene Pond Joullian [b. 12-11-1898; d. 2-25-1965]
|
    Luthia (Dit) Gonzales [b. 7-17-1917; d. 12-17-1973]

    Joseph V. Gonzales [b. 10-12-1920; d. 1-20-2003]

    Leona Gertrude (Nonie) Gonzales [b. 3-25-1924]

    EMANUEL JOSEPH GONZALES, JR. (Gunny)
    [b. 11-26-1913; d. 3-3-2006]
    ——*married* ANNE MARIE BOSARGE (Mama G)
    [b. 5-5-1920 (Bayou la Batre); d. 4-18-2006 (Mobile)]
        |
        Joseph Anthony Gonzales
        —*married* Mary E. (Betty) Hampton
        |
        Elizabeth (Misty) Gonzales
        Joseph A. (Tony) Gonzales, Jr.
        Kerri Gonzales

        John Michael Gonzales

        James Joullian Gonzales
        —*married* Julia Chase
        |
        Kimberly J. Gonzales
        Brian J. Gonzales
        Katherine T. Gonzales
        Michael J. Gonzales

        Margaret Kathleen Gonzales
        —*married* Douglas Collins
        |
        Kelly Collins
        Danielle M. Collins

JOULLIAN

Jacques (Jacob) Joulin [b. 1768 (France); d. 11-26-1844 (Mobile)]

> Francis Charles Joullian [b. 1800 (France); d. 1837 (Macon, Georgia)]
> ——married Sophia Beulah(Beulat)
> [b. 5-1-1801 (Berne, Switz.); d. 1-7-1891 (Mobile)]

>> Charles Alexander Joullian [b. 1823 (N.Y.); d. 1895]
>> ——married Mary J. Pierce Jordan [b. 1833 (Ireland)]

>>> Charles Edward Joullian [(b. 1867]
>>> ——married Leona Gertrude Pond (Irish Ma)
>>> [b. 7-15-1870; d. 3-27-1940]*

>>> Clarice Joullian [b. 2-27-1906, d. 1-11-1995]
>>> ——married Ernest James

>>> Charles Henry Joullian (Uncle Charlie)
>>> [b. 2-27-1906, d. 7-20-1981]
>>> ——married Myrtle Ellen Hasssett
>>> [b. 8-10-1910; d. 12-16-2003]

>>> URSULENE POND JOULLIAN (Nannie)
>>> [b. 12-11-1898; d. 2-25-1965]
>>> ——married EMANUEL JOSEPH GONZALES

>>>> Luthia (Dit) Gonzales [b. 7-17-1917; d. 12-17-1973]

>>>> Joseph V. Gonzales [b. 10-12-1920; d. 1-20-2003]

>>>> Leona Gertrude (Nonie) Gonzales [b. 3-25-1924]

>>>> EMANUEL JOSEPH GONZALES, JR. (Gunny)
>>>> [b. 11-26-1913; d. 3-3-2006]

*Nettie G. Pocase (Aunt Nettie) [b. 4-12-1870; d. 4-10-1955]

BOSARGE

JEAN-BAPTISTE BAUDREAU DE LA GRAVELINE
[b. (Canada); d. 1757 (Pascagoula, Miss.)]
|
　JEAN BAPTISTE BAUDREAU (Beaudrot or Baudrau)[d. (Mobile)]
　　——*married* Catherine Vinconot (VinSonneau)
　　|
　　CATHERINE LOUISA BAUDREAU (Beaudrot)
　　[b. 1742 (Pascagoula, Miss.); d. (Bayou la Batre)]

JEAN BAPTISTE BOUZAGE (Portiers, France)
　　——*married* Marie Jeanne Touche (Portiers, France)
　　|
　　JOSEPH BOSAUGE [b. 1726 (Portiers, France; d. 1795 (Bayou la Batre)]
　　——*married* Catherine Louisa Beaudrot
　　　|
　　　JOHN JOSEPH BOSARGE [d. 5-11-1837]
　　　——*married* Jacqueline Chest
　　　　|
　　　　Joseph W. Bosarge

　　　　Dennis Bosarge

　　　　Pauline Bosarge

　　　　Francis Bosarge

　　　　Iseallie Bosarge

　　　　EDWARD EUGENE BOSARGE [d. 6-27-1876]
　　　　——*married* Lucinda Goulmin
　　　　|
　　　　Edward Bosarge

　　　　Rodney Bosarge

　　　　Cecilia Bosarge (Rabby)

　　　　HENRY BOSARGE [b. 7-10-1854; d. 1930]
　　　　——*married* FLORENCE AUGUSTA
　　　　GREENE [b. 7-17-1859; d. 12-27-1938]
　　　　|
　　　　Mary Ella Bosarge [b. 3-8-1879]

Ida Rose Bosarge[b. 2-20-1882]

MARGARET GERTRUDE BOSARGE
(Aunt Maggie)[b. 3-27-1884, d. 9-4-1963]

Anna Cecilia Bosarge [b. 1-5-1877]

Joseph Homer Bosarge [b. 2-7-1895]

Henry Maurice Bosarge [b. 3-25-1892]

Arthur Edward Bosarge [b. 12-2-1898]

Maude Augusta Bosarge [b. 9-10-1889]

WILLIAM (PESCHEUR) EUGENE
BOSARGE [b. 7-21-1886; d. 5-18-1969]
——*married* SADIE POWELL [b. 11-17-1900
(Dauphin Island); d. 3-10-1974 (Bayou la Batre)]*
|
Henry Maurice Bosarge

Florence Augusta Bosarge

Maude Agnes Bosarge

Wilhelmena Rose Bosarge

Sadie Mae Bosarge

Mildred Inez Bosarge

William Eugene Bosarge, Jr.

Robert Andrew Bosarge

ANNE MARIE BOSARGE [b. 5-5-1920; d. 4-18-2006]
——*married* EMANUEL JOSEPH
GONZALES, JR. (Gunny)

*JOHN COLLIER [b. England; d. Dauphin Island]
——*married* Elizabeth Gatley
        |
        ALICE COLLIER [b. 9-14-1876 (Dauphin Island); d. 6-15-1959 (Bayou la Batre)]
        ——*married* GEORGE POWELL (Poloylessia)
        [b. 3-25-1864 (Greece); d. 12-5-1913 (Dauphin Island)]

|
George Powell

SADIE POWELL (BOSARGE)

Renie Powell (Bosarge)

Octavia Powell (Kennerson)

Sophia Powell (Sprinkle)

BIBLIOGRAPHY & RESOURCES

INTERVIEWS

William Eugene (Pescheur) Bosarge, 1958-1964, passim.
Sadie Powell Bosarge, 1958-1964, passim.
Charles Caminas, November 27, 1988.
George A. (Tweet) Davis, November 26, 1988.
Jean Gonzales DeKeyser, July 20 & 21, 1995.
Alphonse (Al) C. Gonzales, November 26 & 27, 1988.
Anne Bosarge Gonzales, 1978-1986, passim.
Arthur Sebastian Gonzales, November 27, 1988.
Emanuel J. (Gunny) Gonzales, Jr., 1976-2005, passim.
Joseph V. Gonzales, November 26, 1988.
Leona Gertrude (Nonie) Gonzales, November 26, 1988.
Clarice Joullian James, June 25 & 26, 1994.
Myrtle Hassett Joullian, February 12, 1994, 1979-1994, passim.
Charles H. Joullian, July, 1979.
Joseph N. Langan, February 10, 1994.
Margaret Gertrude Bosarge Verneuille, 1958-1963, passim.

NEWSPAPERS & PERIODICALS

Mobile Daily Register, Tuesday, January 20, 1891.
Mobile Labor Journal, Friday, February 6, 1948, p. 1, 4.
Mobile Labor Journal, Friday, March 26, 1948, p. 1.
Mobile Labor Journal, Friday, August 20, 1948.
Mobile Labor Journal, Friday, September 17, 1948, p. 1.
Mobile Labor Journal, Friday, July 8, 1949, p. 1.
Mobile Labor Journal, Friday, July 15, 1949, p. 1.
Mobile Labor Journal, Friday, July 22, 1949, p. 1.
Mobile Labor Journal, Friday, December 2, 1949, p. 1, 6.
Mobile Labor Journal, Friday, December 9, 1949, p. 1, 5.
Mobile Labor News, Friday, August 20, 1948.
Mobile Labor News, Friday, October 15, 1948, p. 1.
Mobile Labor News, Friday, December 17, 1948, p. 1.

Mobile Labor News, Friday, December 31, 1948.

Mobile Labor News, Friday, January 21, 1949, p. 1.

Mobile Labor News, Friday, April 1, 1949.

Mobile Register, Wednesday, November 26, 1913.

Mobile Register, Thursday, November, 1913, p. 6.

Mobile Register, Thursday, May 22, 1919, p. 1-3.

Mobile Register, Friday, May 23, 1919, p. 1.

Mobile Register, Tuesday, September 21, 1926, p. 1.

Mobile Register, Wednesday, July 9, 1930, Sports p. 1.

Mobile Register, Saturday, July 12, 1930, Sports p. 1.

Mobile Register, Friday, July 18, 1930, Sports p. 1.

Mobile Register, Thursday, July 24, 1930, Sports p. 13.

Mobile Register, Sunday, July 27, 1930, Sports p. 1.

Mobile Press Register, Sunday, September 25, 1932, Sports p. 3.

Mobile Register, Saturday, November 5, 1932, Sports p. 1, 8.

Mobile Press Register, Sunday, November 6, 1932, Sports p. 1-2.

Mobile Press Register, Sunday, November 27, 1932, Sports p. 1.

Mobile Register, Saturday, September 30, 1933, p. 1.

Mobile Register, Saturday, August 24, 1940, p. 4.

Mobile Press, Wednesday, September 4, 1940, p. 1.

Mobile Press, Tuesday, August 27, 1946.

Mobile Press, Saturday, November 9, 1946.

Mobile Press, Wednesday, January 22, 1947, p. 1.

Mobile Register, Thursday, January 23, 1947, p. 1, 4.

Mobile Register, Friday, January 24, 1947, p. 6.

Mobile Press, Monday, February 3, 1947.

Mobile Press Register, Sunday, February 23, 1947, p. 1.

Mobile Press, Friday, April 11, 1947, p. 1, 4.

Mobile Press Register, Sunday, April 13, 1947, p. 1, 7A.

Mobile Press, Tuesday, April 22, 1947, p. 1.

Mobile Press, Saturday, April 26, 1947, p. 1.

Mobile Press, Tuesday, August 27, 1947.

Mobile Press, Friday, August 29, 1947.

Mobile Press Register, Sunday, August 31, 1947.

Mobile Press, Thursday, October 30, 1947, p. 1.

Mobile Press, Wednesday, November 12, 1947, p. 1.

Mobile Press, Friday, November 14, 1947.

Mobile Press Register, Sunday, November 16, 1947, p. 1-2.

Mobile Press, Monday, November 17, 1947, p. 1.

Mobile Press, Friday, November 21, 1947, p. 1.

Mobile Press, Saturday, November 22, 1947, p. 1.

Mobile Press, Monday, November 24, 1947, p. 1, 4.

Mobile Press, Tuesday, November 25, 1947, p. 1.

Mobile Press, Wednesday, November 26, 1947, p. 1.

Mobile Press, Wednesday, December 3, 1947, p. 1.

Mobile Register, Thursday, December 4, 1947.

Mobile Press, Friday, December 5, 1947.

Mobile Press, Friday, January 2, 1948, p. 1.

Mobile Press Register, Sunday, January 4, 1948, p. 1-2.

Mobile Register, Wednesday, January 7, 1948, p. 1.

Mobile Press, Tuesday, January 13, 1948, p. 1, 4.

Mobile Press, Tuesday, January 20, 1948, p. 1.

Mobile Register, Tuesday, January 27, 1948, p. 1, 4.

Mobile Register, Thursday, January 29, 1948, p. 1, 4, 11.

Mobile Press, Friday, January 30, 1948, p. 1.

Mobile Press Register, Sunday, February 1, 1948, p. 22A.

Mobile Press, Monday, February 9, 1948, p. 1-2.

Mobile Press, Thursday, February 12, 1948, p. 1.

Mobile Press, Thursday, March 18, 1948.

Mobile Press, Friday, March 26, 1948, p. 1.

Mobile Press Register, Sunday, April 4, 1948.

Mobile Register, Thursday, April 8, 1948, p. 8.

Mobile Press Register, Sunday, April 11, 1948, p. 1-2.

Mobile Press, Tuesday, April 20, 1948.

Mobile Press Register, Monday, May 17, 1948.

Mobile Press, Wednesday, July 7, 1948.

Mobile Register, Wednesday, July, 7, 1948, p. 1.

Mobile Press, Monday, July 19, 1948.

Mobile Press, Wednesday, August 4, 1948, p. 8.

Mobile Register, Monday, August 16, 1948, p. 1-2.

Mobile Register, Tuesday, August 17, 1948, p. 7.

Mobile Register, Friday, September 3, 1948.

Mobile Press, Wednesday, September 8, 1948.

Mobile Register, Wednesday, September 8, 1948.

Mobile Press, Thursday, September 9, 1948.

Mobile Press, Friday, September 10, 1948.

Mobile Press, Saturday, September 11, 1948.

Mobile Press, Wednesday, September 15, 1948.

Mobile Press, Tuesday, September 21, 1948.

Mobile Press, Wednesday, September 22, 1948.

Mobile Press Register, Sunday, October 3, 1948, p. 1.

Mobile Press, Monday, October 4, 1948, p. 1, 8.

Mobile Press, Tuesday, October 5, 1948, p. 1-2, 4.

Mobile Press, Wednesday, October 6, 1948, p. 1, 4.

Mobile Press, Thursday, October 7, 1948, p. 1.

Mobile Press, Friday, October 8, 1948.

Mobile Press Register, Sunday, October 17, 1948, p. 1.

Mobile Register, Saturday, October 23, 1948.

Mobile Press Register, Sunday, October 24, 1948, p. 16A.

Mobile Register, Saturday, November 6, 1948, p. 2.

Mobile Press, Thursday, November 18, 1948, p. 1.

Mobile Register, Tuesday, November 30, 1948, p. 11.

Mobile Press, Tuesday, December 7, 1948, p. 1.

Mobile Register, Wednesday, December 8, 1948, p. 8.

Mobile Register, Friday, December 10, 1948.

Mobile Press, Friday, December 17, 1948, p. 1.

Mobile Register, Tuesday, December 21, 1948, p. 1.

Mobile Register, Wednesday, December 22, 1948, p. 11B.

Mobile Register, Thursday, December 30, 1948, p. 5.

Mobile Press, Friday, January 7, 1949, p. 1, 4.

Mobile Register, Saturday, January 8, 1949, p. 1-2.

Mobile Register, Monday, January 10, 1949, p. 1.

Mobile Press, Wednesday, January 12, 1949, p. 1.

Mobile Press, Thursday, January 13, 1949, p. 1.

Mobile Press, Friday, January 14, 1949, p. 1.

Mobile Press, Saturday, January 15, 1949, p. 1.

Mobile Press, Monday, January 17, 1949, p. 1.

Mobile Press, Saturday, January 22, 1949, p. 1.

Mobile Register, Saturday, January 22, 1949.

Mobile Press Register, Sunday, January 23, 1949.

Mobile Register, Wednesday, January 26, 1949.

Mobile Press, Saturday, January 29, 1949, p. 1-2.

Mobile Press Register, Sunday, January 30, 1949.

Mobile Register, Wednesday, February 2, 1949, p. 1-2.

Mobile Press, Friday, February 4, 1949, p. 1.

Mobile Register, Saturday, February 5, 1949, p. 3.

Mobile Press Register, Sunday, February 6, 1949, p. 6A.

Mobile Press, Thursday, February 10, 1949, p. 1, 4.

Mobile Register, Tuesday, March 1, 1949.

Mobile Press, Wednesday, March 9, 1949, p. 1, 4.

Mobile Register, Saturday, March 19, 1949.

Mobile Press, Friday, March 25, 1949, p. 1.

Mobile Register, Saturday, March 26, 1949, p. 8B.

Mobile Press, Monday, March 28, 1949, p. 1.

Mobile Press, Tuesday, March 29, 1949.

Mobile Register, Tuesday, March 29, 1949, p. 1.

Mobile Press, Friday, April 1, 1949, p. 1, 4.

Mobile Press Register, Sunday, April 3, 1949.

Mobile Press, Monday, April 4, 1949, p. 1, 4.

Mobile Press, Tuesday, April 5, 1949, p. 1.

Mobile Press, Saturday, April 9, 1949.

Mobile Press, Thursday, April 14, 1949, p. 1, 4.

Mobile Press Register, Sunday, April 17, 1949.

Mobile Register, Tuesday, April 19, 1949.

Mobile Press, Tuesday, May 3, 1949, p. 2.

Mobile Register, Wednesday, May 11, 1949, p. 4.

Mobile Press, Thursday, May 12, 1949, p. 1, 4.

Mobile Register, Thursday, May 12, 1949, p. 1.

Mobile Press Register, Sunday, May 15, 1949.

Mobile Press, Monday, May 16, 1949, p. 2.

Mobile Press, Wednesday, May 18, 1949, p. 1, 4.

Mobile Register, Thursday, May 19, 1949, p. 2.

Mobile Press, Saturday, May 21, 1949.

Mobile Press, Monday, May 23, 1949, p. 1.

Mobile Register, Friday, May 27, 1949, p. 1, 10.

Mobile Press Register, Sunday, May 29, 1949.

Mobile Register, Saturday, June 4, 1949, p. 1.

Mobile Press Register, Sunday, June 5, 1949, p. 1.

Mobile Press, Wednesday, June 15, 1949, p. 1.

Mobile Press, Friday, June 17, 1949.

Mobile Press, Monday, June 20, 1949.

Mobile Press, Tuesday, June 21, 1949, p. 1, 4.

Mobile Press, Thursday, July 7, 1949, p. 1.

Mobile Register, Saturday, July 9, 1949, p. 1-2.

Mobile Press, Monday, July 11, 1949.

Mobile Press, Thursday, July 14, 1949, p. 1, 4.

Mobile Press, Friday, July 15, 1949.

Mobile Press, Saturday, July 16, 1949, p. 1-2.

Mobile Press, Monday, July 25, 1949.

Mobile Press, Wednesday, August 10, 1949.

Mobile Press, Thursday, August 11, 1949.

Mobile Press Register, Sunday, August 14, 1949, p. 8A.

Mobile Press, Monday, August 15, 1949, p. 1, 4.

Mobile Register, Tuesday, August 16, 1949, p. 1.

Mobile Register, Saturday, August 20, 1949.

Mobile Register, Monday, August 22, 1949.

Mobile Press Register, Tuesday, August 23, 1949, p. 1, 4.

Mobile Register, Saturday, August 27, 1949.

Mobile Press, Monday, August 29, 1949.

Mobile Press, Tuesday, September 6, 1949, p. 1.

Mobile Press, Friday, September 9, 1949.

Mobile Register, Saturday, September 10, 1949, p. 1.

Mobile Press Register, Sunday, September 11, 1949, p. 6A.

Mobile Press, Tuesday, September 13, 1949, p. 1.

Mobile Press, Friday, September 16, 1949, p. 1.

Mobile Press Register, Sunday, September 18, 1949.

Mobile Register, Tuesday, September 20, 1949, p. 1.

Mobile Press, Friday, September 23, 1949, p. 1, 4.

Mobile Press, Friday, September 30, 1949.

Mobile Press, Wednesday, October 5, 1949, p. 1.

Mobile Register, Friday, October 7, 1949, p. 1.

Mobile Press, Monday, November 21, 1949.

Mobile Press, Tuesday, December 20, 1949, p. 1, 4.

Mobile Press, Tuesday, January 10, 1950, p. 1, 4.

Mobile Register, Tuesday, January 10, 1950, p. 1.

Mobile Register, Friday, January 13, 1950, p. 1.

Mobile Press, Wednesday, January 25, 1950.

Mobile Register, Friday, February 3, 1950, p. 1.

Mobile Press Register, Sunday, April 2, 1950, p. 1, 18A.

Mobile Press Register, Sunday, April 16, 1950, p. 1, 12A.

Mobile Press Register, Sunday, April 30, 1950, p. 30A.

Mobile Register, Tuesday, May 2, 1950, p. 1, 4.

Mobile Register, Wednesday, May 3, 1950, p. 1, 4.

Mobile Register, Thursday, May 4, 1950.

Mobile Register, Friday, May 5, 1950, p. 1.

Mobile Register, Friday, May 26, 1950, p. 1.

Mobile Press Register, Sunday, May 28, 1950, p. 1, 13A, 18A.

Mobile Press, Thursday, March 22, 1951, p. 1.

Mobile Press Register, Sunday, April 1, 1951, p. 1.

Mobile Press, Wednesday, October 10, 1951, p. 1, 4.

Mobile Press Register, Sunday, September 6, 1953, p. 10A.

Mobile Register, Wednesday, September 9, 1953, p. 1, 4A.

Mobile Register, Saturday, September 12, 1953, p. 5A.

Mobile Press Register, Sunday, September 13, 1953, p. 1, 23A.

Mobile Register, Monday, September 14, 1953, p. 1.

Mobile Press Register, Sunday, May 2, 1954, p. 7A.

Mobile Register, Monday, May 3, 1954, p. 6A.

Mobile Register, Wednesday, May 6, 1954, p. 3A.

Mobile Register, Tuesday, May 13, 1958, p. 1.

Mobile Press Register, Sunday, June 1, 1958, p. 6A, 17A.

Mobile Register, Monday, June 2, 1958, p. 1, 10.

Mobile Register, Wednesday, June 1, 1960, p. 1.

Mobile Register, Thursday, September 19, 1963.

Mobile Press Register, Sunday, May 3, 1964, p. 10C.

Mobile Press, Wednesday, August 18, 1965, p. 1.

Mobile Register, Thursday, August 19, 1965, p. 1D.

Mobile Press, Monday, May 19, 1969, p. 18A.

Mobile Register, Tuesday, March 12, 1974, p. 5C.

Mobile Press Register, Sunday, June 13, 1971, p. 2C.

Mobile Register, Friday, May 3, 1974.

Mobile Press, Tuesday, May 21, 1974, p. 6A.

Mobile Register, Thursday, March 6, 1975, p. 4A.

Mobile Press, Monday, June 2, 1975, p. 8A.

Mobile Register, Thursday, May 6, 1976, p. 4A.

Mobile Press, Wednesday, May 26, 1976, p. 2A.

Mobile Register, Friday, July 16, 1976, p. 1.

Mobile Press Register, Saturday, March 26, 1977, p. 4A.

Mobile Press, Monday, November 21, 1977, p. 4E.

Mobile Register, Monday, October 16, 1978, p. 4D.

Mobile Press, Tuesday, October 24, 1978, p. 4C.

Mobile Press, Tuesday, October 9, 1979, p. 5C.

Mobile Register, Tuesday, October 28, 1980, p. 4C.

Mobile Press, Friday, October 31, 1980.

Mobile Register, Wednesday, January 28, 1981, p. 1B, 2B.

Mobile Register, Friday, May 29, 1981, p. 1B.

Mobile Press Register, Sunday, October 11, 1981, p. 12A.

Mobile Press, Friday, October 29, 1982, p. 4D.

Mobile Press, Thursday, October 25, 1984, p. 4D.

Mobile Press, Tuesday, October 30, 1984, p. 4B.

Mobile Press Register, Saturday, February 23, 1985, p. 12D.

Mobile Register, Tuesday, April 15, 1986, p. 4A.

Mobile Register, Tuesday, April 16, 1985, p. 2B.

Mobile Register, Thursday, April 18, 1985, p. 4A.

Mobile Register, Friday, November 8, 1985.

Mobile Press Register, Sunday, April 13, 1986, p. 13A.

Mobile Register, Tuesday, April 15, 1986, p. 4A.

Mobile Press Register, Saturday, July 12, 1986, p. 1B.

Mobile Register, Thursday, February 16, 1989, p. 4A.

Mobile Register, Monday, July 31, 1989, p. 2B.

Mobile Register, Tuesday, August 1, 1989, p. 6B.

Mobile Register, Wednesday, March 18, 1992, p. 10A.

Mobile Register, Friday, June 19, 1992, p. 7B.

Mobile Press Register, Sunday, March 21, 1993, p. 6B.

Mobile Register, Friday, April 23, 1993, p. 1, 4A, 12A, 13A.

Mobile Register, Wednesday, May 12, 1993, p. 1.

Mobile Register, Friday, May 15, 1998, p. 2.

Mobile Register, Tuesday, January 21, 2003, p. 4B.

Mobile Register, Wednesday, July 27, 2005, p. 2A.

Mobile Register, Friday, March 10, 2006, p. 6B.

Mobile Press Register, April 21, 2006, p. 5B.

Newsweek, July 21, 1997, p. 37.

People's Forum, Monday, August 30, 1948, p. 1.

People's Forum, Monday, September 6, 1948.

The Catholic Week, Mobile, November 10, 1935.

The Catholic Week, Mobile, November 23, 1979, p. 25.

The Catholic Week, Mobile, November 7, 1986.

The Fairhope Courier, Thursday, November 25, 1948, p. 1.

The Mobile County News, Thursday, June 4, 1981, p. 1.

The Mobile Post, Friday, December 2, 1949, p. 1.

Rocky Mountain News, Monday, November 23, 1987, p. 119.

U.S. News & World Report, August 7, 2000, p. 37-38.

Veterans Journal, Friday, December 10, 1948, p. 1.

Veterans Journal, Friday, April 1, 1949, p. 1, 11.

Veterans Journal, Friday, February 10, 1950, p. 1, 8.

FEDERAL COURT DECISIONS

Hunter Davis, Julius B. Cook, Ethel E. Carter, Russell Gaskins, Johnnie Q. Laine, John Joseph Daughtry, Monroe Kidd, W. F. Cunningham, Willie H. Garvin, and Russell July, Jr., v. James E. Folsom, Dan Thomas, Haygood Paterson, E. C. Boswell, Milton J. Schnell, E. J. Gonzales, Mrs. D. C. Randle, and The Board of Election Registrars of Mobile County, Alabama, Civil Action No. 758, 81 F.Supp. 872 (S.D.Ala. 1949), *affirmed, Schnell v. Davis*, 336 U.S. 933, 69 S.Ct. 749 (1949).

Moore v. Moore, 229 F. Supp. 435 (S.D. Ala. 1964).

Reynolds v. Sims, 377 U.S. 533 (1964).

Sims v. Frink, 208 F. Supp. 431 (M.D. Ala. 1962).

United States v. Alabama, 192 F.Supp. 677 (M.D. Ala. 1944).

ALABAMA COURT DECISIONS

Alabama State Federation of Labor v. McAdory, 18 So.2d 810, 815 (Ala. 1944)

Ex parte Rice, 143 So.2d 848 (Ala. 1962).

Opinion of the Justices, 40 So.2d. 849 (Ala. 1949).

State v. Albritton, 37 So.2d 640 (Ala. 1948).

Waid v. Pool, 51 So.2d 869 (Ala. 1951).

FEDERAL STATUTES

Article I, Section 2, Constitution of the United States.

14th & 15th Amendments, Constitution of the United States.

Civil Rights Act of 1870, 42 U.S.C. Section 1981.

Civil Rights Act of 1871, 42 U.S.C. Sections 1983 and 1985.

Civil Rights Act of 1960, 42 U.S.C. Section 1971(f).

Voting Rights Act of 1965, 42 U.S.C. Section 1971.

H.Res.1375, Ninety-fifth Congress in the U.S. House of Representatives, October 10, 1978.

ALABAMA STATUTES

Boswell Amendment, Article VIII, Section 181, Alabama Constitution of 1901 (1946).

Amendment 223, Alabama Constitution of 1901 (1965).

Articles IV, Section 50, IX, Sections 198-200, and XVIII, Section 284, Alabama Constitution of 1901 (1965).

Code of Alabama, Title 17, Sections 12, 15, 17, 31, 32, 33, 34, 35, 43, 46, 52, 53 (1940).

DOCUMENTS & RECORDS

Appointment Certificate, Member of The Board of Registrars of Mobile County, September 10, 1948.

Appointment Letter, Governor James E. Folsom, October 24, 1947.

Photographs and maps, Archives, University of South Alabama.

Births, Deaths, and Marriages records, Augustus Bush Greene & Anna Stevens Fraser Cox family Bible.

Civil War Soldiers & Sailors System, National Park Service.

Cong. Rec. November 18, 2004, p. e2041 (extension of remarks, Hon. Jo Bonner).

Galvez Park Resolution, Mobile City Commission, May 31, 1921.

Galvez Park Petition, April 14, 1926.

Letters and Memoirs, Anne Bosarge Gonzales, 1976-1986.

Letters and Memoirs, Emanuel J. Gonzales, Jr., 1940-2003.

Melton McLaurin Oral History Project, University of South Alabama, Interviews with John J. LeFlore, 1970-1972, Archives, University of South Alabama.

Mobile City Directory, R. L. Polk & Co., 1870-1942.

Mobile County Democratic Executive Committee Resolution, January 17, 1947.

Mobile Municipal & Court Records Project, Probate Court records, City & District of Mobile, 1715 - 1812, Works Progress Administration, 1937.

Mobile Parks & Playgrounds Archives, November 15, 1932.

O. H. Finney, Jr. letter, January 12, 1948.

Press Release, E. J. Gonzales, July 12, 1986.

Record of Trial, *Hunter Davis, Julius B. Cook, Ethel E. Carter, Russell Gaskins, Johnnie Q. Laine, John Joseph Daughtry, Monroe Kidd, W. F. Cunningham, Willie H. Garvin, and Russell July, Jr., v. James E. Folsom, Dan Thomas, Haygood Paterson, E. C. Boswell, Milton J. Schnell, E. J. Gonzales, Mrs. D. C. Randle, and The Board of Election Registrars of Mobile County, Alabama*, Civil Action No. 758, 81 F.Supp. 872 (S.D. Ala. 1949).

Spring Hill High Lights, Spring Hill College, Mobile, October 6, 1932 and June 2, 1933.

BOOKS

Bass, Jack. *Taming the Storm*. New York: Doubleday, 1993, p. 89, 98, 105, 108, 184-196, 340.

Hamilton, Peter J. *Colonial Mobile*. Edited by Charles G. Summersell. University, Alabama: University of Alabama, 1976, p. 190, 285-287, 327-328, 490, 494, 518.

Higginbotham, Jay. *Mobile, City by the Bay*. Edited by Cathy Patrick. Mobile: The Azalea City Printers, 1968, p. 29-35.

King, Clinton P. & Barlow, Meriem A., Ed., *Marriages of Mobile County, Alabama, 1813-1855*. Baltimore, 1985, p. 15.

King, Clinton P. & Barlow, Meriem A., Ed., *Naturalization Records, Mobile, Alabama 1833-1906*. Gateway Press, Inc., Baltimore, 1986, p. 47.

Pickett, Albert J., *History of Alabama and Incidentally of Georgia and Mississippi, from the earliest period*. Charleston, 1851, chapters 16, 21, 23, 25, and 28.

The Annals of America, 1916-1928 World War and Prosperity, Hiram W. Evans: The Klan's Fight for Americanism, Encyclopaedia Britannica, Inc., 1968, Vol. 14, p. 506-511.

Vidrine, Jacqueline Olivier. *Love's Legacy: The Mobile Marriages Recorded in French, 1724-1786*. Univ. Southwestern La., 1985, p. 334-335.

INDEX